Terry Mackintosh

With all good wishes,

Alastair Mackie

November 2007

SOME OF THE PEOPLE ALL THE TIME

SOME OF THE PEOPLE ALL THE TIME

Alastair Mackie

Book Guild Publishing
Sussex, England

First published in Great Britain in 2006 by
The Book Guild Ltd
Pavilion View
19 New Road
Brighton, BN1 1UF

Typesetting in Garamond by
Acorn Bookwork Ltd, Salisbury, Wiltshire

Printed in Great Britain by
Antony Rowe Ltd. Chippenham, Wiltshire

A catalogue record for this book is available from
The British Library.

ISBN 1 84624 056 5

DEDICATION

To our great granddaughter Alice

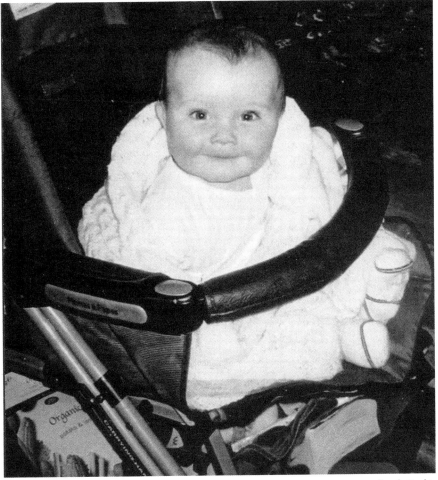

Sarah Mackie

who sees her prospect of the world with the same delight and gratitude
to humanity as I see my retrospect.

Contents

Funtispiece

An extract from a synopsis of *Carmen*, thoughtfully provided some years ago by the Paris Opera for the benefit of its English and American patrons:

> Carmen is a cigar-makeress from a tabago factory who loves with Don Jose of the mounting guard. Carmen takes a flower from her corsets and lances it to Don Jose (Duet: 'Talk me of my mother'). There is a noise inside the tabago factory and the revolting cigar makeresses bursts into the stage. Carmen is arrested and Don Jose is ordered to mounting guard her but Carmen subduces him and he lets her escape.
>
> ACT 2. The Tavern. Carmen, Frasquita, Mercedes, Zuniga, Morales. Carmen's aria ('the sistrums are tinkling'). Enter Escamillio, a balls-fighter. Enter two smugglers (Duet: 'We have in mind a business') but Carmen refuses to penetrate because Don Jose has liberated from prison. He just now arrives (Aria: 'Slop, here who comes'!) but hear are the bugles singing his retreat. Don Jose will leave and draws his sword. Called by Carmen shrieks the two smugglers interfere with her but Don Jose is bound to dessert, he will follow into them (final chorus: 'Opening sky wandering life') ...
>
> AXT 4, a place in Seville. Procession of balls-fighters, the roaring of balls heard in the arena. Escamillo enters, (Aria and chorus: 'Toreador, Toreador, all hail the balls of a Toreador'.) Enter Don Jose (Aria: 'I do not threaten, I besooch you') but Carmen repels him wants to join with Escamillo now chaired by the crowd. Don Jose stabs her (Aria: Oh rupture, rupture, you may arrest me, I did kill der') he sings 'oh my beautiful Carmen, my subductive Carmen ...

Quoted from 'Christmas Crackers' by John Julius Norwich, with Lord Norwich's kind permission.

ix

Chapter 1

Back to Front

I wonder why Dylan Thomas bothered to exhort the old to 'rage at close of day'. I do it anyway. I rage at a droop that owes nothing to brewers, has made Priapus give me up as hopeless, given new edge to the taunt of Weary Willie and turned libido into libidon't. I rage at hernias trying to burst their mesh; at teeth more amalgamated than ivorine; at bladder service, formerly on demand, replaced with while you wait ... and wait ... and wait: the question being to pee or not to pee. I rage at eyes in constant need of screenwash and ears of a fluebrush; at a mind more given to boggling than to comprehension; at the exit of reminiscence pursued by oblivescence. One of my few compensations is Housemaid's Knee, making me a sure-fire winner of a knobbly knee contest should such a thing come my way. Another, far better, is a scar stretching from my cleavage all the way to the bosky region below, obliterating my navel en route, which may yet earn its keep: as a bird-puller, I'm told, it beats etchings hollow.

Physical and mental crumbling in my eighties has inflicted on me a waning capacity to do all the things which I've been doing all along. For many years my most constant companion has been the bicycle I first used for commuting when the London buses and Green Line coaches between Putney and New Oxford Street successively disgraced themselves by late or non-running. The bike offered a constant journey time of 42 minutes and pleasant exercise. And there was even occasional amusement. Buses, for instance, have a habit of stopping too long at stops, owing to neglect of the platform bell-push by conductors selling tickets on the upper floor. When a No. 14 lingered to great excess on the Fulham Road one morning, I performed a notable public service by getting off the bike, hopping on to the platform and ringing the bell twice. As the bus sped away the conductor, descending to discover the source of the outrage, responded less than enthusiastically to my cheery wave. So, on a dark evening in Shaftesbury Avenue, did a swarthy car driver when I pounded on his boot after a cutting-up – the cyclist's term for being forced into the gutter by drivers who turn left, uncaringly and often dangerously, across one's path. When he stopped and got out I sensed that he might have a knife. Without waiting to find out I shot into the enfolding fastnesses of Soho.

1

The bike served, and goes on serving, other purposes. One is beautiful rides round Richmond Park, 10 minutes from our end-of-terrace semi in Barnes and blessed with paths exclusive to bikes and walkers; and an approach road from which golf balls hit out of the neighbouring club ground by incontinent players can be garnered for the delight of our elder great granddaughter (see Dedication). Another is trouble-free mobility in the traffic-infested capital and suburbs, especially for carrying home the produce of our allotment. Yet another is the warding off of pain from the osteoarthritic hip that has plagued me since the 1970s, by helping to keep the ball in the socket.

The bike's climactic purpose, however, is the one my declining energy and muscle power have conspired to deny me. My wife Rachel, being no cyclist and with no great liking for France, turned me loose annually for 20 summers to roam for a few blissful days in Languedoc and Roussillon, still deeply rural and totally captivating. My habit was to fly with the bike to Montpellier, a most beautiful and majestic city and capital in Roman times of their great western province (Provence). After a display for the entertainment of fellow travellers in the terminals at Gatwick and Fréjourgues airports of how respectively to dismember and reassemble the machine, I would pedal off for scenery, sun, sea, wine and leisurely progresses from one camp site to the next; (French sites being quantum leaps ahead of their horrid British counterparts). Being south of the city, Fréjourgues gives easy access to the Mediterranean. Turning left at the coast took me eastwards, by way of the medieval tourist trap of Aigues Mortes to the enchanting twin fishing villages of Saintes Marie de la Mer, little frequented because of indifferent roads and the nearness of the package-toured Roman cities of Nîmes and Arles. Alternatively, turning right at the Mediterranean leads along the sparsely developed coast of western Provence from Palavas-les-Flots, still unencumbered by power boats and other French tat towards Sete. There, in the biggest fishing port in Europe, the trawlermen go in for Baroque-costumed tourneys of doubtful Provenance, as it were, on decorated trawlers. Beyond is the almost deserted shore all the way to Marseillan, where the worst of the local wine gets made into vermouth; and the town's tacky plage, easily skirted. Then comes Cap d'Agde where the nudist camp, also Europe's largest, makes the mile or more of beach look like, and about as erotic as, an enormous display of assorted sausages laid out on a butcher's slab. Further on towards the Spanish border are Beziers, a miniature sand-coloured Paris built in the Haussmann style; Perpignan, another good air terminal for bicyclists; and then the rising ground towards Collioure, signalling me to turn back towards Montpellier.

I know of no more relaxing holiday than sauntering on wheels through this lovely bit of France, all but traffic-free except for tractors and peasants' jalopies because lorries and tourist cars tend to get sucked into La Languedocienne, the motorway to Spain. Such are the quiet and peace that even turning a corner is a happening. Rounding one I found a very small bullring, complete with villagers astride the stockade, a bullock and a combined Picador, Toreador etc. I left as blood began to flow. But I saw enough to get an insight into a sport, so-called, that I loathe. Undeniably, man and animal perform with balletic grace. How sad that the drama's end, a Racine certainty as it were, must be tragedy.

Lingering in bars listening to the denizens has often helped my French; except on one occasion in a small café when I could not identify the patois, as it seemed, of four young men at a table in the corner. As they fell silent I concluded that it was Catalan. That proved not to be so when, *a propos* of nothing, one of them volunteered,

I blime the farking dawg.

Football supporters, perhaps, en route for Madrid and its Reality. At the time I was on the way back to Montpellier, bicycle-friendly and with plentiful parks, superb food and cheap hotels. In a first-floor room in one such establishment, overlooking an alleyway, I foolishly left the shutters open on a hot night. Just as I was woken by a scrabbling noise, a head appeared at the windowsill. A rush at the miscreant and a shout made him lose his grip on the wisteria, fall to the ground and depart at speed.

Disaster struck at the end of the 1983 trip, when for two nights I slept not just badly but not at all. I flew home tired and anxious, just in time to finalise a speech I was due to make the next day for an Ex-Services Campaign for Nuclear Disarmament conference in Central Hall Westminster. While I was dressing at home after a third terrible night, I burst into tears. My wife Rachel's consternation at this unprecedented bit of the eccentricity to which she was well used grew when I resolved nevertheless to try to fulfil my engagement. On the way to Westminster from Barnes, my bike seemed to float on air and the world was my friend. I greeted the police escorting the march to the hall, remarking with peals of merriment that I had never felt safer. On the way through Parliament Square I showered my ex-Service friends with witticisms of a quality far in excess, as I thought, of my usual standard. The hypermania of depression gave me, as it seemed, new insights: how much I disliked one of the veterans; and the goodness of Bruce Kent who, as well as the cornerstone of CND itself, is an ex-soldier and thus one of us.

As the chairman introduced me in the Hall my mood changed to leaden and I was terrified of what I might do. The doubts and fears mounted as he reported that the next speaker, a guest ex-soldier from ANCAC (roughly describable as the French military peace movement) spoke no English. Alastair, he felt sure, would oblige by interpreting. Though well short of bilingual, Alastair miserably agreed to do his best. I first swam through the treacle of delivering my own speech, about the military lunacy of the British so-called independent nuclear deterrent. The audience reacted well enough. Then the Frenchman gave an abysmal address, barely *contre nucleaire* and well to the right of the audience's tolerances. So, as his sentences echoed round the room I did what I could to skew them into acceptability. To my surprise our hearers loved it; but by then I felt too terrible to feel relief and made for the door to the press room where I had asked a friend to wait. In the merciful privacy I again collapsed into tears. He, as Rachel had been, was concerned when I insisted that the ride home would do me good and left. It did; but at Rachel's urging I went to our excellent GP.

Luckily I was his last patient of the day and he gave me an hour beyond the canonical seven minutes. Nervous exhaustion, he explained, had led to hypermania, known in the trade as 'funny jokes', and acute clinical depression. That, I knew from my work in health education, was very common and treatable but prone to nasty consequences. (The long session, I realised later, was to see whether I was suicidal.) It seemed wise to ask our two sons and their wives, all of whom lived nearby, round to hear the news.

That was a bad idea. I was made to recognise that I had brought my trouble on myself by trying to do too much and faced the dreary fact of being too old to do as had been my habit. The next day brought the very antithesis of the quiet I had hoped for. With the best and most caring intentions, the family made the mistake of thinking that depressives are incapable of thinking for themselves. The morning saw me lying in bed shouting witticisms at our two sons and their spouses, assembled by a sequence of misapprehensions in our sitting room and waiting for the doctor whom Rachel, sensibly, had summoned. He turned out to be a young assistant wise beyond his years, exuding calm. He listened to my stumbling explanation of what was happening, which persuaded him not to administer the knock-out pills our GP had prescribed. He gave me a sedative instead; and after a day's rest I was back at what would, for a long time to come, have to pass for normal.

Normal was awful: I knew that something had gone terribly wrong and could scarcely bear it for the five weeks before the first of several drugs prescribed by the psychiatrist to whom I had been referred took effect. Sessions with him relieved the gloom which Churchill, a fellow sufferer, had described so aptly as the Black Dog. But not for long. I was no exception to a condition I later found to be typical when I served as a volunteer at a mental hospital: it is that almost all depressives refuse to believe that they will recover. I could no longer speak or write for the peace movement, or for that matter anybody else. I had to stop working for the Church as a sidesman, cleaner, scene shifter and honorary flower lady (following, that is, the arrangers with a dustpan and brush, picking up floral detritus). I had to neglect my jobs in the small firm which our younger son Gregor and I had started. I could no longer drive except for fetching the car from the garage and returning it, for both of which I had to steel myself. Visitors terrified me. The only lift from the permafrost of gloom came at Christmas, when one of the drugs I was on enabled me to proclaim

Ding dong Merelil on high.

Otherwise the ups of existence were in abeyance and the downs were deep indeed. One of the worst was when, a bit better as I thought, I tried another bicycle holiday in France in 1984 leaving, with incredible folly, my sleeping pills at home. I slept not at all and when I got back to Montpellier I was in such a state that I was lucky to be deemed fit to fly by an apprehensive British Airways official. Even more luckily, the duty doctor back in London was my own GP who prescribed a new drug and gave the reassurance needed to get me back to a bearable state. He retired soon afterwards, and I have found his successor no less skilled and sympathetic. His monthly 'state of mind' consultations (another anti-suicide precaution), very slowly brought me recognition that I was getting better. The process was accelerated by the controversial drug Seroxat which, whatever harm it may do to some people, has given me back my life.

One of the ways of giving point to that life was to try to find ways of putting my experience as a depressive to work. For that I joined a group under Church auspices which supported local people lacking companionship who had asked for visits: most are mentally or physically afflicted, alcoholic or just old. Barnes being the affluent suburban village it is (beneficiaries of the collection for the poor of the parish at Christmas being said apocryphally to include anyone on less than £100,000 a year) most of those in need were wealthy former professionals who demonstrated that the poor have no monopoly of misery. One from whom I gained as much as I gave in

5

friendship was the former chairman of the Pacific region of a multinational firm and a visiting professor of business studies who lacked male company, welcoming the chance to tell of his commercial exploits and share in mutual deploring of what the world was coming to. Another, a former partner in an archetypal small law firm in the City of London, appreciated some small relief from the boredom of partial blindness and was inordinately grateful for such minor help as writing cheques which he could only see well enough to sign. After his sudden fatal heart attack I continued to visit his gallant wife, wonderfully supportive despite a series of strokes; bereft and aimless in widowhood until a final stroke released her.

I stumbled on a chance of complementary work as a hospital visitor in the National Health Service corps of volunteers. That began with ten weekly training sessions comprising everything from NHS-type hand washing, by way of the pitfalls of patronising and insensitivity towards patients and their families to regulations and law. I was glad to be assigned to a small mental hospital within bike range of home and under the guidance of a devoted and amusing chaplain; proof if ever it were needed of the excellence of women priests. My hope that my experience as a recovered depressive would be useful proved correct. I was well received by the patients; and, after an interval for politely disguised weighing-up, by the staff. They belied notions of NHS mental health care: every single one of them in three years having impressed me with his or her patience and devotion. Their common shortage was of time for conversing with patients, which is where volunteers are of value. Like me, the depressives could not accept that they would get better; but almost all, especially the old, were most appreciative of a chance to talk about their joys and sorrows. Even my pathetic conjuring tricks and obsolete jokes came in useful. The one about the young couple, for example, discussing the cost of their engagement portrait with the photographer, who explained that it all depended on what they wanted. 'For instance,' he asked, 'would you like it mounted?' 'No need,' said the groom-to-be, 'arm in arm will do.'

I continued to gain more than I gave. There was Joan (whose name, as well as those of all the others, I have changed), blind, almost stone deaf and doubled up in a wheelchair: she had been a breakfast cook in a Donegal pub – a fine job, she explained, because it got her almost the whole day free for bringing up the enormous family whose members' rare visits meant everything to her. Jim, forever being discharged into flats beyond his ability to cope with and having to return by, as he gallantly put it, popular request. Constance, physically and mentally disabled but still able to enjoy describing, in embarrassing detail, what we could have done if we had met 30 years earlier. She had heard of Clerihews (irregular rhyming couplets said to have been invented by J. Clerihew Bentley), and enjoyed the one about the homosexual Tchaikowsky and his patroness:

'Heck'
Said Madame von Meck
'I should have been a bit more wary
Of the little old Sugar Plum Fairy.'

There was Peter, for whom no amount of support and reassurance was enough to prevent his suicide, and in whose memory we planted a tree in the hospital grounds. Mary, a virago embittered at her many misfortunes, sadly deficient of visitors because of the swathes of plastic sheeting and the scrubbing up that her MRSA infection imposed on them, but loving a chance to reminisce. Elizabeth, cultured and often coherent but given to terrible rages; who, seeing me sitting on a bed with an arm round an old lady in acute distress, shrieked 'Sex games!', to the momentary alarm of the staff. Comparable in its slapstick element was a visit to Dorking Theatre for a musical comedy matinée for which the excellent amateur company gave the hospital free tickets. With six patients and a nurse I marvelled at the courtesies shown to plainly disabled people as we were ushered to our seats. As the show got under way the patient sitting next to me stepped into the aisle and took off his trousers. My race to get them back on before the lights came on was nothing short of enthralling.

Such were the joys and sorrows of a hospital and home superior in some ways to the private homes where I still visit patients; and differing from the latter mainly in that the NHS private spaces have only curtains, instead of the walls of the wealthy. The care and love are the same.

As I was preparing to hand the job over to a younger successor, I found blood in my urine. 'Could be an inconsequential burst vessel,' said the consultant. Of the tests that followed, the most onerous demanded the drinking of almost a litre, as quickly as possible, of unpalatable liquid which would show up in the images produced by a great arched tube that portrays bodies entombed therein as if they had been sliced. Some of my overwrought fellow patients were so incensed by the ordeal and so unpleasant to the superintending nurse that, having imbibed my potion with all despatch, I asked whether she did seconds. That, I hope I can say without sounding immodest, gave comic relief.

An ultrasound test showed a blown-up kidney, meaning suspect cancer and surgery of unforeseeable extent. I was not so much worried as insulted, having the overweening conceit of the very fit. My father, I reflected, had been a doctor who made his children clamber over the Malvern Hills. My schools had had compulsory games and I seldom managed to evade them. As a medical student, I had learnt the bits and pieces of my body and how they should be looked after and I did my best at maintenance. RAF bomber crews, far from being the beer-swilling layabouts of some popular fiction, were exhorted to keep fit. True, I had had an operation on the most southerly of my orifices – the one least likely to be of concern to a dentist. The surgeon later exhibited the result of his prowess to a group of admiring students as I lay in a missionary position with a pillow: the procedure should be called depilatory, but the word is used for a different kind of removal; all of which would scarcely have registered on an illness scale. And anyway it had been my job later on to help the public to learn about sickness and health and I tended to follow my own advice. So the descent into a medical abyss was not so much a worry as a put-down which I had thought fate would never inflict on me.

I duly lost a kidney and some of the associated pipework. I found out later that I was very ill for a few days, not helped by the unnoticed pulling out of a drip as my sheets were changed, and the loss of blood that followed. Also far from a barrel of laughs was a pulmonary embolism, essentially a blood clot on the loose which may lodge in a lung. Such, in the dark of the small hours, was my consequent shortness of breath that I re-experienced the feeling of being about to die that had gone with some of my RAF adventures long before. The plus was that having to have the embolism treated solved the problem of finding somewhere to go until I was no longer too much for my wife Rachel to look after. Meanwhile I rediscovered food, and began to wash and slowly to patrol the ward on the arm of a Junoesque nurse who could have doubled as a nightclub bouncer: so frequent, indeed, were our promenades that we wondered whether people were beginning to talk.

Many who recover from serious illnesses are compensated for the privations and pain by the return of the delights of the world they left behind, much enhanced: everything somehow looks better than one imagined. That happened to me, after another bout of depression caused, I was assured, by the hours I had spent under anaesthesia. It went away as my senses of smell and taste returned; along with all my pleasures of old, buffed up and burnished. The only leftover is a continuing series of tests for bladder and prostate cancer. Every quarter I am privileged, as most patients due for operations are not, by being trollied into an operating theatre fully conscious and thus able to see the festoons of cables and piping, control consoles, trays of instruments and green-gowned-acolytes. Then the problem, but not its subject organ, arises. Like everyone else I have, as Shakespeare put it, my entrances and exits. One of the acolytes, however, makes an exit an entrance, connecting it to a big bag of water hanging from a gantry (after several doses of plain I have been moved to ask for Elder-flower, so far without result). As I get a squirt of local anaesthetic into that sensitive corporeal exit I am inclined to issue a warning that peals of laughter from the nurses at what they see will precipitate a complaint to the Royal College of Nursing; but, again so far, my attendants, bless them, have shown commendable restraint; apart, I fancy, from admiring glances. There follows an insertion of a tube bypassing my prostate gland into my bladder. The gowned and masked surgeon wields a device like a submarine periscope for conning the interior and, if the scrutiny necessitates it, uses minute scissors for nipping pre-cancerous polyps in the bud. He is a former naval medical officer and a qualified diver, which gives a nautical flavour to the display of my innards on a video screen as he searches, to the edification of all concerned, for hostile marine life.

I relish having a tale to tell in the tradition of 'it was agony Ivy' on the radio of the 1940s and Les Dawson's salacious whispers to his fellow drag artist on the telly. I particularly enjoyed inflicting my reminiscences on my fellow workers in the small firm that our younger son Gregor had started in 1983, and in which I was glad to resume working as I got better. Under the name of Ansador Limited we supplied and fitted telephone and video entry systems, having started in a single room in an office block in Battersea with a table, two chairs and a primordial computer. After the first few anxious weeks which Rachel and I spent contemplating a silent telephone and with only VAT rebate as income, Gregor found some custo-mers and fitted a few telephone entry systems. We were literally in business. Our landmark first cheque was for £183 from Vereker Properties for an entry system put into a small block of flats in North London. Susie Vereker, coincidentally, was a wealthy woman whom I knew from my peace work. She had upbraided me for failing to support a Campaign Against the Arms Trade protest run from her big house near the RAF base at Brize Norton; failing to understand the difference between being anti-nuclear weapons, which I am; and anti-Defence or anti-RAF, which I certainly am not.

We had found Susie's block of flats with the computer, the utility of which consisted in writing letters to property people that looked indivi-dual, but which went out in dozens, their addresses having been garnered by me from all the London borough planning consent offices within bicycle range. From the same source came an early order for a domestic video entry system – a device for people with more money than sense – from an Indian lady with a flat in one of the magnificent turn-of-the-nineteenth-century blocks near the Albert Hall. Pleased with the result and infinitely polite she asked diffidently whether we would mind if she paid the £1,500 bill in cash. Would we?!

Our first employee was Luigi, a perky Cockney/Sicilian youth who buckled to as hard as we did when work starvation turned to overburden. Installing a video entry system in a synagogue in Stamford Hill, North London, Luigi delighted the elderly Jews in their rest room where we were fitting a video monitor when I asked him to go for a bag of chips: 'I'll make sure they're not smoky bacon, Alastair.' We were lucky soon to get the London Borough of Hammersmith and Fulham as a customer, installing and maintaining the entry systems in some of their dozens of blocks of flats. The tenants were unfailingly generous with cups of tea, but oblivious of the consequent need, for which I thought it unseemly to ask. I have been reduced instead to purloining a sheet of corrugated iron from a nearby dump, propping it against a wall and cowering under it for a contortional pee. Gregor had another stroke of luck, responding to a request from an old lady tenant to put a new ceiling light fitting in her flat in the block in which we were working. Soon afterwards the minion in Hammersmith Council who dealt with us rang to tell us that she was the mayor's mother. His Worship was duly grateful and there was soon an increase in the council's custom.

One new commission from them, which had to be done in Gregor's absence with flu, was the cabling of a small estate in Battersea for the entry system that we were to supply. Luigi and I spent a fortnight crawling in the darkness of newly built lofts, fumbling for the conduit pipes that were to house the cables, proceeding by God and by guess, and making, as we feared, Heaven only knew what mistakes. Cycling past the estate a year or two later I was much relieved to see the houses being demolished, ending the possibility of lurking residual glitches. Another council job was close by. We had fitted automatic gates at a Hammersmith Borough mortuary, often put out of action by the hearses that kept ramming them as they were backed in. We were suddenly missing the friend who sent for us so often and so profitably to mend the gates, the carefree Australian soldier of fortune who was in charge. The reason for his disappearance arose from the coffins which he had a hand in supplying. These had proved too small for some of the deceased, and his unorthodox remedy of cutting the heads off to make the bodies fit had not found favour with the council.

My miscellany of jobs for Ansador had begun with tea making, cleaning, calculating the VAT and pay, bank runs, borough searches, fetching and carrying, and helping with wiring and fitting. The bank runs meant a lot of queuing, an occupational hazard of lowly messengers. That was aggravated on the morning after the hurricane and floods that afflicted London in the autumn of 1987. Our own bank branch had been closed with its computers down and, having tried two others, I fetched up in Wimbledon. Having paid in cheques for the week's takings of £3,000 or so I presented my wages cheque for about £300. Incredibly the clerk refused to cash it. After much argument I addressed the company in the customers' hall, announcing at the top of my voice the bank's, as I saw it, outrageous action. The cheque was cashed thereupon.

As Ansador expanded we were afflicted by a pool of bad and non-payers. The new job of invoice-chasing and debt-collecting fell to me. Dealing with one particularly piquant case, I used the technique that had worked in the bank. My quarry was Gerard Smith, an American merchant banker with a house in a grand district in which we, to the order of our friend the developer, had put an elaborate video entry system. Smith delighted us by ordering us to take it out and put in a new and even more sophisticated system, highly profitably because the wiring stayed in place and we could still charge for a whole new system. He curtly refused my repeated telephone requests for payment with various excuses, finally telling me to collect the cheque from his office. I bicycled to the Stock Exchange tower in the City straight from a site where I had been painting in my roughest attire. Stalking into the plush reception room of Salomon Brothers, where there were several smart clients waiting, I put a chair in the middle of the carpet and thumbed through *Country Life*, loudly declaiming that I had come to collect a cheque from Gerard Smith, who made a habit of not paying his bills. In a flash the glossy receptionist vanished into the interior, returning almost at once with the boodle.

Preparing for one of the court cases which, to my great joy, gave me a long-awaited outlet for my legal training, I came under public suspicion. I was trying, furtively, to photograph a small office in Fulham whose owner, a chronic non-payer, had alleged intimidation because, when I served the summons in person I had, as she put it, 'peered the office'. That was easily refutable because 'the office' had no front window. Using the Polaroid camera we kept for preparing quotations, I tried to get a decent picture of the windowless wall to use as evidence, darting from round a corner with a scarf over the camera for fear of another peering accusation. Not knowing how to work the camera did not help; and success came only at

11

the cost of arousing the curiosity and derision of the locals, fortunately excluding the defendant who stayed immured in her office. At the hearing I duly gained judgment; as, indeed, I invariably did, selecting only cases that looked likely to succeed.

The biggest of many such cases followed two hearings generated by my opponent, a South African lady with a mansion off Hyde Park let out in flats. She had appealed on the grounds that I had bullied a witness; and that the registrar, as district judges were then titled, had been prejudiced. I had indeed shown up as a fraud her electrician who had alleged that our wiring of the defendant's house had been illegal. Handing him the manual of the Institute of Electrical Engineers, I sensed that he had never seen it before, and sent him chasing after various references showing alternately that we had and had not acted illegally; ending by making him read out a crucial footnote showing that the low-voltage system we had installed was indeed permitted. The appeal hearing took place in No. 1 Court at Wandsworth before the senior Judge, Sir Frank White, who found for me and cleared the Registrar. The case was at the limit of what I could manage, and I was relieved to win. Sitting in No. 3 Court was His Honour Judge David Mackie, our elder son and then a part-time assistant recorder doing County Court work as an elevated temp while still head of litigation at Allen & Overy. He lunched with Sir Frank, from whom he got a good report of my conduct. I was not surprised, because the opposing barrister was most complimentary as he helped me to work out our costs; and because his instructing solicitor, who had got to know me during previous hearings, described me, I blush to say, as a brilliant lay advocate. I continued to enjoy getting money off baddies until, after seven years, Gregor's wife Dianne took over my office work and a newly hired accountant the sums. I retired except for some part-time security vetting of the staff. In the end my nephew Francis Davey, who had joined the firm, and the new sales and technical directors, bought Gregor and me out. The business continues to prosper.

Retiring from Ansador gave me more time for the love affair I had with my allotment. The estate of several dozen 12 rod (two-thirds of a tennis court) plots was beside a quiet road in Sheen, ten minutes by bike from home. My bit of it had a brook running alongside, and beautiful trees round half of it. I took it over as a jungle of weeds that could only be tackled with a flame thrower. I double dug it to two spade depths over the winter of 1981, pulling out festoons of ground elder proliferating 3 feet down. Thereafter, from the first muddy lettuce to the last armful of show-quality sweet peas grown from seeds costing nearly a pound each, the allot-

The allotment, where everything was growing, including our granddaughter Bella. *Author*

ment was a haven of peace. It produced all the common vegetables. Many were of such poor quality that they had to be composted, but there were still plenty to eat and give away, and growing them was its own reward. There were all the usual kinds of fruit, with such surpluses of redcurrants and blackberries that we could hardly give them away. Above all was the quiet, all the more welcome for the occasional interruption. One was the arrival in the road of a police car from which there emerged a young policewoman. She reported on her radio, 'We are pursuin' villains', at which two young men ran up and tried to hide behind my hedge-sized row of runner beans. My 79-year-old neighbour, whose allotment, incidentally, was to sublime what mine was to ridiculous, joined me in cornering one weedy villain with our gardening forks. The police girl, tall and wiry, seized him by the scarf round his neck and, with a cheery 'Come on, sunshine', quasi-frogmarched him back to the car. Her male colleague showed up and chased the other fugitive, of villainous aspect. I ran alongside the constable and was relieved when the villain got away.

As another diversion a motor bicycle ran out of road on a bend near our fence, and the rider fell unconscious into the gutter. My final perk on leaving the health world had been a Red Cross first-aid course, and I took charge of my patient: apprehensive because, as the book said, the most formidable casualty a first-aider can encounter is an unconscious one. Going by the book, I called on a member of the public, another allotmenteer as it happened, told him that I was a first-aider and that the casualty was my patient and asked him to go and telephone 999 for help. 'No,' he said '*you* go and phone. I'm a doctor and he's *my* patient.' I could have kissed him in relief. He was actually a consultant oncologist, himself stricken soon afterwards with colon cancer as I had been with my kidney. When we were both back in action he told me that we were lucky to have been afflicted when we were. Ten years earlier, in the absence of new kinds of surgery, we would both have died. We were friends until, after 21 years, I realised that the allotment was controlling me, having become more than I could keep in good order. I had created, as I saw it, a tiny speck of productive and ecologically well-maintained ground, improved by my years of composting and crop rotation. It needed somebody to keep it going. My neighbour seized it gladly and has done just that.

As we reached our eighties Rachel and I realised that we were free of most of the obligations that obliged us to watch every penny: school fees, the mortgage, helping grandchildren and the like. With the burdens eased we began going to better hotels for holidays. We went to more concerts at the Royal Halls, Festival and Albert, preceding these musical events with supper and enough wine to be, to adapt the notation, *blotto ma non troppo*. We were encouraged to find acquaintances with the same stuffy tastes as ours: we are not alone, for instance, in recognising 'World Premiere' and 'BBC Commission' as signals for placing fingers in the ears and leaving the arena. Others shared our discovery of such musical names as Claudio Arr*au* and Harrison Birt*whistle* as danger signs; and Simon *Rattle* as the rule-proving exception.

We made increasing use of other delights within easy reach of home such as the National and Richmond Theatres, for me requiting a passion that began at the Malvern Theatre pantomime before I reached double figures. Having taken our children, we now take theirs, as well as an annual posse of great-nephews and -nieces to its lineal descendant. Unfortunately real pantomimic mishaps are rare; but one in that specialised repertoire afflicted the Demon King in a Donegal theatre who, consigned to subterranean damnation through a stage trapdoor, was left discomfited by its failure to open. His impasse provoked a catcall:

Praise the Lord, Hell's full.

14

Even more enjoyable because of the pomposity of the genre are operatic gaffes. A classic being the prima donna Tosca at the Paris Opera who had made the mistake of quarrelling with the stagehands. When, crazed with suicidal grief at her lover's death from a gunshot wound that was meant to be a blank, she threw herself over the battlements, it was too late to discover that the fall-breaking mattress had been replaced with a trampoline. Her third bounce back into visibility dampened the dramatic effect. Would that something similar would happen at the English National Opera, memorable to me for a *Macbeth* whose oh-so-clever director had turned Verdi's Highlander chorus into chauffeurs and the set into banal suburbia.

Disinclined in our dotage to wash up into the small hours, we give our dinner parties, mostly familial, at restaurants nearby. One that does away with the drink-drive hazard by being within walking distance is a wonderfully boisterous Italian *ristorante* with a pizza oven. We go often enough to get kissed on arrival by the semi-shaved comedian who does magic with pizza dough before shovelling it into the *forno*, a cavernous oven; stopping occasionally to dance, brilliantly, with young female customers whom he politely hijacks and escorts to the floor. More ambitiously we use some of our prosperous children's patrimony for cruising, appreciating the absence of the jagged edges that go with other kinds of travel and the patently genuine aim of the ships' crews to make the holiday the experience of a lifetime. P & O's *Arcadia* (before it was Butlinised into *Ocean Village*, a witless name for a vessel needing something appropriate such as *Aphrodisia*, *Fornicatoria* or *Apassionata*) and *Adonia* were delights; but *Oceana*, whose vulgarities include the huge 24-hour foodery needed for the American trade, is a disagreeable Leviathan. The show-stealer for us is Cunard's superb *Queen Elizabeth II*, now in her forties, in which our cabin came with a butler, steward and housemaid.

The stops for exploration, we find, are miracles of organisation and the people-watching that offers so much fascination on board is enhanced by the runs ashore. I was intrigued on an expedition through the mountains of Madeira by one of the predators of both sexes in search of a mate who frequent cruise ships. Rachel, not good at heights, had gone off on a lace factory and shopping tour and I was on my own in a coach threading its way along the precipitous mountain roads and through enthralling scenery. At a stop I gallantly met the request of a lady of uncertain age, sharing a table for coffee, to lend her a pen. We were away. The next stop was a *bodega* for sampling the local wine, some of which makes one wonder how they got the cat to squat on the bottle orifice. Disinclined to partake of the tasting, I was dismayed that my new-found companion insisted on my

A P & O stately pleasure boat. *Author*

joining her at the table for two she had seized. Politeness forced me to sit as she poured out Madeira and confidences. As we left I, certain that she would want to visit the shops, mentioned that I was not bothering with them. Alas, nor was she. After her prolonged sojourn in the ladies' lavatory of a nearby pizzeria, during which I cravenly failed to make my escape, I said I needed to sit in the shade. That failed to shake her off, and the only shelter was under the awning of a dockside café. Two beers for me and two Campari and sodas for her later it was time to board the bus back to the ship. There followed more conversational intimacies as we sat next to each other, positioning chosen by her which my courtly nature obliged me not to abandon. Only as we surmounted the gangway did my chance come. She had to turn either right or left at the top; and I, saying how much I was looking forward to introducing her to my wife, had only to go the opposite way. So populous was the ship that I never saw her again. Rachel, for some reason, accused me of having strung her along. Strange creatures, women.

For advanced people-watchers there is ample pabulum. Young ladies habitually favouring tight pants and navel displays turn, on full dress evenings, into elegantly attired diners swathed in taffeta. Their companions cover their tattoos and singlets with white shirts and dinner jackets, forsaking the bars and casinos round which they habitually cluster like suckling piglets. The most striking feature, however is the obesity pandemic – alive, well and manifest in cruise populations. Perhaps half the adiposely challenged are running to fat but have not quite got there; another quarter are colossi whose bellies give advance notice of the owners' arrival and bottoms of their sojourn or departure. Some can manage no more than a seafaring waddle as, replete with Full English, morning coffee and pastries, seven-course lunch, afternoon cream tea with all the trimmings and another seven-courser, they totter into post-prandial theatregoing, gambling and romance (though how they manage the last is a mystery). After which there's always the midnight buffet.

I welcomed the chance that cruises offered to test a hypothesis. I had always got fun out of giving fun to other people; and this, like other aspects of life, had emerged from my travails of illness as even more engaging than before. Dreadful jokes always amused the very ill people I went to see. Handkerchiefs that change colour as they pass through my fist and the coins, eggs and golf balls that vanish and turn up in my quarries' hair or pockets give innocent merriment. So do true tales of derring undo, as it were, from my murky past. Would the infliction of such small change of comedic currency, I wondered, work on my fellow passengers? I knew of the risk that such efforts can go dreadfully wrong. I shuddered, for instance, to remember a well-known professional TV comedian's toe-curling performance at a clients' dinner given by the advertising agents Saatchi & Saatchi years before. He told jokes of deepening shades of blue that got token applause from the well-oiled, flashy company, waning as one dreadful sally after another thudded to the floor.

Our cruises have provided two separate settings in which I can shine – or not. One is the dinner tables where our fellow guests, carefully chosen by the company's social staff to harmonise with each other, stay the same throughout the voyage and cannot readily escape my attentions. The other is the constantly changing breakfast and lunch sittings in the magnificent restaurants, that offer superb service and comfort to those who choose not to patronise the self-service obesitarium on the top deck. In social terms these meals are the shuffling of a gigantic pack of eaters; the result, almost invariably, being different companions at every meal. Each type of sitting, I hoped, would provide its own test of whether my attempts to emulate the three jolly princes of Serendip (dedicated, as Horace Walpole described them, to the revelation of unexpected sources of happiness), would work; or whether, seen as geriatric burbling to be endured, my efforts at entertaining talk would suffer the same fate as had the Saatchis' indijester.

So far, success. Not only intuition and the absence of wifely kicks under the table have told me that my hypothesis is valid. On one voyage a fellow diner, extraordinarily hale at ninety, followed my example. He told a joke so blushmakingly obscene as to blight the occasion. I could do no other than attempt to take the nasty aftertaste away with the mildly lavatorial tale of the GI home from the wars at his parents' primitive Kentucky farm. Having been trained by the US Army in elementary hygiene, he was disgusted by the family privy at the bottom of the garden. He took a Mills bomb from his belt and threw it at the privy, which disintegrated in the explosion.

His taciturn father, removing his pipe from his mouth, opined,

Ye shoun've done that, son.

Adding, after another pull on the pipe,

Yer ma wus in there.

With husbandly solicitude he called out,

Are ye awright Ma?

From the wreckage there issued a faint cry:

Sure. I guess It must've been sumpin I ate.

Not all light-hearted sallies work. For reasons unexplained, neither P & O nor Cunard have yet accepted my suggestion for relieving the shyness of open-sitting eaters who meet in the dining room for the first time. It is to conceal a whoopee cushion on one of the 500-odd seats and connect it to the public address system; the lucky sitter to receive, of course, a bottle of champagne. I live in hopes.

More successfully I passed a different test on a small, very grand ship named *Hebridean Spirit*. Joining a wealthy and refined clientele on a weekend trip to the Scillies and Brittany, we visited the Breton port of St Malo and its asparagus-growing hinterland. My suggestion that the staple product could be marketed more effectively by calling it Brittany Spears was well received; except by one lady of such refinement that she did not know of the eponymous pop singer. Two elderly table companions, however, enjoyed my recounting an incident during the distribution of gas masks for civilians said to have taken place early in World War Two. Three old ladies living together received a summons to the collection point. Only Joan and Enid were well enough to go. After the official had handed them their masks, sedulous for their companion's welfare, they asked him,

What about our Fanny's?

'I'm afraid we've nothing suitable: you'll just have to stuff them with newspaper,' came the reply.

My maritime forcing-house experiments have persuaded me that the hilarity that begins at home can be spread abroad and some at least of the 80-odd years'-worth of what lurks in my memory may be worth recounting. That is my excuse for what follows. Recording it Back to Front will, I hope, make you wonder how it all came about and read on until you get to where you came in.

By way of epitome, let me remind you of Lynn Redgrave as the au pair Georgie Girl, lying face to camera as she first experiences sexual inter-course with, of course, the master of the house. As it gets exciting the telephone rings, the dog barks, the child screams and the mistress, returning unexpectedly, is heard opening the front door. Georgie resignedly observes:

Isn't it odd how there are some people for whom God always seems to keep a custard pie up his sleeve?

There, with the grace of God, go I. Happily, I enjoy custard pies.

Chapter 2

Too Clever by Half

> I remember, I remember
> the house where I was born:
> the little window where the sun
> came peeping in at morn.

Actually I don't but I like poetry. We moved in 1925, when I was three and had yet to acquire a memory. My father, a doctor, had returned from a gruelling four years of World War One commanding a field ambulance in France. No measures to guarantee resumption of pre-war jobs then existed, and he had lost his appointment as Medical Officer to the College, with some general practice thrown in, in the would-be spa town of Malvern. He used a pre-war spell as a house physician in psychiatric medicine to get a job as deputy head of a lunatic asylum, which is what mental hospitals were called in those days; a job not much better, he seems to have thought, than the back legs of a pantomime horse. But it gave him three badly needed years of rest until he responded to calls from former patients and went back to Malvern, breaking medical convention by, as the phrase was, 'putting up a plate' – starting from scratch rather than buying an existing practice.

Malvern has delectable hills and has been my abiding favourite place. My father started work there in 1901 and the *Malvern Gazette* in 2005 recorded the centenary of his having been called to attend a somnambulatory 'domestic' who had fallen from a window. Our elder grandson James went to the College and I am still a frequent visitor; making the family association with the town a long one. The dawn never peeped into my room because the hills were in the way. Instead I looked up over the greenery to the Worcester-shire beacon. My room was at the top of our big Edwardian house with a ceiling just below the rafters. I remember it for the shelves which gradually filled with books and the desk at which I read and wrote. The other side of the house looked down on a superb view of the plain towards Bredon Hill.

I got my too-cleverness-by-half from a family of hustlers and thrusters. The Mackies are a branch of the Clan Mackay, itself a branch of the Clan

21

The house that faced the Malvern Hills. *Author*

Gregor, oldest of all the tribal titles. Being married to a genealogist and the
son of a genealogical dabbler, I know a bit about us. We originated in the
county of Sutherland and our first, probably apocryphal, bit of luck was in
1315, after the Battle of Bannockburn in 1314. King Robert the Bruce, the
legend goes, fetched up for an overnight stay at the cottage of a Mackie
widow and her three sons. They rallied to his cause with their bows and
arrows and one, in a toxophilic exploit, killed two ravens with a single
arrow. The enterprising mother, offered a reward, asked for: 'the wee bit
hassock o'land atween Palnure and Pelkin'. She got it and divided it
between the sons. The marksman, says tradition, was our ancestor and the
transfixees provided us with a family crest; ours by appropriation because
we got it long before the Lyon Herald took charge of Scottish entitlements of
that kind. We moved south-east after the Battle of Flodden in 1513,
perhaps having supported the wrong side; a practice that became something
of a habit. More trouble followed when the Duke of Montrose laid waste the
town bearing his name and the surrounds in 1645. We recovered from that,
prospering as farmers until we got it wrong again in the Jacobite rebellion in
1715, losing our well-gotten gains except for one farm in the beautiful

22

Balmanno, near Montrose, the family home we lost. *Author*

village of Dalally. Pausing only to invent a mechanical corn mill that sold, as it were, like hot bannocks, one John Mackie went into the timber business, supplying Scottish oak to Montrose shipbuilders and later buying ships to carry it to the Low Countries for housing. When the supply of Scots oak ran out, John used his fleet, as it had become, to carry other timber from the Far East to colonists in largely treeless Australia.

Some of John's descendants diversified into ropes, rigging and sails, and their firm still exists in Montrose. Others, including my ascendants, became bankers and doctors. One of the former was my great-grandfather David, three times Provost of Montrose. Like many eighteenth and nineteenth century dignitaries he had his portrait painted life-size and presented to him by the Town. It hangs in our dining room, where it has terrified at least one cleaning lady who thought its eyes followed her round the room. He is said to have had 'a furious notion of dress' ('furious' retaining at the time some of its Latin (*'furiosus'*) meaning of mad); but the large, elegant white tie and fancy waistcoat of his evening dress look sensible enough. He shared with his son Alexander a fondness for claret. I am thankful for having inherited that unquestionable virtue. Less so was

Great Grandfather David, whose eyes are said to follow you round the room.
Artist James Irvine

their shared propensity for hurrying: Alexander, whom alas I never knew, is reputed invariably to have caught the train to Edinburgh preceding the one he had intended.

Grandfather Alexander was another banker whose wit emerges from an extraordinary account, as over the top as the occasion, of the opening ceremony in July 1898 of an elaborate meeting hall, complete with a clock tower, gallery and surrounding chambers, presented by his cousin to the village of Edzell, near Montrose. Cousin Robert Inglis's extraordinary philanthropic venture is the subject of a book with a gold embossed cover giving every detail, from the initial circular to 374 persons offering 581 tickets, all the way to the 28 items in the concluding firework display. The celebratory lunch ended with nine toasts, to each of which there was a reply. Alexander's was the last, toasting 'The Ladies'. His 900-word speech shows traces of what became a family conviction – that our Inglis cousins

24

The Hall at Edzell, a white elephant to this day. *Author*

were a bit odd, and that Robert's venture, philanthropic as it was, was more ostentation than generosity:

> I somewhat envy the community of Edzell in getting possession of that handsome pile of buildings because ... I have been trying for many years to impress upon old schoolfellows ... to give a portion of their wealth for the different institutions we have and which are languishing for lack of adequate support ...

As near, perhaps, as he could get to saying that he thought it was the white elephant which succeeding generations of Mackies know it to be. He went on to chance his arm – straining, as I sense, to keep within the limits of propriety, in the gentlest of lampoons:

> As compared with my cousin I am nobody (laughter) – but ... if there are any good qualities found in us it is because we have been trained in those requirements and because we drank them in with our mothers' milk. With mother wit, and if not with that alone, to a large extent our friend [Robert] has been able to take his place alongside of any body and everybody. (Applause).

25

Would that such mordancy had stayed in our genes.

It was certainly an element in my father George's remarkable élan. True to Mackie form, he qualified as a doctor before he was 21 and legally entitled to practice. Once past that obstacle he hurtled through two appointments at Edinburgh Royal Infirmary and a presidency of the Royal Medical Society of Edinburgh before he settled in Malvern. His World War One record is remarkable for bravery: he earned the Distinguished Service Order, a fighting award rarely conferred on non-combatants. His account of the adventures of his field ambulance, which served as his thesis for the honours degree of MD (Edinburgh), shows a second virtue: ferocious devotion to his patients, and contempt for what he saw as uncaring and idiotic higher medical authority. Of his unit, largely comprising civilians in uniform from architects and engineers to labourers, he says:

> When our methods transgressed the narrow confines of official medical sanction ... the violation was both conscious and deliberate; and it was, in the end, justified by its results.

It was his practice in the front line, in which the field ambulances spent much of their time, to accompany his stretcher bearers; often, I suspect, to help the desperately wounded lying in shell holes on their way:

> ... nothing save mud for miles and miles pitted with myriads of shell-holes close to and cutting each other like the cells of a honeycomb. And if the life of the infantry-man was bad, that of the stretcher bearers was worse and their carriage of the wounded amid constant shelling in the trackless roadless waste remains even now [1922], after nearly five eventful years, a loathsome nightmare of dismay and horror unspeakable.

He applied his talent for hustling to his soldiering. As a volunteer in the Artillery when the war began, he was roped in to help with recruiting. He and his colonel achieved remarkable results,

> by the simple expedient of attesting and medically examining all the volunteers from the audience at our recruiting meetings before their easily aroused enthusiasm had been allowed to cool.

That at least seems to have remained in our genes. I first showed signs, my mother told me, when my vocabulary was still thought to consist only in gurgles. My maiden Aunt Alice, (her position sadly typical because of the surplus of spinsters that the slaughter of males in the war created), came to see me and announced that she had a present for me. I took the attendant baby worshippers aback with,

Get it.

Along with William Collingwood, my mother's son by her first husband who had been killed on the Somme in 1916, and my sister Joanna, I enjoyed the best of everything. Promoted from a grey pram with matching nanny I was given, for two mornings a week, a governess/tutor; another sad spinster whom I remember for smelling of newly sharpened pencils. She toted a pack of small coloured pictures of objects whose French names I was to learn. I was surprised when she took me through them for a second time, having already memorised them. I learnt from her what a metaphor was after a visit by the piano tuner: reproved for fiddling with a pair of scissors, my excuse was that I was tuning them. Later on I applied the coloured picture procedure D.I.Y. to cigarette cards. Film stars, poultry, birds, cars and cricketers still clutter my memory.

Malvern ('Great' to distinguish it from lesser versions of West and North) was in the early 1920s a small middle-class town, noted for its hills, elegant Edwardian houses like ours, and the abbey-sized Priory Church with the second-best stained glass in England. From a well in the hills came its other resource, water thought to have medicinal properties. That gave rise to a clinical procedure comparable to the taking of the waters at Bath, called 'Hydropathy', invented by another local doctor in the nineteenth century and commemorated by an ugly monument recently demolished. My father tried to go one better by adapting, as he put it in a memorandum to the Development Association, the natural features of Malvern to the treatment of many forms of heart disease. In what a 1927 article in the *Malvern Gazette* called 'a lucid and comprehensive manner', he envisaged a therapeutic institute for massage and:

Carefully regulated walking exercise ... shelters where patients can rest in sunshine and pure air with sight of the most wonderful view in England.

Moonshine, as we now know; but full of the spirit of enterprise which I have tried to emulate and which certainly pervades our sons, one on the

The deceased ravens ensconced in the family crest. *Artist George Mackie*

senior judicial bench after a brilliant career as a solicitor, and the other a no-less-successful entrepreneur. Malvern water joined those of Vichy, Buxton and other sources in overpriced bottles; except for a well in the hills where it was to be had in a tin mug chained to St. Ann's Well, since transmuted into a café with tasteful china crockery.

The genteel town itself sported elegant shops passed on my pram itineraries and later serviceable for browsing. One was Alfred Mander the chemist, inventor of Lea & Perrins's Worcestershire sauce, for years misleadingly labelled 'made to the recipe of a nobleman of the County'. Competing with W.H. Smith as Mander did with Boots was Miss Newth, stockist of then esoteric items such as the mauve tissue paper for one of my aunts' Christmas parcels, wrapped and despatched in September to reach the Malay States where the uncle was a colonial servant. He was a huge, agreeable man always good for half a crown when they came home on leave; and later, in what I saw as the ultimate accolade, to have a road in Kuala Lumpur named after him. The grandest shops had double names: Tipping & Morris, patrolled by one or the other in morning dress; and

Cridlan & Walker, where Mrs one or the other lurked in a cabin to take the cash while the husbands clove whole carcasses on wooden tables scrubbed smooth and fissured with knife cuts. Scarcely less impressive was Tilts the Dairy where there was a large marble container from which, with wondrous accuracy, Mr Tilt cut lumps guessed at as weighing a pound, slapped them on greaseproof paper and only occasionally had to add or subtract a sliver. From what would now be called a hot bread shop, came the bread, sold in white (luxury) or standard (ordinary); our usual fare being the cheapest, which was 'stale (yesterday's) standard'. Would that trade descriptions nowadays had the same integrity. Regular customers had their purchases written in small books, and once a week came a round of payments. Elevated from the pram, I accompanied my mother as she did that chore. The other semi-regular visit was to the Westminster, later the West in Natwest Bank, and the overfamiliar clerk Hugh Mermagen. He was the source of the first Awful Worry that I can remember (see below) and I hated him.

On Sundays I was carted off to the regular service of matins at the Priory Church. It lasted over an hour and usually featured a sermon by the grandly named vicar Hubert Humphrey Middlemore Bartleet. His staccato bursts of emphasis sounded like barking, and so deepened the red hue of his face that he seemed at risk of bursting: of which, I half hoped, the wobbling of his pince-nez was warning. Otherwise the boredom was so stupefying that I could have been forgiven for turning to atheism. Only intermittent relief came from choir-watching, close to our reserved and paid-for stalls: one bass singer had an enormous moustache, thrown into disequilibrium in such climactic verses as the last of the 'Te Deum Laudamus' ('We praise thee oh Lord') when he affirmed that he trusted in the Lord and prayed never to be confounded. Otherwise I can remember little except endless maternal exhortations not to fidget; and gazing across the enormous altar at a stone effigied couple lying in their joint tomb and engrossed in prayer. They're still at it.

Three minutes' walk from our house was St Martin's Kindergarten where my formal scholastic career began. In the big house lurked the tall, forbidding Misses Henderson, and Margaret, a pudgy, pink colleague, much younger and sometimes almost jolly, who did games and handicrafts. Of the sequence of ordeals in which being at this grim place seemed to consist, the most wrenching was putting away my outdoor shoes and arsenical green cap: donning elastic-sided pumps seemed to cut me off from the world. Of the lessons I remember nothing except the slow repetition of what my pencil-perfumed governess had already covered. But on an all-too-memorable occasion my father entered the classroom, somewhat flustered as it seemed. Having asked leave to do so of one of the grim sisters, he came over and told me that the house and garden had been scoured in a search for the garage key, for the lack of which he could not go out on his rounds. Could it be, he asked, that by any chance it was about my person? It was in my blazer pocket. In hideous embarrassment I handed it over.

The incident stoked my unpopularity to a point beyond that of a mere swot, and fortified my decision to run away. Once out of the grounds, home, I thought, would be a better destination than the wide world which I had first selected. Duly returned at break time, I was confronted by all the other children who ran at me down the sloping drive. Absconding again, this time at the double, got me the day off. My second, mercifully peaceful, return to the school gave me my first encounter with a concocted collective lie. The children, said Margaret, a good deal pinker than usual, had wanted to show me a pet rabbit. Whining, no doubt, like *As You Like It*'s schoolboy but lacking his shining morning face I left St Martin's at the end of the term. One of the Hendersons, feigning regret, handed me what even then I was school-wise enough to know was my report. Sedulous to spare my parents' distress at what I was sure was unfavourable, I thrust the envelope into the hedge before walking home. To my consternation my father, who had come to the gate to greet me, had seen what I had done. Unpersuaded by my denial, explanation and plea in mitigation, he sent me to fetch it.

Nevertheless I loved Malvern and still do, revelling in being a doctor's son and listening as he told my mother about the patients to whom he was so devoted. As family we all tended to get medicated from the samples he was sent by the big drug houses, and I felt, when I was ill, that I was trespassing on his time.

My half-brother William, son of my mother's first husband killed in World War One and seven years older, had built a wireless set with a cone-shaped speaker slung from the drawing room picture rail. From the set ran an aerial wire, perhaps 100 yards long, through a tube in the window sill and right across the garden to the top of a tree. I was always hopeful that drama would ensue if there was a thunderstorm because of a standing order that the nearest family member must in that event rush to the drawing room and throw a copper isolating switch and save us from being conflagrated by lightning conducted down the wire. Regrettably it never happened. The wireless started me off as the radio addict I have remained. At the time the big night for the National Programme was Saturday. A series called *In Town Tonight*, consisting of a sequence of interviews with the urbane people who foreran celebrities, gave one a marvellous sense of being involved. Then came *Music Hall*, being acts by six or so star and less-than-star performers. Gracie Fields, the Blackpool comedienne, was the star of stars. Others were Sandy Powell ('Can you hear me mother?'); the Western Brothers, Kenneth and George, immaculate in tails and singing songs considered risqué; other double acts such as the predecessors to Flanders and Swann, Flotsam and Jetsam:

> Bound to be notice-ed by anyone who spots 'em:
> He's Flotsam, I'm Jetsam,
> He's Jetsam, I'm Flotsam.

I particularly enjoyed the sending-up of what were then pop songs such as Bing Crosby's 'Pennies from Heaven':

> Every time it rains it rains
> Halfpennies from Hades.
> Don't you know each cloud contains
> Little old ladies?

Another, the dreadfully slushy 'Every time I hear a newborn baby cry', concerned a long-forgotten film star:

> Every time I see a newborn baby grin
> I think of Errol Flynn.

Most deserving of send-up was the plagiarised version of a Borodin string quartet ('Take my hand, I'm a stranger in Paradise') concerning another:

> Stewart Grainger in Paradise.

Which blended well with my father's soubriquet for the same composer's other well-known work – the 'Fallopian Dances'.

Another delight was my Fairy Cycle, a children's bike, lacking the small tutorial side wheels now standard. In their absence Auntie Alice ran behind holding the saddle until she could clandestinely let it go, starting me on a succession of bikes culminating 75 years later in the Rolls-Royce of a Red Feather Dawes given to me by our elder son for my eightieth birthday. Home life also featured a white West Highland White puppy given originally to my sister Joanna, to which she never took. Originally Tinkerbell, she became Tinker, then Stinker; and on occasion, in spite of being almost instantly house-trained and regularly bathed and whitened with special powder, Stencher. We loved each other so dearly that she sensed forthcoming separations days in advance, and moped. As self-appointed guardian of the house, she sat regularly, in Trafalgar Square leonine mode, at the front gate. One afternoon, with my head in its usual post-prandial book, I heard my father's footsteps on the stairs to my room – as unusual during home consulting hours as it was ominous. Tinker, it emerged, had bitten a patient who, idiotically, had tried to pet her, and my father had had to dress the wound. After reproving me he had the grace to concede that the wound was the first genuine affliction that the patient, a hypochondriacal lady named Archer and nicknamed Sagittarius, had suffered in 30 years.

Tinker was later to have mongrel puppies for which, having arranged accouchement facilities, I acted as midwife. Destined from my earliest days to follow my father as a doctor, I dipped into his copy of *Quain's Anatomy* (predecessor to the better-known *Gray's*), and was shown how to study people's physique and gait. He reinforced my interest during a holiday in Edinburgh, showing me the entrance to the School of Anatomy at the university, decorated with the cased remains of Burke and Hare, infamous as 'resurrectionists': they supplied bodies for dissection robbed from graves and boasted to a Royal Commission that there was nobody beyond the reach of their snatching activities. Inside the school was a student exploring the innards of a male subject whose grey, formaldehyde-soaked skin and shrunken organs were a sad sight. My father also took me out on his rounds. I sat in the car and read while he was in patients' houses, hoping morbidly that he would have occasion to sign one of the block of death certificates that he kept in the glove box of his Rover. No such luck. But on a memorable unscheduled stop he answered the urgent plea of the manager of the Leathercraft workshop where there had been a multiple accident. He went in and plied his trade until the ambulances arrived. As a thank-you offering he was later given a handsome blue leather overcoat which lasted him his lifetime.

I pleased my father by diving into the Everyman edition of the sixteenth-century *Organon on the Rational Art of Healing*. It stressed the importance of giving the body a chance to heal itself, still well recognised as homeostasis; but, as I came to know decades later, too often honoured medically in the breach. Another memorable phrase explained the origin of the profession of midwifery, as I told their Royal College students in a lecture fifty years later. Women took to delivering babies because physicians of the day:

32

Would not deign to touch the noisome pudenda of the poor.

They would and did, however, open patients' veins and bleed them in the belief that it would be of benefit. One measure of enough being enough was when the patient fainted – 'bled to syncope' (as, lyrically, in ''twas all over my syncopee'). The term survives in 'micturition syncope' which, I know from experience, means fainting during an unsuccessful effort to pee.

With my younger sister Joanna I enjoyed the Winter Gardens (strawberry or vanilla ices, waitress-served at threepence and sixpence); the Priory Park with concerts from the bandstand, still there, whose evening performances I could hear in the distance from my bedroom window; the ornamental lake with hand-cranked paddle boats on hire as leisurely aquatic bumper cars; and the swimming pool where a fearsome ex-sailor taught me to swim. Also featuring in the pool was the first of the celebrities – the genuine kind and not the phoneys who currently clutter public life – who have always been an interest. He was Bernard Shaw, in the town for the annual drama festivals in which his plays predominated. Bearded and with a bulging belly, he habitually held court in the shallow end for the admirers who were always around. He was also to be seen in the back of a big two-tone brown car being driven to the theatre, where he was said invariably to contrast the excellence of the drama with the poverty of the acting. I remembered parental talk of his biting criticism years later when an occasional pleasure was to read James Agate, drama critic of the *Bystander*. Of a musical comedy not to his liking he remarked,

I knocked everything, even the chorus girls' knees. But there nature had anticipated me.

Best of all in my Malvern childhood were Christmas and the New Year, when the house smelt of the large tree with real candles that took ages to light in the patients' waiting room. Greenery festooned the hall and long staircase. The dining room, promoted from its role as the nursery, had streamers made from hoops of crêpe paper from the picture rails to the central ceiling rose. On Christmas Eve Joanna and I were in ecstasies of anticipation of the contents of outsize woollen stockings retired from our father's shooting outfit of plus-twos (like plus-fours but less baggy). On one occasion, after we had all been kept awake by Joanna's sleepless fretting into the small hours, my father was advancing upstairs with a pad and a bottle of chloroform at the ready when, to huge relief all round, she dropped off. Next morning, after church, came an orgy of present opening. There was invariably an enormous turkey which reappeared in various guises until its final epicurean obsequies as devilled legs. On New Year's Eve, as the only dark-haired Scots male (my father being balding and grey), I had to stand in the cold outside the front door with whisky and shortbread until the church clock struck midnight and I could 'first foot' by knocking for admission.

In the New Year came an expedition to London to see Bertram Mills's wonderful circus at Olympia, with the extra treats of the Great Western Railway journey and a stay at the Regent Palace Hotel. Another routine was the buying of National Savings Certificates with the monetary proceeds of the season, augmented by an old lady who liked me to call on her in her room in a private residential hotel just before each school term began. I had to give her an account of my doings, which I did so softly at first that she would ask me to turn her shoebox-sized hearing aid up. I then spoke very loudly into the saucer-sized microphone, sadistically relishing the consequent convulsion. I still got half a crown.

As these agreeable years passed, I discerned a change. Ever since I could remember we had had three servants: Cicely the cook, of uncertain temper; Doris the housemaid – not Keats's La Belle Dame sans Merci but certainly alone and palely loitering; and Lois, the tweenie from an orphanage, charmingly natured and young enough to be a friend. My mother needed them all because she was practice secretary, receptionist, housekeeper and hostess. All three servants gradually disappeared without replacement, and there was much table talk of money problems. Patients, always tardy with bill-paying, were increasingly often not paying at all. Professional etiquette and the need to maintain esteem made debt collection impossible. All my father could do was to keep sending repetitions of his courteous request: ('Dr George Mackie presents his compliments and begs to intimate that his charge for professional attendance amounts to ...'). Domestic help shrank to visiting dailies and a formidable living-in housekeeper whose dignity demanded that she should be called by her surname, Kemp – forbidding but kind underneath. I learnt a little more of mortality when she slowly turned bright yellow and died of cancer. Her successor was a carer for Joanna and general helper, Kathleen, delightful daughter of a farmer who stayed for many years and was a friend and confidante.

Our situation seemed to stabilise but I sensed that it was precarious. My mother had inherited a holding of shares in her first husband's family business, the Vulcan Foundry, which made railway engines famous for their quality and sold in many countries. The shares brought in a useful £500 a year; but their real value lay in backing the joint account overdraft at the Westminster Bank. Being in hock, I came to realise, did not matter as long as the shares were worth no less than 10 shillings. That was the source of my Awful Worry. At the age of no more than eight I found out how to consult the Iron, Coal and Steel section of *The Times* shares list and did so almost daily. Vulcan shares fluctuated between 9s 6d (panic about the imminence of I knew not what form of Nemesis), and 11 shillings (exultant relief). Whichever obtained, I knew that matey Mermagen, the clerk, knew all about our predicament, and my hate for him grew. I was always as relieved by the paying-in of cheques as I was anxious about their cashing.

I knew far more of money than of sex. As the signs of puberty began, Kathleen, habitually in and out of the bathroom, took to busying herself at the basin and sidelong glancing while I was in the bath. Amongst my voracious reading was a historical novel about Roman times by Naomi Mitchison, and that was useful. More so was combing the Bible, which hitherto I had studied only in the context of the quatrains, handed down by my father, that reminded their learners of who was who:

> Joshua the son of Nun
> And Caleb the son of Jephuny,
> Were the only two
> Who ever got through
> To the land of milk and honey

(Numbers 14:30).

I was soon to know all too well from two disgusting paedophile schoolmasters. I knew what Onan did (Genesis 38:8–10); but I couldn't make much of the Song of Solomon, and it took time to interpret 'known' or 'gone into'. So did 'intimacy took place', a frequent usage in the *News of the World*, favoured with their custom by the maids. Gaps nevertheless remained. Part closure came one morning at breakfast when my father, usually punctual, immaculate and ready for work apart from his spats joined us late, unshaven and obviously tired. My mother asked him how long he had been out. 'Almost all night. I was struggling with what I thought was little [newlywed] Annie Bartleet's huge premature baby. It wasn't till 4 a.m. that I realised it was full term and despatched it with forceps on the kitchen table. *She and Bobby must have started before the gate went up.*' I was beginning to get it together.

Of the very few dislikes of the ways of my parents, loving to the point of doting, the worst was enforced Scottishness. I didn't much mind holidays

The hated kilt. *Norman May*

in Scotland, except that it seemed always to rain. Porridge was bearable and I quite liked haggis, ordered from Gibsons of Edinburgh and fired in salvos at Christmas by my father at other doctors in thanks for help during the year. The bane was my kilt, all the worse because I was expected to be proud and appreciative. Wearing it with a fancy silver-buttoned jacket, sometimes a lace bib called a jabot, a false dagger (*skean dhu*) in my stockings and a fore-and-aft hat called a Glengarry, made children's parties a penance, the incongruous outfit earning the derision of other children and undue attention from grown-ups. Whenever I could I positioned myself behind anything that concealed my horrible skirt. And I was as desperate to get away as I would later be on the sports field. Was it, I still wonder, the origin of a lifelong dislike of social gatherings and a lack of small talk?

Following the St Martin's debacle came Tannachie Court, a small pre-prep school to which I was allowed to go as a day-boy, delivered and fetched 10 miles by one or other parent, eating into their already overfilled time. The school was on the beautiful plain east of the Malvern Hills, with good grounds and classrooms in a former mansion. The work was more challenging but still not enough to extend me. I was at a loss to know why I and two other boys classified as clever had to go for extra tuition during the lunch break with a small general factotum of a master whom, for his descendants' sake, I will call Master Bates. I thought smugly that we, the intelligentsia, should have done less rather than more. In the event the sessions were not so much useful as abuseful, owing to Bates' nasty peder-astic habit. We realised it must be wrong but felt unable to say anything, soon discovering that doing to him as he wanted led to his rebuttoning his flies and getting back to work. He also taught soccer and cricket, which may have had to do with my dislike of both. Soccer I found so disagree-able and the ball so intransigent that I would stand, usually shivering, at left half where I was put because there I was least likely to do harm. I hoped that the ball would keep its distance, aching for the final whistle and relieved beyond measure when the premature arrival of a parental car would provide remission.

Further listening-in at meal times at home established that the headmaster, Keith Bullen, was a patient of my father's. That meant that there would be a file on him in the study cabinet, which I duly rifled. Pale, except for his red nose, and fleshy he had a history of digestive trouble for which he had been prescribed bismuth and my father's home-made panacea, known to the family as 'Dad's headache pills'. (They were a compound of aspirin, phenacetin and caffeine which would nowadays be banned as near lethal, combined in a small machine into scarlet gelatine capsules sealed with a Bunsen burner). Bullen – to come back to him – my father had noted as having little wrong that drinking less whisky wouldn't cure. Remembering his most prominent feature reminded me of:

> And Oh, ho, ho
> His nose doth show
> How oft the black jack
> To his lips must go.

That fascinating nugget, I realised, could cause trouble. I only now reveal it.

Some patients too poor to pay their fees in money did so in kind. One was Mr Tilt the milkman who delivered a whole summer holiday's worth of thick cream in daily half-pints, which cheered up our porridge. Another, an awesome drinker who had a lot of illness, was Mr Humphries, head of the riding school, who gave lessons to Joanna and me. To my great delight, I had found something physical that I could do well on the ample commons of Malvern, where the ponies' homeward gallops were my earliest experience of the exhilaration of speed. I no longer felt just a bookish little swot. My prowess put me on a path marked out by our half-brother William, who was an excellent horseman, hunting with the Croome and getting 'blooded' after a kill and later presented with a 'mask' (fox head), duly mounted on a wood shield. Incredibly in retrospect, I envied it and aspired to one of my own. But we could only afford one hunter in the family. Just as well.

Bookish I certainly was. As well as the conventional pleasures of Sherlock Holmes, Bertie Wooster and Dr Doolittle I was given Hendrik Van Loon's trilogy on *The Story, Home and Arts of Mankind*. Above all, in a house full of books, was an almost complete set of bound volumes of *Punch* magazine. I nourished my precocity by thumbing and re-thumbing through them. In retrospect, most of the jokes are barely comprehensible and ultra-patronising of the lower orders. A beautifully drawn charlady proclaims in 1876:

> I've often heard rumours
> Of wars and contumours
> Sea-Sarpints and comics as lights up the sky
> Steam-hingins a-bustin'
> And banks as folks trust in,
> But they don't never fret a old 'ooman like I!

Nor were the fashionable upper classes spared. Responding to her beau's suggestion that they should sit down after dancing, a wasp-waisted belle, feathered and bustled, replies, 'I should like to; but my dressmaker says I musn't.'

Political cartoons, savour of a primordial *Private Eye*. One lampoons Prime Minister Disraeli's initiative in the Tory Government's sagacious purchase in 1875 of £400,000 of Suez Canal Company shares. Another portrays the perennial problems of Irish home rule, at the time conditional, to the anger of the peasantry, on the Sunday closing of the *shebeens* (drinking parlours). Of the more comprehensible jokes, one was an archetype of precocious me and my pencil-perfumed pedagogue:

The new governess (impressively): 'O Tommy, when I was a little girl and made a blot on my copy book, I used to *CRY*'.

Tommy (earnestly): 'WHAT! REALLY?'

New governess (still more impressively): Yes – really *cry!*'

Tommy (still more earnestly): 'What an awful little duffer you must have been!'

How the readers must have fallen about.

Not much had changed by 1902, when Teddy Roosevelt, President of the USA, is drawn in a swimming costume jumping into a lake full of trust (cartel) crocodiles. Marylebone Council is roasted for refusing a millionaire publisher (Carnegie)'s offer of £30,000 to provide public libraries. As the portly Beadle puts it: 'Go away my good feller! We don't want no books 'ere!'

The apparent birth of the blonde joke emerges in a young lady's reply to her boyfriend's protest, as he missed meeting her at the station because she had not, as agreed, travelled in the slip coach (that is, the last one, detached and separately braked): 'How could I have known where it was on the train?'

A lineal descendant being the young lady who asked the bus conductor whether his open-topped double-decker went to Victoria. To his helpful intimation, 'Outside only', she asked, 'Where does the inside go?'

Precursors, no doubt, to the lady on the westbound transatlantic Jumbo who left her economy seat and sat in the first class. Asked to vacate it successively by the stewardess and her supervisor, she obdurately stayed where she was. Only when the first officer, summoned from the crew compartment, spoke to her did she return to her correct seat. Asked how he had done it, the first officer explained that he had told her that that section of the plane wasn't going to New York. *Plus ça change.*

In 1936 came a black-edged edition mourning the deaths of King George VI and Rudyard Kipling. The butts of two prescient cartoons by the brilliant draftsman Ernest H. Shepard (he of Winnie the Pooh) were Lord Rothermere (*aka* the Pornographer Royal) and his *Daily Mail*'s praise of Mussolini, and the emergent Nazis' tearing up of the Locarno Treaty and rape of the Rhineland.

That was to come. Meanwhile I ascended to a full prep school called Wood Norton. It was 20 miles away near Evesham, and so boarding was inevitable. It had originated as the Priory School, attended by my brother while it was in Malvern. Its motto, kept on after the move, was a middle-class pun rather than a joke: *Priore nil prius* is Latin for 'Nothing before the first' as well as 'Nothing ahead of the Priory'. Kept on after the move, the motto was belted out as the last line of the school song, a paean of praise

39

in Latin for former pupils deserving well of their country which we all had to learn:

Hi bene de patria merentur,
Priore, Priore, Priore nil prius.

For the time being the first hurdle was the farewell parental tea party: so many other boys were in tears at the moment of party that my built-in desire to excel kept me inappropriately cheerful. We were soon shown round the main building, a semi-stately home built for the Duc d'Orleans, a monarchist refugee from the Buonapartes. Many rooms were oak-panelled and everywhere were carved replicas of the Orleans fleur-de-lis. The majestic dining room belied the awful food. The lumpy porridge made me retch daily. Tuesday's sausages tasted of vile things that had floated up from an abyss. Thursday's liver was tough, grey and hard-wired with veins. Friday's fish was slimy flakes in soggy batter that made the ground floor stink all morning. The bony mistress of all this was Margaret Giles, wife of headmaster Claud and billed in the prospectus as a graduate of the renowned Athol Crescent, centre of culinary excellence in Edinburgh. I don't think she passed out top. The only relief was a slap-up Christmas meal at the end of the autumn term; and huge helpings of straw-berries presented by the grower in Evesham, father of a boy, whenever he had a surplus.

The school grounds seemed vast and we were allowed to roam almost unrestricted. In front of the palatial classrooms stretched lawns leading to a balustrade patrolled by red squirrels from the woods below. I liked the staff. Claud was formidable but kind behind the carapace, with a marvel-lous talent for reading aloud and making classics exciting. Ed Osborne, a classicist chain smoker, was agreeable except for the smell. Of Cyprian Wilmot Beale I remember only his explanation of the difference between pathos and bathos, and his ear-splitting laugh. J. Packenham Nangle (I kid you not) of course taught maths. Thomas Paulette Partington had as his mission giving me ever more difficult books to read. A colleague, whose family name I will protect with Pete O'Phial, taught French. All went well at first: he even gave me a prize of Gasc's *Concise English/French, French/English Dictionary* which I still use. But he began punctuating his lessons with indecent exposure and attempting to abuse not just two or three of us but the whole class. Once bitten, as it were, I took it on myself to tell Claud Giles. O'Phial vanished within a day. Not so another Tyrannosaurus Sex: named in mercy Randy Rita. She gave piano lessons but was prone to rubbing her breasts against my back and trying to kiss me. Years later I was reminded of that nauseating experience by a couplet from the comic American poem, set to Tchaikowsky's ballet music, about a small boy's desperate effort to persuade his parent to let him leave the horrible boys' camp Granada:

> Hey dere Momma,
> they won't miss me;
> why, I'll even let Aunt Bertha
> hug and kiss me.

I could not bring myself to shop Randy Rita to Claud Giles, for fear of being disbelieved. The easiest way out seemed to be to ask to give up the lessons without saying why. It worked.

Profane gave place to sacred love with the advent of Joan Pascoe, the glamorous dancing teacher who came weekly from London to give lessons, with piano accompaniment by a butcher's daughter from Evesham. I could hardly wait for my turn to dance with her, my ardour damped only slightly because her navel was at eye level. Pleasurable for hilarity rather than romance was unison singing with Miss Barnet. A fresh-faced ingénue, she told us all about the sea shanties which sailors once sang to help their work along. She then invited the class, some of whom were doubtless enuretic, to sing the first line of her chosen example:

> a wet sheet and a flowing sea.

Unabashed by the ensuing gale of mirth she pressed on with:

> a wind that follows fast.

When the convulsion died down we changed, as I recollect, to something like Widdecombe Fair. The song, nevertheless, was the opening item of the Christmas 1934 concert, the review of which concludes:

> [the performers] can rest assured that their efforts thoroughly pleased their audience.

No doubt of it.

Other unison singing consisted in hymns, rendered at morning prayer on the rainy Sundays that everyone hoped for because they saved us a two-

and-a-half-mile walk to Fladbury Church. At domestic worship we took turns to choose hymns. Chronic trouble resulting from minor offences usually moved me to select *Ancient & Modern* 184:

> Rock of ages cleft for me,
> Let me hide myself in thee.

Fladbury predominated. Every three weeks we were allowed a Sunday out after church after the service; or earlier if one's parents had arrived early and one could contrive a faint, real or simulated. I managed both in my time.

The single playing field was on low ground beside the River Severn. During most winters it was flooded, giving terrible footballers like me the relief of rounders, which was all the higher orchard land could sustain: it was a game I found almost congenial. Not so cricket and soccer matches, which we seemed consistently to lose. The result was a common feeling of failure, echoed in the school magazine:

> We should prefer to pass this term's results with a minimum of comment ... a distressing series of matches ... lack of any real attempt at combination ... proved our downfall and ... an inferiority complex prevented us from doing anything right.

Not all was so miserable. I made my first close school friend, Peter Turley, another loner, whose father had died. His prize possession was a wind-up gramophone and we constantly played his collection of brass band records, wearing 'Entry of the Gladiators' almost to extinction. We were constantly together, inviting each other to our respective homes. We shared dreadful jokes: to a question asking the difference between a post box and an elephant's bottom, professed ignorance elicited a scornful, 'I shan't send you to post my letters.' Worse, if possible, was:

> The boy stood on the burning deck
> Playing a game of cricket
> The ball flew up his trouser leg
> And hit the middle wicket.

I later came to prefer Spike Milligan's monosyllabic second line:

> Twit.

We were both Scouts, under the mastership of a local landowner. Apparently as a Good Deed, he taught us knots and firelighting and set us on the path to a multiplicity of badges on offer. Scouting, moreover, took up one afternoon a week that would otherwise have been used for games; it was worthwhile for that merciful saving alone. Also to be had were carpentry, handicrafts and lectures by interesting visitors such as Tschiffely, well known at the time for riding on horseback across South America. There were picnic expeditions to the Malvern Hills and cinema visits: *Sanders of the River* with Paul Robeson was a film I particularly enjoyed. Claud Giles's readings of classics made them enthralling. All in all, Wood Norton tried to educate rather than merely to prepare us for the Common Entrance exam. I worked hard to get ready, stretched but never apprehensive about it, even though my destination, Charterhouse, demanded 65 per cent as a pass mark, a figure exceeded only by Winchester.

My father, desperately keen that I should do well, was very supportive. He rewarded my slightest successes, once buying me a small silver cup, duly engraved, to augment what he saw as an inadequate prize for winning

The 61st Division memorial at Laventie, Pas-de-Calais. *Author*

43

a three-legged race. He rolled turnips down a hillock for me to shoot at with my four-ten sporting gun before I graduated to rabbits. We fished the River Annan during our Scottish holidays; so boring was casting flies that I resorted to a worm, considered ungentlemanly but highly productive of flounders. Being a member of the Worcestershire County Cricket Club he took me to matches to watch such stars as the Nawab of Pataudi, whose son was later even better than he was; and Wally Perks, a legendary fast bowler. He had had as patients the Foster family of seven brothers, all of whom played for the Worcestershire team, which became known as Fostershire. They gave the coach, John Laker, a silver cup, autographed by them all, to celebrate their best season; he left it to my father and I still have it. My father built for my half-brother William, of whom he was no less supportive, a magnificent model railway in the corner of our utility room, full also of tools which he taught us to use. Responding to my childhood efforts as an entertainer he had a model theatre built in wood complete with torch bulb lighting which we installed, a blue velvet curtain and a

The wreath-laying, achieved with great relief. *The Illustrated London News.*

44

revolving glass stage through which characters could be moved from underneath with a magnet. It, sadly has not survived, but I still have a 4 foot battleship hull which a carpenter had made and to which my father made and fitted the superstructure: it proved to be top heavy, capsizing in the bath; but not unlike the battleship Potemkin to be seen at St Petersburg, it is a handsome ornament on stocks. He and I both enjoyed the General Knowledge paper which Wood Norton set each Christmas holidays, taking great trouble to ferret out the answers. The 1935 exam's 20 formidable questions asked, *inter alia*, for the plants associated with Arran Chief, Madame Butterfly, Cox's Orange, Royal Sovereign and Cup and Saucer; the meanings of quixotic, philatelist, phrenology, ventriloquism and mythological; and definitions of a logan stone, a mortar board, an oast house, a silo and a cromlech. Our joint effort won, two years in succession. I still have the *Oxford Book of English Verse* given as the prize.

My father responded to a request from his divisional commander in World War One for a child to lay a wreath at the unveiling of the division's memorial to the thousands of their dead and got me the job. That meant a memorable trip to France and Belgium where I saw the trenches and absorbed a little of what he as commander of a field ambulance and his comrades had endured. Apart from being the best kind of education, that adventure led to my first experience of the media – a photograph in the *Illustrated London News*, and later a leatherette-bound book of cuttings and photographs. It was also the start of a seventy-five-year love affair with France.

In due course came the Common Entrance exam result. I had passed with such high marks in every subject that Charterhouse put me in Special Remove, a form for scholarship boys in their second or third term. No new boy in living memory had entered it. I was soon to discover that my too-cleverness-by-half had run me into the sand.

Chapter 3

A School of Thought

Some people think of *Nicholas Nickleby* and *Tom Brown's Schooldays* as offering models of public schools: tough places, that is, for small boys with mother's apron strings not long, and often not entirely, severed by pre-prep and prep conditioning. Not so Charterhouse. There the souped, or rather caked-up version of Wood Norton's tearful tea party for new boys was comparatively cheerful and the partings were completed almost with relief. First thereafter came a progress of new boys to the Music School, where our singing was to be assessed for suitability for the choir. Not shanties this time, but notes and short phrases – solo. Master of ceremonies was Dr Fielden, director of music, who eased our ordeals by making kind fun of the awful noises we emitted. Only much later did he emerge as a formidable figure, given to bawling, from behind the organ console in the chapel, corrections to hymn and psalm numbers wrongly announced: it was always pleasurable when one of the chaplains, nicknamed Jumping Jesus and error-prone, got the treatment. For the time being Fielden deemed my strangulated squawk good enough to make me an alto. That earned me a choir seat in the beautiful chapel, opened in my half-brother William's time at the school as a memorial to the boys of whom, like those from other public schools, wars always take a terrible toll. The long list of my contemporaries whose names are on a wall always moves me. It includes one of my heroes as a small boy, Arthur Bean, a top table monitor, brilliant cricketer and above all a good bloke whose posting as 'missing believed killed' particularly saddened me. His fate as a Fleet Air Arm pilot emerged only in 2004, when his body was found still in the cockpit of his previously undiscovered Seafire naval fighter, which had buried itself on the coast of France.

Shoehorning us in was done mostly by mentors, boys in their second or third terms (known, logically enough, as quarters). Mentors befriended the neophytes for the first fortnight and often much longer. They, including the boy I was lucky to get, Peter Laverack, tutored us in the intricate system of privileges: when for instance, one became entitled to a large instead of a small tea mug; and how many and in what circumstances one could undo the buttons of the black jackets which, with striped trousers, were uniform at the time (later to be replaced with tweed jackets and grey flannel trousers, to widespread relief). Mentors also helped their charges to prepare for the new boys' entrance test which included the names, house colours, masters, tutors (assistant housemasters), head boys and second heads of the 12 houses. All except one were '-ites', as in such biblical formations as Perusites, Jebusites and Israelites. I was a Saunderite. Neglectfully I never found out who Saunders was: only that he had to be pronounced as in *Sanders of the River* and never as in 'saunter'. I and everybody else had to know the school's history. Charterhouse, we learned, was founded in 1612 by Thomas Sutton, a prosperous merchant and philanthropist who wanted to help with the education of indigent boys in the City of London. The foundation still exists there but is now residential, providing homes for deserving Old Carthusians and others. There is also a charity in Southwark providing a variety of facilities for needy East Enders. The school itself was moved to Godalming in the 1870s and consists in a cluster of Victorian buildings made to look dowdy by the memorial chapel, a tall, beautiful 1930s building. There are also new residential houses for boys in the acres of green and well-treed grounds. The motto, ensconced below a roundel-decorated shield is,

Deo dante dedi

(roughly) 'God giving, I have given [in return]'. And the toast that accompanies it,

Floreat aeternum Carthusiana domus,

meaning 'May the Carthusian foundation [literally home] flourish forever'. (Eton gets by with 'Floreat Etona' and the Middle Temple with a mere 'Domus', though giving the word a more collegiate meaning. The higher the fewer.)

More mundanely, new boys had to be taught fagging. The system, essentially licensed slavery, entitled senior boys called monitors to trigger, by means of the loudest yell of 'Fag' they could manage, to summon a helter-skelter of small boys supervised by a senior slave known ex officio as Head of the Week. The last boy to arrive in the monitorial presence would get one of a range of permitted menial jobs such as shoe cleaning; buying sweets from the Tuck Shop, which carried a commission; and other fetchings and carryings, which did not. There were also specialised fags with regular jobs. Mine became the cleaning of the large house collection of silver cups and other trophies in Long Room; the task taking an hour or two per fortnight. Long Room was where junior boys lived, moved and had their being: working, reading, playing board games and socialising. But not eating. Unlike Dotheboys Hall and the like, we had a handsome dining room. Meals began and ended with a Latin grace, read in turn by senior boys at a top table. The food was ordinary but much better than that at Wood Norton. Such extras as fried eggs could be bought from the house butler, cantankerous but good hearted.

First-quarter boys slept in small dormitories under the eye of the Matron, Miss Jennings, very well liked and sadly soon to die of cancer. From the second quarter onwards everyone slept in cubicles in rows along the sides of huge rooms. Each had a noisy door bolt, making unauthorised use instantly apparent to patrolling monitors. Attached above each side wall were loose panels held in place with wires extending the length of the room. An attempt to clamber from one cubicle to the next would bring the whole contraption down with dire consequences. That deterrent, however, never went off in my time. There were no such devices in the communal bathrooms, which had open-ended cubicles under similar monitorial oversight. For a privileged quartet of top boys there was a shared bedroom with a battered brass bedstead for the head monitor used by William Makepeace Thackeray when he did that job. Promoted to the same eminence I slept in the bed, finding it less comfortable than the ordinary one. Saunderites, along with the two other houses within the periphery of the school buildings, was regarded as pre-eminent, becoming more so when the headmaster reverted to the practice in Thackeray's day of being also its housemaster.

Absorbing new boy lore was easy. And although monitors' and masters' disciplines were strict in theory, both were applied humanely. I never met or heard of bullying. The only monitor's beating I got, for some forgotten peccadillo, was painful through pyjama trousers; but worth it for the claret-coloured weals on my buttocks, a badge of honour much admired. New boys, like everybody else, had at their disposal the tuck shop, where such sybaritic treats as slices of melon, iced coffee and Mars Bars were to be had; a combination I often wolfed on the spot. There was also a book shop, primarily for supplying text books but also well stocked with other material for browsing.

The terrible exception to my otherwise harmonious start was the schoolwork. Special Remove was the sand into which precocity had run me. I could hardly understand, let alone do, much of the work. Except for Latin and essays, I came emphatically bottom in every test for the single quarter for which I survived. The form master, a shy intellectual of great learning and kindness, was named William Oliver Dickins and nicknamed

WODESQASM, derived from a notice he, as assistant scoutmaster, had put up in the Scout Hut, unwisely initialled and designated. I was greatly relieved to be downgraded to Remove, a form for clever but not brilliant boys, with a seasoning of older proles who had clambered up through the four lower forms during their first two years. The form master became a profound influence on my life. The Reverend George Snow, 6 feet plus, was a revelation. His precise and very demanding teaching methods, implemented with humour and sympathy, were just the stimulus I needed.

The syllabus was geared to the all important School Certificate, somewhere between the later 'O' and 'A' levels. But, with a wide and absorbing curriculum, Remove was far from an exam sweat shop. In 1936 and 1937, Snow set us an extended essay, complete with our own cover, binding and illustrations and known as a *magnum opus* (major work). My first was on 'My idea of photography', illustrated with the results of my small folding Kodak camera undeservedly featured as exemplars of good technique, and a postcard of Charterhouse Chapel pilloried as dull. I answered my own question of why people take photographs with: 'For the same reason that people paint pictures, write music or poetry or indulge in every other one of the arts.' Priggish and too high-flown for such fuzzy images as those of my dog Tinker and the Zeebrugge train ferry, but relieved by an account of an apparatus of strings and pulleys for photographing myself; tragically, it failed. George called my *magnum opus* an excellent work with an amusing style and full of personal touches.

Its successor, 'Miniature Drama', was an account of my model theatre, illustrated with my own photographs and bound in waste suede from the Leathercraft factory where my father had dealt with the casualties of a mishap. It dwelt mainly on how the actors were moved, the scenery made and the lighting operated. But as to subject matter I specified the sources as: 'books full of plays ... obscure magazines and old annals of *The Scout*. As well as this I write whatever extra dialogue is necessary'. The selections were undoubtedly over the top for family and neighbour audiences, but fun to make. The most successful production was 'an old rhyming play [performed in the Middle Ages by travelling Mummers] with the usual story of St. George overcoming evil by fighting various people'. But there were adversities:

I had the programmes professionally printed, a very expensive proceeding. A number of fights had to occur and convincing fights between valuable model actors are dangerous. To overcome this difficulty we had dramatic thunderstorms ... ignited magnesium ribbon was lowered on to the stage, which looked quite like genuine lightning.

The subject matter, as George Snow said, appealed to him enormously and the cover, complete with cut-out comedy and tragedy masks, was one of the best he had ever had.

Out of the classroom George was a man of parts. As a chaplain he far outclassed Jumping Jesus and another insipid divine. His approach to religion was clear and simple, 'Determination plus confidence equals faith' being one of his helpful aphorisms, complementing Paul's definition of faith as the substance of things hoped for, the evidence of things not seen (Hebrews 11:1). George wrote three religious manuals, respectively on *Prayer*, *Confirmation* and *Belief*. They retain their freshness. With WODES-QASM's help he revolutionised the Charterhouse Scout Troop, showing himself to be as dexterous with ropes, knives and staves as he was with words. He lived in a small bachelor house full of gadgets, among which was a self-assembled radiogram with a huge funnel of a speaker in the corner of his sitting room. His boast was that the only way of improving the sound quality lay with the BBC. He had an acute sense of fun. At the risk of straining the bounds of pedagogic loyalty he told Remove of an encounter with his neighbour Colonel Jameson, an old World War One veteran who taught the bottom form, Shell. 'Good morning Snow,' said Jameson one day. 'You must congratulate me; I've become a grandmother.' 'Surely, Colonel,' George replied, 'you mean grandfather?' 'Forgive me,' came the reply, 'how stupid of me; of course it's a little boy and not a girl.'

Another in the circle of masters who did well by me was Norman Chignell, my housemaster until Robert Birley, the headmaster, took over. He was a mathematician and outwardly as grey as John Major. He proved, however, to be good hearted and approachable when I got to know him better, as he prepared me for Confirmation. He is memorable mainly for his hugely fat, jolly wife, whose pince-nez glasses made her look like Billy Bunter in drag. A brilliant classicist, John Waterfield, later to have a successful career in the Foreign Office, wrote of her in a less than diplomatic clerihew:

> In the wishing well
> that the plumber built her,
> Mrs Chignell fell.
> We must buy a filter.

Like John I learnt to love Latin in the ill-tempered care of one Sniffy Russell, who got me a housemaster's beating with a false accusation of erasing a blackboard full of Latin verses: the weals were less roseate than those the monitor had inflicted, but still sufficed as exhibits.

I caught an infectious delight of English from Arthur Irvine, another old stager and an expert in such seventeenth and eighteenth century poets as Milton and Addison, the latter an Old Carthusian. Irvine hated the misuse of words, one being 'glamour', which became fashionable in the 1930s as an epithet for trollopy girls. 'Glamour,' he posited, 'is romance with excitement.' I agree. No less meticulous, but with music, was my piano tutor Arthur Trew. He was primarily a cellist, chosen for me from a selection of four tutors for the worst of reasons: my parents had got to know the Trews through their daughter Patricia, who was a girlfriend of my half-brother William. She was a stupid, mincing girl whose affected accent earned her the soubriquet Twishy Twew. I did not prosper at the piano. At the time (1937) there was a press advertisement for a piano correspondence course with an illustrated slogan guaranteeing astonishing progress:

They laughed when I sat down to play.

With me, they still do.

Although cricket, soccer and hockey were compulsory, the dozens of games on the great steppes of the sports ground made teams of equivalent ability feasible. Playing with fellow duffers was much less onerous than the ineptitude-induced miseries of Wood Norton. Scouting afternoons also reduced the burden, and swimming sessions could be manipulated to the same end. Swimming, learnt as a small boy, boosted my small store of physical self-esteem. So did the shedding of self-consciousness at being naked, erased by force of numbers, familiarity and preoccupation. I recall a moment of hilarity when an otherwise unremarkable boy, having loaded another on his back, staggered towards the dives and as he did so got an erection. It was doused only when, to hoots and whistles, he jumped into the water. Years later, at a comprehensive day school used by the Health Education Council for curriculum research, I realised the value of unself-consciousness. Some of the boys were so abashed about others seeing their genitalia as they showered after games that they went through the deluge draped in a towel or still in underpants, preferring discomfort to embarrassment. I have since wondered what part easy familiarity played in the homosexuality through which most adolescents pass. That phase manifested itself in the overt crushes, distinct and often separate from friendships, which boys got on each other. They included Berner and myself (see below); and between me and another boy, effeminate and petulant, whom I grew to dislike. My own feelings were so scarred and inhibited by my previous pederastic experiences as to make me shy away;

but I think other boys' attachments, like mine, seldom became physical. Certainly the popular idea that the public schools were riddled with homosexuality was false.

My luck continued with two marvellous opportunities for a games-hater. The large school hall had a stage and curtains but lacked proper lighting because drama took second place to undemanding recitals, concerts, lectures and prize-givings in no need of special lighting. One event in which such lights as there were showed their deficiencies was a performance by a cobbled-together orchestra of staff and boys of the works of Vaughan Williams, the best-known Old Carthusian composer. He was present, glowering most of the time, and made a surly speech of unappreciation. Another, much grander, concert came from the London Symphony Orchestra, conducted by Sir Adrian Boult. My enrapturement was disturbed by my fascination with the elastic inserts in the armpits and sleeves of his tail coat; there, as I imagined, to enhance his back view.

Such were the detractions from events like these, and so restricted was the range of plays caused by poor lighting, that the school had a platform built high on the side wall of the hall to accommodate the controls and switchgear for a better system. There was a call for two boys who would work the lights during performances, after first helping with the installation under the supervision of the school electrician Arthur Burgess. John Berner, an older boy from a different house and another fugitive from games, and I got the jobs. We worked with Peter Barton, a maths master with an excellent singing voice and a talent for drama. With him we devised and installed what became a much-admired system. The dominant feature was a cyclorama, a plain white surface at the back of the stage onto which floodlights of variable brightness and assorted colours could be projected. We made them from large cubical biscuit boxes, each fitted with two 150-watt bulbs. All the different circuits had home-made dimmers, each consisting in a standard 3-foot drainpipe, sealed at the bottom and filled with liquid electrolyte. There were lead weights at the top and bottom of each drainpipe, the top weight being moveable up and down in the electrolyte to vary the voltage fed to the lighting and hence the brightness. The moveable weights were worked by cords threaded through pulleys and controlled by wooden wheels, the whole contraption being sited on the back side of the new platform. Doubtless the much stricter regulations for such installations later imposed would have put ours beyond the pale of legitimacy. But for the time being it far exceeded my self-photographing device in Heath Robinson ingenuity. And it worked.

Design and fitting took two quarters' worth of weekday and weekend afternoons. After free tuition in the school carpenter's shop I made the control wheels on a lathe, but Berner did most of the difficult work. We both got acclaim for the result. Another knowledgeable master took the trouble to write to me in the holidays complaining that nobody but the two of us understood the wiring, the festoons of which, as he put it, were enough to hang all the murderers in England. He later helped with improvements. When switch-on day came, the whole of Godalming's lights flickered, and the duty engineer in the town's small electricity undertaking rang to complain of lack of notice.

Far more ambitious productions were now within reach. One was the *Ascent of F6*, by W.H. Auden and Christopher Isherwood; the mountain top and its diurnal variations of background giving marvellous scope for our battery of cycloramic colours. Later, in 1938, we did Shaw's *St Joan*, applauded by all, including professional reviewers, and deemed good enough to go on Continental tour. All I had done was to help to light it effectively; but that included mild risk-taking in a perilous journey, with a hand-held spotlight, along a narrow, slightly bouncy, transverse steel girder which was part of the proscenium support. The object was to highlight, in the centre of an otherwise darkened stage, a kneeling Joan's Parthian line,

How long, oh Lord, how long?

Enveloped in dusty velvet, with my arm round a vertical girder, I found myself asking the same question.

Concurrent with the stage work came another get-out-of-games card: the Film Society, founded as another of his many enterprises by George Snow. He persuaded the authorities of the growing cultural importance of cinema, moving them to build a projection box on to the back of the school hall; and to buy two second-hand, cinema-size projectors. He asked me and another boy, quaintly named Le Rossignol, to become operators and general factota; an attraction being that most of the preparatory work would take place on games afternoons. We back-projected the films on to a screen in the hall, showing them at society meetings once or twice a quarter. The classics we displayed, enhanced by George's excellent programme notes, added to my passion for the cinema. The best-known was *The Cabinet of Doctor Caligari*, a portrayal of the world through the eyes of a madman, the eerie effect of which was heightened by the flickering black and white images. Another was *Turksib*, a record of the stupendous Russian achievement of building a railway from Turkey to Siberia through appallingly difficult terrain. Others still were British documentaries made by the Post Office Film Unit about night mail trains and North Sea fisheries, Walt Disney's *Fantasia*, and masterpieces such as Pabst's *Kameradschaft*, Lubitsch's *Trouble in Paradise*, and Hitchcock's *Sabotage*: their lasting quality is evidenced by the appearance of some of them in our granddaughter's media studies degree course in 2001. Rossi and I, after some ragged instances, became expert in split-second coordination of the two projectors so that stopping one and starting the other between reels showed no trace on the screen.

As a reward, perhaps, for these efforts I was given a place in the *St Joan* company's tour in 1938, with a small part and the job of liaison with the stage electricians at the theatres en route. The first stop was Paris, where on the free night, the boy who played St Joan and I, flaunting our French, wheedled our way into a glorious performance of the *Magic Flute* at the Opera. The company's other stops in France were Nancy and Strasbourg, with enthralling train journeys through the wooded hills of the Vosges. But planned performances in Germany were stopped by the Foreign Office because of rumblings of war.

That growing threat came home to Charterhouse in the autumn quarter, (known as Oration), during which Hitler and Prime Minister Chamberlain reached a so-called settlement at Berchtesgaden, followed by the Nazi rape of Czechoslovakia. Our Headmaster Robert Birley, with his characteristic passion for truth, denounced what had happened in a sermon on liberty. He illustrated his prediction that liberty would prevail in the end with the elegant metaphor of Smetana's tone poem *Ma Vlast* (my country), which includes a thrilling portrayal of the unstoppable rush of the river Vltava from its source in the mountains to the sea. After the sermon the director of music, Fielden, played his setting of part of the Smetana piece on the chapel's thunderous organ, said to have been rejected for the new Liverpool Cathedral because it was too big. I remember no better lesson on liberty, and have seldom been more moved.

At home, I no longer needed to eavesdrop. I shared the family problems. My sister Joanna, spared the horrible St Martin's kindergarten, had gone to Lawnside, a local all-girls private school, where she stayed happily until the time came for becoming a domestic science and drama student. But of course she added to the incubus of school fees: I realised the true extent of the burden only when Rachel and I had two sons of our own to educate. How my parents managed to sustain the way we lived I do not know. The Malvern Theatre, the cinema, Boots lending library, tennis at the excellent local courts, a big house, two cars and much else were all funded somehow.

In lean years, holidays in the Mackie haunts of Scotland were replaced by visits to my half-brother William's grandmother in her near-stately home in Dedham, Constable's village in Essex. As widow of the railway engine magnate Sir William Collingwood, she had a large holding in the Vulcan Foundry, the proceeds of which she lavished on her 22 grandchildren, making no distinction between the real Collingwoods and our slightly alien Mackie selves. In 1937 we stayed with her, enjoying day-trips to prim, respectable Frinton-on-Sea. We went there in her large Armstrong Siddeley with her at the wheel, the chauffeur/factotum having departed. The redeeming feature of these frightening trips was the ticking-off she gave my father if he dared to remonstrate, presuming to point out the merits of the left of the road as opposed to the right, her preferred side. Back at her house, Joanna and I enjoyed exercising her latest gadget, a refrigerator, unknown to us because we had a large, cool walk-in larder. Its ungoverned cooling pump was such that leaving the door open would cause a crescendo of speed and noise as the inside warmed up and it tried to cool the whole world. In better times we drove across Wales over enthralling mountain country to Borth, then an unspoilt seaside village but later to become an overdeveloped plague spot of tack and tat. We rented a house overlooking the low cliffs and the shore: magnificent for us, the children, but as big a burden for my mother as running our ordinary abode; her only relief was from patients.

Back in Malvern I became more and more attached to what was now a study bedroom bursting with books. I had acquired a portable wireless by cashing 5 guineas-worth of my small hoard of National Savings Certificates. It needed a very expensive dry battery as well as accumulators which had periodically to be reinvigorated at the local garage. What I liked was news and music such as that of the resident BBC organists Reginald Foort and later Sandy Macpherson, as well as the dance bands of Jack Jackson, who began the horrible trend of American-accented crooners; and, in contrast, Harry Roy with his inimitably English style. Dance bands were also part of another Terrible Worry, shorter-lived but no less provocative of the anxiety that has plagued me at intervals all my life. This time my parents, not content with all that they already had to do, became prime movers in organising an elaborate full-dress ball in the Malvern Winter Gardens in aid of the Red Cross. There were to be a big-name band, raffles, floor and side shows and a high-class buffet. Attendance was to be by personal invitation to buy tickets, to all those deemed by the committee to be, as dreadful Thatcherspeak expresses it, 'one of us': 'County' was the term of art. County, it emerged, weren't much interested. Nor were big-name bands, even at enormous fees: the best we could get was Marius B. Wynter of whom I and other cognoscenti would, had the phrase been invented, have asked 'Who he?' Everything else from catering to marquees by way of bar stocks and parking seemed to go wrong, and I shared my parents' exhaustion, anxiety and misery. Almost at the point where it would have cost more to cancel than to proceed, the number of takers began to grow. The event scraped through with a derisory sum for its object. But holding it might well have contributed to my father's appointment to the county directorship of the Red Cross and my mother to a lesser post. That in turn was to lead to an OBE for him and a Certificate of Merit for her.

Otherwise home was far from gloomy. Joanna and I had become competent horsepeople. We were promoted from the town swimming pool to the private pool of Dad's grandest patient, Lord Beauchamp, in the grounds of his country seat at Madresfield. Dad had become a confidant and adviser as well as a doctor to the family, who were stricken by the death from an accident in Switzerland of the heir Lord Elmley. They once asked us all to Christmas Day tea; of the expensive presents we were all given, my Tiffany gold cuff-links still survive. The most welcome perk of all, however, came from another pay-in-kind patient: Stan Green, the Malvern College racquets coach, taught me squash. Here, at last, was a ball game which I loved and would continue to enjoy until, at 40, I reached the age which RAF doctors regarded as the safe limit.

As a very different kind of diversion I sat in a stand to see the Coronation procession for King George VI in 1937. The treat was made possible by my Uncle Alex Cavendish who, as a retired colonial servant, had been allotted a seat in the Mall next to the Admiralty Arch. With typical generosity, he gave the seat to me. Apart from what seemed an eternity of waiting from very early morning until nearly noon, it was a thrilling experience to see so huge a sequence of the great and the military pass by to the music of umpteen bands. Years later, while I was driving my ancient and imperious Aunt Jessie down Park Lane, she pointed to the verandah of one of the mansions that line that grand thoroughfare and remarked that she had sat there to watch the Coronation procession. Flaunting my own experience, I questioned whether the procession had passed that way. I was put brusquely in my place by being assured that it had – Edward VII's procession in 1901, of course.

For the rest I walked the hills and rode and bicycled the plains of Malvern at home. At school Charterhouse did its job and I sailed through the School Certificate exams with credits in all six subjects. That meant an end to the Long Room and cleaning silver, and the award of a study. Studies were very small rooms in which recipients were allowed to augment the issue desk, chair and bookshelf with an armchair; and to embellish the walls with pictures and hangings. I put up my Peter Scott prints of birds, accumulated over successive birthdays, and garish blue and orange material from the drapers' cheapest range. The study complemented my room at home and helped with preparations for the next hurdle – the first year of medical education and training, culminating in the First MB: a facility offered only by Charterhouse and Epsom College which provided a reduction of a year of the sojourn, even more expensive in those days, at university.

I felt crushed and offended at being railroaded into medicine as a biology specialist when alternatives were on offer, comprising classics, history, science and a ragbag of subjects for the dim and/or undecided called pre-specialists. The Latin which I was good at and enjoyed, in spite rather than with the aid of the miserable classics master, had gone by the board; as had my chance of the classicist's glittering ascent, by way of a scholarship or exhibition to Balliol College Oxford and thence probably to the Bar. I was left with such treasures as the formula for writing Latin verse, which is based on metre rather than rhyme:

> Down in a deep dark well
> Sat an old cow munching a beanstalk
> Out of her mouth came forth
> Many melodious sounds.

the long and short syllables of which are easy to transpose into the dactyls and spondee components of Roman poetry. No less useful was the guide to the imperatives of certain irregular verbs:

> Dic had a duc with fur on its back
> And that's a fac.

And the aide-mémoire for unruly prepositions:

> *A, ab, absque, coram, de,* [day]
> *Palam, quam, in, ex or e* [ay].

No longer in need of such joyous props for mastering a language I loved, I thought it best to plod on – a decision not so much craven as cognisant of all that my father had done for and expected of me. I came to enjoy the physics, organic and inorganic chemistry and biology in the syllabus. Percy Chapman, zoologist and botanist was likeable, gifted and hospitable in a little house like George Snow's. He was remarkably prescient about the contents of the Cambridge University exam papers which everybody sat, almost invariably predicting which animal would be the subject of the dissection: earthworm, frog, dogfish or rabbit. He was succeeded by Oleg Polunin, an outstanding young botanist who was to become famous as a don. The inorganic chemist was J.C. Thompson, an aristocratic, learned housemaster with a sideline of superb lectures on architecture. The physicist was Reginald Poole, another war veteran thought to have a bladder disability, leaking being triggered by whistling, which gave his lessons a pronouncedly musical character. The most amusing of the team was Professor Teagan, an engaging Irishman, with a brogue so strong that his pronunciations were often distorting of technical terms. We, and I suspect he, enjoyed our efforts to make him say the symbol for acetic acid – CH_3COOH – which came out as,

See haitch three see dubloh haitch.

As the preparations progressed some of us, me included, were offered lessons in chemistry in German to equip us for an exam in that subject which was part of the Cambridge scholarship syllabus. The master, a young priest called Anderson, did his best to interest us more widely in the language to which he was devoted. Too busy to respond properly, most of us stayed within the confines of *stickstoff* (nitric acid), *sauerstoff* (oxygen) and *schefelsaure* (sulphuric acid) and their derivatives. I have ever since regretted my limitation to the argot of Mond, Liebig and other German chemical giants in the language of such as Goethe and Schiller.

I did not sit for the scholarship because of a tortuous diversion. My father, a graduate of Edinburgh University, wanted me to follow in his footsteps not only as a doctor but also as an Edinburgh student. Charterhouse, however, sent all would-be doctors to Cambridge and the Edinburgh and Cambridge syllabi were very different: the latter so much so that the best way to get there was by taking the London University exams which Edinburgh accepted. After deliberations in which I took no part I was tasked to attempt both the Cambridge and the London exams in the same 1939/40 season. Feeling far from confident I sat the whole series, discouraged by being treated as no more than an exam-taking drudge assumed to be capable of performing such academic feats with ease. For the London exams I stayed with my beneficent Uncle Alex, now retired to a flat in Fulham, near the Science Museum where the sittings took place. In Cambridge, I stayed in the vacant room of a student in Christ's College Cambridge and got a feel for how agreeable student life would be.

Charterhouse I continued to enjoy. I had become first a monitor and then head monitor of Saunderites. In the same term Robert Birley, the headmaster, took on the additional job of housemaster. I already knew him as a very tall, shy man whose teaching and preaching were couched in luminous language. He had had the difficult job of succeeding Sir Frank Fletcher, one of the great headmasters, which he did with ease. I now started to work with him, mostly dealing with such trivia as permission for monitorial beatings and approval of boys' engagements and appointments. He remained shy, perhaps because two quarters earlier I had incurred his wrath. There was a path, forbidden to cyclists, which afforded a short-cut from Saunderites to the main entrance to the school. Bent on something urgent I was bicycling along it at full speed. Reaching the road, I pulled up too late and found myself sprawled in front of an approaching car. Out stepped Birley. He took me straight to the holy of holies, his study, selected a cane from part of a bookcase adapted to conceal his collection, and beat me. After cursing my unbelievably bad luck, I recognised the boost to my reputation that would follow from a headmaster's beating. It did. But the afterglow, physical and figurative, soon passed.

Birley, despite his diffidence, was a better housemaster than Chignell. He shone especially in small gatherings of the senior boys whom he invited for discussions of current affairs dominated by the darkening prospect, and later the actuality, of war. His stance was Christian Socialist and I found it difficult to disagree with him. I was an occasional guest after Sunday morning Communion at a breakfast of sausages whose herb-laden succulence was unimaginably different from their sinister Wood Nortonian predecessors. The hostess was Elinor, his porcelain shepherdess of a wife, in all things as bright as she was beautiful. In an effort to help with preparations for my exams, they invited me in the spring of 1939 to stay with them in their cottage in the village of Martock. I worked all morning on practice questions and walked the Somerset lanes with Birley in the afternoons, finishing with pre-prandial ale in the pub. He and Ellie were superb hosts and amusing companions.

So was George Snow, especially in the Scout troop in which I stayed until I had to move into the Officers' Training Corps. The weekly meetings culminated in the summer camps, of which I went on two. One was the enormous world Jamboree of 1937 at the village of Vogelensang

'Be Prepared' is the Scouts' motto: at the Jamboree and ready for anything. *Anon*

('Birdsong') near Haarlem in Holland. It began with an assembly of 28,000 Scouts and Guides from 50 countries for a royal welcome and march past. We had all put up tents and made fireplaces and gadgets using our diverse skills and ingenuity in the complex of fields made available. The only exception was 'Boy Scouts of America', whose luxurious camp had been erected by contractors. It attracted much derision; the tent pegs, set in cement, having been put in sloping backwards instead of in the canonical forward stance, the better to secure the guy ropes.

We entertained each other with a multiplicity of yells and other campfire items: an English one fit for polite society being a variant of a well-known ditty:

> x blue bottles
> standing on the meat
> x blue bottles
> standing on the meat;
> and if one blue bottle

61

should wipe its dirty feet
then xday's dinner
won't be fit to eat.

There was, of course, much matey intercourse and souvenir swapping.

Presiding over the whole affair was Lord Baden Powell, the 80-year-old Chief Scout. I knew him slightly because his wife Olave and wayward elder son Peter were friends respectively of my mother and half-brother William. On a Sunday out from Charterhouse I went to tea at his home, Pax Hill, near Farnham. I found him disappointingly taciturn, very different from what I had imagined after reading his lively, self-illustrated books. I'm sure the fault was mine for being too gushy.

After the Jamboree the Dutch people, some 20,000 of whom had visited the open events, conducted us on tours all over Holland. It was a cleaner, pleasanter and more bicycle-friendly country than Britain; and so it has remained. The entire cost per participant, including rail and boat travel, food, camp fee, sight-seeing and insurance, was £5 10s. I marked the occasion with a scrapbook of cuttings and photographs; my father completing it with a cover specially printed, yet again in lieu of fees, by a patient.

The other camp took place in 1939 in a sloping field near Corfe Castle, Dorset, with an amphitheatrical view of the Channel. Therein deployed was the Home Fleet, then still enormous. The sight of warships of all kinds stretching as far as the eye could see gave a realism to Thomas Arne's 'Rule Britannia' sadly lacking in the shrunken flotillas of the twenty-first century. The one discordant note was the German guest scout invited by WODESQASM'S successor, David Keith. Horst Brandis was a young Nazi and a Hitler Youth member who boasted of what Germany could do and strutted to the point of self-caricature. The textbooks for my German chemistry course had included one titled *Marchen und Erzalungen fur Enfenger* ('Words and phrases for pupils'). Larded with chemical names, the phrase provided shoutable gibberish ideal for aping Hitler's speeches. I used it to the full.

I was rapidly putting away childish things. The camp was my last association with George Snow for a year or two, but we corresponded. He left Charterhouse to become headmaster of Ardingly College in Sussex: a welcome progression on the strength of which we later sent both our sons there. He officiated at our wedding; later himself marrying, quite late in life, a pleasant girl called Joan who made an excellent headmaster's wife. Their children, like so many offspring of parsons, were a mixed blessing.

The eldest overdid, perhaps, his father's precepts of determination and confidence by becoming a Marxist. His brother Jonathan pays tribute to his steadfastness as a hospital porter and trade unionist in his own biography, but confirms the familial unhappiness that Tom's disputes with his father caused. After Ardingly, George was made Suffragan Bishop of Whitby. I felt he should have gone further in the Church. He retired, however, and he and Joan settled in Corfe Castle. He died from a heart attack during a favourite pursuit – an evening walk on the hills behind their house. Amongst the tributes paid to him at his memorial service in Ardingly Chapel in 1977 were those for his

> wise counsel, teaching, preaching, care and concern, life of prayer, overflowing faith and vision of the Kingdom of God.

The least he deserved.

I started driving lessons on my 17th birthday on holiday in Dorset with the local garage man Leo. T. Phear (yes, that was his real name), continuing at home. I passed one of the newly instituted, and doubtless very easy, tests. I was thereby enabled to do odd jobs in my mother's Morris 8, though never in my father's bread-and-butter Rover 12. I had acquired a new girlfriend called Virginia Leigh, a dearth of parties having extinguished the match-making with Eve Perrins of our respective parents. Virginia lived on the far side of Malvern Common, which offered an opening for 'dash and initiative': qualities which, I later discovered, were highly regarded in the RAF. I could gallop across the Common on a riding school pony, tethering my not very dashing and well-off-white charger outside her home. I soon sensed that she had been warned off; and that, until we began writing to each other, was that. The next girl, nearer home but not next door, was the lumpy Mary Behrens. Again, parental *force majeure* saw me off. Virginia later left for the Belgian Congo to be spared, I hope, a white woman's grave. Mary married a gunner officer friend of my half-brother William's: alas, it didn't last.

Out of order but not of ardour, I turned to taking stock of my prospects. Whether I would remain stuck in the toils of the Carthusian Laocoon or those of the Aesculapian serpent of medicine depended, as it seemed, on my exam results. Neither prospect pleased. Luckily, I was to wriggle out of both.

Chapter 4

Blueing the Lot

Blueing in a different sense began in the night sky over Charterhouse. Just as I was in final preparation for my clutch of exams the Home Secretary announced the formation of the Local Defence Volunteers, an unpaid citizen force to help in resisting the German invasion of Britain, then thought to be looming. All the school officers' training corps were at once roped in because we were already trained in fieldcraft and tactics and armed with the Lee Enfield rifle, a World War One relic but still serviceable. Having reached the lofty rank of corporal, I had an LDV badge sewn below my chevrons and shared in the renewed enthusiasm for what had been the lackadaisical weekly training afternoons that succeeded Scouting. We now had also to do night patrols, working two hours on and four off; the latter being spent drinking cocoa made largely with water and trying to sleep in bunks with itchy blankets in the school armoury, pressed into service as a guard room. The task was to scan the heavens for the German parachute troops thought likely to initiate the invasion of Britain. We were enjoined, believe it or not, particularly to look out for parachutists disguised as nuns and equipped with folding bicycles. We also had to patrol the school grounds in search of possible intruders. The LDV soon became the Home Guard and, along with all the other school units, we formed, as one might describe it, Son's Army.

My exam results came first from London University where, unsurprisingly to me but upsetting to my father, I had failed all four papers. Fortunately the opposite had happened at Cambridge, and Christ's College offered me a place for the autumn term of 1940. There followed an idyllic summer quarter unencumbered by pre-exam drudgery. Instead I was given some white mice with which to conduct histology, preparing and reporting on thin slices of their innards mounted on microscopic slides. I read a great deal and did more and better monitoring. Not being under pressure was just as well, because of the depletion of energy that afflicted the Home Guard night owls.

At a loose end one evening I went to one of the voluntary lectures that I had always enjoyed. Instead of the usual general interest topics we were given a good recruiting talk by a Royal Naval schools' liaison officer. I had long felt uneasy at going into a comfortable civilian occupation as a medical student ('reserved' as the term was); unlike my half-brother William who, now a subaltern in the Royal Northumberland Fusiliers, had volunteered for service in the elite expeditionary force formed to prise the Germans out of Finland, which they had occupied when the war began. I must also have been jealous of the heroic limelight in which he, as big a show-off as me, basked. But I also realised that a break from medicine at the embryo stage would give me time to decide whether it was a profession I wanted to pursue.

The lecture precipitated me into wanting some of the action. I thought of the Army, but I was put off by the *sotto voce* assurance that those of us who joined up in the ranks of the local regiment, the 60th (Royal Surrey) Rifles, and behaved would within six months be commissioned as officers. That, I felt, flouted my principle of paddling my own canoe, already wobbly enough. The lecturer was persuasive about the Navy; but life in the Executive (seaman) Branch seemed likely to consist in very long periods of gazing at dangerous oceans and only rare opportunities for the derring do I had in mind. That left the RAF. I consulted my father about deferring my entry to Christ's College, which had been guaranteed for after the war. Convinced that his intense patriotism and his own war record would override his desire to launch me into medicine, I was not surprised that he agreed. He was bitter about it, however, telling my mother that he was sure I would be killed. Back at school, I wrote to the recruiting office in Reading and got a reply by return, summoning me to a medical examination. It was surprisingly thorough, reminding me of the would-be shop assistant in A.P. Herbert's poem:

> And everything there was to know,
> Selfridges knew.

On the way back to Charterhouse I watched a Rolls-Royce entering Waterloo Station. In it was King George VI in Field Marshal's uniform. The encounter seemed a good augury.

It was. I had to leave Charterhouse before the end of the summer quarter, departing with great sadness and replete with good wishes. Still a day under age, I reported to the RAF base at Cardington, well known by its enormous hangar used for research into the use of barrage balloons, but also a recruitment centre. I spent the night in a hut with 29 other aspirant air crew. Almost all slept in their singlets and pants, and there was a consensus that the windows should be kept shut. After a night's smelly stiflement I breakfasted off lumpy porridge, half-cooked bacon and over-fried egg with toasted damp flannel to follow, washed down by tea. Its cardboard taste was said to come from the bromide added to dampen licentious airmens' sexual libido.

Processing took all day. Having agreed to serve on the ground if not acceptable as air crew, I was sworn in and given the traditional King's Shilling. Next came an interview with a panel presided over by a Group Captain Betts, elderly and affable. After lunch (stew, brown or curried, suet pudding and custard) I finished the sequence, only to be told that I would have to stay another night. The reason, it emerged, was that the Flight Lieutenant whose job it was to sign the railway warrants for homeward journeys had gone off duty. No sacrifice being too great to avoid the company of sweating humanity in repose again, I declared my willingness to do without one. The surprised corporal let me go.

I made my way to Ickwell Bury, a country mansion nearby owned by Charles and Mary Wells, old friends of my mother's, who had offered me a bed. She and my mother had been at school together, and he was Wells of Wells & Winch, brewers, who still exist. In their drawing room for pre-prandial sherry was Group Captain Betts, billeted in the house for want of decent accommodation at Cardington. He kindly disclosed that I had been accepted for pilot training. Though innocuous, that morsel of old-boyery reminded me of the furtive 60th Rifles offer. Later came a repulsive strand from the same skein. My father, with the best of intentions, had written on my behalf to a one-time medical colleague, now director of RAF Medical Services, Air Marshal Sir Harold Whittingham; and also to the Air Vice-Marshal commanding the group based in Gloucester, near Malvern, whom he had treated as a patient. Happily these toe-curling, hanky-twisting initiatives turned out to be as unfruitful as they were otiose.

For a month or so I was on deferred service as, what RAF jargon called an 'ach (aircraft hand)/ut (under training) pilot', chafing to realise what the term implied – that I was to be taught to fly. As well as doing the usual enjoyable things at home, I earned a little money. At the Malvern Theatre a travelling company was performing the play of the Bronte novel *Jane Eyre*. Jane was played by a mature lady who had consulted my father, honorary surgeon to the theatre (from which, incidentally, came the complimentary seats of which I had long been a delighted beneficiary). He prescribed for her throat infection a concoction of cocaine to ease the pain, and mildly antiseptic glycerine of thymol – a mixture which he made up himself on the marble counter behind a screen in his consulting room.

The stuff was to be sprayed into her throat from a de Vibiss syringe, which had a rubber bulb pressuriser, a small glass reservoir and a long spout. He deputed me to stand in the wings for the six-night run and treat Jane, whenever she exited left, to ease the pain of the screaming of which she had to do rather a lot. Flounced, ringletted and miraculously rejuvenated with cosmetic filler, she was most appreciative. My £1 per performance came in handy, but the chief reward was relieving my father's burden, however slightly. By now, apart from running his own practice and helping with that of a younger doctor who had enlisted, he was having to do more and more Red Cross work as county director.

There was more to come. A benefactor had given the Worcestershire Red Cross an Austin 18 limousine, gleaming black and complete with a snob's panel. It was to be used as a glorified delivery van for distributing the hospital supplies needed by the emergency hospitals. These were located in a network of requisitioned large houses all over the county to help cater for the thousands of casualties which World War One experience indicated would occur. Drivers were scarce, and I welcomed the chance to help. I ferried bandages, bed linen, splints, woollies and medical miscellanea in the car, which could hardly have been more of a contrast with my second-hand Austin Seven tourer, to pay for which I had raided £30 from my savings. The Baby Austin served me, and later my wife Rachel, well until we deemed its flapping mica windows and draughty fabric roof inadequate protection for our firstborn.

Malvern shared in accommodating evacuees from the big cities thought to be at imminent risk of destruction by German bombs. Amongst the grander of our contingent was a cousin of my mother's and long-term family friend Alan Murray. He repaired to one of the objects of popular derision at the time – a 'safe hotel', in this instance the County, Malvern's best. Formerly a major in the Seaforth Highlanders, he had been invalided out before the war because of an accident involving the loss of an eye. He had turned to augmenting his substantial private income by writing popular songs. He was a hypochondriac with great faith in my father: no doubt that was a factor in his choice of Malvern as a refuge. He was apt to drop in on us for tea or supper, condemning my father, unless he had contrived to be out, to a discussion of the vicissitudes of his colon. For the rest of us, his superb piano playing and ready wit made him a welcome guest. Following the sinking by the German navy of an unarmed merchant ship, the *Athenia*, the German propaganda machine tried to stem the international outcry by blaming the sinking on Winston Churchill, at the time First Lord of the Admiralty. Alan wrote and set to music:

It does seem odd that Winston C.,
Of all sea lords the senior
Should have the sheer effrontery
To do for the *Athenia*.

The best-remembered of his songs is 'I'll walk beside you', which made him a great deal of money from records, sheet music and performing fees. He once heard on William's home-made radio a rendering of the song by Gwen Catley, at the time a well-known performer. Her tempo was not to his liking. Borrowing our telephone, he sent her a telegram congratulating her on her singing of 'I'll run beside you.' He had a reputation as the broadcaster of the series *Whenever I Hear This*, a do-it-yourself precursor of Radio Four's *Desert Island Discs* and Radio Three's *Private Passions*. It led to further work.

Relieved by the call to arms, I went by train to Torquay. Also in the carriage was a brash young man who boasted of his exploits as a trainee pilot. With the rest of a group of uneasy-looking young men I bussed to Babbacombe, a small adjoining resort where the initial training unit was based. Proceedings on arrival began with bare-chested queuing for a battery of injections, blood and urine sampling and the embarrassing liturgy of FFI (Freedom From Infections). The last involved exposure before a medical officer of the armpits and genitalia. At this there was much muffled protest, particularly from those of us Biblically challenged (see 2 Samuel 1:19), for whom there was an added retraction. The orgy of physicality caused some fainting, relieved in my case by spotting that the line-shooting airman of the previous day was no pilot: he was the dogsbody collecting the sample bottles and keeping the queue in line.

We lived in scruffy cheap hotels requisitioned as billets, no doubt to the delight of their proprietors. The rooms, three- or four-bedded, were almost bare but not uncomfortable. We mounted guard on the row of front doors in shifts. Late one evening an old lady, passing the duty sentry, said, 'Oh you poor man, you do look tired!' and gave him a pound note. We devised a crash course in simulated exhaustion; practised, alas, without result. There was little to do in our spare time except to read and spend our 28 shillings a fortnight in the NAAFI. Most of us, strange as it must seem in the twenty-first century, were too young to bother with the pubs. One asset was the YMCA, where a decent bath could be had in private and tea, etcetera could be had cheaply. As a virility symbol I sported a pipe, using Four Square Tobacco branded in various colours. It continually went out and I soon abandoned it. The best amenity of all came from

69

The rookie: butter wouldn't melt. *Anon*

the generosity of the Imperial Hotel, whose palatial grounds adjoined our doss places. Their free swimming, squash and tennis were a real boon.

We drilled, marched at a furious pace, did physical training and learnt elementary airmanship. To bolster our general Service knowledge we were issued with the *RAF Pocket Book 1937*, a compendium of law, cookery, discipline, navigation, explosives, camps and much else. The 320 pages plus supplement offered such gems as the penalty for spreading alarm and despondency, which was penal servitude. In case, as officers, we had to report for duty in His Majesty's ships, it was good to know that we were to:

join in Service Dress before 9 a.m ... there are usually two gangways; that for officers will be marked 'Officers only.' [An officer] will be received by the officer of the watch [who] wears a sword belt and usually a frock coat.'

Both officers and men, we were warned,

must conform to the naval custom of always doubling to obey an order.

Of the 24 recipes, one seemed less than honest. To make lemonade:

Mix two tablespoonfuls of brown sugar and 1½ tablespoonfuls of *lime juice* [my italics] and add 1 pint of water.

But it would be enough, it seemed safe to assume, for sustenance on a landing ground while rectifying:

Damage ... often caused by villagers and their cattle making tracks across a ground which develop into ruts in wet weather.

We couldn't say we hadn't been warned. And it was reassuring to know that the weight, with vehicle equipment but without load, of the 'Car, Staff Hillman type D', was 1 ton, 13 hundredweight, 1 quarter and 21 pounds.

We were supervised by Pilot Officer Aylwin, a pleasant specimen of the middle-aged business men who joined the newly created Administrative and Special Duties Branch of the RAF, much to the benefit of its organisation and efficiency. Our lives were governed by tough, noisy but caring and funny Sergeant Dale and his sad assistant, Corporal Alford, who said almost nothing except 'C'monryurp', irrespective of whether greater despatch was called for or not. Dale's comments as he raised us to really high standards of smartness and drill, and made them fun, were mostly not for repetition – exceptions being 'Look out, there's a sailor behind you' to anyone caught bending, and 'leave your brains alone' to anyone unwise enough to scratch his crutch. He showed his strength when a boy foolishly tried to bicycle across our improvised parade ground: he literally stopped him in his tracks, seizing the bike from behind and dragging it aside. He welded us into a team, of which there was only one recalcitrant member, an older man called Pretzlik. Ooozing money, he had his uniform specially made for him and very smart it was. Well-spoken but slightly foreign-accented, lightly tanned and with film-star good looks, he frequented expensive pubs in Torquay and boasted of his weekend exploits in London. He disappeared overnight as the course was ending for, as we surmised, security reasons. If he was a spy, he could hardly have made it more obvious.

The longed-for next phase soon came. For me, after a short Christmas break, it was the elementary flying training school at Sywell, near Northampton. I was billeted with a kind and, as they seemed, elderly couple who gave me a spotless front room in their house near the airfield. On 28 December, having been picked up by the RAF bus, I began a flying career that was to last 26 years and 4 months. It was to be exactly the fulfilling antidote to my childhood sense of inadequacy, other than as being overly clever, that I needed.

The aircraft was the de Havilland Tiger Moth biplane. That, had I known it, was a bit of luck because it was a classic aircraft, which is still around in the twenty-first century. It is still a safe but demanding trainer. But it is also, as I found out during my several revisits over the years, superb for advanced aerobatics, especially the apotheotic eight-point or hesitation roll which can be executed in the Tiger Moth with a precision exceeded only by the Spitfire.

As the aircraft gathered speed for my first flight ever on that freezing morning, it felt as if it were alive, and I knew I'd found a friend. No less so was Flying Officer David Bamford, my instructor, who followed a precept that I later tried to apply to my own charges: instructors do not teach flying; pupils learn it. With minimum interference to stop me killing myself by not keeping a look-out or allowing the aircraft to lose speed to the point of dropping out of the sky, he let me get on with it. Almost at once it became something I loved and could do. Leonardo da Vinci got it right:

> When once you have tasted flight, you will forever walk the Earth with your eyes turned skyward, for there you have been and there you will always want to return.

A minor but salutary contretemps didn't so much bring me down to earth as disrupt that tricky process. The snow thawed. Hitherto I had relied on a brown ploughed field that stood out among the acres of white ones as a marker. If I positioned the aircraft over it at 800 feet, I could be sure of the respectable approach that would lead to a decent landing. When that egregious helper merged into a patchwork of green and brown I floundered, opening and closing the throttle in overcorrections which caused variations in speed. They were an unfailing recipe for bounces, leading to much chortling from the back seat. In due course the problem solved itself.

On the ground we learnt the Rules of the Air, a three-dimensional Highway Code; more airmanship (RAF common sense); enough elementary navigation to reduce the risk of getting lost (not a serious risk, Sywell airfield having a nearby crescent-shaped lake with the arms pointing towards it); and basic aeronautics. The last I enjoyed, having read the two classics by the patriarch Professor Kermode, *Flight without Formulae* and *The Aeroplane Structure* and dipped into his formidable *Mechanics of Flight*. I passed the ground exams with, I have to say in all immodesty, room to spare.

Living in a single billet made for solitary off-duty time but I was very content with what I was sure was the best bedroom and my hosts' caring concern for all I did. I did some pubbing with friends, but drank very little because on arriving home, whatever the hour, I was regaled with tea and cake and conversation for which I had to be in a fit state. On the few free weekends I drove home whenever the petrol ration would, as one might say, run to it.

My passing-out test with the chief instructor led, contrary to what my burgeoning conceit had led me to expect, a mere average assessment. In retrospect that result and the second one I got after the next stage were cautionary correctives to my overconfidence – a lethal temptress, as poor David Bamford discovered a year or two later when, showing off his capacity for inverted flight, he hit the ground and was killed.

I was blessed with more good luck with a posting to the pre-eminent flying (successor to elementary flying) school at the RAF College Cranwell. The excellent pre-war facilities were still in place, though truncated. The staff did all they could to maintain the standards expected of the pre-war Flight Cadets (less arrogantly titled than their Sandhurst equivalents, including my half-brother William, who were 'Gentlemen Cadets'). Those expectations are clear from a parody of Chaucer that appeared in an early 1920s issue of the *College Journal*, preserved in Hilary St George Saunders's excellent history *Per Ardua*:

> His buttons on parayde were always bryte,
>   His puttyes always laced were y-tight
> And never fowle or muddie were his shoon
>   Hee always did his preparacioun.

Apart from the very few promoted from the ranks, almost all flight cadets were ex-public school boys. After Cranwell, they took up the lordly, leisurely existence, as it was described, of squadron service in peacetime.

Spared puttees (hot and uncomfortable leg bandages which I had worn in the OTC), we did our best to keep pre-war standards up. We lived in comfort in the college, two to a single room. My mate was Reg Langley, older and a Lancashire Lad, unselfish, unaffected and a source of good advice; not least about cars. We were friends for all too short a period because he was to die in action in little more than a year. The food was good. The public rooms, full of portraits and mementoes, were a delight; as, for me and other devotees, were the squash courts.

We marched daily to the college airfield. The college march was 'The Lincolnshire Poacher', with an add-on prelude unsuitable for having disrespectful words put to it. For 'Colonel Bogey', however, there was a choral introit:

> Don't throw the lamp at father;
> Wait till he gets in bed and grab his ...

And thence to the refrain:

> Bollocks, and the same to you;
> Bollocks, they make a man of you;
> Bollocks, I don't mean rowlocks.

By which time the chorus were getting out of breath and left the rest to the band.

We began our advanced training in the twin-engined Airspeed Oxford. Compared with the Tiger Moth, flying it felt like driving a bus, but the closed cabin was a boon in the cold. It tended to swing on landing and had a talent for bouncing. Both could be contained by mentally taking it by the scruff of the neck, with a bit of George Snow's determination plus confidence thrown in, just before touchdown. My instructor, Flying Officer Bill Jolly, was competent and pleasant, and like the rest of us, I did not, I hope, give him the cause for concern for the pupil pilot in another bit of the Chaucerian parody:

> His flying filled his fader with affryt,
> For scarce he seem-ed to remain upryte.

As we toiled at practice circuits and landings we were treated to an occasional diversion. From a hangar remote from the others came a small aircraft, whining as it taxied. It then streaked across the airfield into the sky, returning minutes later whence it had come. Astonishingly, it had no propeller. It was the original jet propelled aircraft, fitted with Air Commodore Whittle's prototype jet engine, invented in the late 1930s while he was still a flight cadet.

After circuits came cross-country flying, putting into practice the elementary navigation and map reading learnt in the ground school. It provided a frightening break in my self-satisfied progression towards getting my wings. Leading Aircraftman Bob Jackson, my earnest but unremarkable flying partner, and I together did the required number of navigation exercises, one of which was along a triangular route south of Cranwell. After doing the sums and plotting the course we set off on a cloudy April day, flying as briefed at 2,000 feet. The cloud base soon lowered and we continued on instruments. I was driving and Bob was navigating with the map on his knee. We descended to 1,500 and then to 1,000 feet and were still in cloud. Then it happened. As we were debating whether to turn for home, part of a huge vertical steel girder flashed into view inches from the starboard wing tip. We both realised that it could only be one of the clutch of 1,300-foot wireless masts near Rugby. At any second we could collide with one of the others. A few interminable seconds later it was apparent that we had passed through the terrifying obstacle. As I was asking what we should do next, Bob vomited. The cloud soon lifted and, knowing from our frightful encounter where we were, we flew back to Cranwell and decided to say nothing. Only now do I reveal the truth.

We soon began night flying at Cranwell's satellite airfield, Barkston Heath. We found it none too difficult because of an overarching fear. One of our number, LAC Patrick (and it would have been a better story had he been Irish), finished his dual instruction and was sent off to do the canonical single night circuit and landing. Having done it, he taxied into the changing-over area, where the ground crew noticed with alarm that his aircraft was spattered with bullet holes. It transpired that a German intruder aircraft, then not an unusual visitor to eastern England, had followed Patrick round his circuit and fired on him. So intent had he been on the task in hand that he had had no idea of what was happening. Thereafter we all practised not just night circuits but also doing them with a swivelling head.

By now we were experienced enough to do the dawn chore of ferrying the aircraft back to Cranwell, longing for food and sleep. That and a gruelling final handling test signified that we were now aviators competent enough to be given wings – yet another priceless boost to my self-esteem. It was still cold; but nothing would have persuaded any of us to put a coat on and conceal the treasured symbol on our chests. Emerging from my airman's hairy serge chrysalis I reflected on how well the RAF had cared for me and my friends. We were made to keep fit, clean and smart. We had to keep reasonable hours. The perception that airmen were encouraged to drink too much had proved false. The medical officer had given us the sort of fatherly talk about sex that few real fathers could have steeled themselves to deliver. Our morale was sky high as we chafed to get into action. Many years later, as a station commander, I was proud to supervise a similar metamorphosis that turned conscript youths from the pond life of urban street corners into fit, self-respecting contributors to the RAF and the wider community.

Briefly at home, I walked the hills with Tinker, made more Austin deliveries and no doubt bored everybody by recounting my unremarkable doings. I was thrilled by the not unexpected news that I would be commissioned as an acting pilot officer on probation on 11 May 1941. On the 10th I went to London to be measured for uniform at Burberry's, Cranwell's tailor of choice, and to open the account at Lloyds Bank in Pall Mall in which all officers whose names began with the letters L–Z had their pay deposited. For me it amounted to 14s 6d per day plus £30 for uniform, the latter's long-delayed arrival putting me temporarily in fear that there had been a mistake and I was really only a sergeant. I stayed the night at what was then the Royal Empire Society in Northumberland Avenue, for membership of which my ever-generous Uncle Alex had proposed me and paid. Such was the noise of an air raid that, unable to sleep, I made my way on to the roof. The view was surreal. All around were fires, the biggest stretching miles eastward. The latter, I discovered years later, damaged much of the Inner and Middle Temples, including the church and the master (vicar)'s residence. I felt more angry than frightened, and glad that my twin-engined training, almost certain to lead to a bomber posting, would offer a chance to retaliate.

So it proved. With Reg Langley and other friends I was sent in June to the RAF Station at Harwell, near Oxford, for operational training on Wellington bombers. That was another stroke of luck. Following the customary principle of safety in numbers that continued into the V-bomber era, the Air Ministry had developed three different types. The Whitley was slow and cumbersome. The Hampden was faster but could only carry a small bomb load and, because it carried no second pilot, was regarded as relatively dangerous. The Wellington, however, was larger and faster, carried two pilots and had a criss-cross duralumin skeleton like an old-fashioned waste paper basket which gave it great strength. The Bristol Pegasus engines fitted to the early version were barely powerful enough, but later ones had Rolls-Royce Merlins and then Pratt & Whitney Twin Wasps, both of which gave it an excellent performance. Nicknamed the Wimpy after the *Daily Mirror* cartoon character J. Wellington Wimpy, it became the staple of the medium bomber force, more than 11,000 having been built before it was superseded by a new trio of four-engined aircraft.

Harwell was one of the network of RAF stations built in the 1930s as a part of the rearmament programme that started after the dream of a peaceful post-war world faded. They were widely separated at different heights above sea level to mitigate the problems of cloud and fog, and to effect dispersal. Harwell had to accommodate many more people and facilities than it had been designed to take, but it was comfortable, not far from Malvern and in beautiful country. My Austin Seven, its foibles seen to by Reg, was an attraction for the ample sufficiency of WAAFs; and although officers were not supposed to consort with them, that edict was honoured in the breach. So well furnished, as it were, was my social life that I dispensed as kindly as possible with the night's assignation with Virginia, now in the Women's Land Army, that had resulted from our lurid correspondence. Wishing her Godspeed on her journey to the Congo, I forbore from advising her to take a solar topee; that, I feared, might smack of taking the pith.

Compared to Oxfords, the Wellingtons were lumbering and heavy to fly. In particular the long sequences of rods and linkages between the throttle controls and the engines imposed an irritating delay, much like the soggy response of a pipe organ compared with that of a piano. Juggling with the power to make the small adjustments needed for a decent approach was formidably difficult at first; not much eased by the instructors who were untrained as such, being bomber pilots who had completed a tour of operations, mostly over Germany. The good ones had useful tips to impart. The others were 'line-shooters', giving exaggerated, ill-advised accounts of their adventures that could be sensed as the 'advantages' that Shakespeare attributed to the tales of Henry V's Agincourt veterans.

Ready for long cross-country flights, the student pilots were paired off and crewed with a navigator, a wireless operator and rear gunner. When, as often happened, the newly trained navigators got lost, the instructor aboard was seldom more useful than the rest of the crew. Help usually came from wireless bearings to augment and rectify the dead reckoning, the name for basic navigational computation. So did the pilots' map reading and the pinpoints identified by the rear gunner, blessed literally with hindsight. Our most spectacular trip, in preparation for the forthcoming ferry flight to the Middle East, took us northwards and into the eastern Atlantic to Rockall, a solitary rock which took skill and luck to find. Then came combat training with practice bombs, air firing from the Boulton Paul turret, a mechanical marvel in itself from which the occupant could swivel, raise and lower his four Browning machine guns. We got much less practice than we would have liked, especially at night, of the bomber pilot's crucial manoeuvre: the seemingly interminable period of steady, straight and level flight which had to be done, irrespective of the opposition, to enable the navigator, lying on the front floor of the aircraft, to take aim with the bombsight and let the bomb go at the critical moment.

I was teamed with Pilot Officer John Tolson, older than me and formerly a junior in the Asiatic Petroleum Company, a predecessor of Shell. In a rare burst of modesty, I have to admit that he was a better pilot than I was; but we shared the flying equally, taking captaincy in turns. He was a charming, effervescent man, full of energy and humour. We went to London together; joining, greatly daring, the Cabaret Night Club in Beak Street Mayfair. We were entertained by a hostess old enough to have been an aunt, who rendered, to modest applause, 'Tonight I see a message in your eyes', primordial pop. The message we got was that the club was far too expensive for anything more than a couple of drinks. John entertained me, in return for being driven there, at Asiatic's hospitality centre on the Thames, full of jolly gels and gilded youths exempted, presumably, from military service because their job was maintaining fuel supplies. Treating us as the heroes we weren't, they gave us too much to drink, and beds to sleep it off in. During a scarcely less bibulous weekend, I acted as best man for Reg Langley at his wedding to his delightful Eileen in Blackpool; the reception in the Tower Ballroom mysteriously lavish at a time of severe shortages of food and drink. No mystery was the plenitude of beer during weekends too short for the trip to Malvern, which I spent with the Wells's at Ickwell, their capacious home now open to the officer offspring of their many friends.

At the end of the Harwell course we were all deemed fit for operational flying. My 70 hours in the Wellington flying brought my total to 230 – very small compared with those of most new pilots by then (1941) coming off the production lines in Canada, Rhodesia and the USA. British-trained pilots, however, had the advantage of being acclimatised to the European weather and thus needing no weaning off the endless blue skies in which overseas training had been done. I felt confident, pawing the metaphorical ground to close with the enemy, and thankful that a Major Anxiety – that we might run out of war before I got to it – had proved needless. Now with a permanent crew, I was thrilled to have it confirmed that we were to ferry a brand new Wellington to the Middle East via Gibraltar and Malta, thereafter being posted to one of the squadrons based in the Suez Canal zone. The aircraft was to be a Mark Two, fitted with Merlin engines, sprightly sports models compared with the labouring Pegasi. Planning for the awesome trip in concert with John and myself were the navigator Sergeant Bolton, wonderfully precise with his charts, no doubt because he had been a trainee town planner; Sergeant Jimmy Worden, formerly an office boy at the *Daily Mirror*, streetwise and cocky; and Louie Warren, much older and a former layer of granite floors in Belfast. He liked the job of rear gunner, being, as he explained, indifferent to where he was going but keen to see where he had been. Before trips he habitually peed on the undercarriage for luck, (a superstitious practice later banned because urine damaged the metal), flaunting his penis and boasting in his thick brogue of its exploits.

I drove the whole crew into Oxford for what would later become known as a bonding exercise – a pub crawl. After we had all gained beerage way, the car's gearstick came off its stub at Carfax, a main City crossroads. In those days a uniform did marvels for sociability: a knock at a nearby door produced a man who gave us just what we needed – a length of piping ideal for putting over the stub, functioning as a jury rig that would get us home. Had the breathalyser been invented and applied on the way back to Harwell, it would certainly have exploded.

During my final few days at home our august evacuee Alan Murray told us that he had stirred from his lounge lizardry in Malvern and got a job with the BBC as a news commentator; at, of all places, Wood Norton, requisitioned when the school closed and now a centre for overseas broadcasts evacuated from London. It seemed an odd appointment because he knew only what other wireless news and the papers had to offer. But he made up for that, perhaps, by his wide experience and good mikeside manner. At last, my departure mourned by Tinker, I drove via Harwell to the nearby house of a doctor whom my father knew, glad to have my car parked in his drive until my mother could collect it. He asked me in and listened to my story so far, moved and blushmakingly appreciative. He was sure, I sensed, that I was going to be killed. That insight made me write a posthumous letter to my parents, happily never to be posted. It ends:

... in my 19 years I could not have had a happier life ... I have thought of you and home as a steady, different world to which I aimed to return and looked for support; having that behind me, my job has been easy ... Think of all that I've had in my life, not what I've missed. My death was probably in the thick of a raid or in the instantaneous finality of a flying accident – painless and probably happy.

Wilfred Owen it isn't. But not too bad, perhaps, for a teenager. Thus my youth ended.

Chapter 5

Thither, Hither and Wide Blue Yon

At last. On 29 August 1941 we left Hampstead Norris, satellite airfield for Harwell, Gibraltar bound. At full power, in which state the Pegasus engines gasped and clattered, the Merlins purred and we left the runway like a scalded cat. The easy bit was finding Bishop's Rock lighthouse, west of the Scillies and turning for Cape Finisterre at the north-west tip of Spain. Getting there was the difficult bit because it meant passing the French port of Brest to our left and evading the attentions of the German fighters based there by getting under their radar. The standard way of flying as low as possible was to wait for the long aerial trailing behind us to earth, or rather sea, itself and put the radio out of action. When that happened, John Tolson and I enjoyed more low-flying practice in an hour than we had done in weeks of training. Remembering that the 29th was my father's 63rd birthday, I reflected that it would be as well not to get killed, and so took particular care as I savoured the intoxicating thrill of going faster and lower than ever before.

No fighters appeared and we rose to a sedate height, Bolton's skill taking us to Finisterre and thence to Cape St Vincent, the south-western extremity of Iberia. We had been warned of Gibraltar's Levanter cloud, which sometimes enveloped the Rock for days, as well as the capricious winds. Neither materialised. We rounded the Rock at Europa Point, getting a northerly view of the beautiful natural giga-sculpture. The day's last obstacle was the very short landing run of 980 yards on the Colony's racecourse. Neither of us had ever landed a Wellington on less than twice that length, and we knew that the text book minimum was 1,000 yards. But we also knew that we were the umpteenth aircraft on delivery by inexperienced crews, all of whom had landed successfully. So did we. As we taxied to a halt the Merlins made their alluring tick-over sound: 'Big bugger little bugger big bugger little big bugger little bugger.' But out of the exhausts came wisps of white vapour as glycol from the cooling system evaporated. That was a symptom of the overheating that later caused the Wellington II's confinement to operating in temperate zones.

We weren't expecting a civic welcome and parade, but the lack even of a

'Hello, glad you made it' was daunting, and there was no sign of an officer in a frock coat. The officers' and sergeants' messes, contrary to custom, were unwelcoming and we were given beds in hot Nissen huts. The town was partly blacked out but replete with shops and bars. The drink of choice was John Collins, mixed initially with proper gin but changed, as the rounds continued, to hooch. To my shame I did not explore the hinterland either then or during many later visits, until as guest of Gibraltar CND, I was shown round by my hosts. In later life Rachel and I, on a jaunt from a cruise ship, shunned the apes (actually monkeys), and explored the bay from a boat, the water effervescent with dolphins.

As we waddled to the take-off point on the following morning, what had been wisps of glycol vapour turned to clouds. Having decided that to go back for a top-up would be self-defeating, we rationalised the cause as overfilling. It wasn't, and we flew the whole trip with hot engines, causing worries that one or more of the 32 cylinders might seize, happily unrequited. On the way to Malta, one of Bolton's rare miscalculations took us too close to the Italian islet of Pantellaria, putting us at risk of interception from the mainland. That possibility became a certainty when, fascinated finally to have got to the war, we encountered the enemy. It was an ancient Italian flying boat (very similar, for the experts, to the contemporary Saunders Roe London of the RAF). Louie Warren was desperate to get his guns on it; but the right course was not to dally by turning, but to make for Malta as quickly as possible, hoping that the fighters which the flying boat would summon from Sicily would not jump us. There was an added risk that we might miss Malta and fly eastwards to perdition, mitigated by the powerful radio beacon that Malta kept going come what might. We finished the trip at sea level, mightily relieved to pull upwards to land at Luqa, the main RAF base, its runway a prominent brilliant white. We were lucky that all was quiet, because Italian intruders could range over the island almost at will. Until shortly before we arrived, the only defence other than anti-aircraft artillery had been three antique Gladiator biplane fighters known as *Faith*, *Hope* and *Charity*.

After another tepid reception we looked round the sleazy town down the hill. I learnt from many later visits that there was much of interest further afield, notably the racecourse, where all the races were said to be fixed. There was the opera house, from which tinny-sounding singers could be eavesdropped from the street outside, belting out the Italian classics. The leading haunt of sin was the Floriana Gut, a steep hill lined with bars. They all had whores in attendance, many with an opening gambit of unsolicited groping. One establishment, run by two middle-aged homosexuals called Mitzi and Minko, was known for their rendering in falsetto harmony of:

They tried to tell us we're too young, too young to reely be in lurv ....

An unfailing bringer-down of the house. The area was patrolled by British naval police who knew exactly what to do with drunken sailors earleye in the morning.

For the time being there were no such frolics. Impressed by the fortitude of the resident RAF personnel in terrible conditions, we slept in stone huts surrounded by rubble. Next morning we shook the dust (metaphorical only – the real stuff got into everything) from our feet and flew uneventfully to El Fayoum, a desert airfield and distribution centre for Wellingtons of the Middle East Air Force.

I had to make that glimpse of the enemy last. Instead of being, as we had hoped and expected, welcomed as a much-needed resource to be harnessed and whipped into instant action we were, to mix a metaphor, shunted into a horrible siding. It was the Middle East Pool, a large tented camp in the desert near Kasfareit, in the Canal Zone. The truth was that the need was for aircraft, not crews. We would have to take our turn for squadron service when losses or tour expiry created vacancies.

In the event the ghastly sojourn lasted only three weeks. While we were there every new arrival got diarrhoea, in some cases with vomiting. 'Gippy tummy', as the affliction was called, could either be left alone to get better, which I was sure was what my father would have prescribed; or if one was so unwise as to go to the sick bay, treated with a dose of castor oil. Either way, constant visits to the foetid chemical lavatories with insanitary wooden sitting holes were a penance, as was the consequent sore bottom. The food introduced us to bully beef (low-grade corned beef) from tins said to have been left over from World War One; and the sweet potatoes that went with it, having the texture of unpicked knitting and a cloying flavour that I came to loathe. Apart from whisky, which I did not drink, there was only Stella, locally brewed beer infamous for its disgusting onion after-taste. The weekly ration of 50 V for Victory cigarettes, also locally made, we all found unsmokeable. Even the bearers (Empire-era speak for batmen) would not accept Vics as tips.

Worst of all were the morale problems. The pool staff had been soured by multiple encounters with young aircrew frustrated by inaction. Many, especially the Antipodeans, reacted against staff incivility with misbehaviour. Profuse disciplinary action followed: formal reproofs for officers and charges against NCOs. Very late one night there was unison singing outside the CO's tent:

> The MEP's a failure,
> A failure and a farce ...

followed by another rhyming couplet suggesting where it should be put. Wisely, the CO did nothing.

A small boon was the crackly BBC Overseas Service, whose nightly news programme ended with Alan Murray's comment. He was no Alastair Cooke nor, another giant of those days, Raymond Gram Swing. But he was a welcome link with home. He remarked on the hilarity of the description by a subaltern in the van of the headlong advance of the Eighth Army, referring to the military map:

> The second 'B' in 'Buq Buq'.

All I could offer him by way of response, again a place name, was:

> El Wak beside you.

I was, of course, in touch with home as the mail began to come through. But Alan provided a welcome extra link. One way of relieving the boredom was exploring the local Arab villages. Dressed in long robes known variously as *dhotis* and *galabeas*, the men wore white skullcaps and

Author   *Author*
The delightful locals of the Nile Delta.

84

the women headscarves. They lived in primitive huts and cultivated land made fertile by the periodic flooding of the Nile. They looked well fed, never begged and were welcoming, especially enjoying having their photographs taken.

Dredged at last from the rank pool, our crew were posted to Shallufa, a pre-war station near the Great Bitter Lake. We were to join 70 Squadron, a famous unit based for many years at Heliopolis, the much-sought-after base adjoining the city of Cairo. There were still some officers in the squadron who had served there before the war, when their existence had been even more lordly and leisurely than it had been in Britain. The squadron had converted locally to Wellingtons from their ancient Bombay bomber transports, memorable for their fixed undercarriages. Though much friendlier than our quasi-hosts at Gibraltar and Malta, the 70 Squadron officers and NCOs clearly saw us as Johnnie-come-latelies. I also sensed that the locally converted crews were insecure, conscious of the probability that Harwell training had made us better qualified than they were. However that may have been, we and other new crews only lasted days at Shallufa. With a seasoning of seniors we moved a few miles round the lake to a half-built base called Fayid. The object was to re-form a squadron with an old and honourable number: 108.

Our most intriguing senior figure was Flight Lieutenant Robert Alexander, who was a brilliant pilot, an unstuffy Scot and a source of anecdotes, particularly about the recent evacuation of Greece, enforced by the overwhelming German forces of invasion: a glimmer of fun during that tragic operation being the source of the award of a Distinguished Flying Cross to the captain of a Sunderland flying boat which he had rescued from under the Germans' noses. Handing over control to the second pilot during the flight, he had paid a courtesy call to see that all was well with the sole passenger in the back, a female British refugee. Together they created a unique circumstance for the award, fully complying with the requirement that it should be earned in action.

The 108 squadron commander designate was Con Wells, a buccaneering scion of the Norfolk squirearchy with a humour that did not detract from his stern authority. He and my flight commander, a shy New Zealander called Ken Vare, obviously relished leaving 70 Squadron to set up shop on their own. Apart from our crew and others fresh from Harwell, there were senior captains from earlier outputs. Con revived the 108 custom that all captains grew moustaches. After six weeks of omitting my upper lip from my hardly-needed shaves, my baby face got me a special dispensation.

85

Two duly hirsute captains concerned me; but not, it seemed, Con and Ken. One, halfway through a second tour, had shattered nerves, forever fidgeting, chain smoking and giggling without cause. The other, his antithesis, was in depths of gloom emphasised by his drooping moustache. He laboured under some never-clarified financial burden such that he was permanently broke, reduced to borrowing money and scrounging cigarettes. I worried for their crews and was relieved to be wrong about their fate when both completed their tours unscathed.

The adversities of a half-built station still peopled with Arab workmen none too fastidious about where they performed their bodily functions had a unifying effect on the squadron, determined to do better than the haughty 70 and put 108 back on the map. The messes were in half-completed barrack huts and everybody lived in tents appropriate to their ranks. The station commander was Group Captain Oliver Gayford, a majestic father-

Arthur Read, a station officer and talented portraitist, at work. *Author*

figure, well known for an astonishing long-range flight in 1933. Using an adapted Wellesley bomber, a predecessor to the Wellington, Whitley and Hampden, he and his co-pilot flew from Cranwell to Walvis Bay in South West Africa, staying aloft for over 57 hours and landing with fewer than 10 gallons of petrol left, having covered 5,341 miles. Under him were the station staff, there to provide supporting services for the squadron and again friendlier than their Shallufa equivalents. The adjutant, assistant to Gayford and general factotum, was an oldish coffee grower from Kenya, one of many colonial denizens who had felt the urge to join up. The cipher officers, whose sole job was to encode and decode messages in round-the-clock shifts, were middle-aged Australian business men. Another kiwi, so-called not because of Antipodean antecedents but because he had no wings, was an administrator, lovelorn and newly married. We shared a tent and I was surprised when he asked me to photograph him naked so that he could send the print to his wife. I wondered, since he was neither an Adonis nor a David, how it might be received. There was also the medical officer, not given to overexertion. When I told him of my medical ambience, he was glad to let me give the airmen their annual injections, and to assist with health checks on the airmen (FFI's – Freedom From Infection), where I first saw the lack of male genital hygiene that became a health education concern years later. Undiagnosed venereal disease was rare because, very sensibly, having it was not an offence but concealing it was. For most officers the main duty other than ordinary work was to censor the airmen's outgoing mail to weed out place names, numbers or other material that might be of use to the enemy. I came across one letter so sexually explicit that I sent for the writer and asked him whether he really wanted it to go. He almost fell on my neck in gratitude, having written it while drunk and worried about it ever since.

When troopships arrived at Suez some of us would be detailed to meet and greet contingents of arrivals destined for Fayid. The airmen were always tired, anxious and sweaty in calf-length shorts and pith helmets, at once discarded. They were appreciative of being met and welcomed into the station's personnel. They were encouraged to get fit, using the sand football pitches; and tanned enough to withstand the searing sun. We aircrew also did our best, being made to do physical training. My parents were delighted to be sent a copy of a photograph in the *Egyptian Mail* of me at the head of a line of sweating, squatting pilots. Other pleasures were the cinema, one of a chain covering several stations run by the brothers Shafto, said to have bribed their way into the contract; and an old relic of an aeroplane, a Fairy Gordon, on which some of us amused ourselves. It was a biplane light bomber of the 1930s, delightful to handle and the first in the RAF to be fitted with wing flaps to reduce the landing speed and provide an easier landing attitude. Sadly some idiot crashed it, damaging it beyond repair.

The station ran the Air Force equivalent of a Naval liberty boat, a lorry with rudimentary seating that made a trip once a week to Ismailia, an elegant town in the Delta with a French Club of which officers were made honorary members. Our horrible diet in our mess made the Club's cuisine all the more of a delight. Another lorry made jaunts to Cairo, 100-plus miles away, where most of us stayed in the New Zealand Club, cheap and comfortable because it was subsidised by the Government of that country. It served the best soft drink in the world: fresh lime.

I used one such visit to follow a family tentacle. I had had an invitation from a Monty Massey-Dawson to stay in Cairo for a weekend. Monty turned out to be an attractive 30-something-year-old woman related to my mother's closest friend and our hostess in Dorset. I stayed in her luxurious flat. I decided that any romantic initiatives must come from her, fearing that mine, if refused, would be reported to Dorset and thence to Malvern. She evidently decided that I was a boy unsuitable as a toy, and we confined ourselves to seeing the sights of Cairo and dining in sumptuous restaurants. She worked for the British Government; as what, I never found out. Following another tentacle in the beautiful city and port of Alexandria, I stayed with Brigadier Ronald Collingwood, a cousin of my half-brother William. He had been an engineer in Egypt for many years, helping to design and construct the Nile Barrage, a huge irrigation project that brought prosperity to millions of the *fellaheen* (peasant people) of Upper Egypt. When the war came he was conscripted as a brigadier, becoming the DCRE (Deputy Commander, Royal Engineers) for the Upper Egypt military zone. On the first evening he plied me with aperitifs and we later joined a dinner party in the awning-covered roof restaurant of the prestigious Turf Club. I was already a bit woozy and halfway through the meal I realised that my entrée was just about to exit. Excusing myself I made for the passage leading back into the building, where both the situation and my stomach went out of control. In the merciful absence of passers-by and the providential presence of a large ornamental brass pot on a plinth at just the right height for a vomitarium, I found blessed relief, returning unruffled and unsullied to the festive board.

The route back to Fayid ran along the Treaty Road connecting Cairo and Suez, built as part of the Anglo-Egyptian agreement for the stationing of British troops in Egypt. A landmark was the checkpoint halfway along the road used to stop traffic when it was militarily necessary. One day during a ban the sentries stopped a large car carrying a single, very fat passenger. On being told to turn back, he protested that he was Farouk, King of Egypt. The soldier replied that he was Winston Churchill and repeated the order with a threat to shoot if it were not obeyed. The incident was said to account for the fact that British forces in Egypt received no thanks, let alone the medal that would have been appropriate.

Our first venture as a crew was to fly up and down over Cairo at night to give target practice to Egyptian anti-aircraft artillery. Just before we began the necessary straight and level runs, at sitting-duck height, an Egyptian voice on the common control radio frequency was heard to ask whether live or blank ammunition was to be used. We sheered off until a British controller assured us that the gunners now knew it was to be the latter.

It was a relief to start proper operations. Preparations for a raid began in the morning with flight planning and main briefing. Then came oversight of the bombing-up of our aircraft and often the stowage of bundles of multilingual tract-like leaflets intended to subvert the opposition and any pro-enemy Senussi tribesmen. The Wellingtons were well-worn Pegasus-engined specimens, with a performance made worse by the anti-sand filters fitted to the engine air intakes. Fully loaded and fuelled, we seemed to stagger into the air in the blinding heat of the afternoon, the cockpit temperature 120 degrees and the engines at full throttle sounding fit to burst. Our destination was one or other of the advanced landing grounds in the Western Desert that would put us within range of our target. On arrival we topped up our fuel from tankers which had only recently replaced the primitive semi-rotary hand pumps and drums which had made refuelling an ordeal. There was then a final briefing and a wait for the time set for take-off by the group headquarters (205).

The main advanced landing ground was at Fuka, but we were usually directed to others to disperse the force, such as it was, and reduce the damage if, as happened from time to time, we were attacked by intruders – initially Italian but later Junkers 87 dive bombers of the Luftwaffe. The makeshift airfields had few facilities other than fuel tankers, a handful of ground crew, a workshop and rest tents. Those near the coast had excellent sea bathing, but the inland ones were so short of water that washing was out of fashion. The airfields were managed by crews on temporary respite; a very popular intermission on return from some of which it would have been apposite to echo, had it been written, Dylan Thomas's apology:

I'm sorry I smell so much, it's Margate.

We all enjoyed our turn when it came, escaping one of the torments said to be prevalent: crab lice, which attached themselves to the crotch and scrotum and caused intolerable itching. The cure was reputed to be rubbing the affected area with whisky and sand so that the lice would get drunk and hurl rocks at one another.

We welcomed the operational routine. At the appointed time the elderly Wellingtons staggered across the uneven sand into the night air. On moonless nights, keeping the aircraft in the climbing attitude in the blackness using only the instruments was a skill underemphasised in training. One danger for inexperienced pilots lay in momentary disbelief of what the artificial horizon and the rate of climb/descent indicator showed; another lay in opposite correction which, by making a dive or a bank steeper, could turn an aberration into a disaster. But such momentary terrors and the risks of an earthward plunge were mitigated by the spare set of senses of the second pilot. A few raids were enough to make them disappear. Once safely aloft, flights to and from the target were the acme of boredom. Keeping a look-out and awake were not enough to fill the time, and the temptation was to muse. Sexual fantasies were a well-recognised danger, later becoming the subject of a poster for aircrew showing a pilot with a floozie and a glass of champagne reflected in his goggles.

During the autumn of 1941, our targets were usually chosen to support the Eighth Army which was continuing the series of advances and retirements across the desert that had started in 1940/41. Our object was to erode the air support of the enormous Italian army by attacking airfields along the North African coast such as Derna and Berka, the latter a hornets' nest of fighters. The raids were frustrating because our photographs showed little damage, the fighters being well dispersed and the cratered sand runways easily repaired. More usefully we kept pounding away at the Italian supply base at Benghazi, capital of Cyrenaica and a major port. So frequent, indeed, were the attacks that they became known as the Mail Runs. The 70 Squadron had a version of 'Oh my darling Clementine':

> Seventy Squadron, Seventy Squadron,
>   though we say it with a sigh,
>   we must do the fucking mail run
>   every night until we die.

suitable for unison bawling after boozy dinners on nights off.

I hope we gave some relief to the much-tried ground forces. Their first 'push' westwards, in 1941, was commanded by General Archibald Wavell,

Back from a raid, trying, at 19, to look macho. *Anon*

an author and intellectual as well as a brilliant tactician, whose force almost reached Cyrenaica, taking thousands of Italian prisoners and staying in occupation until lack of resources forced a retreat. Wavell was also that rare asset, a popular commander. Formerly a cavalry officer, he was known for a report on a less than satisfactory subordinate:

> I would not breed from this officer.

He was ignominiously sacked, later becoming Viceroy of India, where he put together a famous poetry anthology with memoirs, *Other Men's Flowers*; not unlike a printed form of Alan Murray's radio programme *Whenever I hear this*.

A degree of variety came from such raids as those on the Cretan airfield of Maleme, a heavily-defended town and fighter base later to become a target for terrifying daylight attacks in Liberators. One compensation

الى كل عربى كريم

السَّـلام عليكم ورحمة الله وبركاته وبعد فحامـــل هـذا الكتاب ضابط بالجيش
البريطانى وهو صـديق وفيّ لكافة الشعوب العربية فنرجو أن تعـاملونه بالعطف والاكـرام .
وأن تحافظوا على حيـاته من كل طارىء ونأمل عنـد الاضطرار أن تقـدموا له ما يحتاج
اليه من طعام وشراب .

وأن ترشدونه الى أقرب معسكر بريطانى
وسنكافئكم ماليا بسخاء على ما تسدونه اليه من خدمات .

والســـلام عليكم ورحمة الله وبركاته ؟

القيادة البريطانية العامة فى الشرق

To All Arab Peoples - Greetings and Peace be upon you. The bearer of
this letter is an Officer of the English Government and a friend of all Arabs.
Treat him well, guard him from harm, give him food and drink, help him
to return to the nearest English soldiers and you will be rewarded. Peace
and the Mercy of God upon you.

The British High Command in the East.

Useful Words

English	Arabic	English	Arabic
English	Ingleezi.		
English Flying Officer	Za-bit Ingleezi Tye-yar.	Water	Moya.
Friend	Sa-hib, Sa-deek.	Food	A'-kl.

Take me to the English and you will be rewarded.

Hud-nee eind el Ingleez wa ta-hud mu-ka-fa.

PME/1554-9/41

A so-called goolie chit for aircrew shot down to give to capturing Senussi tribesmen.
Crown copyright (expired)

92

during my Wellington days was that opposition on the way to the targets and back was much less severe than it was during the ordeals over the Ruhr which our comrades at home in Bomber Command had to undergo. On the other hand, our numbers were pathetically small. Con Wells sometimes began his briefings with: 'Tonight lads we're going to saturate the defences with no fewer than four of us', making the concentration of anti-aircraft fire on such small targets much greater than it was in Europe. Amongst the ironmongery hurled up at us there were so-called 'flaming onions', small spherical missiles chained together and useful for slicing off wings; heavy anti-aircraft shells which could reach well above our operating heights of around 18,000 feet; and below them light flak consisting in ordinary shells interspersed with beautifully multicoloured tracer rounds in patterns like seaside illuminations. The Italian fighters were, to my personal chagrin, Macchi (*sic*) 200s and 202s, inferior to the Hurricane and Spitfire but still lethal to the lumbering Wimpies. They were later reinforced by the twin-engined Messerschmidt 110 and the superb Junkers 88 of the German Luftwaffe. The former inspired another squadron lyric, based on 'Somewhere over the Rainbow':

> Somewhere over Benghazi,
> way down low,
> there's a Wimp on one engine,
> chased by a 110.

> Somewhere over Benghazi,
> that crew's blue;
> if they go any lower
> they'll catch the light flak too.

The ditty was not totally unrealistic. Our arrivals at targets, and by no means only Benghazi, would be signalled by aircraft fire. A way of trying to avoid it was to 'jink', involving dives, climbs and banking one way and then the other. Another reputed remedy was to drop empty beer bottles down the flare shoot, a tube about 9 inches wide amidships, which were thought to make a whistling noise as they fell, confusing sound-directed guns. An anti-fighter manoeuvre was the corkscrew, similar to jinking but with longer periods between changes of height and heading. None were demonstrably effective; and there was no escaping the long, straight and level bombing run, essential before the final release of the bombs from the actual racks and the crew from the figurative rack. Like everybody else I found bombing runs terrifying. Unlike other tasks incumbent on bomber crews, experience didn't help: the more one did, the greater the tension as the navigator intoned:

Steady, steady ... steady ... steady ... steady ... steady ... BOMBS GONE,

instantly followed by the blessed relief of a steep diving turn and escape for home.

On the journeys to and from the Western Desert targets lay a different hazard – that of Tobruk, by-passed by the Italians as they turned the tables on the Wavell advance and left as a small British enclave. The garrison commander made it clear that any aircraft, friend or foe, that came within gun range would be fired on, inspiring another verse of the 70 Squadron song:

Navigator, have you lost us?
Do come up and have a look.
Someone's shot the starboard wing off.
Very well then, that's Tobruk.

Our aircraft were chronically unserviceable. We frequently had to cancel flights, apprehensive that if we did it too often we would be accused of shirking. Robert Alexander, respected for his integrity, once had to abort twice on the same night. Stung into indiscipline, he abandoned the standard letter code for his stricken aircraft:

W for Whore's Ghost, back to dispersal again.

Our percentage losses were less than those over Europe, but more distressing because of the smaller numbers. I was very upset when my former captain and co-pilot John Tolson, who had taken over another crew, was killed over Benghazi; and no less so when my Cranwell room mate Reg Langley, who had been posted to the torpedo-armed Wellington squadron at Shallufa, failed to return from an attack on shipping in the port of Piraeus, near Athens. I could not bring myself to tell Eileen, with whom incidentally I kept in touch until her death in 1969, that his survival chances were negligible.

Not all the consequences of enemy action were tragic. One captain, a tough little man from New Zealand called Anderson, had his aircraft so damaged that the undercarriage wheels flopped out of their casing. The

Andy's desert crash, so near and yet so far from the airfield. *Author*

increase in drag was so severe that he ran out of fuel and had to alight (though light was not the word) on a soft patch of desert within sight of the advanced landing ground. Unhurt by the belly flop, the crew, with as much paraphernalia as they could carry, traipsed forlornly over the soft sand until a rescue lorry could reach them.

Like others of the youngest pilots I was made to stay a 'second dickie', as the jargon was, for much longer than I would have liked. It had hardly mattered with John Tolson because he and I had shared the captaincy as a two-man soviet. But when I changed captains the new one, quite properly, asserted his authority. He was the older and much more experienced Sergeant Tony Kayll, also an Old Carthusian and a contemporary; but in a different house and three years older, an enormous difference at school. He was an excellent captain, one of several aircrew NCOs I met whose potential as officers had gone unrecognised.

I chafed on, sustained by the knowledge that a good second pilot can be an asset to his crew. Barely 20 and by no means as good as I thought myself, it was 19 raids before, in February 1942, I got my own crew and was charged with dropping the usual load of eleven 250 pound bombs on a familiar enemy air base at Martuba. Two days later we were delighted to attack Tobruk, now in enemy hands, and to get a direct hit on a ship in the harbour estimated to be a 5,000-tonner. I had reported a probable hit, happily confirmed by photo reconnaissance. My parents were no less delighted when the feat, not without luck, was reported in the *Daily Sketch* as:

Tobruk's worst raid of the war ... a young Pilot Officer from Malvern, captain of a giant bomber scored the hit on the cargo vessel.

A less fortunate adventure was an engine failure while we were on the way, fully loaded and fuelled, to an advanced landing ground. That was a

A newly arrived US Army Air Corps B-24 being re-marked as a RAF Liberator. *Author*

considerable emergency. The Wellington could barely keep height because the device for streamlining the failed propeller, known as feathering, was not fitted. With the blades milling round and causing enormous drag, I wished I could have resorted to Con Wells's half-serious remedy, which was to carry a machine gun and shoot the offending member off. Having practised the emergency many times, but acutely aware that there could be no second chance, I landed with the same mixture of skill and luck that had favoured us at Tobruk.

There was soon great excitement at the news that our ancient Wimpeys were to be replaced with four-engined American B-24 bombers delivered directly from the Consolidated factory in America. They began to arrive, bearing US Army Air Corps markings and flown by American crews whom we had envisaged as like the film portrayals of aces. Not so. Their flying, to put it kindly, was amateurish. The essence of a good bomber pilot, for instance, was to land with as little delay as possible after the tightest possible circuit (to which, remembering the shooting-up of LAC Patrick at Cranwell, I gave special attention), plonk down at the beginning of the runway, pull up quickly and dash for the dispersal. The Americans' circuits seemed to take in half the locality. They would then make long, low, laboured approaches and, as the phrase was, creep up on the runway as if trying to surprise it. Having learnt the essentials of the Liberator we could soon manage better for ourselves. We marvelled at its luxurious appointments and even more at the long range which made it possible to attack targets such as Misurata near Tunis, far to the west of Benghazi, which was the Wellington's limit. It later became clear, however, that these directly delivered aircraft were themselves semi-obsolete, having been made to an order from France before the German occupation of that country in 1940.

A characteristic of all military service is vacillation by those on high, such that a question exchanged between lowlier beings so often as to have achieved cliché status is, 'Don't you know it's all been changed?' Among the sufferers was 108 Squadron. Instead of settling down to our change of type, we were to return to England for formal conversion to more modern Liberators and bring them back to Fayid. Con Wells was himself to fly one aircraft load of picked crews home, leaving the rest to follow as air passengers to West Africa and thence by troopship to Britain. Our crew was one of the also-flews. So were those of Alex and of Derek Duder, another experienced pilot and a former instructor at a flying training school in South Africa. At Heliopolis, sinisterly as we thought on the Ides of March 1942, we boarded a Pan American DC3 for Lagos. We followed a route across Africa made famous as the Takoradi Run, for the delivery of aircraft shipped to Lagos in crates, assembled and flown to the Middle East war zone by way of Kano, Geneina, El Fasher, Midougri, Fort Lamy and Khartoum. The new aircraft, mostly single-engined fighters, were flown in convoys led by Blenheim bombers whose job it was to navigate and shepherd their charges. The losses from engine failure and losing the leader were large. Some of the returning ferry pilots were our fellow DC3 passengers. Still at the great age of 20, I was struck by their youth and saddened by their prospects.

At Lagos, where we landed at Takoradi airport, we expected the prompt embarkation for Britain which our operational importance, in our own estimation, entitled us. The opposite happened. As what was to be a very long wait began, we were shocked to hear that Con Wells and all the others aboard the Liberator had been killed when it hit a hill in Northern Ireland, far off course and doubtless short of fuel. It could only be concluded that bad weather had compelled Con to descend blind, hoping to break cloud and find somewhere to land. All pilots know that such action is folly. All have taken it.

For the first fortnight we lived in messes in Apapa, the agreeable suburb of Lagos where the RAF station was. The resident officers, equippers and engineers were there to supervise the unloading and assembly of the reinforcement aircraft. They were as remote psychologically from the war as they were physically, and showed their dislike of their enforced guests. Not, of course, that we were without fault. We were soon relegated to a local boarding house where we chafed at having to wait for a troopship to arrive. There was little to do except to explore the bush country, made hazardous by snakes, malaria and other flora and fauna including predatory prostitutes. We were told that they were 'full housers', meaning afflicted with all the prevalent venereal diseases. There were no other sports facilities; but a local priest lent us his sailing boat, which we greatly enjoyed, Derek Duder knowing enough of sailing to make it safe. The one source of relief for the boredom of the evenings was the cinema, where film changes were so infrequent that some of us were reduced to seeing a terrible film called *Babes in Arms*, starring the dreadful Mickey Rooney, three times.

I might have endured a fourth but for getting malaria and being admitted to the civilian hospital in Lagos. I lay in luxury in a single room, my aches, shakes and debilitation worsened by diarrhoea, dealt with by excellent black male nurses, all enormously tall. As I was beginning to get better, I was horrified to see from my window the arrival of the *Georgic*, a White Star liner converted to a trooper, in the docks which the hospital

98

adjoined. Desperate not to miss her, and bolstered by being out of military jurisdiction, I discharged myself. Ignoring the advice of my kind attendants, I lugged my bag out of the grounds and across the quay, feeling more and more faint but just able to establish that I was on the passenger list. I was virtually carried aboard, but soon recovered.

The *Georgic* was fast enough to sail unescorted and still luxurious. All went boringly well until two nights before we were due to dock at Gourock, on the Clyde, when the ship began to vibrate violently. Most of us were enjoying a post-prandial brandy in the saloon when the captain, his mien no less majestic than that of Group Captain Gayford, joined us. He explained that the ship was prone to vibration at full speed, adding almost casually that the haste was necessary because we were being pursued by a submarine. Happily we outstripped it.

I caught a troop train from Glasgow to Birmingham where in the absence of evening transport to Malvern, I was stuck. I went by bus to the suburb of King's Norton, having remembered the address of my half-brother William's in-laws. The father, Meaburn Tatham, the overseas director of Cadbury's, greeted me as if I had been invited and I was fed right royally and given a room in their galleried mansion.

My disembarkation leave was a joyous interlude, especially for Tinker. I was flattered that my newly gained status earned me an invitation to see one of my father's odder patients, George Hinds, an inventor. He had made a model of a bombsight in which he hoped to interest the RAF. Was it, he asked me, likely to work; and, if so, to whom he should address himself? It was similar to, but simpler than, the standard RAF Mk IX sight to which I was used. I told him he might be on to something and undertook to find him a contact, with no idea of how to set about it. He was exaggeratedly, almost feverishly, grateful. Sadly my task never materialised: on the same night he had a violent manic episode, having to be certified and, as the phrase was, put away. I wondered whether genius had been extinguished and heard no more. More agreeably, another patient, quaintly named Otway Lely, came up, years after I had admired it at his home, with an offer of his American organ; pedal operated rather than blown but with several stops and a good tone. I had hoped that it would make my poor piano playing sound better; but it seemed inappropriate to accept it at that stage. I had to wait 14 years for another chance to play an organ.

Leaving home for another tour of operations was strangely upsetting. In uniform, I was ready for my mother to drive me to the station when a family friend dropped in to see her. While we waited for her I offered our guest a glass of sherry. As we drank she wished me well with some emotion and burst into tears. This time it wasn't 14 but 44 years before I had a similarly lachrymose encounter after I had spoken in a debate in the Oxford Union

My immediate destination was RAF Station Burn, near Selby in Yorkshire, where there was a Liberator conversion unit. Most of the clientele were crews from Coastal Command to which Liberators in the European theatre were to be assigned; because, as were to learn to our cost, their poor performance at height made them suitable only for the literally lowly job of submarine hunting. The station was typical of the many thrown up rather than built early in the war. It had corrugated iron hangars, Nissen huts and rendered brick buildings, a style popularly known as 'piss and plaster'. Their depressing ambience, combined with what seemed incessant rain, induced near-desolation. That state was not improved by terrible food, including pint tankards of milk served at lunch to all air crews: our nutrition, some mogul at the Air Ministry having decreed, had thus to be augmented. Nobody asked for seconds. I was reminded of the Cub mistress who had exhorted her charges:

Come, come, Robin Patrol, not drinking up our cocoa is no way to win the War.

Worse still, we were already converted, sort of, to the Liberator. Repetition, we thought rather cockily, was a mere device to cover higher authority's back. I was further miffed by relegation to second pilot, penalised by my youth and the lack of a vacancy. But I was pleased to have as my captain Ted Dupleix, an older and unusually quiet Australian whom I had respected but not known well at Fayid. The new crew went to RAF Station Lyneham, then as later the main base for overseas departures and arrivals. It was another of piss and plaster construction, soon to be an example of what a little money and a lot of ingenuity could do for amenities. We celebrated the 4th of July 1942 with an overnight train journey, Ted and me sharing a First Class carriage with two female passengers, one unduly skittish, eventually arriving at RAF Station Prestwick, the reception base for transatlantic aircraft deliveries. We collected a Liberator Mk IV, much superior to the airborne jalopies we had left in Egypt and so fresh from the Consolidated factory in San Diego, California that there were scrawled messages of goodwill still in the small metal cups in the centres of the pilots' control wheels. We flew the gleaming monster back to Lyneham, one pilot a little frayed after the frolics in the train, for primping and testing, leaving for the Middle East a few days later.

We followed the route of my Wellington odyssey of the year before but did the journey in two hops via Gibraltar, now much improved by an ample runway extended by a stone peninsula built out into the bay. Our new base was at St Jean in northern Palestine, its good facilities available because of the longer range of the Liberator. Unfortunately the rebirth of 108 Squadron had been aborted by the deaths of Con Wells and the prime Liberator crews. Two other squadrons, 159 and 160, had taken its place, the former destined for India when it had been manned and bedded in with operations; I was glad to stay in the Middle East with the latter. Each squadron had a former Cranwell cadet as commander; both having reached wing commander rank in the Empire Flying Training scheme, by now in full swing in Canada, South Africa and Rhodesia (later Zimbabwe), as well as the USA. Skinner of 159, dull and pallid with a stage colonel moustache, made no bones about learning from his operationally experienced juniors. McNair of 160, pugilistic and insecure, took advice with a bad grace but followed it. The general old sweat opinion of these senior tyros was that we could have been saddled with worse.

My first Liberator sortie took place in daylight. That was an interesting change, being a resumption of the disastrous and long-abandoned RAF raids on France and Germany early in the war; and, had we known it, a trial for the vast-scale US Air Force daylight raids over Europe which were later to complement the night raids of the RAF. Our first target was the harbour at Heraklion in Crete, attacked in formation with an air gunner fire controller coordinating the anti-fighter defence. Both the enemy's fighters and their anti-aircraft guns, perhaps affected by the surprise of the change to daylight, were too feeble to matter. Next came six seven-hour shuttle flights in just over a week carrying naval torpedoes, partly dismantled and slung from our bomb hooks, to Malta to sustain the very successful naval submarine operations from there. With the official loads picked up at Gibraltar and Fayid went as many cartons of cigarettes as we could cram aboard, meeting a need said to be as important as that for munitions. After that interesting experience of seeing how, in spite of extreme tiredness, it is still possible to operate with acceptable efficiency, 160 Squadron concentrated on Tobruk, familiar from my Wellington days and still a vital base for the Germans, who had largely taken over the whole theatre from the Italians. Before they too were ejected, they were much fiercer opponents than their predecessors, a view of the harbour and the rusting hulk of my ship during our daylight attacks being a far from adequate compensation for the fury of the opposition.

My last sortie with Ted Dupleix, and indeed as a second pilot, was a night attack on the Corinth Canal a year to the day after I had done the same in a Wellington, when our bombs had blocked the canal at both ends and sunk a ship in the middle. On this second occasion we were briefed by an RAF intelligence officer of Greek extraction who was in touch with the local resistance movement. He told us that there would be the extra navigation aid of fires on top of the mountains on the north side of the canal; and, with relish, that the German garrison were to hold a ceremonial re-opening of the canal on the morning before our raid. We each carried six 1,000 lb bombs with 72-hour delay fuses for the unbenefit of ships trapped by other bombs dropped at the ends of the canal. The fires guided us as forecast. But there were also guns in them there hills, the more menacing because the gunners knew that our line of approach and release could but follow the canal. Nevertheless, the losses were light and the bombing a complete success. Forty years later on the way from Athens to a peace festival at Olympia, I had a fascinating walk round.

My captaincy this time was of a crew of young sergeants and a newly commissioned navigator, Taff Thomas. We did a sequence of raids, mostly alternating between Benghazi and Tobruk. On one of the latter we were attacked by a Junkers 88 which, having hit one of our engines, used a spin as an evasive manoeuvre from our gunfire: it was not, as the sadly deceived mid-upper gunner thought, a plunge to its death. Miraculously our injured engine suffered only a fractured oil pipe. The fire extinguisher did its job and I shut it down before it seized. I was glad that the Liberator performed almost as well on three engines as it did on four, except for increased fuel consumption and a tendency to swing on landing.

There followed a mixture of day and night sorties, the former in tight formation to concentrate the fire power of the two four-gun turrets in each aircraft. On what should have been an easy daylight attack on a pair of merchant ships in the Mediterranean, we were jumped by two Messerschmidt 110s and a Junkers 88. One of the pair was destroyed, to cheers of all over the gunnery control radio. My aircraft suffered only the loss of an aerial, in tragic contrast to that of my neighbour in the formation, captained by the gallant Flight Sergeant Wilkes, whose aircraft was destroyed. I had been one of several captains who were his passengers on a night ferry flight from Gibraltar. As he began a difficult and dangerous take-off from the still incomplete runway, he broke the mutual tension and made light of what we knew to be his long experience with:

It's all right gentlemen, I've done this before.

In the same month, October, we were rewarded on the way from St Jean to Tripoli with a memorable view of a line of flashes stretching as far southwards as the eye could see. It was the enormous artillery barrage preceding the launch from El Alamein of the third and final push westwards of the Eighth Army which opened the way for the invasion of Italy.

This time the Army commander was General Bernard Law Montgomery. He got the job as a replacement for General Gott, nicknamed Strafer, who had been killed when his car was destroyed on the way to taking over. Monty, a showman with a gigantic ego, began by sending a trainload of canteen supplies along the supply line to the Western Desert bases, deprived of them for some time because of the prior need for ammunition and petrol. That, with attendant publicity, established him as a benevolent boss. (Over Christmas I was glad to be asked to do a similar job in microcosm, taking a Liberator full of seasonal stuff to two advanced landing grounds.) I encountered Montgomery when he welcomed me as the guest RAF participant in a short course for junior Army officers in Cairo in December 1942. It consisted in twenty lectures, only eight of which I reported as being worthy of attention. Monty's opening address, which I deigned to describe in my report as having been of general interest, was on leadership. He exhorted us to ask ourselves, 'Am I making myself sufficiently offensive?' later electrifying the soldiers by telling them that the only thing he would not tolerate in a junior officer was failure. That assertion gained a certain piquancy two years later when, as commander of the 21st Army Group in Europe, Monty made the epic mistake of ordering the First Airborne Division and their supporting air forces, me included, into the disaster of Arnhem. During the course I again stayed with his namesake Monty Massey-Dawson – happy for her that she had married a dashing infantry officer called Derek Lang. Unfortunately she later divorced him. He went on to become a general whom I next met sixty years later at a meeting of Generals for Peace, of whom he plainly disapproved.

As the Monty push gathered momentum, our attacks on the Wehrmacht's bases became more intense and the Luftwaffe's opposition more effective. At a time of worrying losses we were visited by Marshal of the RAF Lord Trenchard, founding father of the RAF. By then in his seventies, he had lost none of his talent for building morale and cheering people up, praising us for the way we were doing a dangerous and difficult job. We were glad that somebody had noticed. One measure of attainment in a military career, he suggested, was being paid a pension for at least twice as long as one's period of active service – a desideratum which he had long ago fulfilled. So have I.

During this intensive phase the dozy RAF 205 Group Headquarters despatched us to bomb the airfield at Maleme, Crete, the raid skilfully timed to prevent the moon from making it easy for the resident fighters to intervene. One tiny detail which escaped the staff was the sun, in the dawn light of which, in a disorganised gaggle, we were chased across the Mediterranean. At full speed and corkscrewing in a gradual dive our losses were small; but the appalling error made a transfer from the group's control a welcome change. Our new masters were the 98th Heavy Bombardment Group, US Army Air Corps. They controlled the much larger US force of Liberators, designated B-24s. Their aircraft, newer than ours, had turbo-blown (better supercharged) engines, giving them a 10,000-foot height advantage over us. That meant near-immunity from anti-aircraft fire and a reduced threat from fighters whose performance was sluggish at their operating height of 30,000 feet. We seldom met the American crews except at advanced landing grounds, where they left us in no doubt of their superiority in accuracy (true), efficiency (untrue) bravery, alcoholic capacity, sexual prowess, beauty and every other airman-like attribute (doubtful). Their commander was Brigadier General Timber-lake. Never honouring us with a visit, he reminded me of a maritime counterpart described in a US Navy ditty:

> Oh they tell us that the Admiral
> is as nice as he can be;
> but we've never seen the Admiral
> because the Admiral has never been to sea.

Our lowly function, literal and metaphorical, was to absorb most of the opposition, continuing to attack the usual targets plus some new ones, more interesting and exciting, within the Liberator's enormous range. Examples were the ports of Tripoli, Misurata, Sousse and Sfax, in support of the Anglo-American troops massing in north-west Africa. Their job would be to attack the north-west Mediterranean coast, later known as the soft underbelly of the German/Italian Axis.

As I approached my fiftieth raid I sensed a bothersome anxiety, well known and common in the much more demanding circumstances of bomber crews operating over Germany, and defined as being 'operation-ally tired'. The feelings were said, almost superstitiously, to be followed by a succession of frightening incidents which in my case proved to be true. However, I had been lucky enough to acquire a new second pilot. A towering figure, younger than me, memorably named Bateman Champain and son of the Bishop of Knaresborough, he gave me just the support I needed for my final baker's dozen operations. One, trouble-free, was an unopposed daylight raid on Benghazi, worth a mention because of the view it afforded me, at last, of the beautiful city, set in the greenery of Cyrenaica, which had received so much of my attention at night.

Benevolent fate didn't last. A raid against Maleme airfield in Crete needed two agonisingly long bombing runs to get a decent result. At the same spot two nights later our load of 12 anti-personnel bombs 'hung up' on a first run at a dangerous 11,000 feet, only falling, most agreeably, on a park full of Junkers 52 fuel tanker aircraft after a dive and pull-up to jerk them free. Thereafter we had another lot of hang-ups, this time with an engine failure thrown in. Unlike the Wellington, the Liberator had feathering propellers which greatly reduced the drag and we were in no great difficulty other than being short of fuel. We diverted to Fayid, now finished and a major base complete with a South African Air Force Spitfire squadron for the defence of the Canal Zone. On the final approach the combined strength of two pilots, beefy Bateman included, pushing on the rudder pedals could not stop a swing. That would normally have caused only a run across the hard sand airfield, almost as serviceable as the runway. Instead we collided with a Spitfire parked for swift take-off beside the runway, breaking its propeller and chopping off our wing tip. My chagrin eased when the station commander, successor to Gayford, accompanying the fire engines and ambulance, almost welcomed what had happened, having asked the South Africans time and again to park well away from the runway to prevent just that occurrence. True to the SAAF's reputation for bolshiness, they had ignored the order.

As if by malevolent magic, Mediterranean winter weather plagued my closing exertions. Its speciality was thunderstorms, a succession of whose mighty clouds dogged a long trip to the Tunisian port of Sousse just before Christmas. After three attempts to find the harbour I did a Con Wells dive, letting down low because the land was flat for hundreds of miles, and we did a successful drop. We found out later, with mixed feelings, that we had been the only aircraft to get to the target. We followed that on New Year's Eve, another murky night, with an attack on Sfax, another Tunisian port. Four of the six bombs plunged into the sea; but the other two hit the quay, causing explosions, fire and a lot of activity. In the apparent absence of opposition I let down low over the sea and flew back over the port at ground level, giving the delighted gunners the chance to strafe the warehouses, shipping and people. We returned for second and third helpings. During the departing climb the top gunner, with a well-merited expletive, reported a barrage balloon. I remembered the Rugby wireless masts.

On a winter's night 26 years later, an Alitalia pilot told me, as I waited for weather fit to take a Hastings load of passengers from El Adem to Lyneham, that the Gulf of Sirte was a boiling cauldron of thunderstorms (which he, in a Caravelle jet, could surmount and I could not). His description exactly fitted the weather that for our next two raids, respectively against Tripoli and Misurata, with heavy icing, lightning and St Elmo's fire silhouetting the guns and canopies in fluorescent blue light; boons because they grounded the fighters. These picturesque conditions had cleared for my 53rd and last bomber sortie, which was an attack on Tripoli at 10,000 feet. We got away with a single run and good hits. In a fitting illuminated address, as I saw it, the searchlights gave me a farewell bath of light for an eternity of seconds before seeming to wave us away.

That was that. After a few non-operational chores and with, at last, an above-average assessment, I was sad to leave the Liberator, a delight to fly and in many other ways a superb aircraft. Throughout my two bomber tours the RAF, as always, had kept me in order and looked after me. My youthful conceit and impatience, potentially lethal, had been curbed by good captains. Once I had been launched as a captain myself, my flying had been unobtrusively supervised. I had had excellent support from well-chosen crews. With a lot of luck and a little skill, I felt I had not done too badly in the bomber business. Above all, I was elated that there was now every chance of my fulfilling my parents' hopes, expressed so often in their inexpressibly precious letters, that I would be home for my 21st birthday four months later. Surfeited with astra, released from ardua and temporarily out of ardour, as it were, I departed for Suez; and then, as if it had been prescribed, a long sea voyage.

Chapter 6

The Carriage Trade

I got carried away – literally, in the USS *Mariposa*, a former luxury liner of the Matson Line plying the San Francisco to Hawaii route. We passengers weren't told at the time that we were to sail round the Cape of Good Hope, calling at Massawa, Port Sudan, Bombay and Cape Town en route for Britain. Nor did I know that, being now an American troopship, *Mariposa* was dry. For the next six weeks I was to share a double first class cabin with seven US officers. We filled it to bursting, which was also true of the rest of the ship. There was almost nowhere to sit except on the decks, and even they were off-limits during the ferociously enforced blackout. The food was excellent but served only twice a day, which made the time drag even more.

My cabin mates included a bumptious lieutenant from Chicago, much given to expatiating on the pleasures of the flesh including the chops and spare ribs offered by his city's hog inhabitants. Another subaltern, huge and well endowed with sporting sweatshirts, regaled us with tales of his exploits at volleyball; it emerged that he had been a student on a sporting scholarship at Notre Dame University; 'Noter Daim', as he pronounced his alma mater, made it difficult to identify at first. In a late stage of invalidism was a charming Southern-accented medical major, stricken with heart disease but still chain-smoking. No less companionable in his brash way was a marine major, formerly a senior cop in the Pennsylvania state police. He and I got on so well that I have a standing invitation to visit, guaranteed a motorcade. We all realised that the cramped quarters, featuring quadruple-stacked bunks, could only be endured with harmonious teamwork. That was just what we practised and it worked very well. There was no organised shipboard activity other than frequent boat drills. Fortunately there was plenty to read. My literary fare included Daphne du Maurier's *Rebecca*, which I read aloud, slowly and with frequent stops for elucidation, to a young Polish soldier anxious to improve his English. He and others enjoyed an account of the lady friend of Daphne's relative, a long-forgotten impresario:

There was a young lady called Gloria,
who slept with Sir Gerald du Maurier.
Then six other men,
then Sir Gerald again;
then the band at the Waldorf Astoria.

Massawa was a sleazy port at which we could only gaze from the portholes. It was known to pilots of my vintage as a place from which most aircraft of the day were just able to climb sufficiently fast to land at Asmara, capital of Eritrea, 7,000 feet and 100 miles later. Another gazing point was Port Sudan, main outlet for a country once a pillar of Empire. More intriguing but still not accessible except for a handful of disembarkers, was Bombay. We all had a close and alluring view of the docks and their magnificent British-built red brick warehouses, evocative of famous British companies of the Raj such as Jardine Mathieson and Sime Darby which had originated as successors to the East India Company.

Mariposa was fast enough to sail unescorted and the trip to Cape Town, with all aboard now well used to the routine, seemed less tedious. On arrival for a 12-hour stay at Cape Town everyone went ashore, where there awaited the cars of the many South Africans renowned for their hospitality to visiting troops. Almost all the enlisted men (American for troops) were collected at random and taken for a day's sightseeing and jollification. Officers, who by convention left this privilege to their juniors, tended to sightsee on foot. The mass return to the ship was an awesome sight. Almost everybody was drunk and many were incapable. Following what was clearly a routine, the US equivalent of the Royal Navy's Master at Arms and a squad of naval police at the gangways hauled the celebrants aboard and apparently threw them into the protective custody of the brig.

The last leg of the voyage, thought to be the most dangerous, became tense after a visit from a Focke Wolfe Condor, a four-engined Luftwaffe transport (a type used, incidentally, by Hitler as a personal conveyance), adapted for long-range maritime reconnaissance. Fortunately nothing transpired and we duly docked at Liverpool. Waiting briefly in the reception unit, I felt unequal to the situation when a distraught middle-aged flying officer, an ex-ranker, imparted to me that he had just rung his wife, to be told to push off because she now had another man. Lacking the nous to help, I could only suggest the chaplain. I was reminded, perhaps unfeelingly, of the sardonic skit under a cartoon in the *Tatler*, then as later a gossip magazine:

Seen dining at Quaglino's: Mrs Smith and her escort Major Brown. Major Brown is, of course, serving overseas.

Arriving at New Street Station, Birmingham too late to get home I repeated, almost to the minute, my unexpected arrival at the Tatham mansion the year before, to be greeted and looked after with the same unruffled kindness.

At home – and by now it was March – I again felt strangely distanced by all that had happened since I was last there. I walked the hills, at their best in the early spring, relishing my surroundings as they recovered their familiarity. Food was scarce but my mother did wonders at eking out the rations. My father was doing more and more for the Red Cross and my sister Joanna, no longer a child, was bursting to develop a contact our father had with Sir Barry Jackson of the famous Birmingham Rep, and frustrated at the prospect of a domestic science course. I was flattered to be asked by the editor of the *Malvern Gazette* to review a biography of a fighter pilot. The author was Hector Bolitho, very well known in that capacity, and the subject John Simpson, whose letters to him made up most of the book. There were accounts of Simpson's destruction of 13 German aircraft in the Battle of Britain, as well as of his innumerable parties and drinking sessions. For me the book's greatest interest lay in a parallel with myself:

The tiredness that comes to seasoned pilots is not easy to explain. It seems that they live so violently during their combats that they squeeze ten years of experience into the space of two,

being one of the chord-striking excerpts.

Being, like almost all bomber pilots, jealous of the glamour boy fighter pilots, I ended the review sniffily with: 'No better book has been written for readers interested in Fighter Command.' Three years later Rachel and I were to get to know John a great deal better.

I had feared that my next job would be on the ground. In the event I could scarcely have been more pleased. I was now to serve in the newly formed Transport Command at a station in Northern Ireland, quaintly called Nutts Corner. I was to be a founder member of a new operational training unit to train air crews, mainly from Bomber Command and the Empire Flying Training Schools, for employment in civil aviation, then kept going by the successor to pre-war Imperial Airways, British Airways. Part of my job was to familiarise pilots with the Wellington Mk IV, this time fitted with

109

American Pratt & Whitney Twin Wasp engines. Like those of the old Pegasus, the cylinders were disposed radially round the main shaft, making for better cooling than the in-line cylindered, glycol-cooled Merlins. The engines, superbly reliable and with thrust equal to that of the Merlin, made the super-Wimpy a joy to fly. I was also supposed to help to bond the crews and try to set examples of good captaincy, not unlike the staff at Harwell during my bomber apprenticeship. As an extra, I began my lecturing life by conducting courses on airmanship.

The station was built during the renewed expansion of the RAF just before World War Two, when Rothenstein's elegant designs had given place to utility rendered stone shoebox huts, dispersed in widely scattered clumps all round the estate. It was close to the vintage station Aldergrove, a luxurious Coastal Command base. Both adjoined Lough Neagh, in a beautiful bit of Ulster; but we had the hazard of an 800-foot hill, an offshoot of the Mourne Mountains, too close to our circuit for comfort. Our base had a second function as reception airfield for most of the transatlantic salvoes of aircraft on delivery from America, often by inexperienced crews who had never before left their homeland:

Ireland? Is that near London?

The station commander was Group Captain Roger Ford, well known for his long service in that capacity and experienced enough to let everybody get on with their jobs while he devoted his office hours to constructive thinking. His adjutant Paul Hill, fat and hail-fellow-well-met, was highly competent but later turned out to be a rogue. Supposedly in charge of the technical side of transatlantic reception were a dreadful couple of engineers who did nothing but sit in a block near our flight's clump of offices doing nothing: the American new arrivals were always technically self-sufficient. One, the loquacious Flight Lieutenant Jarboe, was himself an American who, he maintained, had so admired the RAF that he crossed the Atlantic to join up. He sported a row of medal ribbons, his entitlement to which was in doubt; but neither Ford nor Hill, whose job it was, did anything to find out. Jarboe had a bedroom near mine in a block of bachelor quarters. When, for no apparent reason, he asked whether he could move in with me I realised, amply experienced in the ways of Tyrannosaurus Sex, that he was a potential homosexual predator. I kept refusing until he sought other prey. He dominated his middle-aged assistant, one of a rare type commissioned from the ranks who, having reached officer status, were content to do nothing and go no further.

In total contrast was a charming locally enlisted Ulsterman, a solicitor, in charge of major disciplinary matters for the clutch of stations in the Province, living locally and grandly titled Assistant Provost Marshal. During his boozy visits he would flog sides of bacon from the boot of his RAF car, the illegality of black marketing meat leaving him unconcerned. Important operationally was George Harding, Senior Air Traffic Controller and highly gifted in the art of 'talking down' pilots in bad weather using the primitive radar device Ground Controlled Approach (GCA). While the training unit built up its staff, he and I did a lot of practice, forming the close air-ground partnership needed to make GCAs work well. The practice honed his skill in helping new American arrivals and later gave our students confidence in operating in the often bad Irish weather. Scarcely less important in his way was Warrant Officer Slater, in charge of the day-to-day maintenance of our Wellingtons. Very skilled and hard-working, he had a habit of lingering over-long at the sergeants' mess bar at lunchtime on Saturdays. He would ring up in mid-afternoon asking semi-coherently for a lift back to the cottage where his wife lay in wait. On arrival I would give this terrifying lady what I later came to know as a plea in mitigation of Slater's bibulous misdeeds.

Most important of all to me was my temporary boss, until the unit was fully formed, Squadron Leader John Bowie, officer in charge of flying. He was a middle-aged South African with Mills & Boon good looks, greying hair, a genial manner and great skill as a pilot. We flew together on various journeys, often in the station runabout, an Airspeed Oxford. In his office was an attractive young clerical assistant, Leading Aircraftwoman Rae Goodson. She reacted to seeing me in his office, as she told John, by wondering why, at that critical stage of the war, I was not in front-line service instead of sheltering in the non-operational backwood of Nutts Corner. John explained that I was on a rest tour after two successive bomber tours and would no doubt embark on a third as soon as I got a chance. I found pretexts for visiting their office on most days. Associating with her off-duty, which I soon began doing, was of course as prohibited as it had been at Harwell; but we did not allow that to get in the way of being together whenever we could. We had picnic suppers on the Ulster hills, and often went to Belfast in the bus. There the main attraction was the Ritz cinema with the great asset of Joseph Seal, an organist second only in renown to the great Reginald Dixon of Black-pool. He would ascend, to universal acclaim, at the illuminated console of the mighty Wurlitzer, often more of an attraction than the films. When I could afford it we went to the Carlton Restaurant whose enormous steaks were no doubt of common origin to the Provost Marshal's dodgy viands.

The Wellington unit was soon complete, acquiring a commanding officer, Wing Commander Tom Llewellyn. He had a background in civil aviation but was less than familiar with his job, having been commissioned directly into his rank. His very experienced assistant was Squadron Leader Herring – 'Kipper' of course – with a brilliant record and highly decorated. Tragically, he was later to be killed as he took off from Gibraltar in a passenger version of the Liberator, plunging into the sea with all aboard including General Sikorski, head of the Polish Government in exile. The cause was almost certainly sabotage. Under Kipper was my flight commander, Flight Lieutenant Dicky Daw, a meteoric harum-scarum-devil-may-carum former fighter pilot of engaging charm. How he became a Wellington instructor I never discovered; but his exuberance proved to have been brittle a few years later when, back on fighters, he took a Meteor jet, flew eastwards over the North Sea and was never heard of again. He almost certainly committed suicide.

Although untrained as an instructor, I took to the doing of endless circuits with the students, trying to follow the precept that it was more for them to learn than for me to teach. The syllabus also featured long day and night navigation exercises, of stupefying boredom because of the repetition and the need to intervene only if the pupil crew got into dire difficulty. Having a 'screened', as we were called, captain aboard gave them confidence, not always justifiable; but having done the main night exercise from Nutts Corner to St Abb's Head near Edinburgh, thence to Chicken Rock at the southern tip of the Isle of Man via Bardsey Island and then home many times, I often came in useful as a getter-out-of-trouble.

Variety came from trips to the mainland on various pretexts. At Christmas time we ferried plane-loads of turkeys, cheap and plentiful in Ulster, for posting on the UK mainland to the homes of the many airmen who took advantage of our offer. Through it Paul Hill's skulduggery first emerged. In a letter of thanks, an airman opined that 1 shilling per turkey posted was a very reasonable reward for the air crews. We had, of course, made no such charge: it was Hill who had collected and trousered the money. That led to a court martial which exposed many other swindles. After his sacking, Hill was said to be living in Morocco in one of two night clubs bought with his illicit gains.

Rae – later Rachel because she hated that name – and I spent more and more time in each other's company, achieving informal recognition as 'going steady'. Instrumental was her widely popular WAAF officer in charge, 'Gillie' Potter, nicknamed after the then well-known fictitious denizen of an imaginary village and given to writing to *The Times*:

Sir, this is Gillie Potter writing to you from Hog's Norton in English,

going on to expatiate on topics of invariably penetrating relevance.

Our being a stable couple meant that Rachel was allowed to come as my guest to an officers' mess dance: not, as I feared, causing jealousy among the other WAAFs, but rather shared delight. And on a rainy evening, in the romantic setting of Belfast bus station, I proposed to her and was accepted. I made two conditions, also accepted: that neither of us would learn golf or bridge. That harked back to the Old Boy system at which I had riled at Charterhouse, both games said to be a catalyst for advancement in the RAF. The engagement made it politic for her to meet my family, for which purpose I flew her in the Oxford to RAF Staverton, near Gloucester and a short drive from Malvern. She showed great éclat during the introductory weekend. But she is a slow eater and all Mackies are vulpine. As Rachel coped with polite questioning my mother, with characteristic tact, kept back a piece of potato and chased it round her plate as the poor girl struggled to cope. On the way back to Ireland the weather closed in and, while we were at sea level near the Isle of Man, Rachel was airsick. Not knowing how common this was or of the fact that the ground crews, glad of the unofficial clear-up rate of half a crown, would deal with the detritus, she attempted a do-it-yourself job with her lingerie and a bottle of lavender water. Preoccupied with trying not to collide with the Isle of Man, I fancied that I had done so and entered a lavender-perfumed Heaven.

My thoroughly enjoyable tour of duty continued for just under another year, lacking incident other than the announcement in April 1943 of the award to me of a Distinguished Flying Cross for my work in the Middle East. I, said the citation:

> made a number of daring attacks on Tobruk, Benghazi and later on Tripoli and carried out a daylight operation against shipping in the Mediterranean. On every occasion ... exhibited great perseverance and tenacity, remaining in the target area until certain of the results of the bombing. In December last, after delivering an effective attack on Sfax, he descended to 400 feet over the harbour to observe the results of his attack and obtained valuable information.

In retrospect all very well; but not fair to the crews whose lives I risked and who went unrewarded.

I was given leave for my long-anticipated 21st birthday on 3 August, celebrated at the County Hotel, still the residence of Alan Murray. My father designed and had printed an illustrated commemorative menu which details the preliminary sherry party, the meal of salmon, followed by chicken or duck and then fresh fruit; and the services of Reg Marsh and his band, Reg being the manager of the local branch of Boots. There also appeared an account of my schools, holidays and RAF career so far, which had just included elevation to acting flight lieutenant. I was humbled by my parents' touching effort to make the occasion every bit as good as its peacetime predecessor, comparatively easy to arrange, for my half-brother William in 1939.

I had made noises at Nutts Corner about getting back to bomber operations but nothing happened until the end of the year. I could have gone along with the students into civil aviation but I found the prospect of airborne bus-driving unattractive. I was delighted in February 1944 to move instead into an operational transport squadron. I joined the force of Douglas Dakota (DC3) aircraft being assembled at RAF Stations Blakehill Farm, Down Ampney and Broadwell to initiate the invasion of Europe, the long-awaited 'second front', as part of a major airborne assault. Each station had two squadrons of 30 aircraft – puny compared with the enomous Dakota (DC-3) force fielded by the United States Air Force, a recent metamorphosis of the Army Air Corps. Nevertheless, forming and training our own RAF transport support force was a formidable commitment, especially because it was very urgent. The air crews were a mixture of ex-bomber pilots, ex-instructors from the now vast Empire Flying Training organisation and others of miscellaneous antecedents; few, unfortunately, had combat experience. Our common task was to learn, as quickly as possible, to drop parachutists and their accoutrements and to deliver the gliders of the recently formed Glider Pilot Regiment. As my single conversion flight showed, the Dakota, whose superb quality as a beast of burden had been apparent since 1932, was an easy aircraft to fly. Dropping and delivery, however, needed faultless day and night navigation at low level and steady, accurate flying, often in formation, akin to a bombing run. Nobody knew when the invasion would start; we all knew it would be soon.

We all worked hard to get ready, supposed to observe strict secrecy. Radio messages, we were told, would be intercepted by our own intelligence as well as the Germans, so that breaches would be detected and the perpetrators punished. Here, in the first signs of how stupid intelligence authorities can be that I discovered later, the code word for a glider on our radio frequencies was 'match box'; and for landing it 'quilt'. There could hardly have been a more obvious giveaway.

The station commander at Blakehill, Group Captain William Kennedy was a grey man showing his humanity only through the attractive Wren (Women's Royal Naval Service) girl who visited his hut near the officers' mess from time to time. The Squadron, 233, had been a Coastal Command unit equipped with Lockheed Hudsons. Our first commander was Wing Commander Nigel Morrison, a Cranwell graduate, later to have the distinction of leading the very first stream of aircraft of the initial airborne assault on the French coast. Another ex-cadet, later a close friend, was Harry Jenkins, formerly an instructor in Canada who had married a charming girl, Marion, from Prince Edward Island, tragically to die of kidney disease a few years later. Amusing and super-conscientious, he was dominated by desire to emulate his father, a distinguished World War One pilot and later a regular. Harry was at heart a field sportsman and naturalist, not really suited to being an airman. My most interesting comrade was my flight commander Geoff Lane, very bright and wonderfully funny, dashing frequently to London to take law exams. Forty years later, after a brilliant career at the Bar specialising in aviation cases, he became Lord Chief Justice of England.

Rachel and I feared that my posting would separate us; and, sure enough, along came a posting for her to the RAF station at Hendon, in London. Being about to marry we could no longer serve at the same station, but there was no objection to the stationing of spouses nearby. Gillie Potter found a girl at Down Ampney, 3 miles on the opposite side of the village of Cricklade to Blakehill, who was glad to take Rachel's posting to Hendon. Thus we could not have been luckier. The path of true love, however, soon ran to traditional form. Although Rachel's introductory stay in Malvern had gone well, my father showed the same determination that I should not marry her as he had in forcing me into medicine. Instead of Hitler, this time my mother came to the rescue: if, she told him, he went on with his stated intention neither to support nor attend the wedding, she would leave him. It worked, but the rancour took time to go away. One of his reasons, characteristically paternal, was doubt of my judgement. Another, unworthy, was snobbery: Rachel, a draper's daughter, was 'trade'; we, superior, were 'professional'. A third plea was that wartime marriages did not last. At 60-plus years and counting, Rachel and I have put that observation where it belonged. The final blow to his stance came when my Uncle Jim Cavendish, brother of Alex, who at 43 had been held up to me as an example of the wisdom of waiting, suddenly fell for a widow and tied the knot.

We went some way towards easing familial anxieties by abandoning a plan to marry in late 1943 and drive the Baby Austin, now geriatrically unreliable, via the ferry from Stranraer to Larne. Instead, the wedding was fixed for spring 1944 in London. In those days marriages could only be solemnized, as Cranmer's prayer book dauntingly puts it, in the home parish of one or other partner. That rule, rather like the methods of proving adultery needed at the time to dismember marriages, could be got round by dumping a suitcase in a hotel within another parish. We did so in that of St Peter's Church, Vere Street. George Snow assisted in the conduct of the Service and Robert Birley was there, with Kenneth Milne and other Old Carthusians. The reception was at the nearby Welbeck Hotel, later The Londoner. Briefer and cheaper than the bacchanalia of later celebrations, its centrepiece was a tiered wedding cake; but such were the privations of the day that all the tiers except one were cardboard. And instead of the RAF motif which our hardworking mothers had ordered, the decorations featured the Royal Navy. Nowadays, I suppose, such a mistake would have led to litigation. We were too happy to care.

We lunched at Waterloo Station, which then had an august restaurant, and entrained for Guildford, convenient for the Bramley Grange Hotel, the poshest of the places to which I had been taken out to lunch on Sundays off from Charterhouse. We tried to register and dine as unobtrusively as possible, only to be greeted and congratulated:

We read the Evening Standard, you know.

Therein was a photograph and the caption, 'DFC officer's WAAF bride'. A clear sign of a shortage of copy.

After a two-day honeymoon, short even for those days, we went back to work, staying at the White Hart Hotel in Cricklade, run by a Mrs Croucher, as Dickensianly forbidding as her name. Wanting a home of our own, we were knocking at doors in the village when we ran into a Mrs Armstrong, a widow looking after two grandchild evacuees. She let us the main bedroom, with use of the sitting room, in her cottage by the church. She seemed reluctant to charge but, when pressed, hoped that 3 guineas a week would be all right. Extraordinarily kind in a kind community, she often found excuses to go out in the evenings to give us privacy; and somehow adapted her own routine and that of the children to suit our working hours, which did not coincide and were, as the jargon would now describe it, unsocial. We felt guilty at trespassing on her generosity and unselfishness and kept an eye open for somewhere else.

As always I was lucky with my crew. The second pilot Jock Hunter had been a junior in the Bank of Scotland in Edinburgh. The navigator, Joe Proctor, had had the privilege as an office boy of changing the film

116

magnate Sam Goldwyn's blotting paper daily. The wireless operator, Darkie Goodwin, was an older man, married and another of the steadying influences that I was fortunate to encounter. I was one of a minority with experience of being shot at, and worried at the lack of it among some of my fellow captains.

Rachel worked shifts as a clerk and receptionist in the Air Despatch and Reception Unit (ADRU) at Down Ampney; like Blakehill, gearing up for dealing with the thousands of troops who would emplane for departure and the casualties expected to return. When I could not drive her to and fro she commuted by bicycle, armed for night journeys with my Colt 45 blunderbuss of a revolver. My exiguous quarterly supply of petrol soon ran out; and when that happened there was nothing for it but the mischievous delight of collecting her in a Dakota. It was a time of our lives as demanding as it was idyllic.

There came, as a welcome break, a summons to Buckingham Palace for an investiture at which I would receive my DFC. We were all delighted that my father, who had been awarded the Order of the British Empire for

Sister, mother, father, son and wife after the joint investiture. *The Malvern Gazette*

his services to the Red Cross, was to receive his decoration at the same investiture. He, far ahead of me in the queue because of the seniority of his award, duly received his word of appreciation from King George VI. Just before he got to me the King's aide-de-camp, an admiral, whispered a reminder that this was a father and son occasion. The King, suitably gracious, remarked on what a happy occasion it must be for us both. Which it was, for us all.

Blakehill Farm expanded with the erection of a large, tented transit camp for parachute troops in final training and awaiting the launch of the invasion. Two other senior pilots and I were invited to the camp mess for lunch in return for the welcome we had given to the commandant. He was Major 'Slapsie' Bailey, broken-nosed, cauliflower-eared and so named because he had been boxing champion of the Army. Whisky (scarce) flowed. Of steak (rationed) there was plenty. After the brandy (scarce) and cigars (very scarce), I found to my consternation that my car, in which I had given the others a lift, had been filled with petrol (strictly rationed). Well under the influence, Brailey told us not to worry. He had, he said, sources and nobody would find out. About 40 years later they did: Lord Brailey, prominent and successful in business, was gaoled for the same sort of thing, dying soon afterwards.

By early June it was all coming together and we were sealed into our bases. The large casualty reception unit was fully staffed (Rachel giving the surgeon and nurses something to do by having her appendix out). We were all briefed for the enormous airborne operation in Normandy, comprehensively except for the date and time. The squadrdon's task was to drop the paras of the 3rd Parachute Brigade of the Sixth Airborne Division on to a field near the villages of Ranville and Colombelles, respectively north-east and east of the city of Caen. The Division as a whole was to protect the eastern flank of the seaborne main force operating to the west, along the coast towards the American force, itself covering the next stretch of coast towards Cherbourg. There was a plenitude of goodwill messages of which Montgomery's reverted to the questionable habit of invoking the Almighty; in this instance on behalf of his new command, the 21st Army Group:

> The time has come to deal the enemy a terrific blow in Western Europe ... Let us pray that 'The Lord Mighty in Battle' will aid us in the struggle.

At the back of the folk mind, perhaps, lingered traces of the ferocity of World War One reflected in the Advent sermon preached in 1915 by

Winnington Ingram, Bishop of London, recalled in Niall Ferguson's *The Pity of War*:

> A great crusade – we cannot deny it – to kill Germans, not for the sake of killing, but to save the world; to kill the good as well as the bad, to kill the young men as well as the old, to kill those who have shown kindness as well as [the] fiends ... and to kill them lest the civilisation of the world should itself be killed.

A long way from the studied neutrality of a prayer on a slip of paper dated August 1914 tucked into my mother's Bible:

> ... stretch forth ... Thine Almighty Arm to strengthen and protect the sailors and soldiers of our King ... Shelter them in the day of battle, keep them safe from all evil, endue them ever with loyalty and courage and grant that in all things they may serve as seeing Thee ...

To which modern prelates, thank Heaven, have returned. Archbishop Runcie, to the relief of many, exemplified that stance by his refusal to countenance thanks for victory in the Falklands War. He rightly stopped short at peace.

On 4 June the mighty force was alerted for a launch that night. On the list of troops allotted to my aircraft I found the name of my half-brother William Collingwood, then brigade major (pivot and general factotum) of the 3rd Parachute Brigade. The commander was Brigadier James Hill, already well known and decorated for his bravery and leadership in previous launches in North Africa and Sicily. I sought William out in the transit camp; and although I kidded him that he should stay in my aircraft and enjoy the quality service on offer, we agreed that, for family reasons, he must go with someone else. Hill, later a family friend for many years, agreed at once and William was transferred to an Albemarle squadron at RAF Fairford which was to drop in the same area. I was apprehensive because Albemarles were reputed to have been assembled from flatpack kits supplied by the Times Furnishing Company, and were highly unpopular.

We were all relieved when bad weather forced the postponement of the launch on the night of 4 June. On the 5th everybody boarded their aircraft, the entire Blakehill complement of which were parked alongside the runways, with gliders adjacent to their tugs. The deployment, long planned by a Royal Army Service Corps captain assigned to that single task, was orderly and rapid. The take-off was punctual almost to the second. The circuitous route, planned to enable 1,300 aircraft to form up as planned, took us northwards to Shropshire, south-eastwards to East Anglia and thence south-west to the Channel and Normandy. The radio silence was broken by a flustered officer in charge of night flying as we passed over the training airfield at Shawbury, near the Wrekin, who had no idea of what was afoot:

I think we'd better cancel flying for tonight.

Nobody else said a word.

For success we needed a cloud base over the dropping zones of not less than 700 feet, with decent visibility underneath. That was just about what we got. I saw the coast and our destination field, studied beforehand in minute detail. I glanced anxiously westwards towards the area prohibited by the Royal Navy, who had announced that their gunners would fire on any aircraft, friend or foe, which violated their space. Along came the dropping zone. As I put on the green ('jump, jump') light I was confident

The death of Dakota KG 429 and all aboard. Mine was KG 430. *By kind permission of my friend the artist Jean Maubert*

120

that our lads would land on the appointed spot. After the familiar agonising seconds, reminiscent of past bombing runs, I put on the red 'stop' light. One poor man had failed to emerge, having tucked his release strop (a long ribbon of thick canvas webbing) under instead of over his belt, and he begged for another chance. I let down from 600 to 400 feet, near the safe limit for him, and again flew over the zone, now thick with small arms and light anti-aircraft fire, from which it was obvious that there had been casualties. That run was not accurate enough for me to allow him to drop. A third run succeeded as far as I could tell, but I have never been sure. We flew clear of the lively party at sea level, climbing away near Fécamp, whence came searchlights and shells. Corkscrewing probably played a part in helping us to escape without a scratch. The same may have been true on the following night, when we did a supply-dropping trip over the beach head dropping large panniers of bedding and stretchers, using the roller conveyors that made the job a quick one; (even quicker if anybody despatched himself accidently by setting foot on the rollers). This time there was fire, presumably German, from near Caen; and, undoubtedly British, from the Royal Navy into whose Tom Tiddler's ground I had strayed, causing minor damage unspecified in my log book.

Not so my unfortunate brother. William's Albemarle had been hit as it approached the dropping zone and at the moment when William had jumped, complete with vital planning documents and a 60-lb kit bag. As he did so his release strop jammed; and he, complete with his bag and case, was left dangling in the aether as the aircraft turned for home. The crew of course tried to haul him back inside. They did not succeed until shortly before the aircraft made an emergency landing at RAF Odiham in Hampshire; and in doing so they dislocated his right hip. Desperate to get back to France because of the documents, and in order not to miss the action, William got in touch with the brigade major of the air-landing (glider) brigade, his friend Major Napier Crookenden, who gave him a lift in his glider. As James Hill later described what followed:

On D+1 who should hobble into my headquarters but Bill Colling-wood with his semi-dislocated hip sticking out sideways? Unfortunately you could not have a brigade major or chief of staff whose leg stuck out sideways and 36 hours later the medics took him away. What an extraordinary feat of mental endurance and guts that was ...

And all he got, to adapt a phrase, was this lousy MBE – a sadly junior Membership of the Order of the British Empire.

121

After the launch and follow-up there were two unexplained and irksome days of inaction. The reason soon became clear. It was that the planners had allowed for many more casualties than there were. It was as discomfiting to realise that we were meant to be dead, as it was relieving to get back on the job as all-purpose carriers for the forces with a foothold in France. We were at first blessed with fighter escorts, flying in formation over the Channel to the series of temporary landing grounds. They were laid with lightning speed by the Royal Engineers, using the ingenious PSP (pierced steel planking) which made a major contribution to the advance. The landing strips soon became a numbered series, prefixed 'B' for British. On the return flights we carried casualties, often including sick and wounded German prisoners of war. There were many desperately wounded patients, but a few cheerful exceptions: leaving the flight deck to chat to them I found a colonel apparently doubled up in agony. As I sympathised he grinned, undoubled himself and showed me the bottles of brandy which his contortions concealed. Like all the casualties he was attended to in the air by excellent nursing orderlies and delivered to Down Ampney, where Rachel was often among the reception staff with the job of helping to classify and despatch the casualties to appropriate hospitals, mostly near Swindon or Oxford. She did a number of frightening night journeys to keep the over-stretched attendants and WRAC drivers company.

By August there were 21 B and at least 50 A (American) landing grounds. To many of both we carried a miscellany of goods: bombs, mail, 15 cwt. trucks, blood, newspapers, tank spares, biscuits, sausages, ammunition petrol and starter cartridges being among the items I bothered to record. As the Allies advanced the place names became evocative of holidays and World War One: Brussels, Orléans, Vitry-en-Artois, Ypres and Poperinghe among them.

At home in Cricklade we ceased taking advantage of dear Mrs Armstrong by finding a bedroom at Abingdon Court Farm, nearby. Farmer Jones and his family were archetypal, as were their mucky farmyard and spotless milking parlour. There was even a dairymaid – fat, smelly and to be found every morning at the kitchen sink, literally red-handed from the soda which was all she had for degreasing the pots and pans. The household was refreshingly remote from the war and the Jones's were very kind. Mrs Jones, however, was pushy: one afternoon literally, into our bedroom on a rare coincidence of days off. Bursting with, as it were, enthusiasm, we were at a loss as to how to oust her, being reluctant to get out of bed naked and usher her through the door. 'Oh well, must be getting on,' also seemed somehow inappropriate. At last, bored with the inactivity, she abandoned her prurient voyeuserie.

In the autumn Wing Commander Morrison vanished to a ground job. His replacement was a glamorous figure, already known for his bravery and excellence as a pilot. Wing Commandeer Bill Coles, who had started working life as a policeman, was a plain-spoken disciplinarian with a Wiltshire accent, whose fierce manner concealed great kindness. He was just the man to lead us through a sticky period. Sticky it was. It emerged that we had not done well on 6 June. James Hill and his staff had had a terrible job gathering the troops together and regrouping them because of the grievous inaccuracy with which many of them had been dropped. Some of our young crews' lack of steadiness under fire for the first time was doubtless a contributory factor, of which I and many other seniors felt ashamed. We needed pulling together; and pulled we were.

The summer wore on and the Allied advance slowed. General Eisenhower, Supreme Commander of the Allied forces in Europe, saw a way of regaining momentum by means of an airborne coup in Holland that could open the way into Germany. The US 82nd Airborne Division were to land in central Holland near Njemegen, not far ahead of the main land force. The British 1st Airborne Division, at the bidding of General Montgomery, had as its objective the bridge over the River Waal at Arnhem. This was an even bolder stroke because the main force front line, west of Utrecht, was a long way west of the Waal. By now an acting squadron leader and flight commander I felt that the squadron, well knit after three months together and in action, would acquit itself better than the undertrained, unseasoned unit that had stumbled at D-Day.

For the launch I had a fully loaded glider in tow. The lumbering take-off reminded me of my struggles aloft on hot afternoons at Fayid. Later it was gratifying to hear of a young Army officer's report:

We dropped on the DZ [dropping zone] absolutely perfect, just like an exercise.

Very soon, however, it was evident that all was not well at Arnhem because Montgomery's main force was taking unexpectedly long to catch up. Four days after the launch we were asked for a maximum effort to replenish the beleaguered force, now contained within a small perimeter round the bridge. I carried 16 panniers, each of 350 lbs of petrol and ammunition. The dispatchers did their job wonderfully quickly in a single run over the DZ. That was a relief because the anti-aircraft fire was the thickest I had ever seen and the Dakota casualties were high. One reason, we later discovered, was that the German anti-aircraft guns had been augmented with field artillery elevated skywards. Together they were firing at the predictable line of approach that we were forced to follow.

Even that frightening task was not without light relief. As we sped away our regular dispatcher, an Irish private in the Royal Army Service Corps as it then was, shouted from the plastic dome which was the sole way of seeing behind: 'Bandits!', which was code for fighters about to attack. We had taught him the standard way of reporting their whereabouts (port, starboard, beam, quarter, ahead, astern, high, low); but nothing but silence followed his shout. The awful gap seemed so long and worrying that I asked

Come on Paddy, where are they?

After a further aeon of seconds came the answer:

There's hunderts of the buggers.

By then I was corkscrewing close to the ground, making the fighters' task nearly impossible, and once again we were spared anything but a few bullet holes.

Two days later came the same again. This time Bill Coles was at the head of the main stream and I was leading the formation behind, again with panniers of petrol and ammunition. The anti-aircraft fire was intense but no worse than before, but mishaps in the back of my aircraft meant that it took three terrifying runs over the target zone to get rid of the load. It was a great relief to dive away, this time free from marauding fighters. But it was galling to learn later that the dropping zone was at least partly in German hands.

The three missions, the middle one of which I had missed, took a terrible toll. Flight Lieutenant David Lord of Down Ampney, despite having his aircraft hit and set on fire, carried on with his run and delivered his load before crashing, all aboard being killed. He was awarded a posthumous Victoria Cross. Other awards included an immediate DSO for Bill Coles, five DFCs, one bar to DFC (mine), a US Air Medal and a US DFC.

My parents, avid radio listeners, got a flavour of what Arnhem was like from what became a historic broadcast by Stanley Maxted, a Canadian BBC man embedded, as the phrase became, in the Arnhem ground force. In a moving broadcast he admired the steadiness:

of the air force ... and what an air force.

For the time being we carried on, literally and figuratively, as before. As the

Supply dropping at Arnhem in October 1944. Flight Lieutenant David Lord earning the Victoria Cross. *Artist Wilf Hardy*

B numbers of the landing grounds increased we entered the removal business, shifting whole fighter squadrons and their effects from airfields in Britain to the Continent, sometimes reassured by the presence of their aircraft as escorts. Returning with a load of casualties after one such move I saw, well below and some way on our port side, what looked like a fighter with flame issuing from its back end. It reminded me of the primordial jet I had seen at Cranwell. I broke radio silence to report the possibility of imminent attack, but nothing materialised. At home that evening I heard the news of the arrival and explosion in a field of the first of the V-1s, powered missiles that caused much damage during the next few months.

By now I had begun to feel some of the despondency and exhaustion that had afflicted me in the Middle East. There would, I felt, be more Arnhems and our casualties would continue to be high, even in comparison with the slaughter of our comrades in Bomber Command. In what could have been defiance, and with no clear decision not to go back to medicine, I applied for a permanent commission in the RAF. Soon afterwards came our first wedding anniversary, 21 March 1945. We could not celebrate because I was part of yet another enormous force, now known as the 1st Allied Airborne Army, for what was hoped for as the final assault on Germany. After three days at a semi-derelict airfield at Birch, near Colchester, I towed a glider across the Rhine at Wesel in the company of all the aircraft available and a huge American DC3 armada to the south. We had all apprehended another bloody encounter; but compared with Arnhem, opposition to the Rhine crossing was slight. The losses of 233 were nil, and there were said to have been only 19 aircraft destroyed out of a force exceeding 1,000. Our aircraft fuel tanks had suffered bullet holes, fortunately non-incendiary. Along with several other Dakotas incontinent of fuel we littered B57, the air base at Nivelles, near Brussels. Rachel had been upset by being told that I had been reported missing, soon afterwards to be reassured.

As the Allied domination of Europe became complete, we began the job of ferrying ever-growing numbers of liberated Allied prisoners of war home to Britain, cramming 30-plus of these emaciated men into a compartment meant for no more than 20; my record was 38. Unwashed, in threadbare uniform, they wolfed the Dundee cake they were offered and were promptly sick. We took them to a specially adapted airfield at Wing, near Aylesbury, where they were deloused, cleaned and, as they deserved, well spoilt. During and after VE Day, 8th May, we conducted business as usual. Unusually, I was required to go on a confidential mission to B156, the German airfield at Luneberg near where one of the surrenders had taken place. The job turned out to be to collect no fewer than 19 German generals and a colonel, plus a well-armed escort, and deliver them to Croydon, the pre-war civil airport for London, undulating and devoid of runways. The captives were docile and we were polite except to one general, ignorant of quarantine rules, who protested at being deprived of his *kleine hund* (little dog). Lassie didn't come home.

In mid-June 1945, 233 Squadron had itself to move to Odiham, an old-established permanent station, comfortable but, like Croydon, uneven and all grass. It had as a runabout an Auster, a puddle-jumper meant for light reconnaissance for the Army; and, nostalgically, another Oxford. Both were fine as runabouts and fun to fly. The domestic consequences of the move were mitigated because Rachel, promoted to corporal, had celebrated it by adopting the most effective way of leaving the WAAF – getting pregnant. Scarcely less welcome was solving the housing problem. The bachelor station commander at Odiham, having no use for the large CO's residence, very kindly lent it to us. He turned out to be Group Captain John Simpson, the subject of the Hector Bolitho biography which I had reviewed. I was saddened that the booze had taken its toll. After what passed for work, John's invariable habit was to repair to the bar in the officers' mess, where he drank whisky until closing time. That was when he, fit only to be shepherded to bed, said it was. He gave off emanations of homosexuality and astonished everybody by proposing to, and being accepted by, Gillie Potter, who had moved to Odiham as chief WAAF officer. They married amidst much alcoholic celebration. Rachel and I were very concerned about Gillie, now a dear friend. There proved to be ample cause. Very sadly, John shot himself a few years afterwards in Green Park, having left a suicide note, pathetically, with the barman at Shepherds, a flashy Mayfair pub. Our sadness for Gillie, with whom we kept in touch until she died in the 1990s, was infinite.

The work load lessened and we soon found out why. The squadron was to move again, this time to the Far East where, of course, the war continued. Our hearts sank at the prospect of a two-year separation; but they soon surfaced again when, because of the two overseas tours I had already done, I was deemed ineligible for another. Not so poor Harry Jenkins, who suffered a further blow on his final day with Marion: he had been debilitated by the multiple injections prerequisite to service in the Far East and could not play his part in fulfilling their dearest wish, which was to procreate an heir or heiress. I suppressed an urge to oblige a pal with the offer of a surrogacy.

My new posting was another pleasant surprise. I had felt sure that I would have to go to a ground job. Instead I was to join, as a flight commander, another Dakota squadron, 525, at RAF Membury, in the middle of nowhere on the Wiltshire downs, the name later preserved as that of the nearby motorway services stop. The squadron's role was long-range transport. Just as we moved I, to my amazement and delight, was awarded a permanent commission amongst the first 20 or so successful applicants. Soon afterwards came a bar to my Distinguished Flying Cross. Mentioning that I was on my third tour of operations, Bill Coles's citation reported my three runs over the dropping zone on the D-day assault; similar actions at the battle of Arnhem; and ended, blushmakingly, with:

> an outstanding operational pilot, his keenness, determination and devotion to duty set a most excellent example to other members of the Squadron.

The taciturn Group Captain Kennedy, in a rare burst of enthusiasm, endorsed Bill Coles's encomium in similar strain.

Our cup of joy was full except for the problem of where to live. We had left the CO's residence to make way for, as we hoped they would be, the happy Simpson couple. Rachel had gone to live alternately in Malvern and at her family home in Glastonbury while I combed the Membury area, if not for a nest at least for a perch. After much knocking on doors I found room in a large farmhouse at Ogbourne St George, a village near Marlborough, 16 miles away. Our fellow lodgers were a senior Army doctor and his wife who went out of their way to be kind, especially to Rachel during my prolonged absences. Like the Jones's, the Ogbourne farming family were hospitable but remote from our world. On VJ day, 8 August, when we had planned to move in, I rang to ask whether it would still be a convenient day. 'Yes,' was the reply, 'we're not celebratin', we're 'arvestin'.' They also kept pigs, one of which was butchered for the benefit of all, on the kitchen table. Neither Rachel nor I could touch our sanguinary share of the spoils.

Commuting to and from work through the Wiltshire lanes added almost an hour to my longish days, sitting in the umpteenth-hand Morris 8 that had replaced our now ancient Austin. The engine behaved like a diesel, burning vast amounts of oil and emitting enough smoke to confuse any enemy. Eventually rebored and with new pistons, it ran well enough.

The station commander at Membury was Group Captain G.A.G. Johnson, an old no-nonsense administrator who asked for and got help in turning the station from what he called a muck heap into a reasonable roost for the Dakota. Years later I was to meet him again in Nigeria, transmuted into a Foreign Office official. Wing Commander Roy Dutton commanded 525, the third of the Battle of Britain pilots whom I came to know well. There was also a fourth, who had shifted from fighters to transport, getting my personal unaccolade as the worst aircrew officer with whom I served: stupid, idle, barely safe as a pilot, he had clearly contributed nothing to the battle; but he shared in the glory, in his case wholly reflected. He, Dutton and Simpson confirmed my impression of 'The Few' as a tribe: the best, such as Simpson and Dutton, were very good indeed. But there were others who did little of the fighting and were dissolute and contemptuous of authority in a way that would not have been tolerated in the rest of the RAF. Roy, like John, had married an older woman, a charming Scots RAF nurse. After his good fighter record he did even better, getting a DSO for leading an airborne stream from Broadwell in the Rhine-crossing operation. He was full of roguish humour, drinking to excess but apparently without any adverse consequences. I was in effect his deputy, and found him a pleasure to work for.

I revelled in the long-range transport work. Malta's tintinnabulating opera house continued to afford morsels of Traviata, Cav and Pag to eaves-droppers. The delights of the Floriana Gut, the haunt of sin that had amused me years before were still to be enjoyed. Less delightful was Sardinia, whose airfield at Cagliari smelt of drains, fry-ups and garlic from 7,000 feet. Cairo's foetid airport demanded of captains a signed assurance that they had not imported any sources of infection into Egypt and, uniquely, the filling-in of a form on which had to be entered particulars of the aircraft's whereabouts for the previous ten nights. Iraq boasted the best station in the RAF – Habbaniyah: every known sport, polo included, was to be had; and to get there after a boiling hot progress along the desert pipeline from Cairo, doubling as a navigational aid, was to have reached Nirvana. We used it as a 'slip' stop, giving crews a day's interval before taking on the next aircraft to arrive. Our easternmost stop was at Allahabad; but those hoping for the glamours and amours of the Orient were dismayed to find themselves in a spotless boarding house run by the draconian widow of a British servant of the Raj. She locked the doors at ten: willy-nilly, as that practice might very aptly be described.

Helping to keep the squadron running gradually kept me more at base than on the routes. Again I became a quasi-instructor, checking captains' flying and supervising crews' continuation training. But I kept one trip for myself. Every Sunday, very early, I flew a load of newspapers to RAF Buckeburg in Germany. Amidst the big bundles there were two complete sets of all the papers. One was for General Montgomery, still commanding the 21st Army Group: the other for me. At home Rachel and I gorged ourselves on the prurient rubbish. Her pregnancy went well and, great with child, she went to Malvern where my father, now happily reconciled to the marriage, kept an eye on her. He asked his favourite gynaecological colleague to deliver. He did: to our boundless joy, a boy.

Before I could finish my tour I found myself posted to what I had been lucky enough to avoid for the whole war and until then for the peace – a ground job. I could hardly complain. In the air the trivial round, the common task, as a hymn ancient and modern (*A&M 4*) puts it, had furnished all I needed to ask – and a great deal more. Now, as the phrase became, for something completely different.

Chapter 7

Special Pickings

My half-brother William and I, like most sons, in the eyes of our mother could do no wrong. When we both became serving officers, she went further: we could do nothing but right. So much so, that for every job assigned to us we were, for her, 'specially picked'. To be fair, that was true of William when he volunteered successfully, at the start of World War Two, to join the *corps d'élite* for the liberation of Finland, occupied by the Germans. But for me, so far, that maternal conviction bore no relation to the facts. And it could be embarrassing. On a holiday in Mull my mother and her best woman friend had stayed in a grand guest house with a quiet man and his wife, who disclosed that he was an airman. He seemed interested in my mother's glowing account of my service as a bomber pilot, specially picked, of course, for the Middle East; and much more besides. When I asked who they were, she said she thought it was a name like Tedder. Trying to contain a splutter of embarrassment, I forbore to tell her that Sir Arthur Tedder was an air chief marshal, at the time Chief of Air Staff.

Once in a while Mum's boasts were near the mark. In 1946 some mogul at the Air Ministry had been empowered literally to specially pick founder members of the new RAF Selection Board, if necessary in the middle of other tours of duty. That happened to me. The board formed at Framewood, a less than stately manor near Slough. The president was to be Air Commodore George Beamish, bachelor scion of a famous Irish RAF family also comprising, two fighter pilots, Charles and Victor, the latter killed in the Battle of Britain; Cecil, a dental officer, with whom I later served in the Far East; and a formidable WAAF sister, said to look exactly like George in drag. He was a large man who had boxed and played rugger for the RAF, attested to by a broken nose and cauliflower ears. He was still a good golfer despite a hip injury which gave him the rolling gait of a seafarer. He was cantankerous, but also funny and kind. He had conducted the evacuation of the RAF from Crete in 1941 with great distinction, but seniority had kept him from aircrew operations at which he would undoubtedly have distinguished himself as had Victor. He retired as an air marshal, later standing as a Tory candidate for Belfast, to the amused stupefaction of all who knew him; and, to their unsurprised regret, failing.

The rest of us were a cross-section of the RAF emerging from the war. Beamish's deputy was Group Captain Paul Holder, an outstanding former bomber pilot and staff college instructor, exactly right as the brains to complement George's brawn. Down one level were the wing commanders: David Evans, unmemorable except for his wife's expressed enjoyment of a cup of post-coital coffee; William Nicholas, a former Halton apprentice who became an air gunner with an excellent record in Bomber Command; and David Scott Malden, a very successful Battle of Britain pilot and with an intellect of great depth, tragically to die of lung disease a few years later. The rest were lowly squadron leaders. One besides myself was John Preston, an RAF fencing champion and an example of what sporting prowess can do for otherwise unremarkable people. The opposite was Lawrence Reavell Carter, a shot-putter at Olympic level, blessed with native wit and cursed with a flighty wife. He had shown his stamina and guts as one of the heroic escapers who had survived the shooting of 40 comrades as, with 60 others, they escaped through a tunnel from a German prisoner of war camp. Another veteran of Bomber Command, festooned with decorations earned on multiple raids over Europe, was Roger Reece, of great modesty and with concealed depths later apparent when he took holy orders. Subsidiary advisers included a RAF consultant psychiatrist, and a civilian polymath, Maurice Backett, later to come my way as a professor concerned with medical training and health education.

As I was buckling down to an unfamiliar job, our family were stricken by my father's death at 67. He had been failing for months, struggling with great fortitude to work while suffering with what he called cardiac asthma – akin, as I understood it, to emphysema. Its origin lay in the gassings he had endured during a four-year period of gallant service in command of a field ambulance. When his final illness began, I helped my mother to find a locum tenens to look after the practice. He turned out to be a newly demobilised RAF doctor in the rank of wing commander. He at once took to the work, but found the burden which my father had been bearing for years almost more than he could cope with. He was so impressed that he bought the practice and the house, where he stayed until his retirement 20 years later.

My father's life had been rewarding in everything except money; his £1,000 life assurance benefit just covering his liabilities. His funeral service in the abbey-sized Malvern Priory Church was packed. We were delighted that he had survived long enough to know David, our elder son. Unfortunately he died before the christening, which George Snow was glad to conduct after:

> Alastair's note, all bursting with joy [which] gets better every day ... the priceless adventure of the start of the family.

George had married the kind and hospitable Joan, whom we had met at Ardingly. Sadly, the paternal joys of George's own family were not undiluted. Of his three boys, Tom, as he told us with chagrin, became a Marxist hospital cleaner. Although high-principled Tom caused, as his brother Jonathan's biography records, much family discord during his childhood. Jon himself became a broadcaster, vying with his cousin Peter, who looks much more like George than he does, in televisionary fame.

The three of us, as we now were, had great difficulty in finding anywhere to live. The problem solved itself in less than three months when the owner of Framewood Manor, which had been requisitioned for the duration of the war, suddenly wanted it back. We moved the Board to another home, this time of full stately status near Ascot and Sunningdale. Sunninghill Park had magnificent grounds and a lake with a bridge into which the resident swans, belying their reputation as good aviators, regularly crashed on alighting. The house and outbuildings offered excellent facilities and our work prospered. It was to select, from as much of the cream of Britain's youth as the RAF could attract, candidates for Cranwell – back in business much as it had been before the war but with the great advantage of a more catholic field of choice. We were also charged with selecting officers from those who had asked for their short-service commissions to be made permanent.

We used practical tests with logs, planks and bricks, usually involving some form of contrivance and absorbing enough for candidates to forget themselves and help the watching testers to distinguish the pushy from the diffident, and the bright from the dim. There were discussions in small groups and in plenary sessions; and interviews decreasing in length with the seniority of the interviewer. The candidates were put into numbered overalls to promote literal uniformity and to secure anonymity. At the end of the four-day cycle we reviewed all we had learnt of each candidate at length, not looking at other sources such as school reports until we had reached consensus. We ended by classifying candidates in suitability for cadetships or commissions in categories A to F (with an unofficial self-explanatory extra F-OMDB, meaning only acceptable Over My Dead Body

– in case of benefit-of-the-doubt tendencies at higher level). The system, said to have been invented in Nazi Germany, had been in use in the Army before we started. I was sent to a WOSB (War Office Selection Board) on a study visit, picking up tips, some of which we used. Although the system, later adopted by the Civil Service and the Police, has its defects, it undoubtedly does better than the previous procedure of a single interview with a panel of senior wiseacres which had produced so much ullage.

There was much interest from on high. One VIP visitor was our ultimate boss, Air Chief Marshal Sir John Slessor, a former bomber pilot, an intellectual and, most rare in that exalted category, a most likeable and modest man, at the time responsible for all RAF personnel. His reaction was to thank his lucky stars that he had got his permanent commission by having an uncle in the War Office. In diametric contrast was Air Marshal Sir Basil Embry, Commander-in-Chief of Fighter Command and an exemplar of what were known as the Barons – lawless very senior office holders who paid no heed to the dicta of the Air Ministry. His notorieties included wasting, in defiance of authority, a huge sum of public money on blast walls round all the individual aircraft hard standings in his command, subsequently shown to be almost useless. His alternative to our selection process, he told us not entirely in jest perhaps, would be to lock all the candidates in one room for 48 hours and commission the survivors.

Private housing around Sunninghill was as scarce as anywhere in the country. We were rescued by one of Rachel's covey of aunts, who lent us a house at Keston in Kent. The distance meant weekends only at home for me; but it was a very good suburban commuter nest and Rachel had plenty of friends. We soon did even better, finding rooms in the servants' quarters of a mansion with a large garden which shared a fence with the Golden Gates of Ascot racecourse. Our co-tenants in the family rooms were the Deputy President Group Captain Paul Holder and his charming wife Betty and young family. The house, belonging to an ancient admiral with a VC, was lit solely by carbide gas generated in a small plant in one of the garages and piped into the rooms. The only heating was from fires. Almost at once the famously cold winter of 1946/47 set in; and in spite of a doctor's certificate for a priority supply of coal to keep three small children warm, neither Paul nor I could get any; the local merchant's yard being bare. Fortunately there was an abandoned timber-hutted former American military camp in the Selection Board's grounds opposite our front gate. Paul and I, with hammers, a jemmy and a cross-cut saw, spent most of our free time before and after work dismantling the huts and sawing the product into foot-long bits of wood which sufficed to keep us warm throughout the terrible seven-week freeze-up. The work afforded wonderful exercise; and the leisurely hours of work meant that the task was not too onerous.

In the better weather we enjoyed the garden; and, on race days, watching the Royal Family driving through the gates and along the elegant course. Then came the forming-up of the jockeys, who chatted amiably to each other before starts; except for the famous Gordon Richards, whom all seemed to ostracise. The house was big enough to provide tide-over rooms for my mother and sister Joanna, who had left the family house when the Malvern practice was sold and were waiting to move into a much smaller abode in Windlesham, near Sunninghill. They lived happily in the little house until my sister married and my mother sadly succumbed to a depressive illness akin, I believe, to the one I suffered from until my psychiatrist found a modern drug to control it. She went to St Andrew's Hospital in Northampton (for the directorship of which, incidentally, my father had been an unsuccessful candidate). She was very briefly restored to lucidity before she died there in 1960.

Like those of Framewood Manor, Sunninghill Park's RAF days were numbered. The trouble this time was that it had been chosen as an out-of-London residence for the then Princess Elizabeth and her husband Prince Phillip. The Board, having learnt lessons in mobility from the first upheaval, soon re-established itself at Ramridge House, near Andover, again commodious and pleasant.

Reavell Carter and I, roped into help with the transplanting, were taking a final look round Sunninghill Park to ensure that all was well just after noon, handing-over time on the appointed day. Suddenly a large car drew up alongside us. The passenger was King George VI in the uniform of a marshal of the RAF. Reminding us of the time, he asked brusquely why we were still in occupation. 'Because, Sire,' said Reavell, never at a loss, 'we want to be doubly sure that all is in the good order in which you would wish to find it.' Mollified, the King wished us well and moved on.

Our efforts were wasted. The Ministry of Works, into whose care the house was to be handed for refurbishment, had been told of the elaborate fire precautions RAF units always took, featuring airmen detailed in turn as fire picket on 24-hour patrol at short intervals all round the premises; and of the particular hazard of fissures in the timber window frames currently having the old paint burnt off them, creating a need for special vigilance. The ministry, studiedly rude, knew better: the house went up in flames 48 hours later. I remembered that RAF routine included the issue of an anti-fire poster whose standard warning message ended with:

In the event of the fire being too large for the finder to deal with he should at once ...

the remaining space being left for any local provisions that unit commanders might think appropriate. Almost invariably there appeared the scrawled waggery:

Look for a smaller one.

Housing near Ramridge, in the Hampshire countryside, was plentiful. We soon took up residence in yet another set of servants' quarters, again very spacious, on the top floor of a neo-Georgian mansion in the hamlet of Tangley. The original owner's widow, a Mrs Merceron, and her mentally handicapped daughter still lived in the grand parts. We got on well: among other favours we did them was looking after, in their absence, the noisy flock of guinea fowl – admirable guard birds. As David became a demanding toddler and Rachel, to our delight, became pregnant again, we took on a 16-year-old nanny. She looked after David only in the intervals between eating huge meals and lying in the bath for hours at a time, so off she went. We cooked on a large Valor oil stove, never reliable and subject to panic attacks. One struck as we cooked a leg of lamb for a supper party: the indulgent guests valiantly scraped the black grease off their helpings. We were also afflicted with mice until I hit upon an inspired solution: a cat.

I continued to enjoy the selection work and the secondary duty of looking after the catering, run by the amusing and mildly villainous Corporal Tetzel. We both assumed that the candidates, being on their best behaviour, were unlikely to complain of short commons. We saw to it, accordingly, that any shortages imposed by the rationing system, at the time even more severe than it had been during the war, were visited on the candidates and any plenitudes lavished on the staff. To my near despair, that did not stop our presidential boss George Beamish from complaining one morning that he couldn't remember when he had last had a boiled egg for breakfast. In fact he had suffered a one day gap, having eaten his own ration and those of the rest of us. A graver impasse threatened from the serving at lunch of Tetzel's special bacon and onion pudding, consisting mostly in suet stodge. The speciality resided in the serving of all the bacon to the staff and the lavishing of the residual stodge and onion on the candidates. Up spake not an aged pauper but a brass-necked candidate who dared to complain of the bacon deficiency. Fortunately I had not started my own helping, which I used to shut him up and conserve my career.

After just under a year at Ramridge I felt increasing boredom and the urge to get back to flying: a RAF unit without aircraft being every bit as lonesome and drear, as the ditty has it, as a pub with no beer. I had also been troubled by one of the criteria applied to our candidates and often the theme of discussions: 'identification with the Service'. The people we wanted, ran the argument, must have their hearts and souls in the RAF: it could never be enough to remain no more than a contracted employee, however bright and efficient. Reflecting on that point, I realised that my own stance was really no more than that of a contractor, in it for the flying. That, I now see, was the first zephyr of an emotional gale that eventually blew me into civil life. Relief from boredom was at hand: along came another 'specially picked' opportunity that would have warmed my mother's heart. With insight typical of him, Sir John Slesssor had seen the merit of bringing together the younger of the pilots chosen for permanent commissions, and putting them through a specially enhanced instructor's course at the Central Flying School (CFS). Several such courses were arranged and I was to be put on one of them. After some refresher flying I found myself before a board of senior CFS staff curious to discover what sort of clay was to be thrown on their collective potter's wheel (doubtless repairing thereafter to Potter's Bar). Interviewing me, the breezy chief instructor, Wing Commander de Boult, asked:

When did you last show your arse to the Lord?

No such display, I had to admit, had occurred since the brief aerobatic sessions with David Bamford which had so excited me at Sywell. That, de Boult assured me, would soon be put right.

It was. Under various guiding hands but mostly with the deft and sagacious Canadian instructor of instructors Peter Johnson I learnt the professional way of doing the quasi-instructional work I had taken to at Nutts Corner and later done in a supervisory way in 233 and 525 Squadrons. I made friends with the Harvard single-engined trainer. Built in America in thousands as the AT-6, and the mainstay of most pilot training, the Harvard had a Pratt & Whitney Twin Wasp engine, wonderfully reliable and with the single disadvantage of a deafeningly noisy propeller. Gradually mastering the technique of flying it properly from the rear of its in-line cockpits and endlessly practising aerobatics and mock lessons with the long-suffering Johnson, I finished the six-month course as a half-decent instructor. My pleasure was enhanced by the extra type-flying which the Slessor add-ons had provided. I got my hands on the Percival Prentice, an airborne greenhouse and successor to the Tiger Moth as the staple of initial training. I had a most welcome reunion with the Tiger Moth; this time I exploited its renowned manoeuvring and aerobatic qualities to the full. There was the acme of versatility, the Mosquito, admirable as an advanced trainer and no less so in light bombing, night fighting and transport. To my great joy there was the Spitfire, every bit as docile and nimble as I had been led to expect; and at the opposite end of the gamut of fame the Lancaster, mainstay of the post-Wellington generation of bombers and as rough and rudimentary as the Liberator had been smooth and elaborate. All in all my flying was transformed, finishing what Sywell, Cranwell and Harwell had started.

All of which was as nothing compared with the birth, just as the course ended, of our second son, Gregor. Rachel had gone to her family home in Glastonbury when we left Tangley and had the baby at the cottage hospital at Butleigh, on the adjoining Somerset Levels. The hospital had quoted 4 guineas a week for the fortnight's confinement, as the genteel described it: 18 guineas was what the newly formed National Health Service tried to charge. Four, after a tussle, was what it got. Far from being present at the birth, I was at the time doing a low-level solo cross-country flight over the wilds of Wales in a Harvard. The CFS controller had trouble in getting the news to me because the mountains got in the way.

Now a multi-role instructor of the B1 Grade (the lowest, B2, kept for tyros and also-rans), I was bursting for a chance to put my new skill to work. It soon came. I was to return to the RAF College Cranwell, joining the advanced flying squadron on the Harvard ('specially picked' yet again). One of the piquancies was that the cadets were the young men who had passed through the selection processes, affording me the interest of seeing how they turned out. Another was that George Beamish had also been posted to Cranwell as Air Officer Commanding the clutch of units based there and Commandant of the College.

Restored to pre-war status and with a syllabus aspiring to equate with that of a university, the college could hardly have differed more from its wartime guise. From an instructor–pupil standpoint, not all the changes were to the good. One snag was the time sunk into drill and marching to the resident band, far superior to the wartime fife and drum combination but not above rendering the 'Lincolnshire Poacher' with preliminary obbligato and the enhanced Colonel Bogey of my cadet days. There was much ancillary education grouped under the weird title 'Humanistics'. Demanding obeisance from all else was sport. Both of which diluted flying training. The result was a running dispute and a sort of class distinction between ourselves, the horny-handed flying instructor technicians down at the airfield; and the polished, cultured beings gracing the college, headed by the housemaster actalikes known as cadet wing officers, there to instil what would really count towards successful careers. One such, entirely atypical, was Harry Jenkins back from Burma, potency restored and nesting happily with Marion who had not yet become ill. His presence lubricated the relationships between the horny-handed and the elite. But the hegemony of the assistant commandant and the director of studies, the latter somewhere between a headmaster and a vice-chancellor, made training cadets to fly much harder than it was at ordinary flying training schools.

We humble toilers were expected to join the gilded college staff on such occasions as the formal dinners in the large, long-tabled dining hall. Those of us keen to get home would sit near the bottom end, and when there was a moment of diversion such as a speech, crawl under the table to the end, darting thence to the nearest door. But there was no escaping the drill sessions preparatory to the passing-out parades that culminated each course. As some compensation we could use the superb sports facilities; and, to great benefit, the cadet education staff who were a great help in preparing for the newly restored promotion and staff college entry exams.

Life in this setting was none too easy for those of us with young families and in housing well short of luxurious. We had moved into a roomy flat in a small Georgian manor house in Leasingham, 6 miles equidistantly from the college and Sleaford, the shopping town. The lady of the manor was a young widow called Daphne Holmes. She caused us some amusement because Harry Jenkins, awaiting the married quarter at the college to which his appointment entitled him, had stayed briefly in the manor as a paying guest. His experiences led him to opine that no man on his own was safe in the house overnight. Daphne certainly had visitors, most often a burly boyfriend, there at all hours. Calling in to pay the rent or pass the time of day was unnerving: one could never be sure that she would not emerge, somewhat crumpled, performing a sartorial procedure comparable to male adjusting of the dress.

We didn't stay there long. A benevolent Air Ministry, concerned at the plight of young married officers, abandoned the appalling pre-war distinction between the 'qualified' married officers and the 'unqualified', whose much lower allowances kept them in penury. The ministry even went so far as to introduce a disturbance allowance of £20, payable every time a domestic move took place after a qualifying period of six months. Like most of my cash-starved brothers in arms I joined in a sort of general post every six months and one day. This time the result was our grandest home so far – a bungalow in a quiet road in the village of Ruskington. It had a large garden, in which I first fell in love with vegetable growing. Opposite lived another instructor, Dennis Bedford, and his wife Stella. They also had two small boys and we formed a friendship that lasted for the rest of their lives. The soul of kindness, Dennis rescued me from dependence on the tyranny of country buses imposed by our having had to sell the Morris 8 to save up for school fees, and the demise of the motorbike which I had had to buy for weekend commuting between Glastonbury and CFS.

Smarting from the average assessment I had receiving on passing out of CFS, I put in for a recategorisation test during the forthcoming six-monthly visit from the CFS examining team. After a frantic brush-up of my aerobatics by John Gibbons, expert in that craft and a good friend, I was tested in the air by the naval member of the CFS team, a notoriously hard man. He, I blush to record, was favourably impressed, describing my flow of verbiage during a simulated flying lesson as 'Churchillian' and complimenting me on an error-free ground test. He awarded me the next upward category, that of A2, and the norm which competent instructors with experience could expect to achieve. In contrast, I got into trouble for inveighing against the needless disruption of his training caused to one of my cadets, John Danton, who had sustained a boxing injury that kept him on the ground. The trouble was worthwhile because it almost certainly contributed to the boxing ban imposed on cadets later on.

Another of my cadets, Michael Short, indulged in the initiative-building sport of philandering with the assistant commandant's wife. The tolerant view taken was justified, perhaps, by the canon:

To bed the wife of an officer of junior rank is grossly to
betray the trust of those placed in your charge;

To bed the wife of an officer of equal rank is a dastardly
breach of an obligation towards a comrade in arms;

To bed the wife of an officer of senior rank is to take a
necessary but sometimes nauseating step forward in a
successful military career.

It did Mike no good. He killed himself, but mercifully nobody else, in a drink-drive accident in Singapore three years later.

In a lesser venture, two more cadets in my flight had a game of the golf which was such an interference with flying training. Rain stopped play. They were invited by another victim of the weather, the manager of a local colliery, to be shown round and be dropped back at the college. Arriving on the front steps of the college, golf bags in hand, they were met by George Beamish. Sedulous as always to show interest, he asked them somewhat fatuously whether they had been playing golf. 'No, Sir,' came the reply, 'we've been down a coal mine.' Calm was eventually restored. One of Beamish's many endearing traits beside his short-lived bouts of irascibility was humanity, shown at the march-pasts which followed the weekly church parades by his inviting the small children from the Service families who went to church to line up on the dais behind him as he took the salute.

By now a flight commander, I had fewer cadets and more time. Some of it I devoted to teaching gliding in a Slingsby T21 trainer, and thus preparing cadets who had volunteered for it to take part in the annual gliding camp at a mountain site at Scharfollendorf in Germany. Other customers were officers' wives, usually on Sunday afternoons when there was no flying training. Another diversion was parading with the glossy college staff in rehearsing and taking part in the passing-out parades. On one of these, dolled up in my best blue and polished to the nines, I stood last in a line of supernumerary officers (i.e. surplus to the flight and squadron commanders but adding an extra row to the ranks of cadets). We were all waiting for the order to march past that would end the dreadful half-hour or so of standing still while the visiting bigwig did his or her inspection with little chats to randomly chosen lads. I was close to the venerated Queen's Colour, a blue silk embroidered flag on an ornate pole, attended by a colour party and held aloft by the tallest cadet on the course. He was in our flight and his name (yes really) was Mullarkey. I noticed with alarm that his normal healthily pink complexion had turned pale grey and the Colour was gently swaying. Breaching the requirement to stand stock still, I motioned to the magisterial college warrant officer who had, as it were, a roving non-commission on the parade. This lantern-jawed martinet with a heart of gold, George Millis, acting as if he were executing some part of the parade liturgy, marched stiffly across to Mullarkey, and stood behind him with his hands in his armpits. He delivered, *sotto voce*, a homily on the consequential effects on his career of any variation from the vertical. The oscillation lessened; and just before the order to march, the Mullarkey face changed colour for the better. I prided myself with the reflection that they also serve who only stand and wait; especially if they keep their eyes open and their wits about them.

After 17 months at Cranwell my substantive (that is, permanent) promotion to squadron leader came through, ending a two-year dip from my wartime rank. Doubtless because of a good recategorisation result, I was posted to command a flight in the Examining Wing of the Central Flying School; (once more, my mother would have been right to call it a speciality of picking). I flew the Harvard with the team of examiners of whom I was now in charge, having my conceit dashed by discovering how much better a pilot I would have to become and how much there was to learn, profiting greatly from their help. I tried to raise my standard of instrument flying to a point which would qualify me as an instrument rating as well as an instructional technique examiner. After one failure I succeeded and at once began the weekly grind of visits to flying training schools throughout the RAF and the Fleet Air Arm, plus advanced training units using single-engined aircraft: a formidable parish. The other squadron, commanded by another former Cranwell instructor and family friend, Dick Wakeford, covered multi-engined training. In due course we became largely interchangeable. We had as our unit commander by far the best senior officer I ever encountered, Wing Commander John Barraclough. He was later to become very senior and of universally recognised excellence. He was full of wit and humour but sensitive in his dealings with all sorts and conditions of people, often over the drink for which he had a prodigious capacity.

He was contemptuous of unworthy higher authority, almost visibly struggling to conceal what he thought of the CFS commandant at the time, small in mind and stature and compared unfavourably with Charlie McCarthy's ventriloquist's dummy. Preparing for the annual ceremony of the parade and inspection by the Air Office Commanding, John realised that his shoes were far from up to snuff. He borrowed an almost new pair from the only examiner who shared his size, Flight Lieutenant Bert Slade, lending Bert his own shoes in exchange. As the inspecting party comprising the AOC, the Dummy and John approached our serried ranks, John stopped in front of Bert and delighted the rest of us with a solemn warning to him never to appear on parade so badly shod again. As an excellent pilot and a natural leader, Barraclough epitomised the component of the RAF officer corps that did most to win the war: not the polished Cranwell product, good as it was, but the unemployed bank clerks of the 1930s, as they had been unkindly typified, who got short service commissions. Barraclough had started life as a Stock Exchange junior.

At the end of our teams' weekly visits of inspection we reviewed our findings with the Chief Instructor of the unit and usually the station commander. John would often fly up in our runabout Avro Anson to attend the review. After one such visit, to Cranwell, as we were flying home he remarked of the aristocratically named station commander, Group Captain Heber Percy, 'Did you know that Heber Percy's just got married again? This time it's a scrumptious bit of South American crumpet, his third or fourth. I think he just wears them out.' At that moment we both realised that the internal intercom system on which we had been chatting was also in external mode, broadcasting all he had said over a big slice of middle England. From other aircraft came such catcalls as 'Oh my!' and 'Get him!' with other less printable ribaldry.

The weekly visits were interspersed with training sessions at Little Rissington, which made for some sort of home life. But my absences were taxing for Rachel and the boys, especially while we were housed in a small, draughty rented cottage in the hamlet of Maugersbury, down the hill from Stow-on-the-Wold. But it was blessed with a small, safe garden; and there was a good first school for David in Stow. Everything improved when we were allotted a RAF house on the airfield. On the patch, as it was called, there was plenty of company and help of all kinds.

The new neighbours were a boon to Rachel during our periods of absence overseas on visits to a miscellany of RAF and foreign units. For the first one I did, under John Barraclough, we borrowed a Dakota with a cream-walled interior, a carpeted floor and blue leather armchairs. We were allowed to borrow this tarted-up-for-VIPs model thanks to inspired wangling by John and his friends in high places. Most of the route I had crossed and recrossed over the years, especially in 525 Squadron. But this time we took in Ceylon (later Sri Lanka) where there was still a RAF base at Negombo (later Katunayake), reputedly the most beautiful airfield in the world with its sand-coloured surface, palms and lush greenery; (Guam, I later decided, just beat it). There we flew the elderly resident Harvards, testing the pilots of the small RAF detachment, egregious in starched bush jackets in a special off-khaki shade, and their Sinhalese charges. In crumpled shirts and shorts out on licence from mothballed drawers at home, we looked like tropical scarecrows. On the way eastwards we refuelled at the holiday brochure resort of Car Nicobar, later visiting the major RAF bases at Changi and Tengah on Singapore Island and the still primitive, hutted base at Butterworth on the Malayan mainland opposite Penang Island.

There I was landed in two senses. I was asked to test a sergeant pilot thought to be unsafe, having somehow passed through the training system without being rumbled. We took off in a Mosquito trainer happily enough

143

and I spent an hour or so on hot and exhausting dual re-instruction. The session went well and I had thoughts of a successful salvage job. To build his confidence we did a single-engined approach with one engine feathered; an excellent source of self-reassurance, not unduly dangerous if a safe approach speed was maintained but offering almost no possibility of going round again. In the late stages of the approach the sergeant panicked, freezing on the controls as we sank towards Nemesis. My own panic gave me strength as, overriding him, I gave the good engine as much get-out-of-trouble thrust as I dared and we just made it over the airfield boundary. Home he went.

Our Far East extremity, reached via a refuelling stop at Saigon, was Kai Tak, the RAF base in Hong Kong. All the pilots' instrument ratings, in effect licences to fly in bad weather, had run out and we slaved to requalify them; glad to depart for overnight stops in Thailand, Burma and the Indian Air Force base at Calcutta, still with its Raj name of Dum Dum. There were glimpses en route of the glamour of the Orient, sort of. One was the famous Nai Lang night club in Bangkok with a chorus line whose legs, unencumbered with underwear, had skirts that would have struck their occidental sisters as wanting. John resolved to return some time to look at their faces. A more sedate feature was the beautiful Schwe Dagon Pagoda, its graceful gold-leafed tower gleaming in the sun as we made for Mingaladon, a landmark in the war in Burma. Rivalling the Pagoda as we refuelled at Palam, the airport for Delhi, was the exquisite white marble Taj Mahal (the latter word being the source of the horrid word 'mall', as in shopping). The last major stop was at the Royal Pakistan Air Force base at Risalpur, near Quetta; a town well known to old stagers as the home of the alternative, allegedly soft-option British Army staff college. Most of Risalpur's CFS-trained instructors were well up to standard, recategorising successfully in their ancient Harvards and Tiger Moths. So also were the cadets, excellently trained, free from most of the trammels of their Cranwell opposite numbers. I was surprised at the strength of patriotic feeling manifest in the demand, absurd in an English-speaking country, for a translation of the famous CFS pilot training manual into Urdu.

Off duty, to a degree, we had to endure a formal guest night that out-Cranwelled Cranwell with its stiff routine, terrible mess games, overcopious whisky and the absence of any chance of escaping under the table. The best part of the other hospitality consisted in a fascinating day tour of the North West Frontier with Afghanistan. The road ran through mountains adorned with huge stone replicas of crests of the British Army regiments which had defended the frontier for so long. So fixed, in those

144

days, were the defences that the emplacements of the machine gun companies are listed in the classic *Imperial Military Geography* by Major, later Brigadier Cole, studied by generations of would-be staff college students, myself included. At one stop there were tribesmen armed with the home-made rifles that Kipling wrote about; though whether they were akin to the moth-eaten Highlanders stationed at car parks in the Scottish Highlands for tourists to photograph was not free from doubt. Westering home along the familiar route I, as the only Dakota-qualified pilot other than John, was glad to share with him the completion of an onerous trip that had tired us all out.

Now began the first of three bits of my flying career that compete for the title 'The Time of my Life' (the others being the Dakota and the Vulcan periods). Especially enjoyable were the next two of our six-monthly visits to the Rhodesian Air Training group, kept in being there because of the cost savings that the flawless weather made possible. For the first I had the company of John Barraclough's successor, Wing Commander Russell Bell, a humourless Royal Australian Air Force officer who later transferred to the RAF. Understandably he found John a hard act to follow. Unqualified as an instructor, he had been on the staff of the RAF Flying College, a recently established advanced training unit for senior officers. He neither understood nor liked basic flying training. Being insecure and suspicious, he was also irascible. My flight commander colleague and long-term friend Norman Smith had a widower father who had had the classic misfortune of being grabbed by a predatory widow. Norman asked me to take his place on one of his week-long visits so that he could help with and go to the wedding. When we asked Bell to approve the change, he petulantly asked why. Norman's 'So that I can be best man at my father's wedding' did not commend itself as a reply; we both had trouble in figuratively hosing him down.

Qualified on the Dakota (this time a standard model), Bell flew some of the legs of the journey. But such help did not make up for his conduct at the destinations and his embarrassing ignorance during the week-long visits to the training schools at Heany, near Bulawayo, and Thornhill near Gwelo in the copper belt. The routine was as at units in Britain except that work started at 6.30 a.m. and finished in time for a late lunch, leaving ample spare time. At the weekend between the two visits it had become customary to fill the Dakota with instructors and their wives and fly to Livingstone, the airfield for the Victoria Falls and their famous hotel. On one occasion I had been stuck at the airfield combing Africa for a spare Dakota tyre, one of mine having been punctured and mending being out of the question. BOAC, as it then was, offered an exchange but wanted £80 for delivery of the spare from Nairobi. Being at Livingstone for a jolly was condoned but lacking in formal authority, and I was at a loss for a story that would prevent an enquiry. Providence intervened when the Southern Rhodesian Air Force came to the rescue by flying in a tyre and jacks from Salisbury. Pouring with sweat, the crew and I made the change and saved these much appreciated *sub rosa* jollies.

The next trip, Bell-free, was in a Valetta (RAF version of the Viking airliner). We followed the standard route but stopped, nostalgically for me, at Fayid, now a major base. We then, as it were, turned right towards Khartoum and all stations south. On the night trip to Juba, out in the wilds of central Africa, I was concerned at the lack of a signal from the radio beacon there, which acted as an auditory lighthouse in featureless

The lion that surprised the beacon operator at Juba. *Author*

146

territory. I feared that there had been a gross navigational error. I was wrong. The navigation, done by Brian Slater, a multi-skilled pilot and examiner, was perfect, Juba turning up just as dawn broke. It emerged on landing that the beacon, housed at the foot of the control tower, had had to be abandoned in the middle of the night when a lion put its head through the window. The subsequent visits went swimmingly in both senses, with little changed except for Heany's two relief landing grounds. They tested the student pilots' perceptions as well as their navigation, being named respectively Miass and Mielbow. A tiny contretemps afflicted me at the end of another of the intermissionary visits to the Falls Hotel when, having left, I had to dash back to my room to collect a forgotten briefcase. There on the bed, minutes after I had vacated, was a huge, deep pink corset. Out of the bathroom stormed its owner, a vast South African matron of the same shade. Her thick Boer accent added venom to her imprecation as I fled. On my last trip I made up for the gaffe at a stop on the way to South Africa when the distraught pilot of a private aircraft, owned by a South African diamond magnate, told me that he had left the aircraft documents, without which civil aircraft could not move, at Bulawayo. His boss, he pleaded, would sack him if his lapse caused a delay. We flew back there and retrieved them. On the resumed southward journey we flew over the majestic but brutal Kruger memorial, doing a visit to the flying training unit at Dunottar, where the South African Air Force pilots' flying was as awful as their hospitality was lavish.

For the journey home, against my judgement because of the possibility of terminal problems of unserviceability caused by lack of spares, we had a change of route insisted on by Russell Bell. It took us through South West Africa by way of Kasama and Kumalo to the evocatively named cities of what was still the Belgian Congo – Stanleyville and Leopoldville, each with old colonial architecture comparable with that of Bombay. We continued through what had been the White Man's grave, staying overnight in Lagos, drearily familiar. After pit stops at Freetown and Dakar we fetched up at another colonial outpost, this time in Spanish equatorial Africa: Villa Cisneros on the western coastal extremity, with wonderfully cheap rooms and good food at the state-owned Parador. My fears of mechanical trouble did not materialise and we returned by way of Gibraltar, now possessed of a luxurious runway, and Bordeaux.

Rachel and the boys were enjoying plentiful company and amusements at Little Rissington. Mother hen to all was Mrs Kean, wife of the chief instructor of instructors, whom we examiners unkindly referred to as the peasants. Such was Mrs K's zeal for good works by her chickens that career advancement for their husbands lay in the making of soft toys as Christmas presents for the airmens' families. They made so many that each child could have had a dozen for the asking. It was as well that Tom Kean was replaced by Bill Coles, former CO of 233 Squadron and an old friend and his pleasant but mistressful wife, also a former police person.

My taste for the wide world had a final fling when I took an enlarged team to Hong Kong, out by the ordinary route but back by way of Saigon in pre-war Vietnam to Pakistan and thence to Mafraq in Jordan and Rayak in the Lebanon. Hong Kong was about to have its fighter defence augmented with Vampires and I was asked to assess Sek Kong, a small relief airfield near the Chinese frontier, for its suitability for jet fighters. The best available vehicle was an old Beaufighter, whose twin engines were piston operated but powerful enough to give the Beau a performance and handling characteristics not unduly different from those of the Vampire. I took off from Kai Tak, flew round the coast to Sek Kong and did a number of successful tight circuits and approaches within the mountain-sided valley in which it lay.

Satisfied that the Vampires would have no trouble, I did one more approach and touchdown. As I climbed away an engine failed. Doing an asymmetric (single-engined) circuit within the narrow compass of the valley would have been unwise. Little better was the alternative of going straight ahead towards a gap in the mountains, the touch-and-go problem of that resort being whether its very slow rate of single-engined climb would suffice for the Beau to surmount it. I chose the latter, gaining just enough height to scrape over the gap. The relief of making it to the other side was only momentary because I was now over Communist China and liable to be jumped by fighters. I was soon back out to sea, turning towards Kai Tak and landing safely. Having kept air traffic control well informed of what was happening and why, I was relieved but not surprised that the AOC was complimentary. The Chinese accepted the Governor's apology.

On the way home we landed to refuel at Saigon and Lahore. The latter involved a long wait, for the idiotic reason that we had to clear the Pakistani customs in spite of never leaving the tarmac, let alone the airfield. Spluttering with the rage when I enlisted his help, the RPAF station commander tried unsuccessfully to reason with the officials. Their stone faces reflected those of bureaucrats worldwide as we solemnly took all our bags and baggage out, carried it through the customs hall and then reloaded it. There was no such trouble at Mafraq, in Jordan; or at Rayak in the Lebanon, where we did some tests. There I was handed another problem pilot, a young cadet under threat of suspension who spoke only

Arabic. He and I, in a Tiger Moth, managed well enough with signs and motions, and I was glad to have no alternative but to follow the precept of letting him get on with imitating what I did. For more than an hour he flew excellently, perhaps because of the absence of badgering. The Air Attaché, Group Captain Nick Carter, whom I was to meet again as a senior colleague at the Joint Services Staff College was assured that my advice would be followed and his cadetship reinstated.

Home at last, I had time to practise for a long-delayed attempt to raise my instructor's category from A2 to A1. The test could only be conducted by one of my own team of examiners, picked by lot and having it impressed on him that I was to be treated in the same way as all other candidates. He verged on the side of overzeal, but I passed. Every candidate had to produce a personal speciality: I presented, and had accepted, night aerobatics in a Harvard, a sequence of which I had put together on nights when the peasants were night flying and I could be allotted a safe bit of sky, well clear of the airfield. Added to the most welcome A1 accolade was a surprise plus from one of the other baronial Commanders-in-Chief. Air Chief Marshal Sir James Robb, C-in-C of RAF units in Germany, which were almost an air force in themselves, had amongst his acquisitions an unarmed photo reconnaissance Spitfire, painted in the sky-blue used for camouflage and marked with his initials JMR, which he used as a personal transport. As a former commandant, he was fond of CFS, and on relinquishing his command in Germany gave it to us. By great good luck there were only two Spitfire pilots in flying practice on the station: one was the Commandant, Group Captain Jarman, a pleasant New Zealander soon to be in trouble for building a boat in a hangar using RAF materials; and myself. Jarman was busy and uninterested, leaving me to look after and fly JMR, ensuring thereby that it remained serviceable. During its weekly outings I exploited its wonderful aerobatic handling qualities which included, along with the Tiger Moth, easy eight-point hesitation rolls and good inverted flying. I had done the same from time to time in the Spitfire's naval equivalent the Seafire, which had the minor impediment of an anal hook to enable it to be caught and brought to a halt on carrier decks.

The Navy provided other strings to my flying bow. Testing naval units meant getting into practice on their aircraft. One was the Firefly, a lumbering fighter-bomber with a wide, strengthened undercarriage to increase the success rate for carrier landings. Knowing its little ways was essential for visits to the simulated carrier deck at Henstridge in Somerset, to check the standard of instruction in carrier landings: a very dull procedure involving endless approaches and not so much landings as almighty groundward thumps. More refreshing was the Sea Fury, the naval version of the Tempest, the last and fastest piston-engined fighter. Originally intended to destroy V1 flying bombs, it outperformed the Vampire jet fighter. I used it at the naval air station at Lossiemouth, where there had been a dribble of fatal landing accidents affecting cadets who, having undershot the runway, applied too much power too quickly to try and get out of trouble. The sudden surge caused the huge propeller to rotate the aircraft instead of the other way round. The need, for two successive years, was for demonstrations at the runway, before an assembly of cadets, of how to 'round out' (that is, put the aircraft in a landing posture) using safe speed and application of power.

That demonstration needed particularly thorough practice. To get it I went shortly beforehand to Lee-on-Solent to borrow a Sea Fury. Arriving in an Anson to collect it I was agreeably surprised that the naval flight commander had kindly started the engine for me and all was ready for me to taxi away. On the next morning, back at Little Rissington, the engine (a Rolls-Royce Gryphon, essentially a souped-up Merlin) would not start. After a day of prolonged and unsuccessful effort I found a flight sergeant engine fitter who had serviced the RAF version of the Sea Fury, the Tempest. Clinging to the wing as I pressed the starter cartridge button, he hit the starter box hard with a soft-headed hammer. Away went the engine. On returning the aircraft to Lee, I answered my dark blue colleague's disingenuously solicitous enquiry with, 'Oh yes, we did have a spot of trouble, but nothing the RAF couldn't handle.' Far different from that cheerful banter was an encounter after I had done the demonstration at the end of Lossie's runway during a week of testing pilots and recategorising naval instructors. I was shocked by the literal sea fury of the Commander (Air), a choleric figure upset because the RAF was doing the testing and not the senior service itself. My abiding memory of the glorious Sea Fury, however, is the utter exhilaration of a fast run, on a glorious day, along a long stretch of the south coast on the way back to Lee. A big piston engine going flat out has a special quality unrepeatable by the suave, silky jet.

The Wing was lucky to be thrust into becoming familiar with both piston and jet trainers. Less privileged training units were uncertain of how to deal with the transition, and especially the 'habit-patterns' as they were called, formed in flying pistons that could cause difficulty and even accidents in flying jets (a topic I wrote about later in an article for a RAF magazine). CFS did all it could to dispel the illusion, teach flexibility and emphasise the danger of creating a self-fulfilling prophesy. The problem was aggravated by the Gloster Meteor twin-engined jet trainer, a thoroughly unsatisfactory aircraft and, indeed, the only aircraft I disliked. Its worst fault was its very short endurance of only 45 minutes, reducing productive training time to about half an hour. It was unpressurised, causing at height a shortage of wind at one end and an indecorous excess of it at the other. It was poorly heated and uncomfortable. Cadets and some instructors were frightened of it. Its redeeming feature was a superb, easy-to-use, aerobatic performance. One dashing CFS peasant, Flight Lieutenant Graham Hulse, used that quality on a good day for vapour trails to draw a huge phallic image in the Cotswold sky. No doubt he had the balls, temperamental and artistic, to complete the picture. But the chance never came. Before he could do so he was ordered to land and sent away on a punitive posting on the same day.

The far superior Vampire trainer, a two-seated version of the fighter, was all that the Meteor wasn't: side-by-side seating, a delight to fly and throw about and pressurised to make pilots immune to fart attacks. It was so exhilarating that I overdid the antics on a practice solo trip, falling out of the sky with such a sudden height loss that, having a cold, I punctured an eardrum. I terrified Rachel with a big patch of blood on my pillow in the middle of the following night and was grounded for four miserable weeks. The Vampire's only drawback was its awful heating system: the pilot could either select 'hot', in which case the cockpit filled with steam; or 'cold', which provided Christmassy festoons of tiny ice cubes. We cursed the makers, Sir George Godfrey & Partners, who had had the gall to put their nameplate on the cockpit control.

As the age of the piston-engined aircraft waned, I was glad not to have missed it. The Avro Anson, formerly a bomber, a twin-engined trainer pre-dating the Oxford and now a light transport, was so easy to fly that one questioned its moral character: ('Fill me up and I'm anybody's'). The de Havilland Devon, a glorified Anson and the military version of the civil Dove, similarly docile, felt like a sheet of paper to fly. The Balliol and the Provost, respectively attempts to replace the timeless Harvard and the Prentice, were humdrum. The real success was the Jet Provost, used for so long as the staple RAF trainer that it became a classic.

All in all I had a wonderful 18 month tour at CFS, flying over a sizeable slice of the world in a variety of aircraft of which I could hardly have dreamt, competent to test on all of them and able, almost at will, to enjoy them on my own account. Unworthily I lusted after an Air Force Cross, which I knew had often been awarded for much less. That award, however, was rationed; and for what I can only surmise was a matter of inter-service politics, the one available went to a naval lieutenant: a stalwart of the peasants but remarkable only in that he wore dark and not light blue.

All I got was this lousy Queen's Commendation for Valuable Service in the Air. Ho hum, now for a penitential year as a staff college student. Specially picked, of course.

Chapter 8

Careering Out of Control

Golf and bridge I had forsworn. Bedding senior officers' wives did not appeal. There remained the conventional method of moving onwards and upwards in the RAF, which was to go to the Staff College and do well. Thanks to the good facilities at Cranwell for preparation, I had sailed through the qualifying exam and my turn came in 1952.

A stately home in Bracknell, its grounds enormously and hideously built on, housed the main college. The ostensible object was to train officers for higher command and staff appointments; but it also acted as a sifter of wheat from chaff. An even more important function at the time was to indoctrinate the students into the case for the continued existence of the RAF, then as later periodically questioned. The propaganda began during kindergarten exercises in thinking and speaking. One was a précis of an article in a 1949 *Sunday Times* by Sir John Slessor headed, 'Britain needs a Bomber Force'. It was so well written as to be easy to shorten and nobody, I feel sure, thought any more about it. That did not prevent the staff from distributing, eight months later, a minute assuring us that Slessor was still of that opinion and attaching a copy of an official pamphlet, also by him:

> an air force of today without its long range bomber force would be like a navy of pre-1914 days without its Line of Battle ... The British four-jet bombers now flying are the best in their class in the world. Are we to be content to provide as our Pax Atlantica the ground-support and maritime aircraft to defend ourselves? ... If we did, we should sink to the level of a third-class power ... In war, we should have little or no influence ... In peace, we should lose what influence we have on American policy ...

Nationalist spin, very different from his well-reasoned article arguing that the bomber has a place in the balanced air force essential to national defence. The whole pamphlet, a world away from the article, was as pure a piece of propaganda as the leaflets I dropped on many raids, oxymoronically combining nationalist bombast and sycophancy of America. It reinforced the unease I felt about other bits of the course. Meanwhile it was amusing to draw on my Selection Board experience to reciprocate the obvious assessment process applied to the students by the grandly named Directing Staff (DS). It worked well during an exercise requiring us to say whom and what we would most like to be and do. The predictable choices – authors, film stars and other well-known figures – came up, scoring poorly. I got an easily-spotted bullseye with Pygmalion and Galatea.

Boredom waned when we moved on to the formal appreciations, which were the military modality for channelling and disciplining thought. In an elementary setting we learnt to select an aim; state how we reached it; list a multiplicity of factors such as time and space, own and enemy forces and weather; weigh the significance of each in relation to the others and the whole; forecast what would happen; and conclude with what to do and a plan for doing it. The easy one was about settling the hash of a minor oriental potentate called the Fakir of Ipi, the last of the unruly tribes dealt with entirely by the RAF, in 1938: grist, perhaps, to the indoctrination mill. The difficult task, Exercise See Adler (Sea Lion), involved planning the German invasion of Britain in 1940. Most students found both of them instructive and amusing, but a few became overwrought. Applying pressure was part of the sifting process and there were rumours of past breakdowns and even suicides; the latter at the bigger and tougher Army Staff College at Camberley where, incidentally, my half-brother William was on the DS at the time. I saw nothing of that except the anxiety of a friend, a very bright engineer, who spent nights walking about and worrying.

The DS, often being cruel to be kind, were a mixed bunch. At the top was the intelligent and perceptive Air Vice-Marshal Peter Gilmore for whom, when he became deputy head of the Far East Air Force, I gained great respect. Below him was a stolid air commodore and four group captains. One was an over-promoted golfer, all pipe smoke and odoriferous tweeds. At the opposite extreme was Bernard Chacksfield, one of a very select few who, having started as boy entrants, ascended effortlessly through the ranks. Tall, diffident and approachable, he was the best of the whole faculty, eventually becoming an air vice-marshal. Of the wing commander workers, mostly bright, the most interesting was Christopher Foxley-Norris, a prominent Battle of Britain pilot reputed to be legally qualified. Over the years I was to get to know him much better and to like him much less. There was much socialising, part of the assessment process and reminding me of Fred Astaire's:

Looking my best,
perfectly dressed,
calm and assured
to pass the test.

Which socially I never was: habitually untidy, deficient in small-talk, good at getting stranded at cocktail parties. School fees being what they were becoming, I tried to make clothes last and was never quite as well turned out as I should have been; commuting on the Royal Enfield 150cc motor bike doing me no sartorial favours. Rachel made up for me, but we shared a dislike for entertainment that was so obviously used as a vehicle for the gain or loss of social Blueie points (airmens' variation of the Brownie points awarded to deserving junior girl scouts).

We were lucky to get relief from non-college contacts. We had found a spacious flat in a big house in Camberley, with wooded grounds sloping down to the main road to London and opposite the landmark Blue Pool – large, clean and much enjoyed by the boys. One of the other two flats housed the owners, a quiet, mouldering couple whose hobby was drinking. In the third flat, above us, booze was a way of life and potential death. The tenant, a Doctor Rigby, burly and bloated, took his resident girlfriend out every night in their tattered Rolls, both returning drunk and spending the small hours in noisy brawls. For one sad period the early teenage son of one of them came to stay, knocking us up in the middle of a particularly noisy night and asking for a bed, which of course we provided. I ought to have done something about Rigby's drink-driving. I did not; I can only plead overwork and the subject's lack of salience at the time.

We were lucky to be close to my half-brother William, his wife Barbara and their family of four. He could certainly have slipped me copies of the 'pinks', which were the staff solutions to set problems, so named because they were printed on paper of that colour. Neither of us would have done that; but he did pass on what he could find out about how I was doing. The answer, I blush to say, was very well.

Another pressuriser that manifested itself as the weeks passed was having several tasks on the go simultaneously: long-drawn-out exercises, essays and practice speeches being piled on top of each other. That was a feature of lasting value; as was the deliberate racking of nerves in drafting and making speeches. When my turn came to address the whole community for five minutes I had already sat through enough such orations to observe that light and funny topics did much better than solemn ones. Having in mind a lampoon of the staff for which the college magazine editor had asked, I presented it in embryo, ending with a suggestion about how to deal with our mentors in a mock Latin tag, less familiar then than it later became:

Nil illegitimi carborundum,

purporting to mean:

Don't let the bastards grind you down.

To my amazed delight it got the biggest laugh of the course so far, and of my still very slight public speaking career. I owed a good deal to the scene-shifter, stage manager and general factotum for the college hall, an old stager in two senses, aptly called Irish. Moments before I began, he had eased my tremors by whispering 'Remember, Sir, every good artist must have temperament.'

There was soon more pro-bomber indoctrination. We had to do a close study of an analysis of the results of RAF bombing of Germany, set out in individually loaned copies of a book as big as *The Times Atlas* and not much thinner, classified as Confidential. Having signed the Official Secrets Act, I forbear to give away what it contained. But it brought home to me how very little all the early effort and sacrifice that characterised the Wellington operations in the Middle East had achieved. It made light of the fact that it was only in and after 1942, when Pathfinder (guide aircraft dropping coloured flares for the main force to aim at) operations began in earnest, that the bomber offensive against Germany had begun to bite. I cannot remember reading anything about the real effect on civilian morale in Germany, which was to bolster rather than to damage it, as in Britain. Nor did the study make clear that it was the USAF daylight raids, (of which 178 Squadron, myself included, had played an arduous part in trying out), and their destruction of oil resources that had triggered the German surrender. Nothing in the tome, I felt sure, was factually wrong. The flaw was simply that the work was more one of advocacy than of analysis.

Not the least benefit of the course was mixing with the students – RAF, soldier, sailor and American – in a comradeship of benevolent adversity. We were kept together by the senior student, Wing Commander the Honourable Hugh Dowding, bearing that epithet because his father was Lord Dowding, Marshal of the RAF and Commander-in-Chief of Fighter Command when it won the Battle of Britain. The drink of which he later died was evident. He was also truculent with the staff, perhaps because of having been made to feel small by his father (a feature of some of the sons of very senior officers at Cranwell, an incubus which their flying instructors had to try and ease). It was Dowding, on the editorial committee, who had asked me for a lampoon. I offered a half-page of rhyming couplets headed with my laugh-getting tag. Too long and in-jokey to quote in full, it included:

Can they [the staff] simply subside into posts designed for ordinary
mortals?
Or should they be raised at once to the heights reserved for [former
chiefs of air staff] Trenchards, Tedders and Portals?
Surely they should rise to the top, and there settle every major issue
with sublime economy of *nisu* [effort; lifted from the College motto;
also a quotation from one of the canonical Principles of War]

... Should there not be a special new directorate designed specifically
to sort out and expectorate the top chaff,
and replace it with members of the Directing Staff?
... Can it be
that high-ups sometimes think the same as we
and wonder
whether there wouldn't be an occasional high powered blunder
if these, our mentors, were to see the day come
when they were bereft of their roseate *vade mecum?*
[= pinks, see above]

I was pleased to have that offering accepted, because with it in the same issue went a ponderous article of mine about pilot problems in the jet age. That ended:

There is a danger inherent in the nature of an armed Service that new technical developments may outstrip the progress in training and organisation which must accompany them ... The race to deploy supersonic aircraft ... is too fast and too closely contested to allow these habits to play their traditional part in the jet age ... We can avoid trammelling the men we have with a training system out of tune with the times ... Only by doing so can we avoid the penalty of failing to produce the men to match the hour.

Which we did. RAF flying training was adapted and refined. It became, and remains, an exemplar to the rest of the world.

157

Getting two items printed was highly unusual. There would, the tweedy group captain chairman explained, have been a third if it hadn't been for the other two. The subject was nationalism in British Africa, set by the college and accompanied by a long list of references of which I found and read every one. It has not survived. Just as well.

There were occasional escapes from the study grind. One outlet was educative visits. Mine included the Bristol Aeroplane Company at Filton airfield where the mighty Brabazon prototype airliner was taking shape. It was as fascinating from a technical standpoint as was its naming after Lord Brabazon of Tara, a giant pioneering pilot whose licence number, issued at the turn of the twentieth century, was One. The Brab, as it was called, was the forbear of the Britannia, for years a mainstay of British civil and military transport.

A contrasting visit was to a submarine base, where my underwater trip convinced me that I had chosen the better of the fluid media. There was also a tour of *The Times*, taking in the panelled majesty of the leader writers' room. No wonder it's such a pompous right-wing rag. I could not

The glider that landed in a cornfield. *Author*

have imagined that I would later have upwards of 50 letters printed opposite its august opinion columns; almost always of disagreement.

The best escapes were my more or less weekly outings to White Waltham airfield, near Reading, where there were Anson, Proctor, Chipmunk, Prentice and Spitfire aircraft, as well as a T21 glider trainer in which staff and students could keep in practice. I had requalified as a Command Instrument Rating Examiner (CIRE) – a new and even grander feather in my flying helmet – just before leaving CFS and so could renew the ratings of the keen and competent. I was also awarded Blueie points for brushing up the aerobatics of one of the wing commander staffers. I and another CIRE, a fellow student squadron Leader Leonard Cherry, head of the CFS subordinate testing outfit in Home Command, were able, incestuously but legitimately, to renew each other at the end of the course. That was to come in useful in the Far East. I marvel at the conscientious way in which we tested each other. Tragically, he killed himself accidently a year or two later doing a demonstration landing for the pilots of his squadron in Germany, similar to the ones I had done at Lossiemouth. A sour contrast to the other flying was a trip in the glider with a US Navy lieutenant commander student who, he assured me, had ample gliding experience and needed only to be familiarised with the T21. He was so self-assured that I failed to intervene in his poorly judged approach and he landed us short of the airfield in a field of growing corn. With a squad of helpers we humped the undamaged craft 200 yards back to the airfield. As constant unkind reminders ensured, I was not allowed to forget an incident in an otherwise unblemished gliding career.

At the end of the course I was posted to the Far East Air Force (FEAF). A friend and co-student, Derek Thirlwell, was also going, getting the influential job of personal staff officer to the Commander-in-Chief. He was to go by troopship with his wife Jill and their new baby, especially cherished because he had long been tried for; and of whom I had observed, to the proud parents' pleasure, that somebody else would have to be prime minister while he was swimming the Channel. I, as I smugly boasted to anyone who would listen (not many), was needed so urgently for a vital new post in Intelligence that I was having to go at once by air. I left Rachel and the boys in Glastonbury, where fortunately there was an adequate small school near her parents' house. They were to follow by troopship when their turn came. I spent a day in London being briefed by assorted military and civil intelligence bodies listed on a slip of paper marked 'Secret', which to my horror I lost. Nobody handed it in and thus I escaped some condign penalty. From the briefings it emerged that, with shades of the special pickery that had gone before, I was to be the RAF staff officer at FEAF, based at Changi, responsible for the RAF intelligence contribution to the Five Power Staff Agency, the embryo of a Far Eastern version of NATO named SEATO and comprising Britain, the USA, Thailand, Australia and France (the last still with a presence in Indo-China).

I flew as a passenger in a Hastings, the standard RAF transport, on a new, speeded-up schedule with slipping crews. The journey took 32 all-but-continuous, hours' flying. Arriving at Changi, the main base of the three RAF airfields on Singapore Island, late at night I was met by Wing Commander Bill Arney, Deputy Head of Intelligence at FEAF. He was welcoming but mildly surprised at the urgency with which I had been flown out. Next morning I found out why. The Five Power Staff Agency had yet to exist. When it did, it would generate no work for months at least; and even then there would be enough capacity to deal with it within the already more than ample intelligence staff. As for SEATO, such were the disputes among the candidate nations that years could well pass before it existed. It took Isaiah 63:5 to express my response:

> And I looked and there was none to help; and I wondered that there was none to uphold; therefore my own arm brought salvation unto me; and my fury it upheld me.

As I unravelled what had happened, the zephyr of my discontent with the RAF became a breeze. The chief intelligence officer at FEAF was an old, long passed-over group captain. In his bitterness he consoled himself by waging the turf wars that were always fought in large headquarters. The very name Five Power Staff Agency had enough buzz for him to put in for another staff officer; and he argued successfully that Intelligence rather than Planning should be the place to put him. The opposing case went by default because the admirable chief of planning, Group Captain Whiteley, saw through what was happening and would have none of it. The Establishments Committee whose job it was to curb demands for extra staff had also been hoaxed, if not hexed. I was the victim. I used my own arm to bring salvation by looking for something different to do. Bill Arney could not help. He was gentle, good-natured and no match for our appalling boss. He was a pre-war Cranwell product of very modest achievement, and my impression was that he had simply given up. One of the other squadron leaders told me, not entirely frivolously, what he did in Bill's department. Arriving in the office each morning he adjusted the day-to-view wall calendar; having noted the new date, he turned the page in his diary. That was it.

True to Isaiah and remembering the dictum of Jeeves' Aunt which he used as advice to Bertie Wooster, that there is always a way, I found one. Another squadron leader, Philip Gee, had just arrived with his family to become the RAF member of the Joint Intelligence Staff (JIS) Far East, based at Phoenix Park, on the far side of Singapore City and a formidable commute. Gee cared much less about what he did than where he did it, and had just found a house near Changi. Unlike me, he was unconcerned at the prospect of two-and-a-half years in a non-job; so together we asked for a swap and got it. I relished the prospect of having something that sounded interesting to do.

The JIS offered exactly that. I worked with a naval Lieutenant Commander, Pat Dane; a gunner soldier, Peter White; and a Foreign Office Principal, Robert John. Phoenix Park was the headquarters of the commissioner general for South East Asia, at the time Malcolm Macdonald, a former Labour MP of great charm and diplomatic nous. The JIS wrote papers for and briefed the Joint Intelligence Committee (JIC) Far East, servicing its weekly meetings. The committee's main job was to keep watch on the Far East to see who, if anybody, was giving cause for warning the Foreign Office and the local embassies and garrisons. The joint structure replicated on a small scale the JIC and the Chiefs of Staff Committee in London, where the two were linked by the Defence and Overseas Policy Committee, aptly acronymed DOPO. We tried to be particularly vigilant about armaments, oil and a scarcely less important resource – rice. Shortages and even significant changes in sources and supplies of rice could cause riots, revolutions and even wars. One of our regular surveys came last on a wearisome agenda of a meeting of the top body, the British Defence Coordinating Committee, chaired by Malcolm Macdonald. Asked by the Secretary how he wanted the rice paper dealt with, he replied: 'Oh, stick it on the bottom of macaroons.'

Much of our other work included studies for the Joint Planning Staff of what to go for in various contingencies. One was the seizure of a beach head on the Chinese mainland, recommending such suitable entry points as the ports of Amoy and Foochow should so hazardous a venture become expedient. Another was a major conjectural study of a possible Chinese Communist plan for the invasion of South East Asia, anticipating the name of an invalid food with the code name Complan. There was a varied diet of actuality: the Communist threat in Malaya and its suspected supporters amongst venal politicians in Singapore; the Hukbalahap rebels in the Phillipines, sounding as if they were part of a Doolittle voyage; the rumbling hostility between the two Chinas at a flashpoint where Communist artillery habitually fired on the Nationalist Quemoy and Matsu Islands. A spectator sport to be watched through secret sources was the mainland government's clumsy campaign to subvert the Chiang Kai Shek (known as Chancre Jack) Nationalists in Taiwan. The worst worry was the steady erosion of French control of Indo-China manifest in their habitual taking of short-term, soft options and their chronic state of denial about the approaching defeat by the Viet Cong revolutionaries at Dien Ben Phu. Their conduct emulated the incompetence and corruption which did for France herself in 1940. All of which I found fascinating.

For three months I lived as a grass widower in the most beautiful officers' mess in the RAF. Fairy Point, on the eastern tip of Singapore Island, was a large colonial-style building overlooking the bosky Malayan coast across an idyllic stretch of water. We were near Hell on the Hill, the nickname of the enormous FEAF Headquarters. A mile away was Changi airfield, with the notorious Changi Gaol nearby. British prisoners of war built the airfield under Japanese lashes and I still regret that they have no memorial for their superb construction job, terribly costly in lives. Also nearby is Changi Village, a miniature version of the Singapore City shopping area featuring tailors who would run up made-to-measure tropical suits and uniform overnight. Near the surrounding RAF housing was the much admired all-ages RAF school from which our boys were soon to benefit.

I was invited occasionally to the conventional social event, descended from colonial days, of curry tiffin or Sunday lunch. A dozen or so guests would have cold beer and curry followed by Nasi Goreng, easily remembered for its Nazi connotation. It was a small mound of compacted sago drizzled, as the telly cooks say, with diluted syrup. The Arneys asked me to what I thought would be such an event. I was surprised that the only other guest was a youngish, nubile airwoman. Much of the talk was sexual gossip. She was over-familiar and I inferred that her presence was my hosts' act of kindly-meant indulgence of a sexually starved grass widower. Like most of us, I had had my moments. But handing me sex on, as it were, a lunch plate, was not, I decided, going to turn into one of them. I fear I disappointed the company by leaving as soon as civility allowed, recalling two printable descriptions of my companion guest's kind:

> She was only an airman's daughter,
> but now she's the Officers' Mess.

162

The other being the title of Squadron Bicycle because everyone rode her.

Another trial of my chastity began with my passing the time of day with a close friend's wife as she sat in the car and her husband dashed into the Mess to buy booze. She complained of a leg injury and accepted my offer of an Elastoplast, which I fetched from my room. When I applied it, a little north of the skirt line, the lesion looked to me to be slight enough to get better by itself. A day or two later, waiting in their sitting room for her to get ready for the lift into Singapore City in my RAF car which she had sought, she asked me whether I had seen her new swimsuit. Without waiting for an answer, she dashed into the bedroom and changed into it. As I was taking in the unappealing sight of baggy breasts and the rotunda below, her husband arrived home unexpectedly and, pink with rage, escorted her into the bedroom. Excusing myself through the open door, I abandoned the offer and departed, adjuring the driver not to spare the horsepower.

Such unholy happenings were untypical. There were many conventional dinner parties, easy to give because of plenty of Chinese staff to cook and wash up. At one of these we guests were all on our best behaviour for our chaplain host and his wife. After a decorous dinner he invited us to view their slides. It seemed a harmless offer until, as box succeeded box, the true duration of the ordeal became plain. Shortly before midnight, as the ennui became almost unbearable, another holy couple dropped in for a nightcap. With horrifying acuity our host recalled that his new guests had appeared on a slide a box or two back. As the partial repeat performance drew to an end, I wondered what I had done to deserve such a penance.

My working life was full, except at weekends. In the week I left for Phoenix Park early in the morning, getting back in time for a game of squash before dinner. Afterwards I read or did a turn of duty at the Officers' Club as a classical music disc jockey, culling culture from the backs of the LP jackets. On Sunday mornings, still qualified to fly the Valetta transport, I did simulated bombing runs over Singapore City, after the fashion of those I had once done over Cairo, acting as the target for the practice interceptions by the fighters and controllers of the Singapore Auxiliary Air Force. Still entitled to do instrument rating tests, I helped to keep my fellow staff officers and the crews of the Far East Communication Squadron up to date. There were also suspicious-looking ships in the Singapore harbour roads to be photographed at mast height from the Harvard, which I also used for aerobatic practice in skies much less restricted than at home. Derek Thirlwell, settled into his tied house and constantly hospitable, enjoyed my CFS party piece of night aerobatics as a passenger in the Harvard's front cockpit; doubtless recounting the experi-

'... suspicious-looking ships in the Singapore harbour roads. Chinese Communist victims of my airborne camera. *MOD/Author*

ence to others including his popular and well-respected boss, Air Marshal Sir Clifford Sanderson and other worthies: more Blueie points, I hoped.

Life improved enormously with the arrival of Rachel and the boys on the troopship *Dilwara,* known for its rolling. We put up in the Grand Hotel, a glorified boarding house and a rite of passage before new arrivals found proper housing. David, playing in the grounds, was seen by an *amah* (nanny) employed by the Chinese people next door called Lee, and was invited to play with their child in their enormous garden. In the best Intelligence tradition I checked up on the family. As was apparent from a pillar of brass plates on the wall of a giant office block in the city, the Lees had interests in rubber, pineapples, real estate, shipping, oil, wharfage and just about every other major undertaking on the island. We needn't have worried.

We soon found a house on the main Singapore–Changi road. Drawing on the very generous allowances for RAF families I bought a second-hand Ford Prefect for commuting, and other hitherto unaffordable delights including bicycles for the boys. Almost at once David had a puncture, which I duly mended in the boiling heat of a Sunday morning. Gregor, aged six, surprisingly, immediately had the same trouble. I did the same for him, only to discover that the hole in the tyre was self-inflicted, brought on by intrigue at watching Dad's discomfiture. Both boys flourished at Changi School. I was glad to observe in Gregor the dawn of logical thinking. Lounging on our bed as I dressed for a dinner at Changi, he had to be told not to fiddle with the bedside light. Grown-ups, I explained, could get nasty shocks from touching lights; and if children, being smaller, did it they could get badly hurt. After a thoughtful silence, a small voice hazarded:

and if babies did it, they'd explode.

We toured the Island in the Prefect, venturing occasionally across the Johore Causeway into the mainland. Other families, unthreatened by school fees, had new cars such as Rover 75s which they used to explore the whole Malayan Peninsula. For us, unfortunately, the high risk of a breakdown and threat of terrorist action kept us near home. But that did not prevent a lot of fun in such exotic places as the Haw Par Villa, which was a replica mandarin's mansion, the zoo and very good public parks. There was also St Andrew's Cathedral on Sunday mornings; and every day the Swimming Club, which could be joined only after a liturgy of meeting the assembled committee – an inspection, as I later realised, to ensure that candidates were white. Of the marvellous shops, the most remarkable was Tang's, selling Chinese wares of all kinds. Seeing airmen and their families investing their allowances, similarly generous, in huge carved wood chests, standard lamps, dining tables and chairs and elaborate screens made one wonder, unkindly perhaps, how their chattels would look in such settings as a Stockport back-to-back.

We had known all along that living in Singapore could not last long. David had already been to four schools and we knew well how bad discontinuity was for education. The only solution was private education for both boys, meaning that Rachel would have to take them home for a timely start. David, unusually, was upset during their sad embarkation on what proved to be the grubby trooper *Asturias*, knowing that we were facing another year or more of separation.

I had sold the car and handed it over on the way back to Changi. Back in Fairy Point, with my RAF commuting car restored, I continued to enjoy the JIS. To save money and avoid inflicting on the family the irritability said to be part of the process, I gave up cigarette smoking, finding no great difficulty after an unpleasant initial 48 hours. My role in Sunday morning flying had changed from simulated bomber to real fighter, vectored endlessly in a Vampire towards a Valetta flown by a colleague, for the benefit of trainee controllers. The awful turf warrior chief of FEAF Intelligence had departed. His infinitely better successor was Group Captain John Roe, kind, sensible and soon to become a force in the Joint Intelligence Committee which comprised all the service chiefs, the secret departments MI5 and MI6 representatives; and as chairman, a senior diplomat on Macdonald's staff, the flamboyant Scot Andrew Gilchrist. Roe's success, I flattered myself, came partly from the insider's scandal-filled briefing I gave him before each meeting. I thought him high-handed for refusing, on my behalf and without consulting me, the offer of promotion to acting wing commander and a posting to another ground job at the RAF Malayan Headquarters in Kuala Lumpur. (That City had a familial link, having a Cavendish Road named after my generous uncle Alex Cavendish, who had served there as a colonial servant.) I came round to being glad he had prevented me from embarking on what would have meant a two-year-plus separation. Promotion, he said, would soon come along anyway. It did. Meanwhile I was happy for my old friend Dick Wakeford to get the job. Our families had been close since we both commanded flights at Cranwell, and I had done what I could a year before to help with the many problems they faced after his sister-in-law, a BOAC stewardess, had been killed in a Constellation airliner crash at Kallang civil airport, a few miles from Changi.

The Arneys were replaced by George Badcoe, a welcome addition to the handful of Fairy Point residents and a squash opponent of exacting parity for me. Another arrival was Christopher Foxley Norris formerly of the Staff College, to be a wing commander planner in FEAF Headquarters. He brought the ominous news of Sir Clifford Sanderson's successor, so awful that he joked that it was a Communist-inspired rumour to destroy our morale. It wasn't. Along came the most unpopular of a coterie not known for their appeal – air marshals. Sir Francis Fressanges, for he it was, confirmed our fears; not so much by the bullying of subordinates, particularly his personal staff officer Derek Thirlwell, as by his boorishness with diplomats and other Service people, doing his own Service no good thereby. When his tour ended he sought, as did all who bought new cars for taking home, the perk of importing it tax free. Such had been the extent of his use of Service transport for private purposes that his Ford Zodiac remained almost unused; it thus attracted purchase tax, to widespread acclaim. He retired to become a pyrethrum farmer in Africa. If anyone could blight the crop, it would have been our Francis.

Like CFS, the JIS offered overseas intermissions to relieve monotony. One was a do-it-ourselves. We had produced a study of Indonesia's situation, prospects and likely effects on British interests so awful that the ambassador in Djakarta suggested that we should visit the country and see for ourselves. Claiming my turn for a perk granted to the regular pilots of the FEAF Communication Flight, I borrowed the de Havilland Devon and, with JIC Secretary Squadron Leader Howard Lewis, a navigator, flew our three colleagues to Jakarta for a weekend. We arrived in time for a formal Saturday luncheon for about 30 guests in the large Embassy dining room. After a no-alternative slug of gin and lime we sat down, on a boiling day, to soup, roast lamb and steamed pudding, no doubt to impress the guests with what Britishness really meant. We then left for a hilarious two-night stay in the Embassy's holiday cottage in the hills, set in a tea plantation and comparable to a miniature version of the hill stations of the Indian Raj. After talks with the head of Chancery, a sort of diplomatic major domo, and with secretaries graded first, second and third, I flew the party, hung-over but wiser, back to Changi.

Much sooner than expected, the Five Power Staff Agency came into being. The JIS, it was decided, were ready made junior British joint representatives, doing the unfortunate Phillip Gee, whose job it should have been, out of his appointed task. For the connoisseur, as I now was, of trips abroad, this one could hardly have been more idyllic. It was to Hawaii, where we went in a US Military Air Transport Service (MATS) DC4, virtually an enlarged four-engined Dakota. The route took us to Guam, a magic Pacific island of surf and sea birds marred only by the paraphernalia of aeroplanes. On Oahu, the main Hawaiian island, we worked on joint contingency plans which, had they materialised, would have provoked a nuclear war. We were much hampered by French intransigence and the constant referral of trivial decisions to Paris. We worked only from 7 a.m. until 1 p.m., usually spending the afternoons on Waikiki Beach, a large slice of which had been appropriated for their own use by the US Army. One amusement was to walk to the adjoining bit of public beach, where elderly American tycoons were to be seen consorting and often cavorting with young ladies whom they had brought from the mainland and accommodated at the Royal Hawaiian Hotel which backed on to the beach. Another diversion was a tour of Pearl Harbour where the cadavers of the battleships bombed on 7 December 1941 have been left as they lay. Eerily similar, in retrospect, to the gaunt beauty of the ruins of Dresden, also left as memorials to acts of infamy, which I visited years later as a General for Peace.

The US Services gave the delegations a formal cocktail party hosted by the commander of the Pacific Fleet (CINCPAC), at the time Admiral Felix B. Stump. He was an archetypal war lord of the General MacArthur stamp. We were each presented to him almost as if to royalty. If, during conversation, a query or an item he thought worth remembering came up, he would snap his fingers at one of the white-uniformed ensigns standing stock still in the corners of the room who would hasten to the master, notebook at the ready, do his bidding and then hasten back to their station. The only lightening of the Teutonic rigidity I saw was traffic slow-downers on the domestic housing access roads, labelled 'Stump's Bumps'.

The civilians were different. At her cocktail party for the visiting military, a leathery hostess expressed her interest in the love life of the Queen's sister Princess Margaret, who had fallen for an air equerry, Group Captain Peter Townsend, and then under pressure from the Palace and the Archbishop of Canterbury, thrown him over. She had also read about Dr Hewlett Johnson, Dean of Canterbury, notorious for his Communist leanings and known as the Red Dean. She conflated the two in her question to me:

How come the Red Dean won't let that Koin'l [Colonel] marry your Queen?

the unravelling of which taxed my interpretative abilities.

On the way home MATS did us the favour of a northerly diversion across the Pacific to Tokyo where, after a look round the city, we spent a night in the requisitioned Dai Iti ('Itchy') hotel. The US Army colonel who managed it apologised for the lack of hot water, attributable, he explained, to the habit of the large Japanese female staff of helping themselves frequently to hot baths: a lesson, perhaps, for some of their occidental sisters.

My last overseas outing took place across the South China Sea in the Philippines, now a member of the shadowy South East Asia Treaty Organisation, which in the event was to come to nothing. After a reception in the

Advice from friend and colleague Major Peter White, no doubt about a weighty matter.
Pat Dane

presidential palace in the grubby city of Manila and a handshake from the jolly Old King Coal President Magsaysay, we went to work in the hill town of Baguio, a hill resort that had never taken off, in the Pines Hotel, beautifully situated in forest surroundings. I shared a room with Pat Dane, a gentle Old Carthusian contemporary whom I had known only slightly. He was more interested in antique silver than in his career, which was soon to end. The soldier Peter White was highly thought of in Singapore and deserved a better career than he had, after the end of which he went into property in southern Spain. The three of us worked in Baguio on another series of abstruse contingency plans. In our spare time we climbed the beautiful Mount Santa Tomas. The marvellous view of the islands from the summit reminded me of a bit of Isaac Watts' hymn (AMR 545):

> Could we but climb where Moses stood,
> and view the landscape o'er.

169

I wondered for a long time what the Landscibor was. There was much social activity between the five nations, consisting mostly in very trying cocktail parties. I was saddled with hosting and escorting two Thai generals, that rank being considered appropriate to work done for which the other allies used majors. They were charming, medal-bedecked little men with little English and unpronounceable names. They were paroxysmatic with laughter whenever, with their delighted permission, I introduced them at functions using as their names two airfields in Thailand which I could remember and pronounce. I found recollection easy because, had they only known, the airfields had been under surveillance: Prachuap Kirikan and Nakhorn si Thammarat.

We returned to Singapore to find that our diplomat colleague Robert John had been promoted and posted to Saigon, where he and his wife Ann went to great trouble to find their small son a kindergarten, eventually coming across a hugely expensive French establishment. Their reward became clear when the child came home after the first morning: asked what he had learnt, his delighted reply was, 'fighting, spitting and wee-wees in the garden'.

Robert's successor was the plain but incandescently bright Meriel Russell, ill-tempered but highly amusing. She was soon to marry a Mellers figure of a major from the Army headquarters. He was no match for her and I worried about them. She improved the quality of our work, which had earned us a complimentary letter from Malcolm Macdonald, leaving to become high comissioner in India:

> a constant series of weighty matters receiving ... always the most thorough expert advice ... working long and late ... tireless and able assistance ... personally and officially I am deeply indebted.

OTT but welcome all the same.

On the departure soon afterwards of the bearded and oddly attired JIC Chairman Andrew Gilchrist to become Ambassador to Iceland, I circulated farewell blank verse:

> It isn't as if he was going somewhere nice, such as India to work for
>> Malcolm,
> where he'd be sure of a warm walcolm;
> or to a place where he could go on wearing sailcloth trousers or even
>> a *dhoti*
> and not shave off his ghoti.
> No, where he's going they don't like such things, they're all frigid
>> and obtuse,

170

and he'll find it hard work telling dirty stories to a moose.
What's more, it'll be no good trying to be witty
in front of a shower of penguins and such-like instead of a quiet
respectful committy;
and no use making a great fuss over some small thing
and then trying to solve it by lobbying the Althing.
... All in all it's a shame that our oracle, pivot and eminence grise
is bound for the deep frise.

It went down well.

Hoping that my bachelor life might be ended prematurely, I applied for a course at the RAF Flying College at Manby in Lincolnshire, where the frightful Wing Commander Russell Bell, under whose command I had writhed at the Central Flying School, had been on the staff. I was delighted to be accepted, thereby getting home in February 1956 instead of July. The course would almost certainly get me back into full-time flying instead of the job on the side that it was in Singapore. It was also a good career move; but that seemed to matter less and less. Flown home by Airwork in the civil version of the Hastings, I was glad to meet an old master pilot (the highest non-commissioned flying rank) whom I had known at CFS. He had retired to the double job of first officer with Airwork and beekeeper at home. He made me welcome on the flight deck. I had the job of OC Troops, consisting in nothing more than keeping an eye on the welfare of the time-expired Service people and their families who, as I had been told they always did, behaved impeccably. My one service to them took place late on a freezing February night when we fetched up in an almost deserted Customs Hall at Heathrow. Just as a horde of customs men were descending on us, I saw a group of winter sporters passing through untouched. Running across to the head customs officer, I pleaded for my charges just home, I said, from years on the frontiers of civilisation serving Queen and country; and much more deserving of leniency than the tourists, fresh from the sybaritic snowfields. He at once shifted the whole pack from us to them.

During my disembarkation leave we moved from Glastonbury, where the boys had gone back to the Tor School which they had left a year or so before. Our new abode was a charming bungaloid cottage at Saltfleetby, near Louth and within bicycle range of the good permanent station at RAF Manby. At last David could start a continuum of schooling at Ardingly College in Sussex, chosen largely because of the new, reformist head, George Snow. The younger boy Gregor went to the wonderfully good, single-teacher village school opposite the cottage. We were in a

The cottage at Saltfleetby .... *Vyvyn Davey*

charming setting beside a brook, but the cottage had an adverse feature new even to us, experienced in abodes of variable quality as we were. The lavatory, in a converted outhouse beside the cottage proper, had a cistern fed by rainwater from the sloping roof: efficient and economical in rainy weather, but disruptive of good sanitary routine when it was dry. A car, for the time being, was beyond our means, but I bought a second-hand bicycle for commuting. It served well except after a boozy dinner, when, in full mess kit, I found myself in a drainage ditch into which it had catapulted me. It renewed my youthful pleasure in cycling (which has continued ever since), conveying me on Sundays to the churches of Saltfleetby All Saints and its sister St Peter, both equipped with simple American organs of the kind I had been offered by Otway Lely in Malvern but had had to decline on joining up. 'I was glad', as one of my favourite anthems puts it, to help out. But the extent of my amateurish-ness was apparent on the Sunday when one of the hymns was 'Ye holy

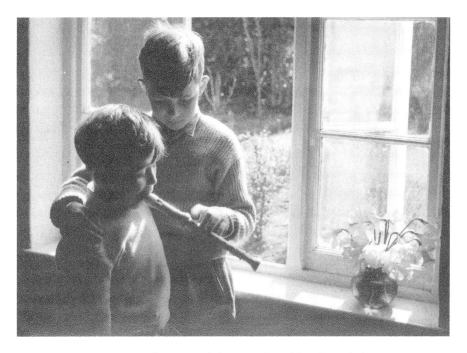

... where our boys enjoyed the springtime of their lives. *Author*

angels bright' (*A&M* 546). Fulfilling the exhortation in the first verse to 'assist our song' ordinarily meant playing in B flat, which imports four black notes. Doubting my ability to remember them, I transposed the tune upwards to Middle C, free from the dark invaders. All very well for me; but when we got to:

> Or else the theme
> Too high doth seem
> For mortal tongue ...

that was just what happened.

Soon we all had bikes and went for expeditions to the small resort of Mablethorpe on the nearby coast. A railway line from there to Louth with a village stop nearby added interest to our lives. It was a great help when Gregor had a prolonged stay in Louth cottage hospital with another attack of a mysterious illness which had afflicted him in Singapore. It eventually turned out to be rheumatic fever, later to prevent him from fulfilling his intense desire to follow me into the RAF.

Work at Manby began with a short refresher flying course which I welcomed because, being already in good flying practice, I could fly for fun. I brushed up my aerobatics in a Meteor IV, a solo version faster and with a longer duration than the Mk VII, at the scruffy wartime airfield used as a satellite for Manby – Strubby. It was an evocative name which I tried to propagate as an epithet for poor flying ('that was a strubby approach you just did'), but I doubt whether it took hold. I was able to repay the flight commander's indulgence when a posse of very senior officers paid an inspection visit. I was deputed to act as exemplar of the high standard achieved by the refresher students by, as that cheerfully disrespectful young man put it, 'making with the circuits'. That meant a succession of approaches, touchdowns and take-offs, known as rollers. By the time the great men showed up, late, I was down to my engines' last gasps of fuel, just getting by and earning whispered thanks.

The commandant was the dapper Air Commodore Paddy Dunn who presided over a wide-ranging course designed to broaden the experience of senior officers and acquaint them with the expanding scope and complexity of RAF flying. We students already had good backgrounds as aviators and were expected to move on to senior posts (more 'specially selected', I thought). Dunn was a perfectionist who, because of my record of high assessments in the bomber, transport and instructional businesses, seemed to ask more of me than he did of the other students. That he did not get, at least at first. I at once took to the superbly smooth handling characteristics of the Canberra jet bomber, reminiscent of the Mosquito but much faster. Its snag was the multiplicity of safety features, not so much bells and whistles as switches, warning lights, 'tits' as they were affectionately termed, and emergency procedures. All of which I, and others, found it hard to master. Compared with some fellow students I knew little of the fighter role; but that was providentially offset by beginner's luck: on an air firing exercise in a Meteor IV I scored 20 hits on a target at which I had fired only 99 rounds.

The besetting anxiety, which had not troubled me since I had overdone it on bomber operations, came back and added to my difficulties. Mercifully it eased as the course progressed. I had as a solid companion Bert Slade, my contemporary as a CFS examiner. Together we did navigation exercises in the Canberra, alternating as captain and navigator. One was a day trip to Malta and back: the island's powerful beacon, as of old, was a great help to two pilots used for much of their careers to the luxury of professional navigators. We all did passenger flights in the Lincoln, last in the line of heavy piston-engined bombers, to experience using the ever more complicated radar navigation and bombing devices. Best of all for me was a brief acquaintance with the Hawker Hunter, the better of the two competitors for the new RAF standard fighter: the other being the Supermarine Swift, which barely saw the light of day. On the second of two Hunter airings I shed my kid-gloved handling of this flighty creature and went supersonic, eastwards out into the North Sea. The bang, from the cockpit sitpoint, was undramatic. But not, apparently, in the wider world. I had forgotten to report it and the local radio that evening mentioned an apparent explosion out to sea which the lifeboat from Strumble Head had investigated without result. It seemed best not, as it were, to bang on about it.

The course ended in December 1956. I got only a chilly 'qualified' assessment, the old categories apparently no longer being used for courses. The compensation was a posting I could hardly have dreamt for. Specially picked, if ever I was, I was to command the second squadron of Vulcan bombers, shortly to form. The Vulcan was already recognised as the best of the three competing types commissioned for the new generation of aircraft capable of carrying nuclear weapons: the first was the Vickers Valiant, a workhorse whose limited performance was soon recognised as inadequate to give a fair chance of surviving the expected Soviet opposition; then there was the Vulcan, immensely sturdy because of its triangular shape and with startlingly good capability; and later the Victor, in some respects more advanced but lacking the Vulcan's superb manoeuvrability.

Like all good things, the posting had to be waited for: a discipline visited so severely on the first choice for the job that, after two years in a hanging-about capacity, he finally passed his fly-by date and gave it up. I was the replacement for the famous, heavily decorated and universally popular Ivor Broom, as it happened a staff member at Manby who had done much to help me on the course. Amongst his qualities was not drinking. I and others could only marvel at the fortitude he had displayed during years of enduring ghastly mess balls and dinners without the analgesia of booze. That virtue was not shared by a fellow student who sat next to me at the dinner marking the end of the course. The main speaker was the loquacious new commandant, Air Commodore Gus Walker. My friend had drunk much too much and had become noisy. To try to save him from last-minute nemesis I said to a waiter standing behind us, 'Please bring the wing commander some coffee.' 'Yes, please do,' shouted my intended beneficiary, 'and while you're at it, bring some toast and marmalade'. Gus shut up within seconds.

My wait, much shorter than Ivor's, was a treat in itself. I was to be wing commander in charge of flying at RAF Waddington, another permanent station and one of the major airfields designated as 'Master Diversion' (MDA), successors to the special relief airfields always open during the war to cater for fuel shortages, bad weather or bases obstructed by crashes. The job also gave me charge of two resident Canberra bomber squadrons, Nos 37 and 38. With them I was able to get plenty of flying in an aircraft I loved. I did many practice bombing runs, not all that different from those in my wartime tours, dropping small practice bombs on ranges near our Saltfleetby cottage. Also at Waddington was the Vulcan conversion unit where crews for the first squadron, numbered 617 after that of the famous Dambusters, were already being trained. The chief instructor was another highly decorated bomber ace, Wing Commander Frank Dodd, an excellent pilot and instructor with a gentility of manner that overlaid steely determination. The two of us made a good team under Group Captain Spencer Ring, competent but boring; more, as it were, a dull thud. Above him was the by now Air Vice-Marshal Gus Walker, newly appointed as Air Officer Commanding 1 Group. The two bomber groups at the time, the numbers kept in being because of their historic importance, were One, known to us, its arrogant members in a football metaphor as First Division North; and Three, known disparagingly as Third Division South. I had come across Walker not only as a long-winded after-dinner speaker but as a noser-round, as opposed to a taker of a general interest in, the college activities, given to describing mundane things as 'fascinatingly interesting'. As a base commander in Bomber Command during World War Two he had lost his right arm in an attempt to rescue the crew of an aircraft loaded with bombs which had crashed. Critics commented that, had he left the rescue to the trained fire fighters and armourers, he would not have been hurt. Having been a top-class rugger player, he became a referee of the same calibre; and despite his disability he flew with remarkable adaptive skill. My first direct encounter with him at Waddington was on a night when I was trying to help the confused American pilot of an incoming transatlantic aircraft in bad weather, as part of my job of caring for users of the MDA. Having been told of the possible emergency by his group Operations Room, Walker turned up in the Waddington Control Tower. I, having done my best to reassure the pilot, had positioned him for a radar-guided approach and landing with our very skilled controller Squadron Leader Peter Jermyn. Walker asked a string of interfering questions. Interrupting his initial instructions to the pilot, Peter, to his great credit, loudly exclaimed,

I must have utter hush.

He got it; and all was well. For me, there was a lot more of Walker to come.

Soon came one of the wider aspects of the general duties (GD) which officers of the flying branch of the RAF were required to perform. Spencer Ring asked me to take charge of the impending visit to Waddington by the Duchess of Kent. I wrote an elaborate operation order and went over the plans with the main participants. The apical item was to be the luncheon (lunch not being an elegant enough term) in the officers' mess. It must, we decided, be rehearsed the day before, in its entirety except for the booze. The menu was smoked trout, rack of lamb and, as the awful faux-dainty RAF VIP catering system had it, 'Delice des Dames'; the last being brought refreshingly to reality by Peter Jermyn the Irrepressible as 'ice cream with bits of Ovaltine in it'. Nothing, however, could deflate the pretentious 'Moka' with which we finished (I wondered whether it was really Nescaf). And nothing could detract from Jerome Kern, Irving Berlin and Robert Farnon, all featured in the tasteful 'Selections of Music' rendered by the strings of the RAF Central Band. What could have been a contretemps was down to the extroverted Sir Harry Broadhurst, Commander-in-Chief of Bomber Command, who had joined the company of dancers of attendance. Knowing better than the airman whose job it was, he ushered the royal aircraft to a point between the hangars from which it would be almost inextricable; saving the royal party a yard or two of walking, but not my nails from several nanometres of biting. We pulled it clear with a tractor. All else went well. I was smothered in thanks. And the officers' mess, like all those that hosted female Royals, got a refurbished ladies' lavatory.

I spent the weekends at the house we had been given at Finningley, the station, permanent yet again, where my squadron, numbered after a famous and long established World War One unit – 101 – was to form. The airfield had just been refurbished and there was rubbish and rubble everywhere. As Gregor, our younger son, and I bicycled across it towards the adjoining village, he fell; revealing, as I picked him up, a huge cut in his thigh from a bit of broken airfield lighting glass. I waved down a van in the middle distance which came to the rescue and took us to the sick bay. As the doctor sewed it up, the wound proved to be no more than a deep flesh one, but there was a lot of blood. I fainted, waking to the doctor's stentorian cry to the orderly to 'Do something about the wing commander.' Rachel of course was present as the twentieth stitch went in. Her maternal 'What do you say?' got a moving filial 'Thank you'.

The house was a pre-war married quarter for a senior officer. Fortunately we had a batman to help with the huge task of keeping it in order. We were also blessed with a good school in Doncaster for Gregor. For David, now ensconced at Ardingly, I was able to keep up the three-weekly parental visits in an Anson borrowed from Waddington, flying to the MDA at Thorney Island and going by train to the school's nearest town, Haywards Heath.

In July I left my job at Waddington to become Frank Dodd's student on the Vulcan, using my last few Canberra trips to try out the new, semi-automated radar descent and landing system (ILS), precursor of the fully hands-off version that later came into general use. With Frank's help I found the Vulcan amenable and a joy to fly. The brilliant control system, so sensitive that it had to be fitted with artificial 'feel', made pilots forget its enormous size; and although far more complicated technically than any aircraft I had come across before, simple once one got the hang. In unbounded exhilaration, I could hardly believe my luck. Never mind the career, I thought. Just let me get on with the job.

Chapter 9

Vulcan Forgeries

My inheritance was no mean one. The first role of 101 Squadron was night bombing in the FE2B, a canvas-and-string stalwart of World War One, under the command of the sonorously named Major the Honourable Twistleton Wickham Fiennes. Thereafter mothballed, 101 re-formed at the famous Norfolk base RAF Bircham Newton in 1928. It was equipped first with Sidestrand and later Overstrand aircraft, still partly canvas but with wires instead of string. The Sidestrand sported a scarf ring, a horizontal circular mount for swivelling the Vickers gas-operated machine gun by hand. The Overstrand had the first Boulton Paul power-operated turret, moveable in azimuth as well as horizontally; later, armed with four Browning machine guns, to become a standard bomber fitment. Named after Norfolk villages, the aircraft survive in silver model form amongst the squadron's treasures. Re-equipped with Blenheim light bombers just before World War Two, 101 took part in the notoriously dangerous daylight raids envisaged as feasible by the pre-war air staff but soon abandoned because of crushing losses. Converting to Wellingtons, the squadron was part of the 1,000 bomber forces scraped together for raids on Berlin and Essen, more for the sake of British civilian morale than for damaging those cities. Re-equipped again with Lancasters, 101 paved the way for the airborne landings in Normandy by flattening houses obstructing one of the dropping zones. After a spell in the job of electronic jamming of German anti-aircraft radar, the squadron resumed daylight bombing. With the Luftwaffe on its last legs, the opposition was inconsiderable. When, after the armistice, Bomber Command joined the transport force to drop food to the Dutch and bring home prisoners of war, the squadron took part. Following a six-year stint with Lincoln bombers, 101 became a jet bomber unit, using their Canberras in the catastrophic Suez Campaign in 1956 and later against Communist terrorists in Malaya.

Now came the Vulcan. The prospects could not have been more exciting, but the foreground was dismal. We chafed at the slow emergence of the new aircraft from the Avro airfield at Woodford, near their Chadderton factory. The ground crews were still learning how to maintain the few we had and the serviceability was terrible. The elaborate facilities needed for a V-Force station were far from complete, except for the new 3,000-yard runway, flat to within a few inches and the object of admiring visits by civil engineers. We managed, somehow, to start on long navigation exercises and practice bombing runs over special radar measurement sites capable of very precise assessment of our accuracy. There were frequent practices of action in the event of war, consisting in hurried dispersal to designated airfields scattered over the UK. More demandingly, we practised emergency take-offs from Finningley in response to a hypothetical crisis so sudden that dispersal would have been impossible. That usually meant leaping from bed, struggling into flying kit, jumping into the waiting cars and thence into the cockpit, starting all four engines at once and rocketing off the runway: all forming so compressed a sequence as to make it feel like a single movement. The scrambles, comparable to those of Battle of Britain pilots, were exhilarating. We became so proficient that on one occasion I was still strapping up as we passed through 30,000 feet on the way to our 50,000-foot operating height. There was a real sense of dedication as we refined the procedures, encouraged by the build-up, at last, to our complement of eight aircraft. It showed in the practice bombing results and the keenness with which we embarked on the rigorous Bomber Command crew categorisation scheme, a ladder with 'Combat' at the bottom ascending by way of 'Select' to the rarefied 'Select Star'.

Finningley soon acquired as Station Commander Group Captain Douglas Haig, another Battle of Britain veteran, aptly named because of his fondness for whisky and with much else in common with John Simpson, he of my book review and later sad marriage and suicide. He knew little of the bomber business but was very supportive. His right-hand man was the chief administrator James 'Mouse' Grant, also well named for his whisky-drinking propensity. I had as one flight commander Squadron Leader Norman Wilkins, highly unusual in that he was a navigator whom I had accepted in preference to a pilot because, though over-anxious to please, he was keen and competent. The other flight was run by yet another whisky-named incumbent, Johnnie Walker, free of its boozy implication. An RAF Rugger Team player from New Zealand, he too was keen and competent. But such was his inferiority complex that there was nothing of him and his that he did not proclaim as the biggest and/or best. In my crew was the radar navigator and bomb-releaser Vic Rollason, ferociously assiduous at the hours of target study that accurate results demanded; and as conventional navigator Bob Harbour, like my former

Wellington navigator Sergeant Bolton, a town planner with meticulous skill. I used a variety of second pilots chosen from the other captains; and having qualified as a Vulcan instrument rating examiner used the tests for ordinary supervisory flying. My charges soon learnt that taxiing the aircraft without allowing the wheels at the centre to move was a category-busting offence, along with leaving the massive cockpit windscreen wipers on when it wasn't raining.

I had doubts about inviting non-Vulcan pilots as guest second pilots because of a major accident that caused a total loss before the aircraft entered squadron service. Squadron Leader 'Podge' Howard, very experienced in multifarious types, was landing at Heathrow. He had as second pilot Air Marshal Sir Harry Broadhurst, who had interfered with my running of the Royal visit to Waddington. The final stages of his approach to Heathrow went wrong and Podge, with on his order Sir Harry, used their ejection seats and escaped. The two navigators were left behind and killed: their only means of escape was by ordinary parachute through the floor hatch, and the aircraft was too close to the ground for that. The inquiry found that Podge had acted correctly. I, not being wild about Sir Harry, wondered how much he had interfered. I made an exception of Duggie Haig who, very keen to take part, soon picked up enough to make a useful second pilot.

We improved in fits and starts. Just as we reckoned ourselves a going concern, 6 inches of snow covered the airfield. We were supposed to be an all-weather force and I decided to try out the small wheels of the Vulcan undercarriage, so far as I knew for the first time, on a snowy runway at night. When my flight plan reached the Group Operations Room, Wing Commander Paddy Finch, an air staff officer and friend, ordered me on behalf of the AOC not to take off because of the snow. When he admitted that Gus Walker had not been consulted and that he had made the decision, I sniffily reminded him that as squadron commander the decision was mine, and that I was ignoring his order. Off we went. After a few acutely anxious seconds and some whooshing, the Vulcan, accelerating comparatively slowly, took the air with its usual grace. Towards the end of a five-hour flight the control centre told me that, as forecast, the whole of the UK was blanketed in low cloud. He offered me as diversion airfields Lossiemouth, still a Naval air station, alongside the Moray Firth which is often blessed with an anomaly of good local weather; or the USAF Libyan base at Wheelus, near Tripoli. I chose Lossiemouth. While we were on the descent from 50,000 feet even Morayshire closed in, reaching a state in which, by the book, we could not land. As Wheelus was now out of range, our situation looked a little bleak. Beginning my ground-controlled approach, I realised that the Naval controller was highly skilled and that he and I had the same sort of compatibility as that which I had enjoyed with another controller, George Harding, years ago at Nutts Corner. The approach, with all due immodesty, was flawless, also doing him great credit because he was accustomed to small Buccaneer aircraft. Just as, in thick snow, his talk-down was ending with a satisfying sequence of 'steady ... steady ... steady', he suddenly said 'You're 25 feet high' [above the glide path]. I felt obliged to ask 'Which bit of us are you aiming at? The Vulcan's 26 feet tall.' Before he could answer, the runway lights appeared and we landed routinely. The captain, who had got out of bed to be present at what could have been a major accident, enjoyed the joke and complimented us both. I heard no more of my contretemps with Paddy.

I felt sad and a little guilty a few days later about a serious Vulcan accident because it might have been a consequence of my own adventure. My erstwhile Vulcan instructor Frank Dodd, landing at Waddington on a snowy runway, swerved into a bank of piled-up snow close to the tarmac edge. The damage was serious but happily nobody was hurt. Like my glider mishap at White Waltham, his error was long remembered:

You shouldn't have put the Vulcan in the bank, Frank.

It would have been uncharacteristic of Frank to have tried a 'Me too'. Perhaps he simply wanted to confirm my result.

As Christmas 1957 approached I anticipated a practice alert during the holiday, so that the group headquarters could satisfy themselves that our state of readiness remained unaffected. Before lunch on Christmas Eve, when the non-emergency part of the station had closed, I found Duggie Haig and Mouse Grant in the officers' mess bar, both drunk on Black Velvet (Guinness and champagne). That made me the only sober senior GD (flying branch) officer available to take charge of an alert for a take-off which I would myself lead. Fortunately nothing happened. Neither of the revellers reacted to my decision, more from funk than compassion, not to shop them as I should have done.

Before we had finished welding ourselves together as a unit we had to divert effort to the displays for which our beautiful white giants were ideal and much in demand. (They were white because that was the best colour to reflect the heat and radioactivity that would ensue after the release of a nuclear weapon.) One daunting job, to which all hands had to turn until better means came along, was to use rags and polish to keep them

Togetherness. 101 Squadron and our first Vulcan. *Crown Copyright/MOD*

gleaming. Another was the mostly unproductive flying involved. Fortunately most displays were local in our terms. We took part in many Battle of Britain commemoration days at bases scattered across the UK, covering half a dozen in an afternoon, with fly-pasts at low level and soar-aways into the blue or grey as the case might be. The four Bristol Olympus 6 engines – prototypes, incidentally, for those of Concord – were quiet enough in the cockpit; but when they gave their all the noise outside was not so much loud as seemingly flattening of everything around. At the earnest entreaty of our two boys I did a similar display over Ardingly College. George Snow wrote:

> Your call very much appreciated all round – dead on time and most spectacular ... the sight against the blue sky very remarkable, and the noise of the climb had to be heard to be believed ...

It was good to know that somebody liked it. Plaudits for displays, more difficult than they looked, were rare indeed.

I later provided a rather different spectacle at the school. Our younger son Gregor very much wanted me to play in the Parents v. Boys cricket match at the junior school. It was, he pointed out, the last chance because he was about to ascend to the senior school which eschewed such larks. In borrowed white trousers, and only too aware of my utter lack of cricketing skill, I joined the other dads in the field; assigned, to my horror, to the perilous post of point, close to the batsman. The opener was huge for his age. The intentionally loose first ball, bowled by an indulgent dad as a long hop on the off side, caused the boy giant to open his shoulders and smite it with all his might straight at me. Smothering a scream I put out both hands in self-protection – and caught the ball. I was far from hero of the match because, contravening parental convention, I had done for the hope of his side.

Overseas commitments gobbled up resources but were great fun. They also oiled the diplomatic wheels of giving away of bits of the Empire, a process in spate at the time. To help to celebrate the freedom of Nigeria, I

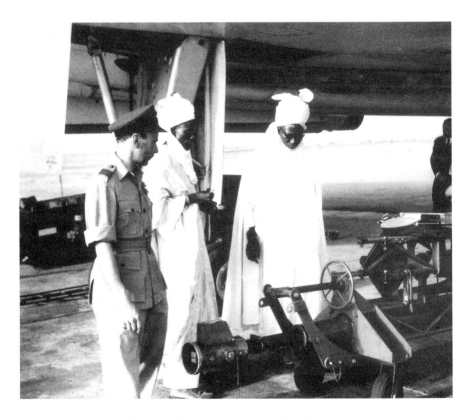

The Sirdana of Sokoto getting a quote for a Vulcan. *Anon*

184

flew a Vulcan overnight to Kano, landing early enough to minimise the local hazard of bird-strike from vultures. That, plus the local solution of piles of carrion for the birds' edification away from the approach, did the trick. The snag was the presence of Gus Walker, much like a booze-free Russell Bell. His presence seemed connected with the dancing of attendance on the Duke of Gloucester at Kaduna to represent the Queen as the Union Jack was lowered and the gaudy Nigerian flag raised. Gus's endless questions and needless warnings were tiresome but didn't spoil the fly-overs of the other main Nigerian towns. One was Sokoto, where we landed at the request of the local ruler, the Sirdana – comparable with the Fakir of Ipi of staff college days but friendly. Using his Oxford-educated son as interpreter, he asked how much a Vulcan would cost. On being told £3.25million plus £600,000 for the radar, he commented that buying one would add a quarter to his people's income tax. No sale.

The squadron attended, as a three-aircraft detachment, a similar ceremony at another former outpost – Kenya, where the opening of the new airport at Embakasi was to be part of the fun. I landed there first. In view of the immensity, as it seemed, of the new runway I decided not to bother with streaming the tail parachute normally used to help to bring the Vulcan to a halt; thereby saving us having to complete a chore done at base by ground crew and not within local competence. What I failed to reckon with was the height of Embakasi above sea level – 600 feet and thus the highest in Africa and most of the world. That meant that our true landing speed would be some 20 knots higher than normal. I touched down accurately at the threshold; but we ran the whole enormous length, finishing with smoke from the brakes, of which I was asking too much. As we taxied majestically to the stopping point where the dignitaries were arrayed, a stroppy controller told me that we had in tow the cables of the lighting system stretching for hundreds of yards behind us. Our arrival thus got something short of a standing ovation. To be fair, the cables should have been buried; but that, I felt, would not be an ice-cutting excuse. Fortunately we were scheduled to leave almost at once. That we did, leaving the air attaché to do the explaining.

Another air attaché had some explaining to do for himself at a later port of call – Saigon – where we were celebrating the freedom of South Vietnam, brief as it proved to be, between French colonial rule and American occupation. When we arrived I was disagreeably surprised to find that, while the runways were strong enough to bear the weight of Vulcans, the taxi ways were not. At terrible inconvenience to our hosts, who were nonetheless polite and welcoming, we parked, refuelled and did

Our Vulcans in formation: unconfined delight. *Stanley Devon/A.V. Roe*

our servicing on a runway. There was general delight with our displays except for the USAF contingent whose C124 and C130 transports, lumbering across the sky, we eclipsed. They, like ourselves, had an eye on the market potential of the dignitaries from India, China, the Philippines, Japan, Korea, Malaysia and others invited to the do.

The best of these jaunts was a transatlantic one done in partnership with a Victor squadron commander mellifluously named Ulick Burberry. We gave joint displays, starting at the annual (later biennial) air show at Farnborough organised by the Society of British Aircraft Constructors (later British Aerospace Contractors). I had long been used to bringing Anson-loads of Cranwell and CFS friends to the show, landing at nearby Blackbushe, later famous as Greenham Common. But taking part in the display myself was new and exciting. I did two fast runs a few feet above the runway with a tightly banked circuit in between. On each run the

186

Vulcan was garlanded with little clouds of water vapour on the upper wings, caused by cooling in the low-pressure areas on which lift, as Dr Kermode had taught me long ago, depended. We clambered away, hampered by the full fuel load needed to reach Toronto, site of the next display. The announcer told the crowd that the time change would enable us to get there before we had left Farnborough. Ulick and his Victor, with much shorter range, had to drop in for refuelling at Goose Bay, for many years a refuelling stop for aircraft en route for Britain. We, too, had a fuel problem. Toronto Control had not been told of my trip and the controller ordered me to conform to the ordinary approach procedure and wait in the holding pattern. After a minor wrangle he got the message and ushered me straight to the waterfront for a fly-past and landing, at our last gasp, at the nearby RCAF Station Trenton. I doubted whether there would be enough fuel left to taxi in, but we made it.

The fault for what could have been a sticky end was that of the officer supposed to be in charge of the joint venture, Group Captain 'Johnnie' Johnson. He was the greatest of all the Battle of Britain aces, draped in DSOs, DFCs and bars. He greeted us somewhat over effusively, nervous because he knew nothing about V-force aircraft; and, as was clear from the absence of preparation for our arrival, about the job in hand. Having got himself the job simply as a jolly he made no useful contribution – a pity, because I could have done with some help with the Trenton locals. They, understandably, were preoccupied with their own display team, the superb Golden Hawks, comparable to the RAF Red Arrows. Ulick and I had the task, on each of the three display days, of doing two sea-level high-speed runs in opposite directions along the waterfront, interspersed by steep pull-ups to 5,000 feet and sharp wing-overs and diving turns to point us at each other again. We passed as close to each other as we dared: having discovered that 'Toronto' is the Red Indian word for 'meeting', I was perhaps slightly more than usually concerned to avoid one with Ulick's Victor. The displays were not entirely suited to taking in the view en route, but I enjoyed, at the top of the southerly turns, glimpses of Niagara Falls in the far distance. We were too busy at Trenton to see round Toronto. But we were invited to an elaborate dinner, curiously named Complimentary, by Toronto's City Fathers and Mothers and attended by the mayor and 18 aldermen and women. The menu varied from the norm with leather beef instead of rubber chicken. The head of the Canadian National Industrial Exhibition, sponsors of the whole affair, was lyrical in his speech about us as stealers of the show from the US and Russian participants and even the Golden Hawks. Less delighted was another speaker,

General Curtis Le May, former head of USAF Strategic Air Command, our competitors for prestige.

As a small and relaxing overseas perk we were allowed a continuation of a long-standing Bomber Command custom: that of a short trip to an overseas destination known as a Lone Ranger. Having hogged several of the glamorous duty destinations, I chose a humble trip to El Adem, one of theWestern Desert airfields that I had known so well in the 1940s, near the Mediterranean coast and beautiful in its own way. It was now a well-developed staging post for short-range aircraft on delivery to Middle East customers. My recollection of the hospitality and the self-maintenance which was part of the exercise was clouded by copious quantities of Oranjeboom, a deceptively powerful Dutch beer. But I'm sure I had a good time.

All these diversions did not prevent a steady improvement in serviceability as we learnt the Vulcan's snags and foibles; and in bombing accuracy and the speed with which we completed practice take-offs. Vic Rollason's devoted target study, and doubtless a bit of luck, led on a memorable night in January 1959 to an almost unheard-of achievement on

An exhilarated crew arriving in Ceylon en route to the Far East. *Anon*

188

a radar target – a direct hit. More typically our errors were in the low hundreds of yards. All the striving for accuracy was partly a leftover from the age of conventional bombing; and partly to allow for the possibility, remote as we thought, but later to materialise during the Falklands War, of a reversion to the conventional role when a Vulcan damaged the airfield runway with the only bomb ever released from a Vulcan in war. The technique, moreover, was used for the annual Bomber Command bombing competition. Thus, like elephants dropping rabbit currants, we showered the ranges near Saltfleetby with 11lb practice bombs.

In parallel, we worked away at our proper job. There emerged, like Whittle's jet at Cranwell, the object of our main efforts – the hydrogen bomb, housed in new buildings remote from most others on the airfield. It was like a huge green dustbin, filling our capacious bomb bays. Its code name may well be still classified, and the Official Secrets Act may thus still apply. It is safe to reveal, however, that it was handled not by RAF armourers, but by white-coated boffins from the Atomic Weapons Research Establishment, later to become infamous as Aldermaston. They hauled it into position and fiddled with thickets of cables and gizmoid linkages. They then left us to practise the arming and release procedures in the air; dauntingly complex but, we were assured, to be made much simpler in the production models. A main prototype safety device, allegorical as I thought, was a huge quantity of stainless steel balls protecting the core mechanism from damage or inadvertent release. Their use chimed with the RAF testicular slang term for a technical cock-up: a 'Hoffmans', after the famous firm that made ball bearings for a variety of aircraft.

We continued to strive assiduously for accuracy in our radar-assessed bombing runs. I had, however, come across an estimate in Singapore of the probable area of destruction of a Soviet weapon of the same order of yield as our own. A hit on London, it indicated, would devastate a circular area with a radius extending to Preston (North End, I surmised in a marginal note meant to leaven the awesome solemnity of the study): Preston North is, of course, a well-known football club. The estimate seemed to make errors of the sort we were used to inconsequential, and our efforts to minimise them nugatory. They became a chore.

Not so another form of practice. Fighter affiliation required protracted flying, straight and level, at heights that suited the fighters using the time-hallowed technique of quarter attacks, curving inwards from the flanks until they were directly astern and affording them as long a period as possible for aiming and releasing their missiles. Such were the Vulcan's performance and manoeuvrability, however, that we were relieved from boredom by a reversal of roles. The fighters did the straight level, that is, and we did the attacking. This game, much enjoyed by all concerned, ended when one of the Javelin fighter station commanders felt it demeaning and bad for pilot morale for a huge aircraft to simulate their role and occasionally to outperform them. That pompous notion originated, unsurprisingly to some, from Group Captain, as he now was, Christopher Foxley Norris.

Immune from such challenges were practice emergencies in cooperation with the Master Diversion Airfields of which my former perch at Waddington was one. An incident that happened in reality from time to time, particularly in Meteors and Canberras, was the practice engine failure known as flame-out. The MDAs' technique for getting single and double flame-out victims down safely was well practised. Thinking that my friends there might like a change, I electrified Waddington control one night by asking, I think for the first time, for assistance with a practice quadruple flame-out. I could picture what was transpiring in the control tower during the brief silence, after which the situation received the calm and efficient treatment I had hoped for as we drifted downwards with four engines throttled back. Though remote, the possibility was not entirely incredible. And trying it out in the flight simulator had shown that the Vulcan was not a bad glider. Survival with no engines would thus have been at least possible. What, tragically, was beyond redemption was the gross electrical failure which caused a freezing of the controls and a fatal dive by an aircraft from another squadron on a liaison visit to the USA. The accident led to extensive modification of the Vulcan electrical system, said to have been powerful enough to light a small town. Mechanical failure, however, was an even rarer cause of accidents in the Vulcan than it was in other aircraft. The common bugbear of pilot error prevailed. One sad instance which illustrated the gossamer boundary between success and disaster was that of Squadron Leader Tony Smailes, a friend and RAF rugger player from another squadron, whose Vulcan clipped a small obstruction short of a runway in New Zealand. The aircraft was a complete wreck. He was so upset that he left the RAF. I thought of the naval tale of the captain of the destroyer escort of an aircraft carrier who crashed his ship, at night in mid-Atlantic, into the carrier's side and sheered away. The infuriated carrier captain signalled,

What are your intentions?

receiving the reply:

190

I'm going to buy a farm.

Frank Dodd had obliged by renewing my Instrument Rating Examiner qualification on the Vulcan. The tests I was thereby qualified to conduct were a good way of keeping up standards and supervising the captains without prolonged sittings in second pilots' seats with a virtual clipboard. Each had to include 'recovery from unusual positions', which required the examiner to throw the aircraft about, finishing in some awkward posture. The candidate, whom one hoped would have been disoriented as he would have been in a real upset, had then to restore the aircraft to an even keel solely by the use of instruments, plus such seat-of-the-pants ability as he might possess. Trying to do that, one second pilot made what the trade calls opposite corrections, thereby making matters worse. Having come to the rescue too late, I could not prevent our speed in a dive from exceeding Mach 0.87 (M1.0 being, of course, the speed of sound or sound barrier), the former being the Vulcan's limit. Fearful that I had made the aircraft unfit for use by overstressing it, I used the Old Boy system – for once, as I thought, justified. I rang up Mike Harrison, a friend from Charterhouse days and assistant chief test pilot at A.V. Roe, makers of the Vulcan. He reassured me with the news that 0.87 was a limit imposed by the RAF. Avro were confident that their aircraft could withstand a much higher figure. My bacon, not to mention my job, was safe. *Floreat aeternum Carthusiana* network.

One of my later instrument rating candidates was Gus Walker himself. His one-armed instrument flying in the Vulcan was as good as it was in the Canberra, the other aircraft in his group. I was relieved to be able to give him, in good conscience, a rating which he used no doubt for the self-promotion at which he was so adept. I also made myself useful keeping pilots with single-engined experience in practice in the runabout Chipmunk trainer, in which I also did part of the job of giving the local Air Cadet members air experience. Waddington continued to favour me with the loan of their Anson for more weekend visits to Thorney Island for take-outs from Ardingly. I was always grateful to the wing commander flying there for never asking why an experienced Vulcan pilot was as much in need as I seemed to be of weekend Anson navigation and sometimes GCA practice at his airfield.

The arrival at Finningley of a second squadron made life more interesting. It was the old-established No. 83, equipped with Valiant four jet bombers, the first and least satisfactory component of the V-force. But a Valiant had the distinction of having dropped the prototype British nuclear bomb at Christmas Island in the Pacific; a doubtful achievement, perhaps, because the radioactive fallout did terrible harm to the people on the ground, some in trouble for years afterwards. The dropper, incidentally, was Squadron Leader Arthur Steele, a former associate as an examiner at CFS. The risk at Finningley was of jealousy-based disharmony between the two squadrons. I was lucky to start a good relationship when, returning from an air test, I came across a stray Valiant, short of fuel and too low to use its many location devices to find the airfield. I earned blueie points for 101 by shepherding it home.

The squadron commander, Wing Commander Derek Roe, was duly appreciative and we made friends when he and Elseretta, a glamorous young Norwegian, moved into the house next door. Unlike the career men who held the much sought-after posts of V-force squadron commanders, he had no long-term interest in the RAF: his passion being boats, one of which he kept in the south of France. His disinterest was just as well, because Elseretta turned out not to be his wife, exposing him to a range of charges including fraudulent occupation of a married quarter. In a reminder for me of the Black Velvet Christmas Eve, Derek and his lady spent most of a day drinking in the Mess bar, finishing only when, responding to a tip-off, I found a tipsy Elseretta with her blouse off and about to divest herself of her skirt; and Derek being, as his shipmates would have said, half seas over. I persuaded them that it might be a good idea to continue the party at their house which, trailed by a salivating entourage, they did. Once again I shrank from a shopping: not that it mattered, because before long he left, with official propulsion, for France and a boat hire business.

As my tour neared its end, two events interacted to fuel my doubts. First came an official visit from a junior minister from what was still the Air Ministry, called Orr-Ewing, later Lord of that ilk. After seeing round the elaborate Operations Room for supervising Finningley's part of a nuclear strike, the spacious new crew dressing rooms and the showers, he addressed all the air crews in the briefing hall. He praised the labours that had made us operational. He exulted in the prestige that came from Britain's having a nuclear strike force of her own, and thanked us for our part in creating it. He stressed that we were just in time, leaving us in no doubt that, at the drop of a hat, we could be on our way to deal with the looming Soviet nuclear threat to our country. Such was his gung-ho nationalism that he seemed blind to the realities of what the consequences of a nuclear strike and retaliation could be. He also seemed in denial of the nuclear pawn in the deterrent game that Britain was. Uncurling my toes, I helped to usher him back to political cloud cuckoo land.

Following that occasion came a revelation from Paddy Finch, our row over the snowy runway long forgotten. The Orr-Ewing visits to us and the other V-Force stations, he knew from on high, had to do with a forthcoming statement in the House of Commons. The terrible delays in bringing the V-Force into being had generated political pressure for a ministerial assurance that the British Nuclear Deterrent was ready for action. *Domestic politics, not the Soviet Union, had created the urgency.* We were victims of a fraud. Silly me, I thought, for thinking we were serving the country. And if there was no urgency for the Deterrent, did we really need it at all?

Coincident with that denouement was a period deficient of enough to occupy my, as always, bookish mind. It needed something to bite on: perhaps, I thought, a qualification that would do as an adornment if I stayed in the RAF and come in handy if I left. I remembered that the only residual benefit of my father's having made me take the Edinburgh First MB was the matriculation to London University that came with it. I asked the registrar whether I could change from medicine (long abandoned) to law. The answer was yes. With the support of the admirable RAF education service and the Metropolitan College of Law, I embarked on a correspondence course for the external degree of Bachelor of Laws. It was slow, absorbing, intellectual pabulum that kept me going for years. Not least on long Vulcan trips when I used case reports written on cards to prepare for the practice exams which I took periodically for the Metropolitan College to correct.

There were still sources of delight. One was a seductive affair with the Victor via another squadron commander, Wing Commander Mike Beetham. Our joint project chimed neatly with a game played after dinner by opposing teams on the Mess carpet. The protagonist, lying blindfold and armed with a rolled-up newspaper, would try to locate and swipe the antagonist, relying solely on the answer 'Yes' to the question, 'Are you there Moriarty?' a successful hit scoring a point and leading to a reversal of roles. For Mike and myself the carpet was an area of the Atlantic Ocean and the newspaper a V-Bomber – his a Victor, mine a Vulcan. In what were very early trials of how to effect long-range interceptions for flight refuelling, we established that getting close enough to put short-range location equipment to use was not unduly difficult: our repetitions of the question being, as we hoped, a source of mystification to transatlantic air traffic controllers unfamiliar with RAF quirks. Mike deservedly ascended to the highest rank, now no longer conferred, of Marshal of the Royal Air Force.

Our final burst of activity as a crew was to get as much practice as possible for the forthcoming Bomber Command bombing competition.

The year before we had come nowhere, not because of any shortcoming of the rest of the crew, but rather from my own enforced neglect. Worse still, we had not been selected to compete in the Bomber Command contest with Strategic Air Command at Orlando, Florida. Determined to do better this time I somehow fitted in a lot of practice. In the competition we came, to our delight, eighth out of the 200-plus competing crews. Our errors were 310, 50 and 210 yards for the first three 'bombs'; but the fourth was 7 miles off because of a technical fault. But for that we might well have won. We had by now been classified in the coveted 'Select Star' category and so could be proud of ourselves. I left elated by the superb flying experience of the previous two years. But I was cast down by the dishonesty of the politicians, amounting, as I saw it, to falsification to the point of forgery.

The ghost of having been specially picked haunted my next appointment. It was to the Directing Staff (DS) of the Joint Services Staff College (JSSC). This middle-ranking establishment, a stepping stone for some to the Imperial Defence College for the very senior, was sited in a grand, rather than stately country house in the hamlet of Latimer, near Chesham. Its object was to familiarise students with the other Services, the higher direction of Defence and Britain's strategic place in the world, thereby fitting them for joint staff posts. The clientele included Commonwealth and American officers. One of the former whom I welcomed particularly was a Canadian wing commander, Al Mackie, having as another similarity to me a transport background in the RCAF. We both contemplated with amused anticipation the oddities and confusions that might follow. They did, but not quite as foreseen. Al was discovered with a Women's Royal Army Corps private in his bedroom, trying to hide her, unclothed, in his wardrobe. The Canadian High Commission did not take kindly to the incident and within hours he was on his way home. For a time, victim of the rumour mill that said I was the culprit, I got praise for a sporting initiative and blame for a disgusting misdemeanour in roughly equal measure.

I had joined the DS without having to do the course; not unique in college history but highly unusual. My worry about not being up to my job soon faded. I found no difficulty in getting on or keeping up with the rest of the faculty; and with the students, some brighter than their mentors. The visiting lecturers were much better than they had been at Bracknell, as were most of the exercises and all visits. Well behind Bracknell, however, was the tempo, which was irritatingly slow. Paradoxically the worst constraint was the grating and inhibiting inter-Service pseudo-bonhomie.

So anxious were we all to appear 'joint' as the term of art was, that such challenging of one Service by another as there was seemed half-hearted. To the collective anxiety not to rock the boat of jointery was added pressure to toe the party line. At plenary sessions in particular I found the same easily perceived orthodoxy for the sake of subliminal self-promotion that had obtained, much more justifiably, at the RAF Selection Board and the single-Service staff college. I was far from guiltless myself. But I did get a reputation as a blurter, perhaps because there was, at the back of my mind, part of a D.H. Lawrence poem:

Fight your little fight, my boy
Fight and be a man.
Don't be a good little, good little boy,
Being as good as you can
And agreeing with all the mealy mouthed, mealy mouthed
Truths that the sly trot out
To protect themselves and their greedy-mouthed, greedy-mouthed
Cowardice, every old lout.

My self-importance vied, as I now see, with my self-satisfaction.

One remarkable figure was the commandant, Air Vice-Marshal Sir Laurence Sinclair: gifted, percipient and almost a professional commandant because of the number of other establishments over which he had presided. He would certainly have gone far but for the allegation that he had blotted his copy book when he was Commander-in-Chief in Aden by cavorting in public with a squadron leader's wife. His wisdom in Defence affairs was lost when he retired to run the United Kingdom Air Traffic Control Service. The Services took it in turns to provide commandants and his successor was Vice-Admiral Jack Scatchard, known inappropriately as Jolly Jack, whose reign was as placid as his contribution to Defence thought was unremarkable. Dutifully, he asked the staff and their wives to dinner; ending the evenings with parlour games, second only in their awfulness to the showing of slides. On one cold evening Rachel and I, with other guests, were bracing ourselves for the post-prandial ordeal of three-dimensional noughts and crosses, played on a plastic gizmo. As we were about to start, the large and ancient Scatchard dog came to the rescue with a fart so suffocatingly malodorous that there was nothing for it but to abandon ship. Seldom can an apology have been accepted with such alacrity as was Jack's. The dog should have had a rosette: appropriately positioned, of course.

We were glad to get home early to the small house in the walled garden that we had accepted in preference to the standard married quarters because the rent was less. It suited us admirably, as did Latimer's location, not unduly far from Ardingly and Rachel's beloved west country.

Scatchard's deputy, appointed on a Buggins' Turn basis from the longest serving four-stripe senior DS member was Group Captain Nick Carter, formerly air attaché to the Lebanon and said to have answered their request for a classical motto for the Lebanese air force crest with the 'Nil Illegitimi Carborundum' of my Bracknell address. He was engaging, studious, funny and a member of the very select circle of writers on military affairs, ideally suited to the job. He was soon promoted and left, to be replaced by the agreeable Hugh Disney, not so suited. The other bright star was Rex Whitworth, a bright, intellectual Guards colonel; he exemplified the leaven said to be mixed into the brave but not very bright lumpen hierarchy of the Brigade. As we departed for one of our three-day weekends he, fond of awful jokes, was heard to quote from a hymn (A&M 545):

Fading is the world's best pleasure.

The senior sailor, Captain Bailey, was on the point of retiring; or, as he put it, choking with unshared emotion when the day came, 'striking my pennant'. During one of what I thought were the really important tutorial discussions, on nuclear warfare and the so-called British Independent Deterrent then due to be transferred from the V-Force to submarines, he came out against it. His reasoning was pragmatic: he and other submariners, he thought, would not fancy being hove-to off the North Cape for months at a time: that, for him, was clinching and conclusive. His successor was Captain Bromley Martin, a little more intelligent but the butt of the lower orders' habit of nicknaming: the 'Bromley', in his case, giving place to 'Remy'. I thought of his colleague in Singapore, Commodore Norfolk, whose unfortunate wife I named 'The Norfolk Broad'.

Some of the rest of us were less well 'identified', as I had known it at the RAF Selection Board with our respective Services. A soldier, the delightful Lieutenant Colonel the Lord ('Reggie') Lydford thought of little other than getting back to his West Country farm. A fellow Colonel, C. Douglas Gill, spent his ample spare time writing a book about stocks and shares, full-time dealing in which he intended to take up as soon as he could leave the Army. An airman colleague, impatient with his job, looked forward to running the steam laundry in Norfolk which he had inherited. And there was me: deceived, as I thought, in my Vulcan days and suspicious of the JSSC and all its works.

That attitude I overdid, losing me blueie points and making it hard to get what I said taken seriously. I railed particularly against the use of DS to micro-plan an exercise involving an airborne and air-transported assault on part of the Arabian peninsula, aptly named Hotpoint by Rex Whitworth. Another RAF DS member with whom I had served before ran true to form, cooing his approval and doing the fiddly, time-wasting job correctly. I, disapproving and surly, did mine carelessly and wrongly. I thought of A.A. Milne's two bears. Good Bear, blast him, was immaculate. But:

> Bad Bear's nickerties were terribly tore.

Good Bear, by agreeing throughout his career with all the right people, rose to Air Chief Marshal rank and did a prominent civilian job before the cancer that killed his much-tried wife did for him as well. Bad Bear used the excellent college library to delve more deeply into the strategy underpinning the case for a British nuclear deterrent. Most of the maps used to put that case, I saw, were Mercator depictions of the world laid flat, distorting the northern and southern extremities by enlargement. The result was a Britain literally writ large; about the same size as India, for instance, instead of the true size ratio of about 1:6. Another distortion was to depict Britain as poised between the two great land masses of America and Euro-Asia, instead of the small offshore island of Europe that it actually is. The two distortions together fostered the illusion of Britain's greatness and importance; just the vote-getting nostrum that an electorate whose pride had been hurt by the loss of an empire and post-war economic decline would lap up. Churchill, in the 1946 speech at Fulton, Missouri, had invented the Cold War. From this flowed the notion that the Soviet Union was on the march and that their hordes might cross the Channel at any moment. How better could Britain regain her standing and prestige than by guarding her shores, buttressed by the atomic weapon which we had invented but had to hand over to America to develop? Perish the thought, the nuclear lore seemed to proclaim, that the Soviet empire felt no less threatened than its American and later NATO opponent. And never let it be disclosed that Britain's Bomb, far from being a deterrent, fostered the very threat it was supposed to forfend.

There were no opportunities of discussing such issues. It was accepted as axiomatic that Britain's forces should remain much as they had been in the glory days of Empire, except for being smaller. The Army, bristling with main battle tanks, must be ready to fight a major land and air battle in Europe that could never happen again. The Royal Navy must attempt the diversity of tasks it had embraced when we were a world naval power. The RAF must be ready to re-fight the Battle of Britain. Above all Britain must continue the obeisance to the USA that had begun when we depended on American sustenance to survive World War Two; now, paradoxically, even more vital because, without American maintenance and navigation aids, our so-called independent nuclear totem could not operate. Instead of considering such issues and even contributing to their resolution, discussions were almost always confined to patsy questions and, as Wordsworth called them:

old, unhappy, far-off things, and battles long ago,

such as an extensive analysis, complete with a lecture room-sized relief map, of the German invasion of Norway in 1940.

Strolling home after each short day's work, I found myself wondering about the value of this leisurely talking shop which could, with sufficient rich productive mess of argument, have made a constructive addition to Defence thought. Instead, constricted by another form of politics, what it did was not so much a forgery of the Vulcan kind as a masquerade. In my final summer, the walled garden a 100 yard parade of glorious multicoloured dahlias, I felt growing doubts about whether I still wanted to be part of Defence at all. For the present, however, I was moving onward and upward. Back in the Intelligence community I had so much enjoyed in the Far East, I was to join, as a group captain, the Joint Intelligence Committee Secretariat in the Cabinet Office in London. Specially, I hardly dare to repeat, picked, disillusioned by forgery and tempered, as it were, in the experiential forge.

Chapter 10

Chairborne, Careworn, Airborne

Emerging like Pooter from his suburban nest, and feeling every bit as much of a Nobody, I crossed Westminster Bridge on my first morning and my cheap new bowler hat flew into the Thames. 'Oh you poor thing,' said a passing woman, but the rest of the world took no notice. The loss, I feared, could have been an allegory; though whether for raising in admiration, doffing in submission or throwing in the air I had yet to find out. Reaching the northern bank I enjoyed the inscription on the Victorian statue of Boadicea:

> Regions Caesar never knew
> Thy posterity shall sway.

Which of course it did, and later didn't, leaving us all with the misguided notion of Britain's place in the world at the root of many of our troubles.

On the previous day I had run into the unforeseen hurdle of an interview with the Secretary of State for Air, one Julian Amery, in the Ministry of Defence. Ushered into the Presence I got a glare and was then asked an inconsequential question and ushered out. His object must have been to establish that my suit fitted and that I could talk proper. His own drawl was not quite plummy: more like chucking-out time at the Carlton Club. Discourtesy among high-ups, I had found, was rare; but when I came across it the experience was etched into my memory. Not that it, or he, mattered on that glad morning, when all I had to do was find the New Government Buildings, a turn-of-the-twentieth-century block in Great George Street.

I duly found my office in the Joint Intelligence Committee (JIC) Secretariat which, as Deputy Secretary, I shared with three assistants. One was a seconded member of the Joint Intelligence Bureau which existed to know, record and collate facts. Another was a young member of MI5, the Security Service. The third, a lieutenant colonel in the Intelligence Corps, was the only other serving officer in the Cabinet Office. All three were highly competent and a delight to work with, each in charge of a segment of the committee's work. My senior was the secretary of the JIC itself, confusingly

199

ranked as an assistant secretary and thus equatable with a Naval commodore, an army brigadier and an air commodore. He was John Hunt, an archetypally chilly senior civil servant. He was, nevertheless, welcoming and soon helped me into harness. He took me to see Sir Norman Brook who was no less welcoming and much more human, making me think that meeting me had made his day. He was, as well as being secretary of (never, as I was told not to forget, *to*) the Cabinet, head of the Home Civil Service. But he took all that lightly and wanted to be seen as presiding over the familial fraternity and sorority of what was then a small concern; and not, as it was to become, a department of state on its own. I was the only four-striper (that is, colonel, captain RN or group captain) seconded member; and, in common with everybody else, free from any of the political pressures that later plagued the JIC and its servants. Alastair Campbell's scheming predecessors worked entirely separately. It was not, indeed, until one of them became my boss at the Health Education Council that I knew what they did: essentially keeping politicians supplied with the two faces and ulterior motives that make up their stock in trade.

The secretarial fraternity/sorority had been like that since the days, during World War One, when records of Cabinet meetings were first kept. The first secretary, Lord Haldane, started a book of memorable sayings of ministers. One was that of Lord Curzon, an aristocrat of an aristrocrat, during a discussion of post-war plans and procedure. Wanting to seem 'with it', as the phrase would now be, he used a word he had seen in print but never heard spoken. He said:

I suppose the common people will want some sort of a bee-arno.

I know exactly how Haldane felt as he smothered a smile and wrote it down. Perhaps he thought of the fictitious occasion when the Duke and Duchess were enjoying each other in bed: 'Do the common people do this dear?' On being assured that they did she observed, 'Well it's far too good for them.'

Such light relief seldom came our way. Our routine work was the task of being constantly ready to enable the JIC to formulate and issue advice about emergencies to the chiefs of staff, the Foreign Office or the Cabinet very quickly. The routine was such that it was a continuing rehearsal, in slower time and within working hours, of the emergency procedure. On the day before the JIC met, staff members of all the committee members' departments met in a lower-order body, the Heads of Sections. Chaired by a middle-ranking Foreign Office official, the heads would review current matters and discuss whether, and if so how much, they mattered. Having done the same sort of thing in the Far East, I knew the risks of missing the significance of small items and, as secretary of the body, built up a reputation for detecting what was important. I was also able to use my experience of the opposite tendency – that of inflating threats, not always for reputable reasons. Deflating usually meant establishing the facts for which, in the Far East, we asked the representative of the enormous Joint Intelligence Bureau in Melbourne; a classic achievement of which had been discrediting an American report of a large force of Chinese Communist heavy piston bombers threatening Singapore. The Melbourne Bureau dealt with this doctored information by pointing out that there were not enough airfields in the whole of China with runways long enough to accommodate more than the British spy-based estimate of ten. From time to time the head office in London did much the same for the JIC.

The Heads of Sections digest drafted by me and approved by the Foreign Office who always held the whip handle of the Chair went to the JIC meeting the following day. There John Hunt and I would be next to the chairman, by custom another Foreign Office official of under-secretary-ambassador rank. They looked at our review plus longer-term material written by the London Joint Intelligence Staff (JIS), grander and idler than their Far East counterparts had been in my time. When a matter came up that was within the parish of my assistants, they would creep in ready with whispered advice, information and sometimes, most agreeably, repartee.

After the meeting came minute writing, finalised by John Hunt who had a talent for making chaotic and inconclusive discussions look suave, rounded and ice-clear. The result would go, along with finalised studies and estimates to the customers, usually the secretariat of the chiefs of staff in the Ministry of Defence. Typically they would use them for writing or revising contingency plans, of which there was a vast array covering what to do and how to do it. One humble example was our very own Far East 'Seizure of a beach head on the Chinese mainland'. A major one, the biggest ever, was the plan for the D-day invasion of Europe in 1944. The range and comprehensiveness of the library of plans was such as to make it odd and perverse that so predictable an adventure as the second Iraq war should have been launched apparently devoid of an intelligence forecast of the aftermath and a plan for dealing with it.

The everyday fare, importing as it did a knowledge of all that was going on in the intelligence world, had great intrinsic interest. But the best part of my work was the people-watching. Top of my personal scrap book was the foreign secretary, at the time Alec Douglas-Home, later to become

Prime Minister. In John Hunt's absence I was summoned to brief him on an aspect of Soviet skulduggery which had figured in a JIC report. He sat at an enormous desk in the Foreign Office which looked as if it had been there since, as the RAF saying is, Pontius was a pilate. He listened, asked good questions and thanked me. Next in my line was Sir Hugh Stephenson, JIC chairman, liked by all of us who had known him in the Far East JIS for his lofty detachment from the plebeian doings in Saigon, where he had been ambassador. In one of the sheaves of telegrams which we had to sift through was a humdrum analysis from him of affairs in Viet Nam, ending with ineffable true blue detachment:

There was another explosion in the city last night but I don't yet know what it was about.

He had the high colour that would once have denoted a bottle-of-port-a-day man, and after a further ambassadorship, this time to South Africa, was said to have died of drink. But while he was with us he did an excellent job. He would certainly have seen off the poisonous attempts at playing politics with the JIC that must have done great harm after the second Iraq war.

His deputy, a duty performed in turn by the Service members, was the Director of Military Intelligence, Major General Lloyd, whose prolix schoolmarm interventions made me put him in imaginary drag. His Naval colleague was Admiral Norman Denning, who spoke seldom; but when he did he was unfailingly wise: not surprisingly because he was one of a trio of brilliant brothers – an outstanding general and a famous judge whose work I had already encountered as a law student and whom I would later meet. One secret department representative was Sir Clive Loehnis, head of Government Communications Headquarters, the nation's eavesdroppers, usually in checks and foulards as if for the races and seemingly bored. Another was Sir Christopher Hollis, very bright but later tainted with a charge of Communist leanings. The third was Sir Dick White, head of MI6, whose name was never mentioned or written other than as 'C', self-effacing and as informative and penetrating as one might have expected. The most intriguing member was Major General (retired) Sir Kenneth Strong, for many years head of JIB. He was tall, amazingly ugly, and well past his best. His main accomplishment was to speak at interminable length off the point. At one memorable meeting he forgot that, as was the custom, representatives of the American Central Intelligence Agency had joined us and spoke at the usual excessive length on a topic classified as UK Eyes Only and thus to be mentioned only in the earlier, Brits-only, session. No amount of paper rustling, fidgeting and even gesticulating could staunch the flow, and my JIB assistant whispered, 'Poor old Kenneth, his brush gets broader and broader.' It was with a mixture of relief and revelation when, afterwards, the head CIA man told us in confidence not to worry: the CIA, he assured us, knew all about it already. That confirmed what I had long suspected: that the CIA were breaking a strict US–UK convention that neither would spy upon the other. So, no doubt, were we. The incident put a gloss on the CIA's habit of generous entertainment of their British opposite numbers. Rachel and I, small fry as we were, were twice dined expensively and taken to performances at the Royal Opera House, Covent Garden.

John Hunt and I worked well enough together and he was invariably generous with his praise. But he continued to lack warmth, notably with me and my lieutenant colonel colleague. When I discovered that he had spent World War Two entirely in the Commonwealth Relations Office, I saw why. Like others with similar backgrounds whom I had met, he felt that we thought the less of him on that score – a totally mistaken idea – and was offhand as a result. Our relationship deteriorated when, on an idle afternoon, I had taken my law books away from my noisy office to the quiet of the JIC meeting room to study. An hour or so later he burst in and stared at the books and papers on the table. On seeing that they were not, as I am sure he suspected, classified papers that I was copying he beat an embarrassed retreat. He left soon afterwards, returning some years later to serve with great distinction as Secretary of the Cabinet.

The most significant figure of all was not the most senior. He was Nicholas Henderson, Chairman of the Heads of Sections. He was an archetypal Foreign Office luminary – languid, debonair and able without apparent effort to convince others of the soundness of his view. I greatly enjoyed working for and with him at his brisk and humorous meetings; and even more his lightning capacity to improve my efforts to reduce the proceedings at his meetings to a concise summation. I came to know him better when a slipped disc confined him to his house in Montpellier Square, where for some weeks I called to keep him up to date and receive his guidance. He went on to achieve the unique distinction of ambassadorships in all three plum posts – Moscow, Paris and, hauled back from retirement, Washington. It was a joy to run into him many years later, when he opposed me in a debate in the Oxford Union, of which he had, of course, been president. He was succeeded by Edward Youde, less effusive but scarcely less able, newly returned from the Embassy in Beijing, where his courage and determination in dealing with the Chinese over the detention of the Royal Naval destroyer Amethyst in the Yangtse River had enhanced his already high reputation.

As a sideline, I was secretary to the Scientific and Technical Intelligence Standing Committee, known as STISC. Like Strubby, the airfield whose name I tried to turn into a derogatory epithet, the acronym with its conflation of 'stiff' and 'brisk', would have done as an adjective for itself. The chairman was a Dr Percival Potts, learned in nuclear matters and anxious not to overstate the extent of the threats the committee dealt with, and the political pressures to do so which I am sure he faced. Though still bound by the Official Secrets Act, I can say that there was nothing in any of our assessments that in any way supported the case for a British independent deterrent.

John Hunt's successor could hardly have been more different or the change more welcome. He was John Roper, a counsellor in the Foreign Office which he had entered after war service in the Scots Guards. It only emerged after his death that his exploits under cover in the Balkans had been legendary. A big, bluff man, he did not so much arrive as burst upon the scene with a porter behind him laden with expensive-looking framed paintings. These, he told us, were surplus stock from his wife's art gallery in Paris, where he had been commercial counsellor in the Embassy. He had permission to use them in our offices as replacements for the dull, cheap prints that had hitherto hung there. They showed to great advantage.

John was less well versed in the ways of the Civil Service than his predecessor and I enjoyed supporting him as well as his breezy company. Almost at once we were rocked by the ripples from the missile crisis in Cuba involving President Kennedy and Secretary-General Krushchev. It began when John asked me to find out at once whether NATO had missiles in Turkey pointing at targets in the Soviet Union. My frantic calls to the Ministry of Defence confirmed that they did; and this piece of, as I imagined, the jigsaw of possible counter-action fell into place. There followed a flurry of lower-level meetings and then, on a Sunday, a JIC meeting. There three flustered CIA men whom we did not know briefed the committee on the now extreme confrontation, illustrating their account with satellite photographs of missiles in place in Cuba. The committee, and especially Sir Hugh, adjured the intelligence community not to drop their guard over other sources of threat that opportunists might exploit. The members left for their war dispositions, all knowing that Britain and her idiotic nuclear deterrent force might well be a first-strike Soviet target. The other staff shared my view of Britain's helplessness and the potentially catastrophic risk created by the so-called independent deterrent. We also shared the minority opinion that what had been crucial in the climb-down was not nuclear weapons but the huge American conventional forces ranged against Cuba.

Domestic life was good. The flat was pleasant despite its suburbanity. Commuting was easy and we were within easy reach of Ardingly. A snag about our property, as we thought, was a set of semi-derelict garages in a corner of the estate on which the freeholders, the huge property firm Freshwaters, were proposing to build yet another block of flats to add to the warren. We were desperate to prevent what we thought would wreck the estate. With gross impropriety I wrote to Freshwater on Cabinet Office headed paper asking them to change their minds. I was at once invited to their offices in Bloomsbury by a Mr Stern, later to break the world record for the size of his bankruptcy. He convinced me with plans and drawings that what was proposed was as much for our benefit as leaseholders as it was for theirs, assuring me that it would put up the value of the whole estate. It did.

The Ropers, highly social beings, soon asked us to their huge rented flat in Charles Street, Mayfair. How a counsellor (equivalent to commodore, brigadier or air commodore) could afford such an expensive dwelling soon emerged. His wife had been a Miss Roebuck of Sears Roebuck, the giant American mail order firm. Anything they needed was flown to them by the firm, and it was her father who had bought her the art gallery to keep her amused in Paris. Midas-like, he had sold it at a big profit. They were a knockabout couple, both hot tempered as their shouted telephone brawls, audible in the offices adjoining his, made embarrassingly evident. But they were both charming and companionable. John eventually left the Cabinet Office for the ambassadorship in Luxembourg, regarded by the gossips as highly suitable for a gifted but lethargic man. Years later he paid me the compliment of congratulating me on my work in the peace movement.

Meanwhile the stimulus of my job waned, as it seemed to have done for my other ground occupations. I seemed hopelessly remote from flying; and having for the first time in 20 years got out of practice, felt the anxiety which I had felt occasionally over the years coming back. Would I, I wondered, be up to returning to high-performance jets; and did I feel able to run the V-bomber station that I was likely to be sent to? Another element was the contempt for British nuclear weapon policy that had grown so much in the light of my JIC experience and the opinions of bright, knowledgeable colleagues. Yet another was the delight of a settled base in which our sons could flourish, if only we could afford to keep it going. We could not.

The problem was solved as if providentially. After a refresher flying course on the piston-engined Varsity, with which I was already familiar, I was to command a two-squadron station of Hastings four-engined transports, the oldest operational aircraft in the RAF. My relief at such an easy flying option, the absence of any conscience-searing armament and a return to the familiar airborne assault role was inexpressible. The station was Colerne near Bath, a beautiful part of the West Country and even more convenient for Rachel's family home in Glastonbury.

On leaving the Cabinet Office I was ushered in to the office of Sir Burke Trend, the new Secretary of the Cabinet, to be thanked. In a sort of abbreviated fireside chat, he seemed genuinely grateful and went on to tell me of his unease that public affairs seemed to him to be on an irreversible downward slide. That view, I thought, was part of widespread disillusion about such affairs caused by the disgrace of a cabinet minister, John Profumo. He had shamed the Macmillan Government by cavorting with *soi-disant* upper-class degenerates and a whore. Such conduct would of course be shrugged off by this century's standards, but at the time it was said to have caused Macmillan such shame and distress that he was for a time clinically depressed. I agreed with Trend, marvelling that both he and Norman Brook, both very busy men, had respectively welcomed and said farewell to a minor functionary: a revealing contrast with the odious Amery who had initially vetted me.

Six weeks bumbling around in the Varsity, tame and staid as it was, I found as refreshing as it was refresher. There followed a longer course on the Hastings, which had a reputation for being difficult to fly. That I found to be so; but its main vice of swinging on landing had also been true of the Harvard. The art of prevention was the same on both: never giving the swing a chance to start in the first place. I never let it happen until a year or so later at Colerne during an experience trip with David, our elder son and then an Oxford University Air Squadron cadet. Such was my flow of parental expatiation that I forgot to keep straight with the rudder. We ambled across the grass, fortunately firm, from which we were delivered ignominiously by tractor.

The Hastings course was at Thorney Island, the pleasant coastal station which had come in useful for school outings from nearby Ardingly. As a group captain I at first found myself being treated as a slight joke. Unlike more junior aircrew mortals, station commanders were not expected to be more than acquainted with their aircraft, a little light practice sufficing to fit them for dilettante participation in their stations' flying tasks: Thorney's commander, it seemed, being a case in point. I would have none of that, setting about qualifying for parachutist and supply-dropping like everybody else; and, as soon as I had the Hastings flying hours required, acquiring a passenger-carrying category.

RAF Colerne was run down. Even our house-to-be lacked the improvements to which station commanders were entitled. The runways, hangars and workshops were adequate but much needed doing for the 1,800-odd airmen, their families and the other Service families, many with no man, on two large RAF residential sites at nearby Pucklechurch which were part of the Colerne estate. The need was for energy and push from the top, which had not been forthcoming from my predecessor. He was a passed-over former fighter pilot who had jogged along, highly sociable and much liked. His hobby had been a land yacht, a large wheeled contraption with a mast and sails in which, when there was no flying, he had cruised the runways on his own. His other fancy, made in the workshops, was a train of trucks like those provided at seaside places, which had ferried guests, suitably fortified, from his house to the officers' mess when there were parties.

Hoping to start with a bit of éclat, I borrowed a Meteor from the Central Flying School, to be greeted on landing by a reception party, suitably impressed, I hoped, by a jet-qualified boss. My predecessor briefed me about our superiors. The group commander was Air Vice-Marshal Leslie 'Duke' Mavor, unexpectedly successful after a bit of trouble at the Bomber Command station at Lindholme of which he had been administrator; a sardonic, humorous Scot who was supportive from his headquarters at Odiham. Above him in what some saw as the ogre's castle at Upavon was the Commander-in-Chief, Air Marshal Sir Kenneth 'Bing' Cross. He was unpopular and much feared because of his ruthlessness and bouts of temper; contributed to, perhaps, by the ordeal of flying Hurricane fighters from aircraft carriers early in World War Two in a desperate attempt to help newly conquered Norway, during which he had flown with great bravery. Rachel and I found ourselves thrust into his company almost at once at a Bath rugger club ball to which the local establishment had invited us. He was as uncivil as his wife Brenda was charming.

Under me at Colerne was a mixed company. The two squadron commanders were Tom Saunders and Bill Dodimead, both solid air crew operators. The chief engineer officer was highly qualified but had served mostly in staff posts and had about him an other-worldliness that seemed inappropriate to the 18 elderly Hastings aircraft in his charge; and even more so to dealing with the airmen looking after them. Many of the squadron air crews had done little other than fly Hastings, and were understandably set in their ways. Most of our overseas scheduled and special flights were routed across France and I was concerned at the high rates of cancellations and premature returns because of perceived unflyable

Hastings transports on a veterans' parade. *Author*

weather over the high ground of the Massif Central on the way. I took the first chance to do a trip myself on a day when the cloud tops were forecast to exceed 20,000 feet, 2,000 feet or so above our usual operating height. My navigator, a senior old transport sweat, was clearly uneasy and his satisfaction was barely concealed when, in severe turbulence and icing cloud, hailstones shattered the plastic dome used for astro navigation. Responding to his bolshily professed doubts about where we were after a long time in cloud, I made use of the self-navigating pilots' friend, a radio beacon near Tripoli. The trip, I hoped, would leaven the lump of reluctance of other old sweats and bolster the notion of a hands-on leader.

Most of my time went on station affairs. The bedrock of morale was good food, and we were lucky to have a catering officer promoted from the ranks as a cook, well versed in all the wrinkles. I often visited the dining halls at meal times, occasionally donning a white overall and encouraging the giving of larger helpings. Scarcely less important was the NAAFI, ready for reopening after being refurbished. I was the first bar customer, downing a pint using the old trick of a throat-opened swallow and earning Blueie points from the airmen and the local press. We gave a reopening concert starring, in her earliest days, the singer Lulu who at the time was backed by three dreadful youths called the Luvvers. Later on *The Times* music critic described her with his usual acuity as possessed of a

208

Excess of enthusiasm in the reopened NAAFI canteen. *Anon*

built-in foghorn. Another musical venture that went down well to which I gave greatly increased support was the small, struggling amateur brass band fostered by an enterprising sergeant. It soon flourished and, by eliminating the need to import one of the RAF regional bands for ceremonial occasions, was a big plus for the station.

Raising a different kind of morale was the revival of the station gliding club, the Bannerdown, which had been largely denied its weekend freedom by the monopolising of the airfield at weekends by my predecessor's land yacht. Reviving my neglected skill as a gliding instructor, I reinforced the junior officer who had somehow kept it going; and we gradually recruited other air crews and even a few wives, to have a go in our T21 trainer. We also had two Baby Grunau high-performance solo models and a pilot of championship quality. The direct benefit was slight; but there in the sky was an outward and visible sign of things happening.

Less susceptible to improvement was the perennial problem of aircraft noise over Bath, unavoidable because the city lay below our aircraft circuit zone. 'Disgusted' was seldom out of the local paper's letters page, and official explanations and a sympathetic ear at the end of a special telephone did little good. The best I could do was to invite the local MPs, Sir James Brown of Bath, Daniel Awdry of Chippenham and Paul Dean of Wiltshire, to fly round in a Hastings with me and have the problem pointed out. This they duly did, with much publicity and an excellent lunch, disposing them to accept that putting up with the noise was part repayment of the debt to the brave boys in blue. The effect, as Boccaccio said of true love, lasted about as long as the singing of the birds.

There were soon rumblings from the Ogre's castle to which, like Childe Harold to the Dark Tower, I came. Sir Bing was furious because, he alleged, I had ignored his injunction to me to look after the Air Training Corps unit at his old school Kingswood, near Bristol. Having expected and got ready for an outcry, I told him that three officers, myself included, had given the boys lectures; that they had used enough ammunition on their shooting range to meet the training needs of 120 airmen for a year; and that some 200 miles of RAF transport had been used illicitly on their behalf. Mollified, he told me to do something about our awful officers' mess.

I did. Using the talents and enthusiasm of a bright administrator with design flair, we spent the small refurbishment funds on wide timber friezes at curtain height round the walls of the public rooms, replacing the institutional green and brown with bold and unusual colours. With new carpets and minor embellishments, the effect was dramatic and widely admired; not least by Sir Bing, who took to bringing small parties of retired cronies to supper from time to time.

I arranged for more of the funds that should have been used for maintenance to be spent on improving the churches. The Anglicans had a literal and metaphorical barn, wartime architecture at its dreary worst, and the Methodists a glorified hut. On the initiative of our vigorous and ingenious Church of England chaplain Peter Grimwood and his Methodist colleague we tidied them both up. Peter found a local plastic moulding factory capable of large-scale works. They made us a blue fibreglass tower about 15 feet high. Welcoming the job and the attendant publicity, the helicopter squadron at Odiham collected and lowered it onto a prepared site on the church roof. The result was a triumph for Peter, a boost for the congregation, and a further success at putting Colerne on the map.

The same object was served by the annual Battle of Britain display and open days that took place annually in September at bases near centres of population. Months of preparation went into welcoming the public in the largest possible numbers to watch aircraft perform and spend money on the ground attractions. The main image-maker was the VIP enclosure to which the Bath establishment and other local big shots expected invitations. Theirs was the most favoured viewing point near the aircraft control tower, part of which housed a champagne bar and buffet. Also worth watching, by us as hosts, was the assembly of the grandees. One was the self-effacing Duke of Newcastle, owner of a Georgian stately home at the foot of our hill, and never known to complain of the aircraft noise which he must have suffered there. Also present was another peer, a young man anxious to get hold of an RAF physical training instructor from the Station for what I gathered were philanthropic purposes, as it were, who had difficulty in taking no for an answer. There were mayors from Bath and Bristol and the colourful chief constable of the former. He had been a sergeant pilot and had a Distinguished Flying Medal. He was given, during his frequent visits for refreshment to our officers' mess, to haranguing anybody who would listen about fast-driving RAF transport on the main road into the city. Soon after raising it yet again with me, he was rendered apoplectic on his way home at 30 m.p.h. when our largest crane, summoned urgently by his deputy, tore past him at its maximum of 50. When he saw it in use for the rescue of an injured driver stuck in his car under the railway bridge in the city centre, his mood changed from 'down with Colerne' to 'drinks all round'.

Our most picturesque grandee was Lord Long of Wraxall, an ancient widower and, as he was fond of telling his listeners, grandson of the politician George Canning (fortunately the question 'Who he?' had yet to be invented). He arrived in a fine old Rolls-Royce landau, decked out in houndstooth check and a bowler, lording it, as it were over the company. He had great old-world charm and Rachel and I got to know him better. We were invited to his large run-down house in Wraxall village, staffed by one old ex-nanny turned housekeeper, and there were signs of neglect all round. The meal, high tea, followed my taking the salute at the march-past of the Wraxall branch of the Royal British Legion (commanding officer Lord Long), and shouting my stirring address to the troops drawn up on the other side of a main road. We then repaired to the Long Arms where he pushed the rest of the clientele aside so that the Quality could be served.

The combined effect of the revival and refurbishments at Colerne brought about a palpable improvement. I had given much less time to flying than I would have liked, which was as well because it had prevented me from getting in the squadron commanders' way. But I did do a representative selection of our overseas trips. I ferried many people to and from overseas postings including Dickie Wakeford and his family whom we had known so well, to Singapore along the well-flown routes to the Middle and Far East. One destination new to me was Khormaksar, airfield for the colony and protectorate of Aden, where I found myself stopping over on the day of Winston Churchill's death. That event, long planned for and kept constantly ready to implement by a one-star general specially appointed for the task, was code-named 'Hope Not', expressing every incumbent's desire that it would not manifest itself on his watch. The plan drew on almost every Service unit in the UK, Colerne's quota being four smart airmen whom we kept earmarked. After the death there was the usual flood of mawkish lament in the media. One exception that appealed to me came surprisingly from the *Daily Mail*, then as now not known for its literary merit:

> So fades a summer cloud away,
> So stills the wind when storm is o'er,
> So gently shuts the eye of day,
> So dies the wave upon a shore.
> The rest is come.

The authorship of which I never discovered. Most of us with wartime recollections of Churchillian leadership recall a specific speech. I, at a terribly dangerous stage of my time in the bomber business, appreciated his tribute to bomber crews, uttered to complement his famous aphorism about the Few. We (they) were, as he put it:

> Unwearied by their constant challenge and mortal danger.

Not true but sustaining. I was glad not to be sucked into the obsequies.

On that and other overseas trips I was irked, as were all the Colerne crews, at having to land at nearby Lyneham for Customs clearance. The station commander, Group Captain Alasdair Steedman, a friend since Cranwell, poured good-tempered scorn on the grubby old Hastings that sullied his immaculate tarmac arrival apron, meant mainly for the Shiny Ships, as the new Britannia propeller-jet transports based at his station were called. Using a base other than our own was tiring, expensive and yet another source of the unserviceability that plagued our ancient craft. (Our longest scheduled service, for the small Army detachment based at Belize, in what was still British Honduras, involved servicing by the USAF who called us the Flintstones.) All of which helped me to put a case, fought for months and in the end successful, for Customs facilities of our own at Colerne.

Suddenly in June 1965, tragedy struck the busy, prosperous and happy station that I and a lot of other devoted people had struggled to create. A Hastings full of trainee parachutists who were about to do a practice jump near the neighbouring RAF base at Abingdon had nosedived into the ground and killed all aboard. By far the worst aspect was of course the human tragedy, and my colleague the Abingdon station commander had to bear the worst consequences such as dealing with the bodies, clearing the wreckage, and a deluge of admin. We, however, had our share, and the first job was to tell the families. Collecting Rachel and the chaplain Peter Grimwood, I toured the married quarters of all who were based at or near Colerne, breaking the news. All the wives except one accepted it with the most moving dignity and calm. For all the stricken families there was massive and immediate support from the close community of RAF neighbours. The exception from the fortitude shown by everybody else was the captain's widow whose paroxysmal reaction called for extra support, which she got. The profundity of her grief could but surprise her friends, who had known the couple as eternally quarrelsome. She later married the local vicar who, it was thought, had somewhat extrapolated the comforting process. The funeral procession at Abingdon was headed by the station commander and me, flanking Sir Bing. All three of us had our best blue uniforms deluged in the pouring rain and were pleasantly surprised that the air blue barathea, to give the material its proper title, dried out undamaged.

The vital job of discovering the cause was soon done. It was the failure, through metal fatigue, of the four large bolts that held the tail in place. Hastings aircraft throughout the RAF, few of which were not at Colerne, were grounded and a 'retro-fit' of much stronger bolts devised. Implementing it on all aircraft would take months. Even as we completed our own share of the funerals and burials in Colerne village churchyard, I recognised the imminent morale problems that would arise on a flying station that could not fly.

They were not insuperable. The air crews were sent on initiative exercises to see who could get the furthest without having to pay for transport: one enterprising young man finished up in South America. There was much make-and-mend to be done and the sub-inspections preceding Duke Mavor's second and inevitably meticulous inspection were looming. The small initial training unit for would-be RAF Regiment parachutists carried on. I could give more attention to the detached family housing sites under my jurisdiction, coming across on an inspection a phenomenon not seen before even by the highly experienced maintenance staff: one problem family, bereft of fuel and having squandered their welfare payments, had sawn up the stairs for fuel and were living on the ground floor of their house.

Another diversion gave me a glimpse of how useful my slowly growing grasp of criminal law might come in. A flight engineer officer asked of his batwoman a service well outside the normal run. Such was the young lady's embarrassment when, with her mother present, I asked what had happened she could only bring herself to describe the object of her attentions as 'his carrot'. I told her that, if she went to court, her evidence would have to include detailed anatomical and physiological descriptions of what she saw and did. She would, I explained, have her own sex life minutely explored during cross-examination and would be accused of provocation. I assured her that I had powers (under Queen's Regulation 1154 as it then was) tough enough to deter any repetition and diminish her abuser's chances of promo-

Keeping busy while the Hastings were grounded. Our two sons enjoyed dual in the Chipmunk.
Anon

214

tion and would use them to the full. She decided not to proceed and I kept a useful officer and saved much adverse publicity.

From the flying standpoint I was one of the lucky ones, using my instructing skill not only in the gliding club but also with cadets including our two sons in the station Chipmunk, which worked overtime with pilot refresher and experience flights. A small museum of aircraft originated by the last station commander but one got a major brush-up and I was able to add a Valetta to its complement. All in all, spirits remained high. In a reply to a signal to all stations in the group asking for the useless information that seemed so important to the staff, I ended with:

Our tails may be off but they're still up.

Earning, I gathered, approbation from Messrs Duke and Bing.

Unctuous joke in return for a compliment from a senior staff officer.... *Crown Copyright/MOD*

About to test the first re-tailed Hastings. *Bath Evening Chronicle*

The technical outcome did not reflect well on the chief technical officer, who had caused me concern from the first, and I was relieved when the tortuous removal procedure that I had initiated months before finally worked. He had, it emerged, failed to act on a file note by a junior engineering officer recommending a check on the very bolts that had failed. He returned to the staff work in which he excelled, to be replaced by a tough, engaging Welsh ex-airman whose rise to wing commander had happened mostly on stations and who knew everything about the Hastings.

The awful non-flying hiatus ended when I tested, with undeserved but useful publicity, the first retro-fitted aircraft; and as we all got under way again I had another piece of luck. One of our fuel-testing airmen discovered a small shortfall in the calorific value in a consignment of fuel from Esso. The defect created a theoretical risk because the consequence would be a reduction in the range of aircraft using the fuel (though in reality the safety margins we always provided would have absorbed the deficiency). The Esso representative, anxious not to lose the supply contract to Shell, called to apologise and, over lunch, asked me to suggest a way in which

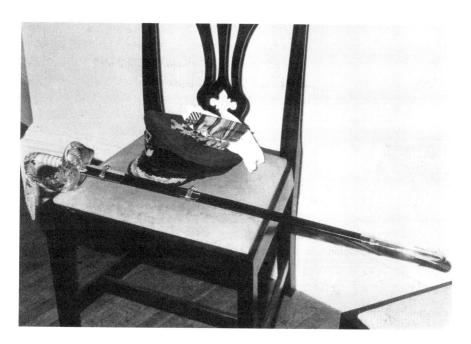

The Esso sword and other clobber in the Mayor's parlour after a march through Bath.
Crown Copyright/MOD

Esso could express their regret. I at once explained that the station commander's ceremonial sword, used for AOCs' inspections and whenever we exercised our right as Freemen of the City to march through Bath, had to be borrowed from a central store of less than immaculate weaponry. Perhaps Esso, I suggested, would care to give us one of our own. Within a day or two I went to Wilkinsons' sword company in London to get one fitted. It was a pride and joy and still rests, no doubt, in the huge reserve depot of such paraphernalia.

There followed a personal plus. I had a letter from Sir Bing asking me to try to recruit, from the 300 or so young officers on the station, more members for the RAF Club, at the time in decline. Knowing that the sole aim in life for many of our air crews, who made up the great majority of officers, was to get lucrative jobs in the crew-starved world of civil aviation, I was not optimistic. However, after months of pleading, cajoling and threatening we had achieved what I thought was a derisory result of about 25 per cent. My devoted henchman Wing Commander John Tipton, chief administrator, remarking that neither he nor I were members, pointed out that if we both joined, the Colerne percentage would rise by a few second places of decimals. That we did and I sent a tremulous reply. To our surprise Sir Bing congratulated me on doing well on a very difficult wicket. Now very different in manner, he was effusively civil when we said goodbye.

Leaving Colerne on promotion to air commodore ended a flying career of 25 years, 5,000 flying hours and 27 different kinds of aircraft. What enormous fun it had all been:

> Oh I have slipped the surly bonds of earth
> And danced the skies on laughter-silvered wings.
> Sunward I've climbed and joined the tumbling mirth
> Of sun-split clouds – and done a hundred things
> You have not dreamed of; wheeled and soared and swung
> High in the sun-lit silence. Hovering there
> I've chased the shouting wind along and flung
> My eager craft through footless halls of air
> Up, up the long delirious burning blue,
> I've topped the wind-swept heights with easy grace
> Where never lark nor even eagle flew;
> And while, with silent lifting mind I've trod
> The high untrespassed sanctity of space,
> Put out my hand and touched the face of God.

Nobody put it better than John Gillespie Magee, 1922–41, in the *RAF Journal*.

Chapter 11

Out of the Blue

Air crew opinion at RAF Thorney Island had it that flying group captains were a bit of a joke. I had done my best to scotch that idea, flying at Colerne as productively as the rest of the job of commanding a station had allowed. Flying air commodores, with one or two exceptions, really were an absurdity. True, we were supposed to keep in flying practice (the highest rank, incidentally to which the rule applied; air vice-marshals and beyond were deemed to be above such a trivial pursuit). But, having done refresher training with senior officers and finding that, for some of them, the job was like trying to turn a prune back into a plum, I dreaded becoming an airborne wrinkly and thought it best not to bother. Instead I faced the fact that I was back in Whitehall. There was no risk of losing my bowler, because Gieves had made the expensive new one I sported to fit my head. When, 34 years later, I took it back to them for reblocking and overhaul, they showed me the measuring machine, now in their museum. The hat spends its declining years as an adornment at peace movement marches and veterans' commemorative parades.

We had to hasten from our comfortable house at Colerne to make way for my successor. Fortunately my new job carried with it the right to a quarter and ours was a senior officers' model at Bushey, near Fighter Command Headquarters at Bentley Priory. The saving grace was an adjacent golf course, trespassing on which offered a semblance of country walks in the suburban wasteland. Behind our house lay a semi-circular tier of other houses on rising ground. Passing our back windows was like appearing in an amphitheatre. Taking Rachel's breakfast tray in the mornings I could feel beady eyes on me; so much so that I was tempted from time to time to play to the gallery with a commentary to go with the performance. We were thankful when we moved to a smaller but more private house at Hendon: the most famous, perhaps of all RAF stations, having been the home of the annual RAF flying display, precursor to the Farnborough display. It was a familiar destination during my Dakota days. Built to accommodate primitive biplanes, it was unpleasantly, if not dangerously, small for aircraft: when taking off in a fully loaded Dakota, for instance, it was advisable, to secure maximum air space for the initial climb, to wait until the adjoining main railway was train-free. Now closed for flying, Hendon housed the huge RAF mainframe computer and later the RAF Museum.

The tube station for commuting to central London was Colindale, and the trains were infrequent. The difficulties showed in acute form on my first morning when a young lady of limited literary attainment doggedly occupied the booking office orifice, slowly scrawling a cheque for a season ticket renewal as the queue behind her lengthened and the train drew out. My journey, when it at last began, was along the ghastly Northern Line, and the destination the Ministry of Defence, housed in half of a huge office block between Whitehall and the Thames embankment. Cuckoo-like, it had soon ousted the Board of Trade from the other half, gaining a northern entrance dominated by stone statuary of obese female nudes. MoD (RAF), the ugly acronym for the old air ministry, was my workplace.

The occupants were segregated by floor in ascending order of grandeur. Being an acolyte of the chief of air staff put me on the fifth of the seven, in a niche of an office overlooking the row of handsome Georgian houses in Richmond Terrace, overshadowed by newer monstrosities and later replaced by an arty office block. Interspersed was a stretch of tarmac used for parking the cars of the mighty, and for parades for visiting foreign potentates. At a right-angle was Whitehall. In the middle of that fine street was the Cenotaph, years later the scene of CND protests and leafletting in which I took part. Opposite was another notable scene: 10 Downing Street, as yet lacking its formidable barriers and gates. Thus there was plenty to look at during idle moments that were to turn out sometimes to be hours.

My job was labelled Director of Air Staff Briefing (DASB). The director-ship originated early in World War Two, when the chief of air staff found his work impeded by too much advice from too many people. He appointed a brilliant young barrister, Squadron Leader Leslie Scarman, who had left his chambers to join the RAF Volunteer Reserve. His job was to dredge and pan all that the staff submitted, gloss it as necessary with his own comments, and submit it in a concise and palatable form. Scarman, soon promoted and appointed as personal staff officer to Lord Tedder began a long succession of DASBs of whom I was the latest. Rank (in both senses) inflation had happened over the years, but the job was the same. There was now a whole Department of the Chief of Air Staff with an air marshal vice-chief, three air vice marshal assistant chiefs and a bevy of air commodore directors down below, with assorted civil and Service staffs as back-up. There was also a deputy chief of air staff; at the time a remark-ably handsome air marshal apart from having apparently helped himself

220

too liberally to cream cakes. Other than a personal staff he seemed to have no supporting lowerarchy. Neither I nor anyone I came across knew what he did; but everybody agreed that it was not a lot.

I, too, was amply endowed with people, with a deputy, two wing commanders and a retired squadron leader who had returned to become a civil servant designated RO (Retired Officer)1, the senior of two grades of these useful people. I had a knowledgeable woman secretary who knew the ropes well, enveloped semi-permanently in a cloud of cigarette smoke. Permeating rather than complementing the ministry's Service structure was a network of civil servants, with a Sir Humphrey lookalike at the top as permanent secretary, running the ministry on behalf of all three Services. Below him were deputy secretaries, under-secretaries and assistant under-secretaries, the last being segregated into single services. Ours, AUS(Air), was Frank Cooper, with a first-class brain that took him to permanent secretary level within a year or two; soon to be succeeded by one of the all-too-common has-beens shunted around the Civil Service until some muggins department got saddled with them. But most of the civil side was remarkably capable and responsive. One striking rise to the occasion was the funding crisis in 1967/68, when the Cabinet suddenly decreed enormous reductions in expenditure on Defence. Voluminous excellent papers on how to set about it appeared within days. The military planners, encumbered with inter-Service brawls and the ponderous chiefs of staff machinery, lumbered along behind.

Presiding over the Colossus were the politicians. At their head was the Secretary of State, a Cabinet post notorious for the rate at which its incumbents changed. Apart from Denis Healey, far and away the brightest, none of the 20 appointed between 1945 and 1966 stayed as long as two years. Two of the better ones, years afterwards, opened my eyes to what was happening. David Owen, later Lord, realised the reversal that characterised the ministry: it was running the politicians, not the other way round, conducting an:

insidious process of military indoctrination, the heady mixture of pomp and secrecy to which most politicians are susceptible [which] tends to blunt one's normal sensitivity. (Owen, *The Politics of Defence*, Jonathan Cape 1992).

Not, as I was later to discover, that Owen had much sensitivity to blunt. A Tory predecessor, Sir John Nott, in a rare burst of getting it right in *The Times* of 10 October 1987, described the ministry as:

a huge supertanker, well captained, well engineered, the systems continually updated – but with no one ever asking where the hell it is going.

The one exception in time served in office and trouble taken was Dennis, later Lord, Healey. I met him while traversing the endless stretches of corridor twice during my tour. On both occasions he asked, apparently with genuine interest, what I did and affably passed the time of day. It was not until years afterwards, when we were both members of the British American Security Information Council, that I appreciated the combination of geniality and intellectual perception that made him so outstanding a minister. Like many staff members lucky enough to receive them, I benefited from his occasional series of personally drafted and beautifully crafted minutes on difficult issues.

My working boss was the chief of air staff, Air Chief Marshal Sir Charles Elworthy, known to all as Sam. Universally popular, full of humour and possessed of a penetrating wit, he was a pleasure to work for. When I briefed him, usually with a bundle of paper, he would cross-examine me on, and often run circles round, my arguments; not surprisingly, in view of his training as a barrister. He was always tolerant and amusing, even volunteering sometimes that he benefited from our talks. He was at his best in small meetings. On the wall beside him hung a framed cartoon of two pairs of feet, the outer one pointing upwards and the inner downwards: The text below read:

Sam, this ceiling needs doing.

He sometimes used a remarkable talent for mimicry on ministers encountered at Cabinet Defence Committee meetings attended occasionally by the chiefs of staff. One victim was the tantrum-prone Commonwealth Secretary Norman Bottomley who, after an outburst brilliantly imitated, 'had to be taken back to nanny'.

I felt that I was of some help to him in the adversarial proceedings of the chiefs of staff. But from time to time he had to miss these preparatory sessions, change into uniform and join the ceremonial reception parade for some visiting potentate on the tarmac five floors below my office. When that happened, as my spies reported, he managed just as well. I was sorry to see him go, promoted to Marshal of the RAF and made Chief of Defence Staff. As such he presided over a new hierarchy supposed to mediate between the conflicting single-Service interests and formulate an agreed view. Responsibility for briefing him passed to Neil Cameron, an air commodore on the central staff. Neil spent much time learning from the single-Service briefers and did his job superbly. He feared that joining the Central Staff would jeopardise his RAF career, but could not have been more wrong. He rose meteorically to become chief of air staff, retiring to become head of King's College, part of London University. Tragically he died prematurely of cancer.

Below Elworthy and my administrative boss was the vice chief of air staff, Air Marshal Sir Brian Burnett. He had recently succeeded Sir Peter Fletcher, another lawyer whom I had known as chief instructor of a flying training school which I had visited from CFS years before. As VCAS he had been chief RAF protagonist in a years-long internecine battle with the Navy, the closing phases of which Burnett had inherited. The issue was whether British defence interests would be best served by aircraft carriers or land bases. It epitomised all that I most disliked about my work. I was being used to do the very opposite of what the JSSC at Latimer stood for and taught: to push the RAF interest and do the Navy down.

Burnett was no Fletcher. His office was always full of files, on the enclosures in which he wrote comments in very small pencil manuscript. I seldom read them and nor, I suspect, did anybody else. He held a weekly meeting of selected air commodore directors, with the assistant chief of air staff (policy), Duke Mavor and me in attendance. Ostensibly a review of current business, it consisted in subtle turf wars and self-advertisement by the directors. I was supposed to glean material for my briefs and to purvey titbits from the Chiefs of Staff Secretariat and other joint gossip centres for the RAF staff. I hope I scattered as much as I gleaned. In striking contrast were similar meetings held occasionally by Elworthy himself. He was adept at using his acuity to put people on their mettle.

Burnett lacked grip and only really switched himself on during Wimbledon tennis fortnights. He had been an outstanding tennis and squash player and delighted in watching the matches on the television set specially installed for that purpose in his office. He left the battle with the Navy to Duke Mavor, upon whom descended a great deal of other work under the catch-all title of Policy. That caused him gross overwork, but he still found time to befriend and advise me; and the regard I had for him as my AOC matured. I used my nascent forensic skill, such as it was, to help with the battle. The RAF case was weak, our prospects for creating an effective strike force having been ruined by the cancellation of the world-leading bomber/reconnaissance aircraft the TSR2. Our main argument, repeated in numerous presentations, was that the TSR2 substitute, the Buccaneer, could provide all necessary long-range support needed for the whole gamut of contingency operations including our obligations as a NATO power. Admittedly, we continued, Britain had to have overseas bases; but these were readily available on our own, Commonwealth, American or other allied territory. The only gap was in the Indian Ocean, and to close that Britain intended to develop garrison rights on the island of Aldabra, virtually uninhabited and a treasury of wildlife. Negotiations with the Treasury and Overseas departments rumbled on.

The Navy staff were withering in their scorn as British influence waned and friendly territory shrank. The Buccaneer made matters worse when it proved lacking in the performance claimed for it. The case for aircraft carrier groups, which included air defence, minesweeping and anti-submarine ships, was that they were almost impregnable. The two groups envisaged, ran the argument, could deal with any contingency. And did not the enormous US Navy, planned to have ten carrier groups, offer proof of their viability and indestructibility? No, replied the RAF, with murmurs of Pearl Harbour and Hiroshima; and what about the enormously higher construction and maintenance costs of a carrier group? I had joined the fray towards its end; but I am as certain as I can be that there was none of the alleged RAF misrepresentation. The Navy were widely accused of exaggerating their own capabilities and denigrating ours; but of that, too, I never saw any evidence. But I had encountered the widespread excesses of emotion-loaded zeal with which other aspects of Naval interests were sometimes presented. I remembered the choleric commander in charge of flying at Lossiemouth. I experienced the heat with which the cantankerous Admiral Sir Caspar John put the Naval case in the Chiefs of Staff Committee. 'My Service, right or wrong' seemed to me, as a mere contract man, as blinkered a way of thinking as the dreadful nationalistic shibboleth (*NEH* 492):

> I vow to thee my country
> All earthly things above ...

Whatever the truth, the whole time-consuming and idiotic internecine war ended in a draw. We got the bases, to my relief filling the gap not with Aldabra but with a right of use of the USAF base at nearby Diego Garcia. The Navy kept their carriers; and later the country was saddled with the enormous cost of replacing them, with delivery well into the twenty-first century.

I was glad to be rid of that task. My other work involved the assistant chiefs of air staff for operations and occasionally operational requirements, though the latter worked so far into the future that I seldom had to bother him. Running day to day operations was Air Vice-Marshal Bob Hodges, bright, popular and as helpful as Duke, later to ascend and join the elite company of presidents of the RAF Club whose main perk is to have their portraits painted. Within the air vice-marshals' stockades were the directors, mostly air commodores but with group captains for the lesser tasks. They varied. At one extreme were those all too anxious to use me as a conduit for impressing the all-highest. At the other were those trying to keep me at arm's-length, apprehensive of thunder-theft. With one of special bombast I had such trouble getting what CAS needed to know that I feared, as we exchanged incandescent minutes, that duelling might result. For others still I could help with foreknowledge of impending horrors. The most memorable was when a storm of economy cuts threatened the famous Red Arrow formation aerobatic team, a hugely popular feature of many displays and universally acknowledged to be an asset to recruitment. My advance warning helped to save the day: the proposal was strangled at birth.

Such achievements were rare. As I learned more of the huge apparatus of the ministry and the extraordinary difficulties of being of any use I became despondent. And as the work of preparation and brief-writing became more familiar it took up less of my time and interest. I had, moreover, an exceptionally bright deputy director, Group Captain John Nicholls, who had been a great help as I learnt the ropes but seemed as frustrated as I was at the lack of an outlet for his abilities. I fretted; but he sublimated his discontent with cheerful cynicism. He was soon posted to command a station, eventually rising high. His successor was the worst instance of a square peg in a round hole I ever came across. Pleasant and willing, he seemed to have passed through the Staff College without touching the sides. He could scarcely put one word in front of another; and his inability to comprehend what was expected of him made him impossible to train. His presence was an advantage in that it gave the two wing commanders working for him more to bite on, and me a chance to add some of what Nicholls had done to my own work. But for my successor's sake he had to go; as at Colerne, I started the long and tortuous process of getting him moved on.

Just as boredom was setting in, I found relief in an extended outing. The chief of air staff undertook periodical visits to overseas RAF units. This time he delegated the job to Duke Mavor, with me to back him up.

We embarked on the now over-familiar eastward route in the glamorous VC10 three-engined jet transport newly in service. It was wonderfully smooth and comfortable, but it broke down at our first stop, Malta. We continued in a Britannia, a successor to the Hastings and, in its trooping mode, at least as uncomfortable. We dropped in at Oman, Sri Lanka, Singapore and Hong Kong, over-entertained at each stop by the resident commanders. I was fascinated to discern just the devices I had used in comparable circumstances to paper over defects and make modest achievements look impressive. A classic lowly instance, I recalled, had been in the tin room at Cardington. The airmen, finding insuperable the task of making piles of dirty meat tins and mounds of amazing grease look tidy, kept a stone on the floor that looked exactly like a potato. When inspecting orderly officers, always young and inexperienced, told them to pick it up they would reveal that it was a door stop. There would be merry laughs all round as they ushered the greenhorn out into the wash-up next door. Of such was the account of his stewardship of RAF Hong Kong given by Air Commodore North Lewis. In place of a potato stone he handed out Chinese extending pointers for use at presentations. Mine came in useful in civilian afterlife. So, in a different mode, did the experience of trying to finish the duty-free gin we had bought to return the hospitality of some of our hosts. Few guests turned up, with near fatal results for the hung-over hosts. I really meant, and have kept to, my 'never again'.

Back home I had two delightful surprises. I had been awarded a CBE (Companionship of the Order of the British Empire). There was no citation, but it was safe to assume that it had to do with keeping stricken Colerne in the best fettle I could manage. Rachel and both boys came to the investiture. This time there was of course no repetition of the two in one feature of the preceding investiture. But the Queen, bless her, managed a nod and a smile. Better still, I found I had passed the Intermediate Exams which I had taken earlier in the year for my LLB degree in all four subjects – Crime, Contract, Constitutional and Roman Law. The results were posted in the Senate House by candidate numbers only; it took three visits to the notice board before I was sure the success was real. Such is *folie de doute*. I at once set about preparing for the Final.

Both events were encouraging, but their effect didn't last. Boredom, frustration and perhaps the absence of flying made me depressed enough to need help; but I was scared of going to a MoD doctor of whose confidentially I could not be sure. I discovered that the head of the private mental hospital where my mother had died, whom I knew and liked, did private psychiatric practice in Harley Street. He prescribed an antidepres-

Both together after the investiture. *David Mackie*

sant that made me too drowsy to cope. But his second attempt worked, and in a few weeks I recovered. I was helped by hearing on my grapevine of a block of flats built in Central London by the MoD for those whose work made quick access essential. Shamelessly I represented mine as one such post and was given one of the flats: to the delight of Rachel and the boys because Ladbroke Square, near Notting Hill, was much more exciting than suburban Hendon. I missed Hendon's squash court and the walks over the idle airfield, but enjoyed the communal garden and welcomed the easier commuting.

With time on my hands I spent more of my half-filled working week with my head in my law books. Having passed the intermediate exams, I thought increasingly of the prospects that passing the Final might open up. At the same time even the bits of work not connected with the naval battle became ever more contentious between the Services and with the civil servants. As a music hall ditty said of the soldiers:

They're not there
To fight the foe
You might think so
But oh dear no.

Instead they fought each other, and I was in the front line. Arrogantly, as I now see, I saw the job as a waste of the talents which a favourite parable of mine enjoins us to conserve.

I was not alone. On the adjoining perch was Air Commodore Angus Nicholson, a friend and former staff officer at 1 Group. He was now RAF member of the Joint (later Defence) Planning, Staff. He, too, lacked enough to do; and with longer experience of the MoD and greater familiarity with joint staff work than mine, was even more contemptuous of the overstaffed and ponderous system. Another good brain bursting to get out as soon as he could afford it was Air Commodore Micky Mount, a qualified solicitor. Yet another was Air Commodore Dusty Miller, an accountant who spent much of his working time making out whole books of cheques, all of which he used to apply for multiple allocations of the many new share issues which, when their prices rose, he would sell.

My required reading expanded into more and more job advertisements. I soon tried for the post of director of the National Association for the Care and Rehabilitation of Offenders. It failed, but the application was good experience. My next target, overweeningly as I later realised, was chief officer of the Welfare Department of the London County Council, as it then was. George Snow, by then Bishop of Whitby, weighed in with:

> ... first class ability, extremely thorough and energetic in all that he does ... will do the job really well ... lively personal interest in the people and situations that come his way ...

the vacuity of which made me realise how little there was to be said for me.

As my ferment frothed, Sam Elworthy was succeeded by Air Chief Marshal Sir John Grandy, who had an outstanding record as a Battle of Britain pilot and had had a succession of highly successful commands. He was charming and good-hearted. Staff work, however, was not his *métier*. He hated having to read his way into topics and was not good at conducting problem-solving sessions. I carried on much as I had with Sam; but I doubted whether he read my briefs, or indeed much of the other paper that passed across his desk. The other chiefs of staff clearly liked him, but he carried little weight. He must have been a burden for his excellent young

Civil Service private secretary Michael Quinlan, who rose to become Permanent Secretary. Like Nikko Henderson, I met Michael, by then Sir, again years afterwards. Once a loyal defender of the so-called British nuclear capability, he later concluded that, had he been able to play his part in bringing it into being again, he would not have been in favour.

One small bit of fun in the gloom came when Rachel, now a part-time assistant at exhibitions, was on a stand in the Royal Garden Hotel, which was part of a display for foreign buyers of export goods. Having undertaken to leave our car in the basement car park for her, I found that I could only get access to tell her where it was by posing as a foreigner. In mixed Euro-speak, appropriately accented, I got past the barrier and greeted her with:

Guten morgen senora, I have-a putta da car in, how you say, slot Five-a. See you soona I 'ope.

Rachel embarrasses easily and was less than enchanted with the performance. As I left I realised that I had to make another entrance:

C'est un grand plaisir, madame, a vous rencontrer encore. I am-a desolée de vous deranger encore but this-a time ees because I forget-a to geeva you da key. Is 'ere. Ciao.

We eventually resumed speaking.

Coincident with the change of CAS came the implementing stage of the 1968 Defence cuts that the civil servants had forecast and planned. At a vice-chiefs' meeting to consider the implications, Burnett had asked 'However are we going to find places for all the people displaced by the cuts?' That did it. In vigorous and, as I hoped, potentially productive middle age, I did not want to be found a job, with all the sinecury which that terrible observation implied. I was finally convinced that the RAF was no longer for me. Civil life, on the other hand, offered a secure base for the boys, of whose school fees we were at last free, and who were at the final phase of entering productive life. David would shortly embark on solicitor's articles. Gregor, at the Regent Street Polytechnic, was a budding businessman. The old life had lost its appeal: the new one beckoned.

I had applied, half-seriously, for the job of secretary-general of the Association of British Travel Agents while I was at Colerne. The result had been short-listing and an interview with the agency advising the association, which went well but came to nothing. Now, after a week of particularly writhing frustration with Grandy, Burnett, Whitehall and all its works, I applied for the job of under-treasurer of the Honourable Society of Lincolns Inn, one of the Inns of Court. Having, as always, done the homework of finding out all about it, I delivered the result to Mr Justice Buckley at the Royal Courts of Justice in the Strand. I thought I had a chance. But, as Hamlet found, the rest was silence.

Not all was wasted. Our elder son David spotted a job advertisement for the equivalent job of Under Treasurer of the Middle Temple. I at once began research, including exploration of the beautiful gardens and buildings which the Middle shared with the Inner Temple (the Outer Temple long reduced to a vestige of offices off the Strand). The Temple was originally the property of the Knights Templar, an order of chivalry dissolved by the Pope and the King of France, and virtually exiled to London. The transfer to the lawyers by Edward III in 1338 and the agreement between the Middle and the Inner of 1732 might, I thought, come up in the interview along with the start of the Wars of the Roses in the Middle Temple's garden. As the Earl of Warwick says in Shakespeare's *Henry V*:

> And here I prophesy: this brawl today
> Grown to this faction in the temple Garden,
> Shall send between the red rose and the white
> A thousand souls to death and deadly night.

With that and a look at the damage to the Temple Church and yard, which, unknowingly, I had seen almost destroyed on the cataclysmic night of 11 May 1941 during a visit to London, I felt once again that I might be in with a chance.

I was. Soon after delivering my application to the Inn's offices in Middle Temple Lane I was invited to a set of barristers' chambers in Pump Court, a blend of old buildings and harmonious new ones replacing those damaged in 1941. I was welcomed by the head of chambers, Hubert Monroe QC, a leader at the tax bar; Sir Leslie Scarman, the first briefer of the chief of air staff and by then a High Court judge; and Martin Jukes QC, who had left the Bar to become director general of the British Iron and Steel Federation, the steel industry's pressure group. We had an agreeable, almost gossipy chat, at the end of which they told me to expect a further invitation to appear before a larger panel of other members of the Bench (government) of the Inn. As I left I saw the beautiful sundial on the ancient wall opposite subscribed:

> Shadows we are and like shadows depart.

The sundial in Pump Court, soon to be the view from our kitchen window. *Author*

I felt it was trying to tell me something but I wasn't sure what.

I redoubled my researches, beating a path between the MoD and the Temple and slavering at the jaws at the prospect of liberation. The summons soon came and I was ushered through the benchers' special entrance in Middle Temple Lane by a black coated and striped-trousered butler, Arthur Cubitt, later to become a friend and domestic mainstay. Assembled in one of the oak-panelled meeting rooms was a group of six of the thirty-odd benchers – judges and senior barristers selected by the old boy system that, I later decided, works very well. In the chair was another friend to be, the Treasurer of the Inn for the year 1968. He was the Honourable Ewen Montagu QC, Chairman (chief judge) of Middlesex Sessions in a handsome building in Parliament Square, and Judge Advocate to the Navy. He was a tall, striking figure, aquiline-featured and with a fearful temper, but full of humour. The others, as I always found

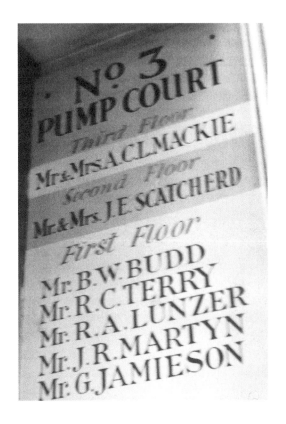

The barrister's version of a brass plate. Good for impressing visitors. *Author*

during job interviews, were a blur. There were none of the penetrating questions I had expected from a bunch of professional cross-examiners. But I did manage to convey my knowledge of the Inn and the law. They ended by inviting me to question them. In view, I asked half-seriously, of the orders made on 15 April 1630 by the Lord Keeper, the judges of both benches and the barons of the Exchequer asserting that the societies (of the Middle and Inner Temples) were instituted 'for the profession of the law and secondarily for the education of the sons of the nobility' what were the prospects for improving the training function of the Inn? The prospects were, they replied, what I chose to make them within the resources available. I had not stopped the show or raised the roof; but my question made an obvious impression.

They offered me the job at a salary of £2,500 a year, a large flat in the Temple with all costs paid and a free car parking space within the often crammed central court. I applied at once for one of the premature releases from the Services, known as Golden Bowlers, thrown up by the cuts in Defence expenditure. They came with an enhanced gratuity and a pension not far short of the full amount due on my normal retirement 12 years later. The vice-chief Brian Burnett asked me why I wanted to leave and I told him as much of the truth as my moral courage allowed, blaming primarily the idiotic RN–RAF clash. An air commodore from Personnel sent for me and asked me to consider changing my mind: 'It's a good record, you know.' Euphoric at the prospect of becoming a civilian I did not budge.

At once came disillusion. Ewen Montagu invited me to meet the office staff who worked in poky rooms below the panelled finery of the Bench quarters. My doddering predecessor, in a room full of mouldering memorabilia, told me of his 46 years' service in the Inn. His next in line, the accountant, glared in hate because his application for the job had been turned down. The students' and chambers renting officers had cubby holes like a film set for the Christmas Carol. Montagu, semi-apologetic, explained that money would be spent on improvements to the building and the training I had asked about. I left in stupefied shame and horror at what I had given up my career for, and went for a long walk along the Thames. I decided to try to call everything off, which would mean crawling back to the vice-chief and grovelling to Montagu at reversing my acceptance. Just as I was about to knock on Montagu's door Lord Donovan, a bustling figure whom I would later regard as the best bencher, arrived and begged forgiveness for bursting in ahead of me. He wanted, he said, to give the Inn the first copy of his Government-commissioned report on the trade unions. I of course gave way. While they talked I decided to abide by my undertakings both to the RAF and to the Inn. The decision made me fear a return of the plague of depression. But it did not materialise; perhaps because I half-sensed the possibility that the result might turn out as it has: the gateway, that is, to the far more useful and edifying life I have since enjoyed.

I slunk back to my office and wrote a minute to the vice-chief, with copies to Duke Mavor and the assistant under-secretary (air), (the dunderhead who had taken over from Frank Cooper), in case Burnett suppressed it. The post of DASB, I said, was justifiable only because of the gross overmanning of the air staff. The first need was to cut posts that existed only for the purpose of taking in the washing of other posts. As to DASB, the rank should be reduced to group captain as a step towards abolition when the badly needed overhaul was complete. I thought of another verse of Lawrence's poem:

> Do hold yourself together and fight
> With a hit-hit here and a hit-hit there
> And a comfortable feeling at night
> That you've let in a little air.

Oh no I hadn't. There were a few reductions, but they were soon restored. Meanwhile, for good or ill, out of the blue I was out of the blue barathea and into the shiny serge of my only suit.

Chapter 12

Lawful Occasions

'Fuck Bates, I'll make my own arrangements for breakfast,' shouted an airman at Fayid in 1941, and some idiot thereupon charged him with mutiny. That was when it all began. Flight Lieutenant Bates had ordered the alleged offender to go to early breakfast before going on duty, and that had riled him into what, it was easy to discover from the Manual of Air Force Law (MAFL), was no more than insubordination. There was no lesser alternative charge and he duly got off. At Cranwell eight years later I had to prosecute a corporal and a young airman for what would later be legalised as homosexual intercourse between consenting adults. Again, the big blue manual came to my aid, enjoining me to do no more than present the facts dispassionately: no histrionics. Otherwise nothing remotely to do with law had come my way until boredom as a Vulcan squadron commander in 1958, coupled with the realisation that I was still a London University student because of the exams in medicine I had taken, moved me to study for a law degree. An unexpected benefit from what I had learnt over the years was an antidote to the terrible feeling of confinement caused by the self-inflicted amputation of my RAF wings and entering the confines of the Temple. Learning the law had left me with a few bedraggled figurative feathers of self-respect for the afterlife.

I took stock of what I knew. It was, of course, scarcely to be compared with the learning of a proper lawyer. It was more like the limited achievement of the patroness of one of the network of American dancing schools:

> Arthur Murray
> Taught me dancing
> In a hurry.

But at least I had fallen in love with the law and I knew what my new friends in the Temple were on about. They kept it to themselves, often using tribal codes. 'Ex parte', for instance means 'Only partly': 'In parte' would make more sense in ordinary usage and it is as well that legal latin has been made obsolete. A contrite bencher confessed that he had made a

235

'Derry and Peake' (1889 LR 14 AC 337) mistake, quoting a leading law case so titled and revealing only to the cognoscenti that he had knowingly made a reckless statement. There were very few books for lay people about the wonderfully rich inheritance of guidance, in statute law and precedents laid down by judges, that keeps lawyers on the rails. If I had had time I would have written one. Very busy mucking out the Augean stable I had landed in, however, I had to confine myself to sharing my enthusiasm with the students, of whom I got to know as many as possible. Most fascinating to me, and I hope to them, was the core of the law of England and the complexities that history and the principles of precedent and procedure had created. The authorities and examples ranged from deeply moving to hilarious. One of the latter was about trespass – originally an ancient writ to remedy any direct wrong but later narrowed down to the right to use reasonable force to repel boarders. 'Reasonable' has often caused trouble and we still know only what is not. In Depue against Flateau ((1907) 100 Min 299) Mr Flateau, assailed by a miscreant who put a ladder up to his first-floor, pushed the ladder so hard that it fell over backwards, causing the unfortunate Depue to fall Flateau, as it were, on his back: too hard to be reasonable, said the judge. Contrariwise, many old cases illustrate the harshness of their times, sometimes through the fictions adopted to mitigate it. One way to avoid the death penalty that applied to many felonies was to claim Benefit of Clergy, which enabled the accused to trial in the ecclesiastical courts which could not impose it. Proof of being a clergyman was to be able to read, or appear to read, a test passage. Evocative and commonly used was the first verse of Psalm 51, known as the Neck Verse:

> Have mercy upon me O God
> According to thy loving kindness:
> According unto the multitude of thy tender mercies
> Blot out my transgression.

conjuring up a vision of a desperate victim coached to recite the lines to the coroner, fluffing them and going the way of all flesh. Savagery continued well into the eighteenth century when, for example, a defendant accused of stealing a pocket handkerchief in Ludgate Hill got a reception on being put up into the dock of 'Ha, we've met before. Stole a handkerchief did you? Seven years. Put him down.' To a response beginning 'But my Lord ...' came, 'Don't answer back: fourteen years.' 'But my Lord, my children are starving,' led to 'Transportation [to Australia]. Put him down.'

No less worth sharing is the rough justice of local courts illustrated by the late Sir Lynden Macassey KC in a lecture on illustrious Middle Templars. In a village court in 1321, Ralph claimed land to which he was not entitled from Rohese. Rohese called him a thief. He called her a whore. Both were fined for a breach of the peace. The court also pronounced on what was to become slander, deciding that Ralph had been wronged more seriously than Rohese. She, accordingly, was ordered to pay him 12 pence in damages. Such processes were soon clogged by the system of writs (originally royal commands) and prosecuted in accordance with strict procedure called forms of action. They formed the basis of a question beloved of examiners:

The forms of action we have buried, but they haunt us from the grave. Discuss.

The forms of action died a slow death. As late as 1941, the judge in United Australia v Barclays Bank ([1941] AC1 HL) doubtless delighted the profession with:

When these ghosts of the past stand in the path of justice, clanking their medieval chains, the proper course for the judge is to pass through them undeterred.

My new (law) lords and masters (of the Bench, as they were called) lived, moved and had their being in a world of which these are microcosmic particles. Some delighted in the forensic athletics of which I had no more than a smattering from exam questions set to test such agility. Into the fastnesses of the ancient Shelley's Case, for example, I never really penetrated, learning by rote what 'words of limitation' and of 'purchase', were and parroting the result on to the page. I wondered, with infinite condescension, how young students fathomed the famous High Trees House case ([1947] KB 130, [1956] 1 All ER 256) in which Lord Dennings's reasoning was too intricate for me. It was to be my privilege to ask him about it, feeling like Father William's young man. He was, as always, very courteous in confessing that he had forgotten his long judgmental essay until, not long beforehand, he had re-read and not understood it. I restrained myself from inviting him to join the Club.

Roman law figured in the LLB syllabus because of the way it illuminates English law, rather as Latin does the Romance languages as a whole. The towering figure is the Emperor Justinian who reigned from AD 527 until

565. His great *Corpus Juris Civilis* systematised and codified the ancient law in a way that has since been emulated in many countries. The Code is of fascinating complexity, comprising as it does public and private rights, legal status and procedures, slaves and their masters, property, succession and commerce. It survived the attentions of the glossators such as the two who might have been in the cast of 'Up Pompeii', Baldus and Bartolus. Purporting to improve it, they merely messed it about. An untouched gem of many is:

Justice is the constant and perpetual wish to render everyone his due.

I enjoyed particularly the legal tags of the sort which I had known as a boy learning Latin. One is:

De minimis non curiat lex:

a pleasing assurance that the law does not bother too much over small matters. Less so, and redolent of political correctitude is:

Mulier et caput et finis familiae suae est

signifying that women then, as later, wore the trousers in the family.
Such trifles enhanced lay instances like the single word telegram sent to London by an empire-building stalwart rejoicing in a new conquest:

Peccavi

meaning 'I have sinned', signifying his capture of the then Indian province of Sind. A poor thing but mine own comes from: 'Tu quoque'. Meaning 'you too'. Although decades of writing to *The Times* have enabled me to indulge a liking for terrible jokes in the headings, which are never published, I have yet to find a context for:

It takes tu to quoque.

I live in hopes. One day I may also find a home for a concatenation concerning our two sons. As the elder, David, was studying a doctrine preventing the repudiation of an act or conduct on which someone else has relied known as Estoppel the younger, Gregor, left for a holiday in the Spanish resort of Estartit.

Thus was Roman law a source of amusement. 1 would have liked to linger and explore its byways.

Criminal law was the stuff of many conversations in the Inn, one big set of chambers known as the 'thieves' kitchen' prospering on getting villains off without regard to the merits of their cases. I had enjoyed the practical experience students were encouraged to gain and the insight it gave into how the courts bend over backwards to be fair to the accused. One case I sat through was that of four yobs jointly charged with unlawful killing. They were alleged to have begun an evening out with eleven rounds of Guinness. On their way to the next pub they met a young man on the pavement who, as they saw it, got in their way. They knocked him into the gutter and kicked his head so severely that he died. The Assize (now Crown) Court judge treated them with great courtesy, seeming to take the blatant lies he was told no less seriously than the other evidence, and summed up with total balance and objectivity. Only after the verdict did he go for them as they deserved, handing down whopping sentences. Not all crime, however, was tried with such impeccable balance. The treasurer of the Inn Ewen Montagu was fond of expatiating on his Middlesex Sessions cases over the Benchers' post-prandial port. He startled his brothers (as judges used to describe each other) when he ended one tale with:

So I summed up for an acquittal and gave him a fiver out of the poor box.

The barristers who appeared regularly before him knew of his furious temper and its value as an aid to getting him appealed against.

Civil law was much more demanding of those who practised it than crime, reflected in the calibre of the common lawyers, as general law practitioners call themselves. I found Contract, being a matter of what the contractor could and could not get away with, the easiest. As every student knew, it is no good thinking, as a shopkeeper for instance, that an order delivered but not paid for necessarily gives grounds for getting the cash. If the quantity exceeds reasonable needs, the much-quoted instance being 22 fancy waistcoats (Cundy v. Lindsay (1878 3 App Cas 459), it did not. For bookies, just as bleakly when it comes to suing, all bets are off; (Hill v William Hill (Park Lane) Ltd) ([1949] AC 530). Though not, on the face of it, the context for humour, the courts often provide it. One instance involved Victor Feather, a rough, tough North Country trade unionist, when he was secretary-general of the Trades Union Council. In the Court of Appeal, one of the three judges, seeking a way out of an impasse and perhaps less than accustomed to the world outside the courts, asked Feather's barrister whether his client was familiar with the concept of *Volens non fit inuria* (an adopted Roman law rule that an act committed wilfully does not constitute a particular type of wrong). In a flash the barrister retorted:

My Lord, I understand that in West Hartlepool the talk is of little else.

Far from relevant to my job or most daily work in the Temple was constitutional law. But it is fundamental to everything in the system, governing as it does how running the country works. Everybody's primer in my day, Geldart's *General Principles of English Law* states says with Justinian-like precision:

The English legal system subsists in the fictitious ascription to the Sovereign of supreme power.

Unlike some of the indigestible tomes I had to consume is Professor Dicey's book of constitutional law, famous for having more footnotes than text. Still being revised and reissued a century after publication, the book's limpid prose explains that Parliament, more expressly the Queen in the High Court of Parliament, is sovereign but far from omnipotent. Power extends no further than its internal limit, the ability of a government to get laws passed; and the external limit of what the people will put up with. With Dicey went Wade and Phillips, to law what the prep schools' manual North and Hillard was to Latin, allowing itself a swipe at the brilliant but arrogant Labour politician Aneurin Bevan's triumphalism when his party won the 1945 election:

We are the masters now.

An assertion, the book says, that has no place in our constitution. The point is an important one because of the frailty of the mechanism of unwritten conventions of the constitution that holds the governmental system together. One in decline, it seems, is the convention of Cabinet unanimity once regarded as fundamental to good government. A succession of bad governments and ministers more akin to ferrets in a sack than a united team may be effect and cause.

All very well and even interesting to some, but not much good in my day-to-day tasks in the heartland of the law. There was much competition between the four Inns to get the best-educated students and as many of them as possible. The Middle Temple had a galaxy of scholarships and prizes, but otherwise no inducement not also to be had from the other three. To improve what it would have been indelicate to call market share at short term I used personal letters to applicants and a better introductory package of information than that of my predecessor. Looking further ahead I tried to recruit benchers to visit and give talks at their old schools of the kind that the Services found effective for officer cadet recruitment.

In order to get to know more students I insisted, to the surprise of the disdainful, on going to a moot, in which a bus-load of students and all too few benchers went to Cumberland Lodge, a residential establishment in Windsor Great Park, for a light-hearted weekend of lectures and the hearing of a fictitious case laced with pitfalls: the imaginary opposing solicitors (Salt, Teares & Co. and Messrs Gastwick, Flue) giving a little hilarity to a case conducted with the utmost seriousness by four eminent benchers. Regrettably, this excellent training modality was a very occasional oasis in a desert of inaction. Otherwise there was only the superb library; and casual encounters with those benchers who bothered to join the students at table after their dinners. My question at interview it was clear, had been only too penetrating. I did effect, however, a small step forward. As the *Daily Express* reported it:

> By courtesy of the [Wells Street Magistrates' Court] stipendiary Magistrates, about 20 bar students will practise delivering pleas in mitigation (statements on behalf of defendants found guilty) in imaginary cases ... 'We go to a good deal of trouble to treat bar students as adults,' said Mr. A.C.L Mackie, Under Treasurer of the Middle Temple, 'if they like it we'll do more of it ...'

There was plenty of more mundane fare on my plate. Urgently needing attention was the administrative mess left by my predecessor The filing system categorised almost everything by initial letter. The crammed cabinets thus jostled unrelated matters together and previous papers on a particular topic were almost impossible to find. I hired a bibulous West Indian student to sort the files out which, by the end of my first summer, he achieved. Catering was little better and especially important because of the students' obligatory dinners and the barristers' lunches. The chef was fully competent only when sober, which was not often. He was assisted in the filthy kitchens by assorted scullions who came and went almost as often as the temporary waiters, often recruited at the last minute by dragnet through the local pubs. The redeemer was Arthur Cubitt, the chief steward, who got on so badly with his wife that he was happy to work all hours. Because of him the ordinary dinners, guest and grand nights ran well. He looked after the cellar, stocked with cheap wine for the students and marvellous clarets and ports for the Bench, and seemed, like Jeeves, always to have a solution to problems.

Lacking the RAF-type authority that would have made rectifications easy, I learnt to cajole and wheedle, and slowly progressed. The result was clean food and better functions. I concentrated on the grand nights to which distinguished guests chosen by the Bench came. They were stress-filled events for me, with the Inn's priceless antique silver in use and on display, and much else that could go wrong. They were easier to run when I managed to abolish the pub press gang and use comparatively clean and honest students, supplemented by our younger son Gregor whose familiar thumb I would recognise as I helped myself from a huge silver charger of such delicacies as whole saddle of lamb. All was much better in time for the annual attendance at a grand night of our grandest honorary bencher, the Queen Mother, accompanied by her Secretary Sir Martin Charteris and wonderfully sociable, especially with the junior staff presented to her on arrival.

Confident that we could do it properly, I convinced the Bench that we should use the hall for outside catering during the long periods out of law term when there were no dinners, hitherto used only for benchers' parties and their offsprings' wedding receptions, on which we made very little. Preparing for our first major occasion I went to the Grand Room at Grosvenor House to watch the controlling of large dinners, done from a pier extending into the enormous dining area with the head waiter, like a captain on the bridge, controlling the serving of salvoes of food and the withdrawal of empty plates and glasses. I adapted the system to the gallery in our beautiful hall, from which I was to direct the first major meal – the 500th anniversary dinner of the Worshipful Company of Musicians, who had no livery hall of their own. A slight complication was the performing of ambulatory violinists during the meal playing squeaky baroque selections. All went well until I ordered the withdrawal of plates emptied of their goujons of sole and the blast-off of the plated roast capon. As one waiter, dodging the fiddlers, approached the swing door to the kitchen at full speed, another, too impatient to wait for my signal, tried to bring his fully loaded tray of capon helpings the other way. Above the chaos of the crash rang out 'Oh bloody 'ell.' Far from being the catastrophe I feared, the laughter made the occasion. The mirth, however, might have been stilled had the diners known that their capon had to be, as it were, recycled from the floor.

We gradually built up a clientele and the Inner Temple soon copied us. That was to the good because it expanded the market and together we were more flexible. Passing engagements that we could not fulfil to them, and their reciprocal action, were examples of cooperation which, I have to say in all humility, could not have happened before I came. There was an enmity between the two Inns that harked back to the eighteenth century when one Inn called in a mortgage granted to the other. It lingered in the folk mind of both Benches; my predecessor, who told it to me as if it were an achievement, had hardly ever set foot in the Inner Temple or spoken to its sub-treasurer in all his 46 years. I put that right during my first week by calling on Commander Rodney Flynn RN, the prickly but good-natured incumbent. We became almost close, swapping tales of the misdeeds of our respective benchers and working together when we could. A particular success, achieved by subterfuge, concerned a large block of chambers at the bottom of Middle Temple Lane, owned jointly by the two Inns. Having obtained identical competitive tenders for the stone-cleaning of the block, we submitted them to simultaneous meetings of the two executive committees and manoeuvred them into accepting the contract we both recommended. Each added the rider that the Inner/Middle would never agree.

But we had made sure that they would. The result was a building restored to its Victorian splendour of gleaming white stone. With that venture went a continuum of cooperation such as the joint administration of the Temple Church. The master (vicar) showed his diplomatic talent at joint meetings of benchers. That was a much-needed attribute for the incumbents who, it seemed, suffered from the occupational hazard of dancing in chains. One vivid precedent revealed itself in crumpled letters that I found at the back of a cupboard showing that the master at the time of the *Lady Chatterley's Lover* trial (1960) had been thought to be out of order and eased out of office because he had let slip his opinion that the book was not obscene. In doing so he had done no more than accept the relatively enlightened spirit of the Obscene Publications Act of 1959 and side with the trial jury. Getting rid of him, I thought, disgraced the two Benches and I was glad that there was less pompous self-righteousness in my time. The new master, Alan Milburn, became a friend, as did the world-famous organist of the Temple Church, Dr Thalben Ball. His wonderful recitals and playing at services were a continuing delight. But he constantly complained of the foibles of the organ, comparing playing it with driving a vintage but temperamental Rolls-Royce.

I managed also to refurbish links with the other Inns, Grays and Lincoln's. With a Service quadrumvirate (Grays had an ex-soldier,

Lincoln's a marine, the Inner a sailor and the Middle an airman – myself), we dined occasionally, vying with each other with the best of our masters' wines. We mitigated the nuisance of multiple applications for membership by would-be students, whose action contravened their signed undertakings on the application form that they had made only one. The oddest, duly signed, was one I received on an Inner Temple form but specifying Grays. For the sake of symmetry I sent it on to Lincoln's. The applicant's name (yes, really) was Juggernauth.

Less felicitous and more significant was the application of Samuel Shitta, an overseas student who brought home to me the terrible shortcomings of a system which left many overseas students to fend for themselves. He had come from one of several countries, mostly in Africa, where graduate barristers had a scarcity value sufficient to earn them public office or lucrative private practice. Lured thereby, and with minimal qualifications, probably false, he had settled in lodgings in London, studying for several years with no guidance other than tips picked up in the library. Inevitably, he had failed the intermediate exam repeatedly. His allowance from his country having dried up, he was reduced to penury, and had eventually written to his MP, Stanley Ewens. Ewens's letter to Montagu arrived while he was on holiday and I drafted an emollient reply for him to sign and forward. Shamefully, we simply paid his fare home.

Shitta's story prodded me into trying to get more personal support for needy students. That meant not only getting to know more of them, but also more of the masters of the Bench, from whom I had tended to remain a respectful distance, in spite of a standing invitation to join them in their hours of ease in their drawing room Most respect-worthy, perhaps, were the oldest. One of the three so-called 'naughty nineties' was Lord Goddard, a former lord chief justice and a widower who seldom left his large flat at the top of our newest and grandest block, the Elizabethan building. When I called on him I found him full of remorse about the death sentences he had passed, and very lonely: one of the trophies in my office being the black cap he had used on those occasions. Often in the Inn for a game of chess was the amazingly youthful nonagenarian Cyril King QC, who set a valuable example to his fellows with a large donation to the students' welfare fund I had started in my post-Shitta zeal. As his shaky hand made out the cheque, I passed some unctuous remark about the survival period needed to avoid the tax demanded by the Administration of Estates Act. 1925 (subsequently 1971). I quoted the wrong section and was brusquely corrected. His chess opponent was Lord Denning, a regular visitor from the Inner Temple and a most friendly man.

Not looking his great age, lacking judicial adornments other than that of Queen's Counsel but just as respected as his fellows was Master Carpmael, who with huge labour had directed the rebuilding of the parts of both Inns damaged in the wartime bombing. The result was greeted with unanimous delight. In his late seventies was Lord Justice Sachs, said to have reached that eminence by marrying Goddard's daughter. He was a former treasurer who had revived the ancient title of 'Master Treasurer' for himself. He was passionately keen on the Inn and the moving spirit of the decision to appoint me in the face of Montagu's opposition. More direct, sardonic and a bully was Lord Justice Salmon, from whom it was difficult to get a civil word. But he redeemed himself during a committee discussion I initiated about the low standards in the 'A'-level grades and subjects offered by prospective students, mentioning that I was having to draw the line at beekeeping and carpentry. A suggestion that a letter to *The Times* might help was rejected on the grounds that the chances of publication were no more than one in thirty evoked from the usually silent Salmon:

Not if you ring up Rees Mogg they aren't.

Lord Rees Mogg, as he later became, was of course editor at the time: he was also amongst the most brilliant of Carthusians, following the classics route to Balliol which I was denied. In contrast to Salmon was Lord Justice Donaldson, later Master of the Rolls, who began as an external student while serving in the Army and showed in a brilliant career what self-teaching can achieve. He and his wife, the large and formidable Tory Lady Donaldson, were keen to back me as a candidate for the Court of Common Council, local authority for the City of London, until I revealed that I would stand for the Labour Party. Collapse, as Punch would at one time have put it, of stout party.

We had several sets of father and son, the most friendly being Big and Little Latey. Old father William as he was called was an authority on defamation sufficient to displace his ancient predecessor in the students' desideratum of yore:

Shakespeare, the Bible
And Odgers on Libel

Latey Junior, a High Court Judge, very kindly took David, now a solicitor's articled clerk, on circuit as his marshal: a task akin to a pupil and personal assistant combined. Also hospitable was Lord Justice 'Scottie'

245

Baker, with two sons at the Bar, who invited us to the races with all attendant delights. Seldom seen in the Inn, but remarkable for hilarious mischief, were two brothers. The more eminent was Owen Stable who, as judge in an epoch-making prosecution of a leading firm of publishers in 1954 (R v Martin Secker and Warburg (1954 WLR 1138)) paved the way for the relatively enlightened Obscene Publications Act, 1959. Another eminent Middle Templar, Louis Blom Cooper QC, recalled in an article Stable's 'enlightened and simple eloquence' in his summing up:

> we should achieve some conception which will lead to great personal happiness between individuals of the opposite sex ... which, after all, is the only possible foundation upon which one could build a vigorous, strong and a useful nation.

and thus to the Lady Chatterley acquittal.

Less impressive was a Stable companion, as it were, an Old Bailey judge regularly lunching at the Inn, whose alcohol consumption limited him, as some who appeared before him said, to fog service only in the afternoons.

The practising barrister benchers were mostly highly successful silks (Queen's Counsel). One jovial example was Desmond Ackner QC, later an outstanding Law Lord whose holiday car crash in France ended, as he put it, with a Citroen pressé. Another was Hubert Monroe QC, who with his friend and fellow expert Heyworth Talbot QC, dominated the tax Bar, appearing alternately, it seemed, for the tax commissioners and their quarries. Robert Askew QC, a retired common lawyer, chaired the Wine Committee, amply equipped to control the Inn's large and diverse cellar, for which I did the buying. I learnt both from him and from the visiting representatives of the merchants with whom we dealt. One of them regularly left small sample bottles of high-grade clarets for the committee to taste over lunch. Of one batch of three he selected two. Not wishing to waste the third I drank it with my sandwich. To my dismay the committee changed their minds and sent for it. Responding to my frantic call, Arthur Cubitt collected the empty and returned within minutes with it refilled and magically sealed. The committee rejected it declaring it a good claret but a little past its best. Arthur explained that he had just happened to be sampling one of a huge parcel of Chilean plonk for the students and had used it as the replenisher. Only Heaven and Arthur knew what else disappeared in that fashion.

My funds for students grew and my circle of acquaintances widened, especially amongst the barristers with whom, as I was required to do, I

Middle Temple Hall, transformed by new lighting presented by Sir Jules Thorn. *By kind permission of the Honourable Society of the Middle Temple*

lunched almost daily (my predecessor having honoured that obligation in the breach, with a Guinness and a pork pie in his office). I picked their excellent brains and enjoyed their ribaldries about the benchers, whom some of them joined as they advanced in their profession, undergoing a call ceremony involving an after-dinner panegyric and a speech in reply. In that respect they needed no help from me.

There was, however, a special category of lay candidates who sometimes did. They were the ones selected for honorary membership of the Bench because of their distinction and/or because they could do the Inn a bit of good. The candidate least in need of my help and most appreciative of the little I did for him was Cardinal Heenan, then archbishop of the Roman Catholic Church in England. In a teasing reply, no less eloquent than the paean of praise from his proposer, Heenan said that he feared that what had been said would endanger his humility – until he recalled that the company were all barristers and thus akin to actors. A more demanding candidate was Walter Annenberg, US ambassador and a billionaire. At his request I gave him a very thorough guided tour of the Inn. He asked many questions, especially about the special features of the beautiful hall. I soon knew why. A week or two later I was showing some other distinguished visitors round when I saw him ahead of me regaling a posse of his own guests with regurgitations of my spiel.

The most interesting candidate, and one whom I liked at once, was Sir Jules Thorn, retiring head of Thorn Electrical Industries. When she rang for advice, his personal assistant told me he was terrified of making speeches and had no idea what to say. After a bit of research I wrote a simple account of how, as a young man in Germany after World War One, he bought surplus and salvaged electrical equipment and sold it, refurbished, into the European and British markets, which were starved of just what he stocked. He soon prospered; and with superb business sense never looked back. The Benchers liked nothing better than that sort of unvarnished tale, and his speech was very well received. I refused a fee. Instead, after lunch at Stone's Chophouse off the Haymarket, he conducted me round his pride and joy, a new automated plant in North London for making large fluorescent light tubes. As we reached the climactic stage when the tubes were ejected from a large rotating drum for packaging, each was being neatly snapped in two. Reminding me of an enraged air marshal and, standing ankle-deep in broken glass, he became as incandescent as his products as they disintegrated in dozens, and stormed off. We were overtaken moments later by an underling to be assured that the malfunction had been rectified.

Ewen Montagu, having ended his stint as treasurer, was succeeded by Lord Donovan of trade union report fame, for what was to be my halcyon period in the job. His duties as a law lord took much of his time, obliging him to refresh his learning in a wider field than that of commercial law in which he had specialised as counsel and judge. He left more to me than had Montagu, was supportive and appreciated the benefits now apparent: clean food, largely free from pilfering, an efficient office and a better spirit all round the staff. He revealed the irony behind the agonised dilemma of my appointment. Had he not interrupted my moment of crisis at Montagu's door, my wish to withdraw would have been agreed with and welcomed. On a divided appointment panel, Montagu had opposed my appointment because he thought I was overqualified. Sachs, as a former treasurer and a power on the Bench, thought nothing was too good for the Inn and had forced my acceptance.

Donovan was succeeded, under the Buggin's turn rule, by a leading land law QC whom I prefer to leave anonymous. He had rarely spoken during his infrequent appearances at the Inn, knew very little of how it worked, and was obsessed with minutiae; at committee meetings, if he spoke, sousing his colleagues in detail. Having laboured mightily over the guest list for a grand night, he insisted on testing my pronunciation of the names. He treated me like a butler and the other staff like vassals. And on one matter of personal detail he was neglectful: he smelt. During his awful regime I reflected that, for all the improvements I had attempted, the care of students was much as it had been, apart from a few lectures by well-disposed benchers and my welfare fund. And my own legal training, such as it was, had very little outlet. I wished I had been more adventurous and done more about my half-formed scheme for giving a series of elementary courses for students, which would have put the Middle Temple well ahead in the competition to attract students.

Suddenly the Bar Council, then an otherwise somnolent body, shot my fox. They announced a plan for an Inns of Court Law School which would open as soon as possible, first for the voluntary and later for the compulsory training of barristers. That meant poor wretches such as Samuel Shitta would no longer languish in bedsits. It also meant, however, that an extension of the personal effort I had had in mind – involving an unofficial panel of proper lawyers to provide a more elaborate course – had been aborted.

Disappointed by the announcement, self-reproachful at having failed to push my ideas harder, and smarting under the new treasurer, I answered an advertisement for a registrar of the Architects Registration Council of the United Kingdom (ARCUK), required because of the retirement of the incumbent, a barrister. The need, it said, was for an administrator of the council's affairs able to implement its policy: being a barrister or solicitor would be an advantage. To my surprise I was interviewed by a small group of architects, chaired, in the cloud of pipe smoke that invariably enveloped him, by Robert Foster FRIBA, chairman of the council; and, as my now habitual researches revealed, senior partner in the famous Tooley & Foster Partnership of Buckhurst Hill. I did not understate my legal background or cloak my grasp of the council and its controlling statute, the Architects Registration Act 1953. I was sure, nonetheless, that a properly qualified lawyer would pip me to the post. I was astonished when I was offered the job at a much higher salary, offset in net terms by our having to leave our beautiful flat in the Temple. (I had, incidentally, not bothered to take my LLB final because it seemed that my training had fulfilled its purpose of getting me established in the civilian world; and because I had intended to get called to the Bar in due course).

I soon decided to accept, and resigned as under-treasurer. Much as I had done in the MoD, I wrote a Parthian paper called 'What went wrong'. The Parliament of the Inn (the Bench in plenary session), received it cordially but it was clear that many liked neither the paper nor the way I did my job. Some, like Lord Justice Scarman as he now was, had seen it as similar to that of an Oxbridge college bursar and were disappointed that I had been so stand-offish. Montagu refrained from the 'I told you so' to which he was richly entitled. All, it seemed, saw my going as a slap in the face for their beloved Inn. Only Lord Justice Donovan was more than politely grateful and complimentary. He also proved an ally when our first choice of house fell through and we were outstaying our welcome in Pump Court. Eventually we found a pleasant end-of-terrace house in the sleek suburb of Barnes and handed the flat over to my successor, a retired Naval captain appointed without competition because he was a friend of a senior bencher. For fear, perhaps, that I might contaminate him, there was no office handover. As the sundial outside our kitchen window, slightly modified, put it, 'Shadows we are [were] and like shadows depart[ed]'.

My quasi-legal career as a registrar began with an early-morning arrival at the converted ground-floor flat in Hallam Street, near Broadcasting House, that served as offices. The staff, comprising a deputy registrar Mrs Noel Dawson, an accountant and half-a-dozen junior staff, were assembled in a central area opening the mail. That daily liturgy had to be performed collectively because many envelopes contained cheques or cash in payment of the retention fee required of an architect wishing to stay on the register and thus be eligible for the council's help. I joined in the togetherness, creating, I later realised, a precedent. Once the mail had been dealt with I tackled my proper task of investigating complaints and offences. There was so little work that I wondered what my barrister predecessor, whom I never met, had done; the only certainty being that it had been not much. Some of the offending architects had simply not paid their fee. A few others had been accused of the classic offence of recommending materials for such corrupt reasons as having a wife on the supplier's board. There were many complaints of wrongdoers having represented themselves as architects when they were not. That was odd, because only the word 'architect' is protected by the Act; and such entirely legitimate alternatives as architectural planner, technician or assistant are enough to fool most would-be clients.

For difficult cases we had the services of a specialist consultant solicitor, amongst whose achievements had been catching the notorious John Poulson, a villain specialising in corrupt planning applications in the North East. For difficult pursuits of defaulters we had the sonorously named Inspector Bolongaro, a retired policeman of great skill and persistence. There was not enough routine work for Noel and myself, and I welcomed another all-hands-to-the-pumps task, which was to convert the paper-based register of 7,000 or so architects to a computer database. That involved completing, in minute detail and without even the smallest error, a conversion form for every architect. The job took months but saved much effort and expense.

At long last there appeared a chance to put my legal training to direct use. There was a change in trade union law, doubtless stemming from Lord Donovan's report, requiring professional bodies to register as trade unions and thereby to have imposed on them heavy loads of restrictions and expense. I knew of doubts as to whether the professions were really caught by the Act; and whether, however that might be, architects were really within the Act's definition of a profession. I plunged into the standard works on that topic and other sources, and wrote a sort of pastiche of a counsel's opinion, concluding that an appeal by the Royal Institute of British Architects against registration as a trade union would probably succeed. Nobody took much notice except Patrick Harrison, the sagacious secretary of the RIBA; the architects' learned society, the Architectural Association, who kindly made me an honorary member; and ARCUK itself, at whose next full council meeting I was thanked. The members proceeded with their routine duty of confirming or otherwise our recommendations for the striking from the register of the more serious offenders, almost always with a metaphorical rubber stamp. We at staff level dealt with lesser offenders with Magistrates' Court prosecutions, which were time-consuming and often pointless. One repetitious offender, found guilty after weeks of effort and modestly fined, shouted to a colleague in the gallery, 'Pay the man out of the petty cash.'

I did the profession a minor service when I spotted a series of articles in *The Times* praising the merits of individual architects currently in practice to such an extent as probably to amount to advertising – at the time prohibited by the Code of Conduct. I wrote to the paper's solicitors suggesting a suspension of the series while I sought advice. *The Times* complied with my suggestion and later, without any further request from me, terminated the series. *Building Design*, the industry's Mirror/Sun readalike printed a lead story – 'ARCUK Registrar exceeds his powers' – with a lurid and entirely false account of what I had done. And all I got was this lousy retraction.

Such futile activities confirmed my impression that the real power in the profession rested with the RIBA. Patrick, indeed, said over lunch one day that mine was really a non-job. At about the same time Noel let slip that her disabled husband could no longer cope with his job, putting them in financial difficulty. Almost at once my friend and fellow sufferer, the registrar of the General Dental Council, David Hindley Smith, told me of a forthcoming vacancy at the British Dental Association which would arise when the secretary, Jack Peacock, retired. The successor, the BDA envisaged, would not necessarily be dentally qualified. I went through the now-familiar researches and applied. The hired consultants shortlisted me; but after a subsequent interview with the dental grandees I felt sure that one of the dentist candidates would get the job. I was wrong. Having accepted their offer, again at a better salary, I told Bob Foster that Noel could easily do both our jobs – at, of course, a suitably increased salary. He and his executive agreed and were duly grateful, as was Noel.

So I left the law, my study of which had done its job as an attention- and job-getter, and remained a long-term fascination. Its one great advantage, I like to think, is that it might have influenced David, our elder son, to take up a career in the legal profession to which his outstanding record as a leading solicitor, a Queen's Counsel and a judge testify. I hope it did.

Building Design marked my departure with another headline:

Mackie Succeeded.

I'm not sure I did.

Chapter 13

Health: Grinning and Bareing

During a game of hockey a teenage schoolgirl got a full-force hit in the mouth from the business end of a hockey stick. Her front teeth were knocked out, her lips and gums cut and bruised, and her good looks ruined. The playing fields where the accident happened adjoined the new St George's Hospital in Tooting. There the girl's luck began. As she arrived in Casualty so did the Professor of Dentistry. They were joined in the theatre by a consultant anaesthetist and a consultant maxillo-facial surgeon who happened to be doing a clinic. After a long operation the poor girl's mouth looked worse than ever, with stitches and contused tissue everywhere. Three months later she was still badly disfigured, but much improved. After six months she looked better than she had in the first place.

The story and the grisly pictures appeared in an issue of the *British Dental Journal* which, owing to an editorial hiatus, it fell to me to check and send to the printer soon after I started working for the BDA. It showed vividly how much more there is to dentistry than the drilling and filling that afflicts most of us; and how far it has advanced from the 'blood and vulcanite' practices that improved the matrimonial prospects of young North Country women by taking all their teeth out and providing dentures to save further expense. It was such a good story that I put it on a press release and got good coverage in the lay press. To my surprise this useful little plus for the profession received far from an ovation in the British Dental Association building in Wimpole Street whose portals I had so recently entered. It was the first of many signs of how hidebound and inward-looking the profession was. Indeed, so self-pitying and condemnatory of the cruel world outside were some of their discussions that I wondered whether self-defence was all the BDA was for. In that role I was soon apologising to the media for a member in St Albans who refused to accept a patient for NHS treatment, offering her acceptance only as a private patient. Stung by her angry response and afflicted with a speech defect, he told her that if she wanted the NHS she could go to:

H ... H ... Hell or H ... H ... Hemel Hempstead.

As the first non-dental BDA secretary I expected opposition, and wanted to fulfil the expectations of those who had supported my appointment. A good first step seemed to be to get to know them and to be known. I toured as many branches as possible, giving a talk about the professions, drawing on my work for the architects and the outstanding 1970 BBC Reith Lectures by Donald Schon about change and how to effect it. It went down well, with appreciation of such of my tributes to the profession as:

> ... what you are – a group of concerned individuals making a very special contribution to society and with a consequential right to respect and to be heard ...

I went on to suggest more contact with the media and meetings with local branches and other professional associations locally, chiding them with dealing with difficulties by hoping they would go away:

> Perhaps it's pertinent to remind you of the drunk found looking for his wallet in the street in the light of a lamp post. Asked where had lost it, he replied, 'Down at the corner, but it's easier to look for it here.'

And giving myself a puff with the hoary nostrum that the way to win the rat race they were in was to use a fast rat.

My more immediate advice was for my ally Ronnie Allen, chairman of the Executive and wonderfully disloyal about some of its awful members. His *bête noire* and my arch-opponent was the grim-faced Lionel Balding, a dental GP whose own dentition, as I learned to call it, featured two yellowing false front teeth contrasting with the grey of the neighbouring real ones. In contrast was the statesmanlike Robert Hunt, from a big West Country practice that gave him time off for his BDA work, who was the chairman of the Representative Board, the Association's governing body. His was a hard job, because too many of the members had, as Ronnie put it, their heads in people's mouths and their hands in the spittle and were thus ignorant, soured and obstinate. One without those excuses was the professor who had operated on the schoolgirl. His ingratiating overfamiliarity aroused my suspicions. A powerful counterweight was Rodney Swiss OBE JP, a man of parts whose geniality did not detract from his authority.

My new friends and foes and the *lumpen dentetariat* spent four weekends a year meeting as the Representative Board in the basement hall of the magnificent headquarters building in Wimpole Street, wringing their hands, airing their grievances and agitating for more NHS money. The

Another unctuous joke for a superior (see page 215). *Anon*

chances, I feared, of bringing them to reality and modernity in a decade, let alone the year to which I was committed, seemed slight. The nay-saying element led by Lionel Balding included a lady practitioner from the shires; half-listening to her interminable diatribes led me to naming her Dental Floss, the Representative Bawd.

I went to as many meetings of the planetary system of committees as I could, getting to know and getting known. One working party was chaired by Professor Aubrey Sheiham, who shared with his fellow members the aim of doing away with dentistry by helping people to look after their teeth themselves. I shared the enthusiasm for this intriguing work with the well-named assistant secretary Alex Maclean, who facilitated the production of the posters, leaflets and other aids that helped the work along. What most interested the general run of members, however, was not preventive dentistry. Their concern was the rates of payment for items in the NHS Dentistry Schedule of Procedures whose chairman and another assistant secretary worked in and for the much larger rate-fixing body the General Dental Services Committee (GDSC). They negotiated rates at the Department of Health and were worryingly close and secretive. I tried hovering over their work, but never did find grounds for my unease. The GDSC itself was a paranoid body, fearful of opprobrium from the profes-

255

sion at large, for whom the rates negotiated were never enough, and anxious to keep their personal details confidential. When, during the summer, I received a request from the small, as it was then, and hostile General Dental Practitioners Association for the current edition of the BDA members' diary, I only needed to glance through it to find out why: within was a list of GDSC members whom the GDPA were anxious to identify and pillory. After a visit to the stationer nearby I replied with an apology that we were out of stock and enclosing, with compliments, a Schoolgirls' Diary given to me by an admirer and surplus to my needs, which I hoped would be of help. The ranks of Tuscany forbore to cheer, but they were certainly amused.

By the end of my first quarter there were straws in a favourable wind. One was a Radio 4 *Today Programme* item in which I spoke of the frustration of dentists at the laziness and indifference of patients on whom they lavished dental care, only to see it ruined and having to be done again because of lax hygiene and excessive consumption of sugar. Another surprised and delighted the Executive, some of whom seemed never to have heard of letters to the press. In a long letter to *The Listener*, then a well-read middle-class vehicle, I embarked on the long standing problem of putting fluoride in mains water:

> all we want, as a body of people concerned with reducing dental disease, is to be free to apply a well researched and totally effective means of controlling dental decay permanently [and] cheaply.

Thereby stirring a pot in need of it.

Yet another was a successful complaint to the Advertising Standards Authority about an appalling ad from Nestlé asserting that their white chocolate was just the thing for children to cut their teeth on. I also had a modest success at the annual conference in Cardiff, mostly a junket but also a chance to meet a great many members. I gave an address asking them, as it were, to open wider please; haranguing the membership on the need for change and its urgency; and pointing out that some reforms introduced by members in their forties would, at the current rate of progress, have little effect until they were due to retire. Discussion was lively.

So, in a more refined fashion, were the question-and-answer sessions following the annual celebrity lectures given by the General Dental Council to which David Hindley Smith, the Dentists' Registrar, invited me. The most memorable was that of Lord Wolfenden, he of the eponymous report which led to the legalising of homosexual acts between consenting adults.

In a brilliant analysis of the 'sodality' of the professions he called for more and better assertions of their place in society. He admitted in an aside to changing the hobbies section of his entry in *Who's Who* each year to find out which issue those who referred to him had consulted: not a custom to which I or our elder son David, both with entries therein, have yet resorted.

As I began to wonder how the year of mutual probation between the BDA and myself would end, David Hindley Smith, well informed as always, told me of a row in the Health Education Council which had led to the sacking of the director general Dr Bill Jones. At the same time he regaled me with a case history of his which showed how much more fun it was to be a dental rather than an architectural registrar. A dentist had just been tried and struck off for the all-too-common offence of sexual assault on a woman patient under an anaesthetic. On hearing that he would no longer be allowed to practise, she was much disappointed: he was, she said, the only dentist in whom she had confidence.

I had lusted after the director general's job because the council was responsible for influencing and giving information and advice across the whole health spectrum, and thus a macrocosm of what had interested me in Aubrey Sheiham's work. When the advertisement appeared I applied. The consultants' interviewer was Group Captain Ian Slater retired, whom I had known as Sir Clifford Sanderson's son-in-law and a Canberra pilot. We chatted and he did his best not to be influenced by friendship. I was – I am sure fairly – summoned for the crucial interview with the council itself. It was chaired by Professor Charles Fletcher, vice-chairman of the council and a world-class specialist in his own affliction, diabetes. It blighted his career by debilitating him and obliging him to inject himself frequently. The panel's questions seemed cursory and the atmosphere flaccid. I left feeling that I had been interviewed for the sake of it and stood no chance. Apart from the briefest acquaintance with Aubrey's work, I reflected, the sum of what I knew of health education was comprised in the infomercials of the American Forces Network, relieving the boredom as I flew in the night skies over Europe:

Flies spread diseases; so keep yours buttoned.

Remember, soldier, a blob on your knob means no demob.

And the even more primitive and wholly misleading jingle about Andrews' Liver Salts on Radio Luxembourg in the 1930s:

257

Oh a glass in the morning
will soon stop you yawning,
for Andrew's will brighten you up every day.

As well as the adaptation of the sign on the itinerant ice-cream seller's bicycle:

Stop me and buy one.

into the condom maker's slogan:

Buy me and stop one.

I was wrong. Along came an offer which I accepted at a salary of £6,000, much more than I had been paid at the BDA. It was linked to the Civil Service grade of senior assistant secretary (air vice-marshal), and soon increased. I exercised my right not to renew my 12-month tenure at the BDA and was flattered by the disappointment, especially from Ronnie and Robert Hunt. The one exception was the ingrate professor whose bonhomie evaporated when, before he knew of my decision, he warned me that he would make trouble for me if I stayed on. I wrote it down as he spoke and told him how strong an incentive to remain that would be, realising how much I disliked him. The professor himself departed soon afterwards, reportedly under a cloud.

My new employer, the Health Education Council, had been conceived by a committee charged in the 1950s to see what could be done to improve preventive health services, chaired by one of the great medical peers, Lord Cohen of Birkenhead. They proposed in 1964 that the lore about health education, scattered about in various forms of medical, paramedical and academic teaching, should be unified in a body, 'seeking to counteract pressures which are inimical to health'. Which I thought highly prescient. The new body, in a confidential document of 1960 was:

to select topics for special educational campaigns, conduct research and arrange the training of health education organisers.

It started work in 1968 under the chairmanship of Lady Serota, soon succeeded by Alma Birk, a life peer and wife of the prominent solicitor Ellis Birk. Alma had edited *Nova* (feminine of *novus*, meaning 'new'), a glossy magazine for titillating semi-educated female readers and soon replaced in that capacity by *Cosmopolitan*. Her chairmanship had been difficult from the start. The staff, with a few shining exceptions, were throwouts from the Department of Health, glad of a chance to get rid of its duds. Of the recruited staff, the director general Bill Jones was a New Zealander versed in public medicine who seemed to have got on adequately with Lady Serota but whose differences with Alma had caused long periods of not speaking. Nevertheless, against the odds, he and Alma had two signal successes. In conjunction with the Family Planning Association (FPA) they had devised press advertisements featuring Casanova, said to have invented a primitive condom made of sheep intestine, about to make another conquest. Following up the welcome furore, the council issued a poster depicting a pregnant man with the slogan:

Would you be more careful if it was you that got pregnant?

The result was widespread publicity for the council and the FPA, and the sort of hullabaloo that does wonders for attracting public attention.

The chief medical officer, Arthur Dalzell Ward, was widely experienced, having commanded a field ambulance in World War Two and done several public health jobs. Author of the standard textbook on health education, he was widely read, fond of Baudelaire and a delightful and universally respected colleague. His companion, Director of Education and Training Ian Sutherland, was a former public school headmaster and professor of classics. He developed school health education from a casual activity into a fully developed curriculum, as well as establishing graduate and post-graduate training as a well-recognised discipline. He edited and contributed to a seminal book of essays on advanced health education by most of the best known authorities. He, too, became well known and liked for his learning and quirky humour. Less endowed was the third director, Dr John Dale, a friend of Jones, who created a Research Division detached from the main body of the council to Bristol specially for him. Amiable, carefree and, as I decided, totally untrustworthy, Dale had embarked, with a multidisciplinary team of young people, on a huge research exercise on accidents in the home, none too closely associated with health education and liable, it seemed, to grow into a tail that would wag the council dog. Closing his division down, I decided, must be one of my first tasks.

My first encounter with Alma Birk was over open sandwiches at her opulent house overlooking Regent's Park. She had been away from the council for some weeks, suffering from nervous exhaustion, and I wondered

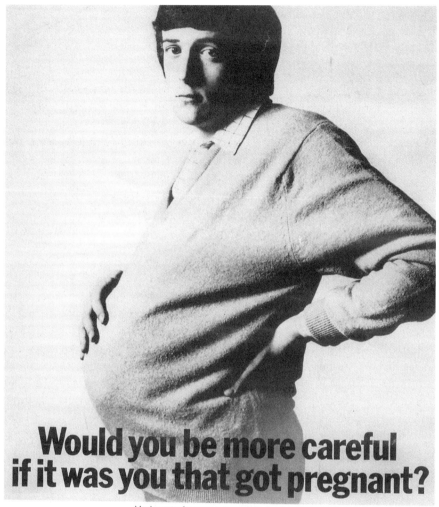

Would you be more careful
if it was you that got pregnant?

It's a lot easier for a man to have a baby than for a woman.
She's the one who has to hump it around for nine months.
She's the one who has to grin and bear it. Backache,
morning sickness and all.
It's not a lot of fun being pregnant, if you don't want the
baby. It's not a lot of fun being an unwanted baby, either.

The Health Education Council

Anyone married or single, can get advice on contraception, from their local family planning clinic.

Crown Copyright/Department of Health

260

which of us was the more tense. We talked about the press coverage of my appointment:

No doctor in the House?

was the *Guardian*'s headline expressing 'some surprise', shared by other heavies. When I suggested to Alma that there would have been a lot more in that strain if they had bothered to discover that I also lacked every one of the advertised desiderata (experience in preventive medicine, social science, teaching, journalism and working with local government, etcetera), the atmosphere lightened. She was supportive, insisting on coming to our offices on my first morning to welcome and introduce me. That she did, helped by a large whisky from the bottle kept by Jones in his office cupboard, staying for the welcome party with dancing. The jolly jiggers included a Junoesque Polish girl named Bednarska – a name open, as I cogitated, to prefixes.

The offices were in the top three floors of a repulsive multistorey block, later described in the *Sunday Times* as a 'canal-side slum', in Alperton, North London. I wondered how we came to be there until I had a conversation in one of the lifts – so few and slow, incidentally, as to be a major waster of time. A very odd middle-ranking (HEO) civil servant, John Pottinger, who I gathered had been very friendly with Jones, first explained to me that his half-bronzed face was awaiting another pot of false tan of which, preparing for his holiday, he had run out. When, as a topic to chat about, I railed against our awful offices, he volunteered that leasing them had been his doing, following instructions from Bill Jones to find offices for the council as near as possible to his house in Harrow. (It was no surprise that the accountant and I later caught Pottinger forging invoices and got him sacked and prosecuted.) The effects of this corrupt arrangement included our having almost no important visitors, because we were ashamed to invite people who, in any event, would have thought twice about making so long a trip from central London. In reverse, distance involved us either in a long tube journey or in using expensive minicabs. I soon started agitating with the money men at the department for a central, and sane, location.

My view of our terrible situation was heightened early one morning when I arrived for work before most of our staff and that of the North Thames Gas Board, who occupied the rest of the building. Floating in the canal that ran alongside it was a body. Reaching out with my umbrella to pull it ashore, I was stopped by another oddball, a security guard and former RAF sergeant and passing acquaintance, who rushed up and jumped into the canal. Having done so, he shouted, 'I can't swim.' I then hauled both the live and the dead body to safety and told another security man who had joined in the fun to telephone for an ambulance. One of the small company of fascinated Alpertonians by then assembled had already done that. It soon arrived, freeing me to go. About six weeks later the sergeant accosted me to show me the letter of congratulation on his brave action which he had received from the Metropolitan Police.

It soon emerged that my task was not only, as in previous jobs, to know and get to know people, but also to disabuse them of the malign influence of Jones who had found an obscure job with a local authority ending, sadly, in his drink-related death. The most awkward of the many concerns that mattered was that of the all-important health visitors, whose access to private homes made them cardinally useful health educators. Jones had accepted an invitation to give a lecture at their institution and turned up drunk. Their secretary Miss Wilkie, comparable in bearing with James Robertson Justice's *Carry On* films' doctor, took a lot of winning over. After our reconciliation, theirs became one of a growing number of bodies to whom I gave talks. Of the hundred or so texts, which I usually tried to memorise, the most important still extant include those for the Royal College of Midwives, the Conservative Back Bench Health Committee, the Socialist Medical Association, the Sports Council, the Independent Television Authority as it then was, the Environmental Health Congress, the Health and Safety Executive Conference, a Commons Select Committee, the American Cancer Society and, most significantly for my future, the International Union for Health Education (IUHE) which the council had slighted by ignoring: Jones again. My texts were usually militant in tone on behalf of health education as a many-faceted modality with great potential for easing the burden on the NHS clinical services. It took me time to recognise that some of those services were by no means keen to be relieved.

That and other useful points got a potentially fruitful airing in front of the House of Commons Social Services and Employment Sub Committee on Violence in the Family, offshoot of the important Expenditure Committee on Violence in Marriage. The sub-committee, chaired by Renee Short, included Sir Ivan Lawrence QC as he later became, and Nicholas Winterton of the husband-and-wife MP duo. Backing up two council members, I drew on my experience as a member of the International Committee for Parent Education, a tiny body with an office in Paris which I had been asked to join. Trying never to miss the chance of a puff for the council, I answered a question from Winterton about parent education:

... we regard [it] as terribly important [needing] an awful lot of work ... a slightly larger subject than that which ... you are addressing yourselves but it is very material [to you] too.

The result was a recommendation for putting more resources into parent education. Instead of providing the wherewithal, a dismissive, disingenuous Department of Health shrugged it off with, 'The Council can formulate its own priorities.'

I put progressively more effort into these egotistical forays as the reforms I had introduced began to take effect and my administrative burden eased. My professional colleagues, too, found themselves relieved of some routine drudgeries freeing them to work more efficiently. I lacked much of a role other than one comparable, perhaps, to that of a trainer helping gymnasts over a vaulting horse. At the same time I began to recognise the enormity of the quasi-curriculum running counter to health education operated by the tobacco, booze, sweet, food and drug industries; and the public fixation, sedulously kept in place by the clinical professions, on medicines, treatments and hospitals as sources of health. Almost all, of course, are no more than alleviators of disease. Health, to quote the World Health Organisation:

is not only the absence of infirmity or disease but also a state of physical fitness and mental and social well-being.

Much as peace is a great deal more than the absence of war. Here, it seemed, was an unfulfilled duty at which I could have a go – that of countering the counter-curriculum that blighted our efforts; thereby exactly matching our founding fathers' aspirations.

I set to. I wrote a 'treatment' or synopsis for a film to be called *Only One Earth* dwelling on the analogy between the earth and the body/mind as dual outfits of resources in need of proper care if they were to survive. It included basic environmentalism in 55 contexts such as the huge increase in the garbage disposal problem, the misery of tenants in high-rise blocks and the known effects of noise on other animals, making them sullen, unresponsive and violent. We commissioned the National Coal Board film unit, recommended by the new chairman, Sir Harold Evans just as he arrived, to make the film. The result, in rough-cut form, departed radically from my treatment into a Rich v. Poor polemic at body and terrestrial levels. When we showed it to a representative team of council members there was an ominous silence. It was broken by one of our more reactionary members, scion of the banking house of Coutts, named, aptly to excess, David Money-Coutts. '*THIS*,' he exclaimed in thunderous tones, 'is *Socialism*.' The film sank deeper than did ever plummet sound.

Other bits of health promotion went well. With the help of a new and reinforced press staff I got some texts of my talks published in such trade papers as the *Journal of the Royal Society of Health* ('Other ways of saying 99'), the *Health and Social Services Journal* ('Any number can play') and even the lay *Time and Tide* ('Traits in the Ashes'). The team got me many broadcasts, mostly on local stations but also national such as Radio Four's *Today*, then as later a flagship programme, and its television cousin *Nationwide*. I also did soft science features; one on sex caused a small furore because, arguing the disadvantages of coy euphemisms, I exemplified the word penis as a perfectly acceptable alternative to the earthy synonyms. The reaction to my broadcasts was often critical and sometimes abusive, making it a pleasure to hear again from George Snow:

We were thrilled to see you on our colour television last week ... You hadn't change a scrap since we last saw you in the flesh, ages ago ...

And, responding to a long article in the *Sunday Telegraph* colour supplement from Robert Birley, Sir as he now was:

If there is one thing which pleases me more than anything else it is to hear of people who were at Charterhouse with me ... who are doing original and constructive work. You are certainly doing that.

There was still a lot of house-ordering to do. For much of it I was well supported by the new chairman Sir Harold Evans (not to be confused with his namesake, a well-known journalist), who joined in the hunt. He had been made a baronet by Harold Macmillan, to whom he was the respectable prototype of the horrible political advisers who now infest high places. He had then become public relations director of Vickers, based at the top of their huge blue tower on the Embankment. I went there weekly to brief and consult him, enjoying the Tate Gallery on the way home. After several rejected proposals the department gave approval for the leasing of a small, modern, self-contained office block in New Oxford Street, in central London. After the ardours of the move, our fortunes and morale were transformed by the central location, convenience, comfort and extra space, including a ground floor shop and mezzanine floor for displays and a drop-in information centre staffed by a nurse. Apart from dispensing advice to the clientele, she regularly gave first aid to the fallers-off from motor bicycles that often skidded on the street outside when it rained.

I had reined in the Research Division with laborious day-visits to Bristol, succeeding eventually in forcing the home accidents project into a form that led to tangible and useful results. I encouraged the highly employable young scientific staff to look round, and almost all found jobs at once; and with the help of a jobbing scientist who had done other work for us, I achieved the closure in spite of Dale's characteristic attempts to block it with misleading press statements. His most influential quarry was Adam Raphael of *The Guardian* who, after grilling me, came out in support of the closure. We replaced it with farmed-out research projects under the guidance of a committee for whom I was very lucky to get as chairman Sir Robert Black, chief scientist to the department and later an ally.

Sir Harold had some latitude in the choice of council members. He deadheaded adeptly, but was not invariably felicitous in his choice of replacements, formally appointed by the Departments of Health in England, Wales and Northern Ireland. His long standing vice-chairman was Leslie Baines, chief secretary to the Isle of Wight Administration and the powerhouse under the sinecure governors. He had endured Alma's upsets and Jones's misdeeds with great tact and aplomb and was a source of strength much missed later on; as was Daphne Elliott, chief nursing officer to Croydon Area Health Authority. In mid-spectrum of utility was Professor Wedell, a polymath with a chair in management studies. He was enormously erudite but his advice was as difficult to interpret as was his mood, invariably disguised with a fixed smile; he meant well. Less congenial was Professor Kessell, a psychiatrist much given to destructive comment. When, after a minor difference, I tried to get in touch with him, he sent a message that he was available and willing to see me only as a patient. I forbore from reporting him to the General Medical Council for touting for patients without referral. Also in the Awkward Squad was Sir Lincoln Ralphs, appropriately resident in Unthank Road, Cambridge, whose response to something I said in council was to call me, abusively in intent but accurately nonetheless, a thrusting executive. The rest were mostly unremarkable and susceptible, at their quarterly meetings with a good free lunch, to persuasion, especially post-prandially, to do as they were told. To that end I took great trouble to draw on my Cabinet Office committee experience, sending out voluminous multicoloured meeting papers, rather longer than most members would read, ending in short, very clear recommendations for action. It usually did the trick. We kept them informed with a monthly report, a little too long to read. And we

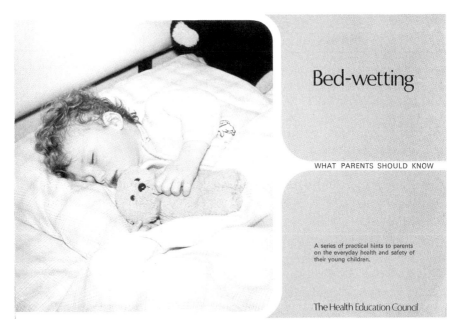

A sample leaflet, undeservedly modelled by our elder grandson.
Crown Copyright/Dept. of Health/author

laboured over the annual report; attractive, detailed and a lot too long to read other than by investigative journalists.

A more honest literary venture was the greatly expanded and improved range of posters and leaflets for health and education departments of local authorities and free distribution to the public, usually written by specialist consultants, polished and issued by a staff working party which I chaired. Their subjects stretched from head lice to foot care with stops on the way down for dental and skin care, breast self-examination for lumps, smoking, diet, contraception, sexual health, constipation, piles, jogging and foot hygiene, and across the alphabet from accidents to zoonoses (diseases caught from animals). Our new products became a self-inflicted burden because of the greatly increased demand. Surveys gave some guidance about their effectiveness. But in one more telling instance I had a personal letter from a lady asking for information about contraception, to be sent as soon as possible because, she said, she couldn't wait much longer. I obliged, resisting the temptation to deliver it in person. Responding to what I under-stood to be a dilemma amongst the family planning clinicians about a contraceptive device for sexually inexperienced females, I devised, for the

266

amusement of our circle of professional friends only, a fictitious master-piece of the Italian school – Caravaggio's *The Virgin and the Loop*.

Some of these materials figured in campaigns, complemented by commercial advertising in the press, on television and in cinemas (the last showing, incredibly, reluctance to accept commercials about contraception even though cinema back row seats had provided sexual gymnasia for decades). Our main positive effort was about personal responsibility for self-care, many months in preparation and eventually called, unimagina-tively, 'Look After Yourself' (LAY). It comprised all the important self-care steps that people and their children could take. It took all our campaign money and some extra, wheedled from the department. Its intended motif portrayed an energetic young man leaping over a fence, reminiscent of Sunny Jim on the breakfast cereal Force. In the only intervention I can remember from him, the motif was scotched by Arthur Dalzell Ward's pallid medical successor as chief medical officer on the ground that the jumper might injure his testicles. Despite its mind-numbing stupidity, I had to accept the point and we redesigned our materials accordingly.

In the LAY campaign we tried to strip personal health care to simplicity, freely adapting one of the early mass investigation of 800 guinea pig people in Alameda County, California. The findings show the remarkable results of a good night's sleep; a decent breakfast; consistent and vigorous exercise to the limit of individual capacity; the avoidance of visible salt and sugar; minimum intake of fats, especially hydrogenated ('high cholesterol') fats; a plentiful intake of fruit and vegetables and other sources of fibre; moderate drinking of alcohol; and, of course, not smoking. Coupled with avoidance of exposure to sunlight, investigative fumbling of breasts and testicles and washing under their foreskins by uncircumcised males there is little more for individuals to learn. It was the inability of the stupid, the indolent and the otherwise disadvantaged to do so that prompted my friend and colleague Dr Harry Crawley, head of health education in the Republic of Ireland, to open a conference in Limerick with a sort of dedication:

Let us be thankful for all the people whose smoking, drinking, greed, promiscuity and other filthy habits keep us in business.

He it was who invited me to help in judging a students' competitive health education display competition in the Republic. It paid for a delightful bicycle expedition to the south-east of Ireland. Stopping on the way back in Dun Laoghaire I followed Harry's advice and visited the James Joyce Museum. As it was a very hot day I followed his further suggestion of a swim in the Forty Foot, a small rocky inlet with a drop of that depth from a natural platform to the sea. Entering through a door with a high surrounding wall, I was startled to find myself in company with 50 or so other men, all naked. I joined them in a freezing cold plunge and swim, sharing in an ancient, very Irish, men-only privilege.

Much of my other activity was less adventurous and unavoidably negative. The biggest was campaigning about the deterrence of cigarette smoking, at which our best and most expensive efforts were as nothing compared with the tens of millions spent by the tobacco industry, still little restricted in, as it were, puffing their product. Our one demonstrable victory was over the elaborately trumpeted launch of allegedly safer cigarettes filled with what was called New Smoking Material (NSM). The industry, in a prodigious press-release barrage, proclaimed NSM's merits, describing lorries racing through the night to stock up retailers gasping, as it were, for the chance to sell it on launch day. On that special day, we lavished our scarce resources on full-page advertisements in all the national daily press. Smoking NSM, they proclaimed, was like jumping out of the 36th instead of the 39th floor of a skyscraper. The undeniable scientific basis of our allegation survived the industry's onslaughts, and NSM disappeared within days. To our delight the wounded giant Imperial Tobacco Limited also used full-page newspaper advertising in a specious effort to answer the unanswerable:

> The introduction of cigarettes containing NSM has been followed by accusations, often in intemperate terms, of misleading the public including accusations made on behalf of a body appointed and financed by the same government with whom the policy which led us to introduce NSM was agreed.

Their paranoia was ambrosia. So was that of the retailers' trade paper *Contob* which, in denial, attributed the disaster to: 'mismanagement of the whole tobacco substitutes experiment'.

Nastier tactics were to come. I had joined, (along, incidentally, with other health-promoting bodies whom I hoped to enlist as allies), Action on Smoking and Health (ASH), chaired by Dr John Dunwoody MP and run with great panache by a young executive called Mike Daube. Stung by ASH, tobacco moguls sponsored and funded an ostensibly independent body, the Freedom Organisation for the Right to Enjoy Smoking Tobacco (FOREST). With a small paid staff, a grant from the industry and good public relations advice, FOREST became an effective pro-smoking lobby. The chairman, to the surprise of few except me, was Air Chief Marshal Sir

Switching to a cigarette
with tobacco substitute is like jumping from
the 36th floor instead of the 39th.

You may have got the idea that the new tobacco substitutes will make your
cigarette much safer.

Not so. The dangers of smoking won't go away so easily.

In the first place, most of these new cigarettes contain only 25% tobacco
substitute - the rest is all tobacco.

And secondly, tobacco substitute itself produces a certain amount of tar.

Some of these new cigarettes - in the low to middle tar group - have a higher
tar yield than some existing cigarettes.

That means the risk of getting lung cancer, heart disease, bronchitis and
emphysema from smoking them could be greater than from smoking a low tar
cigarette without tobacco substitute.

The truth is that the only safe substitute for tobacco is no tobacco.

The Health Education Council.
78 New Oxford Street, London WC1A 1AH

The press advertisement that did for synthetic cigarettes. *Crown copyright/Dept. of Health*

Christopher Foxley Norris, recently retired, under a cloud, from a senior post in the Ministry of Defence. I greeted his appointment with a light-hearted letter in *The Guardian* welcoming a Freebooting Officer Really Expert in Selling Tobacco. He responded with a salvo of malice. Mike Daube, now a senior lecturer at the Department of Community Medicine at Edinburgh, wrote:

> I have recently been corresponding with a character called Sir Christopher Foxley Norris who is Chairman of a Maverick outfit called FOREST. Since he seems to have an almost obsessive interest in you it seems only right to send you copies.

The items were allegations, copied to other influential people, that I had used my rank to create an impression that I was a former RAF doctor;

269

was unqualified to act as spokesman for the HEC; and more in that strain. Having long apprehended just that possibility, I had never used my rank in any working capacity whatever. The council's very sharp solicitors replied on my behalf that I was entitled to damages and a gagging injunction; but that I would accept an assurance that he would utter no more. I got it and silence reigned. Later on we were both offered fellowships of the Royal Society of Arts, essentially the right for those of us vain enough to want them to put more letters after our names for £50 per year. The answer was Yes and No – him and me respectively. He has perpetuated his phenomenal vanity, worse even than mine, with the Foxley Norris Memorial, which is a slab of granite paying tribute to pilots killed in the Battle of Britain, towards the end of which he flew Hurricane fighters.

The incident continued the cigarette industry's sorry tradition of resisting anti-smoking action. When, after seven years' delay, the Department of Health accepted Sir Richard Doll's discovery in 1950 that cigarettes are a carcinogen, the industry hired a bent statistician to 'prove' that the cause of the cancer was air pollution; and a tame physician, otherwise of distinction, to declare that Doll had made: 'a staggering and most unscientific claim'.

Also worthy of powder and shot was the food industry. My quarries were an unsavoury, as one might say, couple – the Food and Drink Industries Council (FDIC) and the British Nutrition Foundation (BNF). The former, run by an errant former Tory MP Tim Fortescue, promoted those industries and parried their critics. In a dust-up with him I criticised the blatant and express denial of responsibility for the health consequences of the enforced over-consumption of the sugar and fat in their products. I also had a go at the BNF, in decline after the retirement of my friend the incorruptible Marjorie Hollingsworth, for asking its panel of eminent scientific advisers questions to which the answers could but be favourable to the food industries – not surprisingly in view of the many senior industry notables then in the BNF hierarchy. In a furious response at a conference at the Royal Society, Fortescue reeled off very badly informed criticism of our work on the dietary effects of fibre ('Bran in the bend of every bowel', as I had, infelicitously perhaps, expressed its message). Unknown to him I was in the audience and, having insisted on joining him on the platform, delivered a robust reply. To reinforce it, and after chuntering by the solicitors, I got the offending passage deleted and a correction circulated to those who were there.

Having enjoyed offensive action in those fields, I turned to others. One was cigarette advertising, which the makers had changed as little as possible from the time before the health risks emerged. One issued in the 1930s was:

> Mine's a Minor
> The ten minute smoke
> For intelligent folk,
> Won't anyone have one of mine?

Which must have helped to dispose of millions of De Reske minors and their victims. Carreras, later to be absorbed along with De Reske by one of the giants, comforted its customers with,

> Smoke as much as you like but keep to Craven A for your throat's sake ... as a doctor I am glad to notice more and more Craven A smokers.

On mortuary slabs, perhaps.

I was glad of a skirmish with the advertising agents Allen, Brady & Marsh, rivals of our own agency, the rising stars Saatchi & Saatchi, who had produced the Pregnant Man and much other outstanding material. Peter Marsh, an even worse show-off than I am, was unctuously described thus in the *Financial Times*:

> Charm and bombast conceal one of the shrewdest minds in advertising.

Balanced with my description of his agency and its output as:

> full of nauseous and self-regarding cant.

They had advertised State Express cigarettes as 'Mild but not Meek'. I was moved to suggest in *Campaign*, the advertising trade paper, that Gentle Jesus would forgive Marsh for virtually plagiarising a childrens' hymn in return for a give-away prayer book in every packet. Complementing a call to save litter by reducing the number of bits of paper in cigarette packets, I suggested tidying up the mortuaries by leaving out the contents as well. Replying to a charge from Peter Simple, a *Telegraph* columnist, I denied that the council was responsible for the health warnings on cigarette packets, suggesting that in any event the need was for action rather than warnings. One such action, I proposed was for Simple to bend over so that he could put his allegation where it belonged. Unfortunately the rest was silence.

Not so when it came to booze. In a *Today Programme* discussion on Radio 4 about drink advertising I castigated Martini:

There is a spiced wine which is put over very extensively as 'The Right One', and associated with sex, upmarket luxury and keeping up with the Joneses. In fact it's right only for the makers. It tastes like washing-up water and will only sell because of advertising of that kind.

Which irked Martini and Rossi, who asked for an apology. They got one, but the truth had outed.

There followed a banquet of protest from the booze and food industries that sufficed to salve my conscience over such egotistical lunges. One resulted from a satirical poster featuring the male symbol of a circle with an arrow projecting from it upwards. Our arrow, however, was drooping; and the slogan, based on one current in lager advertising, was:

If you drink too much there's one part beer can reach.

which won two awards. When the managing director of Seagram took exception to the 'sexual overtones', I thought of the precocious child in the film *Paper Moon* whose con man companion said he had scruples about selling defective bibles to a small religious community in rural America. She replied:

If you've got scruples, they must be somebody else's.

I was able to respond with:

... the lofty moral tone you have adopted ... [is inappropriate] ... to the head of a firm expert in advertising products, presumably unsaleable on their intrinsic merits, with such slogans as 'You don't say hello sailor to a Captain Morgan drinker' and enquiries about how much yo ho ho people have had recently.

No less succulent was the result of a television discussion in which I slated the drink industry for so intermingling sex and drink that we all think you can't have one without the other, and none of us get enough of either – a taunt, incidentally, that I used nearly to death for years afterwards. I again went for spiced wines and the irresponsible pushing of drink at young people. In a pained letter to David Ennals, secretary of state for health,

Vice-Admiral Colin Madden, director general of the Brewers' Society, expressed his

'despondency' at 'the attitude of a senior official of an important public body'.

Ambrosia.

Determined not to relieve the gloom, I turned to the fat content of so-called lean meat and elicited a refreshingly furious letter to Sir Harold from a beef baron, as one might say, about what I was doing to the poor, afflicted meat industry. And when, as part of the 'Look After Yourself' campaign, we sponsored a strip cartoon in a women's magazine giving the facts about sugar, a new kind of opponent emerged. He was Michael Shersby, director of the British Sugar Bureau and a puppet MP who never failed to speak up for sugar in the House of Commons, but did little else. He wrote us a four-page letter disputing what our consultant, one of a battery of experts on whom we could call, had approved. Also in apparent denial, the Cocoa, Chocolate and Confectionery Alliance put profit before the dangers to children's teeth by defending:

A finger of fudge is just the thing to give the kids a treat.

And:

Whenever you feel like a treat, have a Crunchie.

In a similar strain I inveighed against a sugar culture which started with the slug of sterile dextrose given to newborn babies instead of the mother's colostrum, an excellent first nutrient. Thereafter, I pointed out, parental treats and punishments consisted respectively in giving and withholding sweets, which evolved at teenage into sex symbols. The results were obesity and dental caries levels higher than those of most comparable countries. With other counter-curricular jousts, these efforts provoked Gilbert Lamb, director of the Incorporated Society of British Advertisers to tell Sir Harold that:

Some ISBA members are extremely angry.

A benison. With it came an invitation from the Office of Fair Trading to join a working party looking at the degree of compliance of the industry with its own code of conduct. That we were highly critical did not stop its publicity managers from calling our report a vindication and a source of strength. Commenting on that lie I wrote in *Campaign*:

> Perhaps the trouble lies in the narcissists that advertising attracts ... Perhaps the cure – is to take a hard, full-frontal look at what advertising does to people; and what more of them than our tiny sample think of it.

As the consistently tough and supportive Sir Harold's term of office drew towards its end, I valued those qualities even more. Our 'Look After Yourself' campaign prospered, with much press coverage as a bonus. Even the *New York Times* praised it, wrongly but flatteringly reporting us as having lined up the Army, the TUC, MPs and the television industry in a mass effort. One component was a poster about the risks of smoking to pregnant women and their offspring. It was to have featured a female nude, her decency preserved with a superimposed diagram of the lungs, umbilical link and foetus. At the last minute our Saatchi account executive Alex Finn (later a prominent football writer) reported that technical snags with the diagram would delay its release. Very preoccupied, I told him to omit the diagram despite his warning that the result would be a pregnant nude complete with pubic hair, still not accepted as something to the existence of which polite society could admit.

When I warned Sir Harold of an impending rumpus he welcomed it, pointing out that it would get the whole country talking and that we would hardly need the posters. So it proved. We got our best ever media coverage, some scandalised, some laudatory, but all most welcome. Much more importantly, the survey of results showed, incredibly, that there had been a behaviour change among pregnant women of 10 per cent; 1 or 2 per cent would have been a fair expectation. An independent check confirmed the result.

I was soon invited to join a small party of visitors from the Department of Health to attend the annual conference of the American Cancer Society (ACS) in New York. I did a presentation on the success of the pregnant nude to an ACS plenary session, as well as a great many broadcasts including an appearance on the prestigious nationwide television *Today Show*. Many interruptive requests for broadcasts by me came over the announcement system during conference sessions; and it soon emerged that I had, unknowingly and unintentionally, displaced from pole position the chief British visitor, the department's chief medical officer Sir George

Is it fair to force your baby to smoke cigarettes?

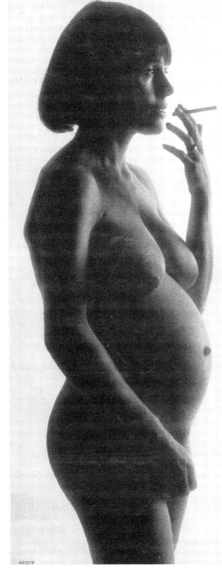

This is what happens if you smoke when you're pregnant.

Every time you inhale you fill your lungs with nicotine and carbon monoxide.

Your blood carries these impurities through the umbilical cord into your baby's bloodstream.

Smoking can restrict your baby's normal growth inside the womb.
It can make him underdeveloped and underweight at birth.
Which, in turn, can make him vulnerable to illness in the first delicate weeks of his life.
It can even kill him.
Last year, in Britain alone, over 1,500 babies might not have died if their mothers had given up smoking when they were pregnant.

If you give up smoking when you're pregnant your baby will be as healthy as if you'd never smoked.

The Health Education Council

AS227P

The pregnant nude, perhaps the most successful health education poster ever.
Crown copyright/Dept. of Health

275

Godber. He was a tall, forbidding man with a patch over an eye socket resulting from a rugger field accident in his youth. I thought that his brusque manner when we met at the innumerable parties marked displeasure at his ouster; but I was assured that he was like that anyway.

Back home I ran into another dust-up, as it were, this time with the Flour Advisory Bureau, the respectable face of the English and Irish Millers Association. The director was Vice-Admiral Martin Lucey, a former student of mine at the Joint Services Staff College whose invitation to lecture at the bureau's conference I was glad to accept. Having sent him a script for advance publicity purposes and gone on holiday to the south of France, I was surprised by a telegram, laboriously hand-delivered to our rented holiday cottage up a hill above Menton:

Your lecture ... is a crusade against food industry and its Advertising. Could not let you deliver it or I would get sack ... either recast to my guidelines or stand down.

What a gift. I gave the text maximum publicity, receiving such headlines as the *Daily Mail*'s:

I was gagged, says Health Chief in food for fatties storm.

And having described Mother's Pride white bread as deserving of the label 'Mother's Shame, tasting like Polyfilla', got a sequel:

What to do when you run out of filler.

The lecture was a serious piece deserving of a hearing. I quoted the terrible figures for childhood dental disease: 31 per cent of under-fives, for example, having five or more rotten teeth.

On another nutritional topic:

The decline of the breast from a nutritional organ to what Margaret Drabble called magic putty had more to it than a bonanza for the artificial baby food industry ... interfering with one part of a complex natural structure ... [may] have unintended effects you will greatly regret.

The Butter Information Council's answer to the ... cholesterol controversy [includes] the statement that butter does not contain [any] ... hardened fish or vegetable oils whatsoever ... that disreputable half truth ... evades the fact that the cow is a natural hydrogenator ... butter is what the statement implies that it isn't – a hard fat.

The Milk Marketing Board represents milk as 'natural and wholesome among today's multitude of processed food with additives' ... That baffles me ... the only natural milk product for man is breast milk ... conversely cow's milk is natural only to a calf.

The doctors' glossy magazine *World Medicine* sucked up to its clinical readership with characteristic hostility, the aptly named author of their article Fred Kavalier bitterly criticising the use of campaigns. The admirable Sir Douglas Black, later to turn up in the peace movement, began a meeting of the Research Committee at the height of the row in his cultured Scots brogue with:

Alastair, to have had a vicious article about you in *World Medicine* is to have *arraived*.

My relationship with another knight from the department was very different. Not long after the New York encounter with him came the announcement that Sir George Godber, on his retirement from the department, would take over as Chairman of the HEC. He soon turned up, having given a farewell party at which he, as was his lifelong habit, did not drink: nor, by his decree, did anyone else. Gone were the weekly consultations. Instead Sir George barged, from time to time and usually without notice, into my office. I usually stood up and almost clicked my heels; but on one morning I was in the middle of a conversation in French with a colleague in the IUHE in Paris. My continuance of the dialogue with the director of what he had described as 'a bunch of French geriatrics' did not find favour. And so often did we find it impossible to agree, that I resumed a practice reserved for talks with the disputatious – that of writing down what he said in a special book. In time we settled into icy cordiality. To be fair, he made very useful contributions from time to time, drawing on vast knowledge and experience and a wealth of contacts. But he was egregiously bad at chairing the quarterly council meetings, which became fractious and seemingly interminable. Part of the cause was that, try as he did, he never grasped the difference between a big organisation and a small one. Personal letters for him, for example, he passed on marked 'treat as official'.

The burden to which Godber added most was that of planning, two years ahead, the next international conference of his so-called French geriatrics; actually for health educators from about 90 countries which I had got authority to stage in London in 1979. Having been elected to the Executive of the International Union for Health Education soon after I joined on Britain's behalf, and incidentally polished up my French, I saw the London conference as a way of putting this country back on the health map. So it proved. As a preliminary, Ian Sutherland and I learnt how not to organise an IUHE conference at its chaotic French predecessor in Paris in 1988. We both played our parts in the proceedings; but my most vivid recollection is social. At a huge French Government reception in the Palace of Versailles I met an American physician professor with whom I had corresponded about his family health encyclopedia and his daughter, a lady of uncertain age, overweight and not blessed with good looks. Not, perhaps, used to champagne on the lavish scale that obtained, she first became talkative and then amorous, literally pursuing me as I socialised with groups of acquaintances. So pressing were her attentions that, to avoid a scene, I literally ran out of the palace and went back to Paris for a quiet dinner. Using the very different example of the next conference in Ottawa, superbly organised, we pressed forward, booking the Royal Festival Hall and parts of King's College on the opposite side of the Thames.

Meanwhile life under Sir George became harder. Much had to be done, as Lord Donovan would have put it, *sub silentio*, and our encounters became more acidulated. Having barged into one of our weekly management team meetings, he was told of a decision we had just reached. His thunderous reaction was:

I make all the decisions.

That called for an entry in my book, which I made with surly deliberation. Thinking better of hitting me, he stormed out. What remained of the relationship soon evaporated. During a press conference at the Royal College of Nursing, David Ennals, about to lose office in the coming election, announced portentously that health warnings on cigarette packets would now include 'seriously' between 'Smoking can' and 'damage your health'. Referring to research into the effectiveness of health warnings, I questioned whether the change would not either have no effect, or make matters worse. Having met him once or twice and knowing that he expected the so-called independent council to criticise him, I did not doubt that he would take my question in good part, which he did. Soon afterwards I heard that Sir George had apologised to him on my behalf. I wrote complaining of the gratuitous and insulting action taken behind my back, and asking for a hearing of my complaint at the forthcoming council meeting. After asking me to withdraw my letter and being refused, he duly put it before the council.

The hearing was pantomimic. As director general, I had first to advise Sir George not to chair the meeting because he was the object of the complaint; and then, as Alastair Mackie, step as it were into the dock. The Vice-Chairman Leslie Baines took over and I went for Sir George, growing more voluble as I got angrier, and broadening the scope of my complaint. The upshot was of course inconclusive and Leslie wrote me a mild reproof for being too rude in my spokesman role. I ignored it; half aware, perhaps, that outspokenness had already been my undoing.

A chance for defiance soon came. The Research Committee had commissioned a study of the effects of sugar advertising on children's health from my friend from dental days Aubrey Sheiham, now a professor at the London Hospital Medical College. With a co-author he came up with a gem of a report on the harmful effects of sugar entitled 'Sweet Nothings', notably condemning Mars Bars. As a research document awaiting formal release by the council, we put a copy as usual in the library for use by the health professional clientele. Our astute librarian reported visits from a suspiciously unprofessional individual who studied the report assiduously. I soon had a letter from the managing director of Mars Confectionery asking me, in effect, to withdraw 'Sweet Nothings'. I refused, referring him to our policy of publishing robust comment; and authorising him personally, as special favour, to consider himself one of the privileged few entitled to read it. We later splashed it all over the lay press, one organ of which embellished it with a photograph of monkeys enjoying Mars Bars in their cage.

Sir George departed to widespread rejoicing, replaced by Dr Brian Lloyd, a physiology and mathematics don and Director at Oxford Polytechnic. He was a most agreeable man, but inclined to push logic too far towards its conclusions for health education, an inexact art and science, to bear. He at once set about helping with the IUHE conference, now looming and worryingly low in bookings. He was also particularly supportive of Ian Sutherland's curriculum development project, nearing fruition, and engaged in ordinary business competently and with humour.

The delegate numbers for the conference at last rose enough for respectability, partly because of the generosity of the IUHE's wealthy French treasurer, who funded 200 health educators from African countries. They had made their way to London hoping for free seats which we could not give. They were as delighted to get in as we were to have their contributions to our work. The opening address was by Patrick Jenkin, Secretary of State for Health in the new Government. He spoke very well, praising our 'Look After Yourself' campaign and pointing out the 'chance to share ... experience ... gathered from all corners of the world'.

Which is exactly what we did. After visiting as many of the activities as possible, and endless, as it seemed, bilingual socialising, I gave the closing address. The location being a musical centre, I entitled it an obligato to the conference themes: these were to see how much regard for health education figured in national planning in the member countries; how, in the International Year of Youth, children's and young people's health was being served in their school and family surroundings; and, as always, how successfully health educators everywhere were doing their job. I posited the idea of a 'Health Voice', meaning that health as an entity had a case which it should be entitled to put whenever and wherever the need arose.

In my normal work I continued to plug and articulate that idea in a growing number of media activities. In a copiously illustrated article in the

Garnished with the results of other people's work. *The Sunday Telegraph/Ian Murphy*

280

Daily Telegraph colour supplement ('Here comes the Health Man'), Elizabeth Dunn called me 'something of a fighter. In his job he needs to be.'

In a similar London *Evening Standard* feature article ('The Holborn Bodyguard') Maureen Cleave, accurately airing my prejudices, ended with:

> One can only hope that New Smoking Material, rickets, smoking, Mothers to be, dental caries, parent education and contraception will continue to engross his daring spirit.

Obverse flattery came from Anne Edwards, columnist of the *Sunday Express*, who quarrelled with the 'purblind assumption' that 'some superior body' should have the right to take over a parent's responsibility, advising Mrs Thatcher to:

> chop out this Council – futile lock, stock and dangerous barrel.

I hope it made her feel better. Also better out than in was the refusal to rest, as John Gordon, Anne's frightful editor, had resolved, until he had rid the country of the pregnant nude poster. I'm sure their advertisers were grateful. 'So, doubtless, was Mrs Valerie Riches, dauntless head of the smugly named Responsible Society. Responsible indeed it was – for the result of never allowing its ignorance of the adolescent world to prevent it from inveighing against anything we or the Family Planning Association put out to help young people cope with their sexuality and limit their offspring by knowing more about sex. Very different were the genuine worries of a serious young peer, Lord Hilton, who took the trouble to come and see me. He left content with my assurance that nothing about sex left the building without personal vetting by me.

I kept sowing the seeds of my own destruction. Patrick Jenkin released, on the Friday afternoon before a bank holiday, a report by Sir Douglas Black, now retired, with Professors Townsend and Morris, respectively giants of sociology and community medicine. What Jenkin was anxious to smother came to be known as the Black Report, whose thrust was that the poor, and especially the unemployed, were being let down by the health and social services, suffering disproportionately from illness caused by poor diet and inability to fend for themselves. On the council's behalf I gave the report as much publicity as we could muster. The Health Voice, as I saw it, was speaking:

> Features such as work accidents, overcrowding and cigarette smoking, which are strongly class-related ... have clear causal significance.

281

> Thirty years of the welfare state and of the NHS have achieved little in reducing social inequalities in health.

Another nail in my coffin was driven home when, to a man and woman, my fellow workers and I refused a direct departmental instruction, the first ever, to mount a national publicity campaign about rickets and its adult clone osteomalacia. Our reasons were that the target public were all Asian, largely illiterate, blessed with tight-knit extended families; given personal advice on preventing these afflictions by health visitors; aware of the problem from the vernacular press; and consumers of the vitamin-irradiated ghee that warded it off. All of which were factors bringing about a steady decline. The instigator, we suspected, was the new minister of health, Dr (later, of course, Sir) Gerard Vaughan, who saw the campaign as a useful vote-getter in his largely Asian constituency.

When the moment came, Brian Lloyd proved to be my benevolent assassin. Had he been less well-disposed, I would have been tempted to tell all, make a lot of money and risk damage to the council. As it was, we negotiated a decent but not greedy package for my departure. I would be given an 18-month paid sabbatical, working as necessary for the IUHE of which I was on a three-year term as President, and a pension equivalent to what would have been payable if I had retired at 65. Meanwhile a director-general designate would be recruited. Predictably, there was a fuss. A tame MP called James Pawsey (should it have been cat's-pawsey?) complained in the House of Commons of the arrangement and asked Dr Vaughan whether he would cease to fund the HEC. No, said the minister, in an answer that I had helped to draft, the Secretary of State thought:

> the arrangement ... will be well justified by the work in this field to be carried out by the present Director General in his office as President of the International Union for Health Education.

I was sad to leave this, my longest and most fulfilling job. I continued to do what I could, including a couple of letters in *The Times*. One, sending up the unintentional copying of our 'caring hands' symbol by the Northern Ireland social service authority, was meant to buttress the council by calling for 'hands off'. The other, questioning whether there is a life *before* death, went on:

> and should we live it for ourselves or hand it over to the drink and tobacco advertisers?

With my IUHE Presidential hat on I got another one printed, harping on my favourite theme:

It is all very well that low fat spreads should be exposed as an expensive way of buying water, just as slimming breads offer comparably expensive air ... [but] what the food industry's customers really need is a simple guide not only to the fat content of what it dishes up but also that of other substances of which the most notable is sugar concealed ... in ... foods.

which came about: *post hoc*, certainly; but *propter hoc* I very much doubt. I think Lord Cohen, founding father of health education would have been pleased.

Working for the union and using the pleasant presidential perk of taking Rachel, I chaired an executive meeting in Perugia and lectured to students of the giant university there, later touring Umbria and speaking at the jazz festival village of Spoleto. On another Italian sortie I presented a lay paper about smoking deterrence at a medical conference about smoking in youth. Dwelling on the counter-curriculum run by the tobacco industry, then spreading to the Third World, I instanced the member of the European Parliament Sir David Nicholson who, as late as 1980, continued to deny the validity of the medical evidence of the toxicity of cigarettes without bothering to mention that he was chairman of Rothmans International; and four British MPs paid as advisers to British American Tobacco – Sir Anthony Kershaw, R.C. Mitchell, Teddy Taylor and Michael Martin (later Speaker). We worked on the enchanting islet of San Giorgio Maggiore, exploring Venice, almost devoid of tourists, in unbroken November sunshine. On a similar jaunt, also sunny but insufferably hot, was Athens where I gave a similar lecture, getting a privileged sightseeing tour in return.

There were also agreeable sorties into Eastern Europe. One was to chair a meeting at the Black Sea resort of Varna, in Bulgaria. With a colleague from Finland I ventured out of a comfortable but hideous shoebox of a multistorey hotel to the public beach. It was packed with sweating humanity, most of it obese. We sat briefly in the last two buttocks-sized spaces before retreating to our respective balconies. On leaving I was embarrassed to have to declare more money than the statutory maximum with which I had arrived, having earned a fee for a broadcast in English. While two hulking border guards were discussing, as I thought, what fearful fate was to be mine, there appeared a Bulgarian-speaking French air stewardess. She explained that they were wondering how to ask me to spend the excess in the airport buffet, so that they would be freed from their obligation to report it. Smiles and thanks all round. And some terrible red wine to take home.

Initially more alarming was going to Moscow in 1975 to make a speech at the Central Institute for Scientific Research in Health Education as part of the celebration of its 75th anniversary (in common, incidentally, with the host of Soviet institutions founded at the time of the Soviet Revolution). A grim official at the passport barrier in the VIP reception lounge looked at my passport and ushered me into a small room furnished only with a chair and a very young armed soldier. He stood and I sat in silence. We awaited developments for about half an hour and I, mystified and getting mildly desperate, was about to get up and try to leave when a formidable woman, not unlike Lady Donaldson of the Middle Temple, burst in and said something very rude to the soldier. She then apologised for being late in arriving to meet me. The trouble, she explained, was that my visa did not become valid until midnight on the day of my arrival; the official action, had she not intervened, would have been to keep me incarcerated until that time. I stayed in nineteenth-century luxury in an enormous hotel, each of the many floors of which had a *babushka* (literally 'grandmother', but also meaning a formidable female) on duty to ensure propriety. The institute was an immaculate mansion of the same period as the hotel, faultlessly maintained and decorated. In a large, round gilt and red hall I greeted the audience by saying what a pleasure and privilege it was to be in Moscow, a city I had been planning to visit for some years. I watched a smile spreading along a row of seats at one end of which was my friend Professor Loransky, head of the institute, to whom I had disclosed that Moscow had indeed been a city I had been planning to visit – in a Vulcan with a hydrogen bomb. He was sharing the joke with guests in the adjoining seats.

From time to time my presidency gave me contact with the high and mighty. One such occasion was at a conference of doctors in Amsterdam wanting to learn more about the techniques of patient education which the union had developed. Just as the proceedings began an elderly lady dressed in expensive tweeds walked into the auditorium and took a front seat. No announcement, no ceremony, nothing but genuine interest: it was Queen Wilhelmina of the Netherlands. Impressive in a different way was President Giscard d'Estaing of France, addressing the third of the annual series of conferences of international experts on the environment organised in Paris. Instead of the formal opening that heads of state customarily perform, he gave a brilliantly well-informed 40-minute lecture, remarking at the end, 'I wish I'd had more time to work on that script.' He continued ad lib for a further 20 minutes on the exemplary environmental work going on in France: the only European country, to quote but one of his instances, with more deciduous forests in 1979 than in 1900. The two eminent professors between whom I sat agreed afterwards that the lecture had been 'inspired'.

The next, and for me the final international conference, was to be in Hobart, Tasmania where I arrived early to give the president-to-be, Paul Hindson, a hand. We were intrigued by 20 or so applicants for admission from France and the USA, lacking health education credentials, whom we accepted for the sake of their fees with some unease. It turned out that they had been sent by US and French official organisations to vote down a resolution which I, in cahoots with my colleagues the heads of health education in the Irish Republic, East and West Germany as they then were, Italy and the Soviet Union had concocted:

> The General Assembly ... addresses itself to all ... member Countries, asking them for active support of the struggle for the banning of nuclear weapons ...

The resolution was carried with acclamation, to the fury of the specially imported phonies, ending my career in health and starting my work for the peace movement.

I had ended my Presidential address, acknowledging our perennial indigence by commending a starving eagle as a better educator then a fat hen, with:

> Establishing a Health Voice is the final *tutti* of my *obligato* ... Countering the counter curriculum and putting health and non-Health in perspective constitute ... [for the IUHE] ... a serviceable perch for an international, non-official, non-Establishment, loose-limbed eagle with sharp claws, no objection to losing a few feathers and a good loud squawk.

Which it still is. My own squawk, silenced only for the time being, my feathers bedraggled but still there and my pecker up, I reflected that grinning a great deal, bearing quite a lot and laying bare as much as I could had been fun enough to make me continue. So I did.

Chapter 14

A Peace of My Mind

'I knew you wouldn't last long after the Tories got in,' said David Ennals, now a Lord. 'Godber kept telling me he wanted to get rid of you but we wouldn't have it.'

Ennals, knowing I knew something of Defence, had asked me to go with him to see Michael Heseltine, then Defence Secretary, to talk about the Bomb. At the ministry door an acolyte from the sixth floor told us that Heseltine would not receive us. Having given our names in advance, we had, I feared, been brushed off because of me, a renegade and thus a Jonah. Anyway, that did it: I decided to join the Campaign for Nuclear Disarmament. I had long admired its work but felt uneasy about some of the oddballs on the fringes. It wasn't that some were Communists: I had had sympathy with Communism as a boy. But I was no anarchist and not a Trot. Bruce Kent, I realised, was a senior Roman Catholic priest and was variously president and secretary. Having him at the centre counterbalanced, I decided, any peripheral deficiencies.

I hit the CND ground running, having spent the year or so since I had finished my presidency of the IUHE reading as much as I could to refresh my knowledge of Defence, the Anglo-American relationship and the Bomb. Perhaps because of a press report I was asked, almost at once, to give a talk at a CND-group run by a Mrs Prins in the familiar city of Bath. They liked the talk and she put me in touch with her son Gwyn, a don at Emmanuel College Cambridge, from whom I later learnt a great deal and with whom I did some tutoring myself. Soon after the Bath talk I gave another in Portsmouth, using a quotation from the Articles of War of 1652, which define the Royal Navy as protector of the 'safety, honour and welfare' of the nation. Trident submarines and missiles, I argued, negated all three. It went down well, particularly with Bruce Kent who happened to be present. Bruce went on to support me as he did many others, and I was soon in demand from CND groups.

Within weeks I was elected to the CND Council, the main organ for making decisions apart from the annual conference. Decisions were not its strong point: it was more of an incubus left over from CND's inception.

Modelled on typical trade union structure and cursed with excess of democracy, the council was a magnet for bores, log-rollers and obfuscators; Heaven for finders of difficulties for solutions; and Hell for the chair, secretary and committee chairs trying to run the show. Later, having been elected a vice-chair myself, I was greeted by *The Guardian* and *Daily Mail* with 'CND General on the Warpath' and 'DFC is the voice of CND' and soon had backers keen to see me as chair. That provoked an interview with *The Guardian* in which I was glad to be quoted:

> The country still thinks that patriotism and nuclear weapons are ... intertwined ... We are the only country where there is no progress – only retrogress ... We, like an ageing whore, are importuning to get more garrisoning from the USA.

They doubted whether I would take the job. After a long dither and consultation with Bruce I turned it down. That cleared the field for Marjorie Thompson, also a vice-chair, a previous staff member of great ability, and an American of right-wing upper-class parentage which gave her added attraction. After her tearful start at chairing the council, Bruce and I took her to a pub for a calming lunchtime drink. The pub turned out to be a local IRA nest, into whose coffers a menacing collector importuned us to put money. Marjorie served well but was under great strain, arguing on television with politicians about the first Gulf War and putting up with internal dissensions. She eventually left for a job with Saatchi & Saatchi, having become as fed up with the awful council as I was. I devised a simpler and cheaper form of governance which, once officers had been chosen and elected, would have allowed them to get on with their jobs without interference. It went straight to oblivion.

More agreeable and easier to run was one of CND's fraternal offshoots – Ex-Services CND. Its origin, in 1984, was fury amongst anti-nuclear former members of the Services at the propaganda that oozed from the Thatcher government vilifying CND as a bunch of Communists, cowards and even traitors. Its founder, the heroic and self-effacing John Stanley, suffered as a Jewish child in Nazi Germany, escaping to join the British Army. As a member of the First Airborne Division, he later fought with great courage and fortitude with the beleaguered ground force at Arnhem. Its membership included two fellows of the Royal Society, Robert Hinde and Hugh Tinker; Horace Dammers, dean of Bristol Cathedral; Olive Price, a former Service chaplain; Commander Robert Green, a former Fleet Air Arm navigator; and the rest of us, numbering about a thousand at our zenith. No less welcoming was Christian CND, known for the well-researched articles in its excellent *Journal* and the impressive annual gathering on Ash Wednesday at the Ministry of Defence to protest against nuclear weapons in which I regularly take part.

I put out another tentacle. Hearing Brigadier Michael Harbottle talking about Generals for Peace on the radio I got in touch and was invited to join. Formed by Michael and General von Meyenfeldt of the Netherlands in 1981, it was an association of retired field, flag and air officers from Britain, France, Germany, Greece, Italy, the Netherlands and Portugal, of which I became the fourteenth member. All from NATO member nations (except of course France, but she was in the Western fold), we were in touch with a corresponding group of generals and admirals from countries of the Warsaw Pact. One of the attractions of membership was that a leading searcher for Reds under the bed and a paradoxical figure, Lord Chalfont, had taken a hostile interest. He had, *inter alia*, expressed great concern from the libel-proof shelter of the House of Lords in 1984 (Hansard 30 October 1984, col 434ff). During question time he had first given vent to grievous worries about a Libyan girls' school in Chelsea. The minister of state, happily, was able to reassure him that the little girls were not a menace to the Body Politic. Turning to Generals for Peace, he asked another minister of state whether she would not agree:

> that ex-NATO generals who held very high positions should now be meeting serving Soviet generals for discussions about western Europe is a matter of grave concern?

She, too was anxious about our meetings in Vienna, having been misinformed about them. She and Lord Chalfont were reassured by two famous ex-MPs, by then lords, Fenner Brockway and Hugh Jenkins, who told the House that all of us, Soviets included, were retired; that one of our purposes was to prevent a nuclear war with all its threat to mankind; and that, as our brochure in the Commons library showed, the policies we put forward were

> almost identical in many respects with those of Her Majesty's Opposition.

Chalfont had retired from the Army as Lieutenant Colonel Alun Gwyn Jones to enter journalism. As Defence correspondent for *The Times*, his views at the time seemed to correspond with those of CND. Concluding an article on the idiocy of the French *force de frappe*, he wrote:

CND leafleting in Putney with Lord (Hugh) Jenkins. *Wandsworth Courier*

... I seem to be suggesting that the French nuclear tests are being carried out in pursuit of a policy which has no military significance, which is based on a false sense of national pride, and which puts existing arms control agreements at risk. Well, actually I am. You may further suggest that everything I have said applies equally to the British nuclear striking force. Well, actually it does.

An odd change of attitude was to come. In a later letter written to *The Times* as president of the House of Lords, he ended with:

... the argument that there is also a threat from nuclear terrorism ... does not mean that, just because we cannot defend ourselves against *all* threats, we should not defend ourselves against *some*.

'Shome mishtake shurely?' as Private Eye's Ed might have put it. Chalfont later went into business, chairing or becoming a director of companies in the security and private police industry, omitted from the many other directorships listed in his *Who's Who* entry. He was also associated with the Coalition for Peace and Security. The coalition, said to have been financed by various right-wing private organisations in Britain and the United States, went in for disrupting CND meetings:

> with a retinue of sniggering storm troopers from the Federation of Conservative students

as one report described it, and of which I had personal experience. The prime mover in the coalition was Dr Julian Lewis, an MP described in his parliamentary profile as 'to the right of Mrs Thatcher', who had described its object as being 'to counter unilateralist propaganda'. At the opposite extreme in doing and being just what it said, and later to flourish as a well-regarded source for all concerned with Defence and peace studies, was the British American Security Information Council (BASIC), originated by Dan Plesch, who went on to become a peace studies authority of great potential.

Thus I acquired a catholic acquaintance with the arrogantly self-styled 'peace movement' (many people and associations, not least the Services, can legitimately claim aspiration to peace). I began a life of writing, speaking and broadcasting not unlike that of my time in health education, but free of the trammels of being a director general.

The core of what I sought to achieve in the peace movement ('The Cause', as a mildly mocking article in the *Catholic Herald* engineered by Bruce put it), was, strangely enough, peace, narrowing down to the abolition of nuclear weapons and especially directed at the so-called British Bomb. The origin was my fury at having to lug the hydrogen bomb about in a Vulcan for no reason other than the access of pelf which it brought to the politicians. To round my knowledge out I had begun delving into origins and causes at the Joint Services Staff College, and later in the Cabinet Office and in the Ministry of Defence. My convictions strengthened as my knowledge broadened.

A harmless delusion of grandeur became, I realised, a menace when, having invented the atom bomb and handed it over to the Americans because they had the resources to develop it, we British were refused access by the US McMahon Act of 1946 to what we regarded as our own weapon. The British Government, reflecting hurt national pride, decided that we must take part in it by developing a Bomb of our own. As Ernest

Bevin, a great foreign secretary in the Attlee Labour Government, put it to the Cabinet Defence Committee in 1947:

> I never want any Foreign Secretary to be treated as I have been [by his US opposite number] ... we've got to have this thing over here whatever it costs ... We've got to have the bloody Union Jack flying over it.

A later Tory Prime Minister, Harold Macmillan, said it was:

> on account of the influence and prestige that we should gain.

His Minister of Defence, Duncan Sandys, Churchill's son in law, feared in a secret meeting revealed in 1989 that:

> dropping out might lead to a Pacifist outlook.

Another Churchill, Winston's eponymous grandson, took a wider view. The bombing of Hiroshima and Nagasaki, he maintained in a letter to *The Times*, had been:

> a correct and necessary expedient.

I managed to get a letter published with a quotation from his grandfather's memoirs:

> It would be a mistake to suppose that the fate of Japan was settled by the bomb. Her defeat was certain before the first bomb fell and was brought about by overwhelming maritime power.

That did not stop young Churchill from asserting in a later defence debate, in 1987, that:

> Those countries that do not possess nuclear weapons or do not have the privilege of belonging to a large nuclear alliance ... are pygmies in defence terms.

He followed that, oxymoronically, by describing Britain as:

> a nation that aspires to be the world's greatest policeman, second only to the United States.

Thus having our own bomb did not arise from fear of Soviet hordes pouring across the Channel, but from the need to assuage hurt national pride. Further rationalisations were inevitable. The dottiest was that the British Bomb would provide a 'third centre of decision-making'. When mounting tension between the USA and the USSR caused the imminence of a nuclear exchange, ran this nostrum, the Soviets would face the added dilemma caused by not knowing whether the British would enter the fray. Nobody I knew doubted that, as the giants reached the stage of eyeball to eyeball, a midget tripping around their feet could but make such uncertainty worse and a cataclysm inevitable. Myopia of that kind permeated defence politics, many of those who practised them having an outlook still conditioned by the glory days of empire. As the V-force became obsolete as a weapons system, it was beyond debate that nuclear-armed submarines should replace it. Harold Wilson, later prime minister, recorded that Macmillan,

fearful of a revolt from his right wing, managed to wring from a reluctant President Kennedy an undertaking to provide the know-how for the building of Polaris submarines together with the missiles to stock them.

That is a pointer to the political impasse that has plagued Britain ever since. The politicians have implanted in the electorate the notion that a nuclear capability is integral to Britain's greatness. Imbued with that notion, voters will not tolerate a political party that does not support it. Thus the voters and the voted-for alike are stuck. And while most voters remain unable to distinguish a deterrent from a detergent, no way out is in sight.

Polaris itself soon became obsolete and had to be improved in secret with Chevaline. Then came Trident, no less American than its predecessors. The warheads, though made in Britain at Aldermaston, are of American design. The missiles are made and maintained in America. The two together cannot operate without navigational guidance from satellites whose owners, the US Defence Department, can switch them off at will.

Knowing all of this tended to improve the content of my talks and writings. So did a study of what the military thought of nuclear weapons and what they could do for us. They were divided. At the very beginning the chief of defence staff, Lord Mountbatten and Sir Gerald Templer, head of the Army (though not their Naval and Air Force colleague members of the Chiefs of Staff Committee) were

293

absolutely opposed [to] the concept of an independent nuclear deterrent.

Mountbatten later flip-flopped, joining a later set of chiefs in telling the Prime Minister Harold Wilson in 1964 that they were:

> unanimous ... that the only practical defence in military terms against direct attack or blackmail is the possession of our own nuclear retaliatory capability.

But shortly before his assassination, Mountbatten reverted to his original view in a famous speech at an international peace conference in Stockholm in 1979:

> As a military man who has given half a century of active service I say in all sincerity that the nuclear arms race has no military purpose. Wars cannot be fought with nuclear weapons. Their existence only adds to our worries because of the illusions which they have generated.

Field Marshal Lord Carver, the best military brain of his generation and a lifelong friend of my brother's, was more consistent and succinct, asking of the Bomb:

> What the bloody hell's it for?

He expanded on the theme in one of his classic military studies:

> If one wishes to deter one's potential opponent from embarking on a military adventure by the threat of the possible use of nuclear weapons against his forces or his country, one must appear to be prepared to use them in certain circumstances. But if one actually does so and is answered back in kind, one is likely to finish up very much worse off than if one had not initiated their use, even if the enemy restricts their use to the same level as one has oneself; and there is no way by which one can confidently assume that.

In a Lords Defence debate later on, he had spoken in the same strain and secured the agreement of another senior soldier, Field Marshal Lord Bramall; but he, it later emerged, must have had a less than perfect understanding of what Carver was on about. Doubtless all three great men had in mind analyses such as that of the eminent historian A.J.P. Taylor, writing of World War One:

> The prime cause ... lay in the precautions that had been taken to ensure that there would be no war. The deterrent dominated strategical planning before 1914 ... The deterrent did not prevent war. It made it inevitable.

That wasn't, I concluded, rocket science. I remembered the advice of the canonical strategist Carl Marie von Clausewitz:

> What one protagonist sees as defence the other will see as offence.

In sum, far from working as a deterrent, the Bomb in military terms *has created the very threat that it seeks to forfend.*

Nor does it end there. Britain's Bomb, the progenitor of many others, makes her the founder and exemplar of the inglorious Society of Nuclear Proliferators, of uncertain but certainly growing strength. Having to possess the Bomb warps our politicians' ability to make decisions without looking over their shoulders at what the US will think. The Bomb has made the British known as liars, proclaiming support for abolition and parading the disposal of obsolete weaponry as earnests of compliance, but secretly increasing stocks of those that matter. The Bomb, chiming as it does with our crass electorate's addiction to all things American, blinds them to the European destiny that geography, political nous and common sense demand.

I could have dug deeper but it seemed best to find out more of our lord and master, rich uncle and best buddy America. I discovered a little of the US Military when the awful Army Air Corps (AAC) pilots delivered Liberator bombers to 108 Squadron in the Desert War; and later when, in the 98th Heavy Bombardment Group AAC, 178 Squadron took the flak and the AAC the credit. I worked in 101 Squadron with Strategic Air Command, to be fair very different from their predecessors in their friendliness, efficiency and open admiration for the V-Force, regarding it as small but perfectly formed. I had worked with, and thought highly of, US health educators. I have American family. With thus, I hope, an open mind I could but notice how elegantly their own nuclear weapon affliction reflected their psyche, articulated in 'The Star Spangled Banner':

> ... The bombs bursting in air
> Gave proof through the night
> That our flag was still there ...

As soon as they knew of the work of Rutherford in Cambridge, and that of his two refugee associates, Peirles and Fritsch, America could but seize upon and develop what its inventors called 'an extremely efficient explosive', producing energy that Einstein had calculated as the product of a given mass of Uranium 235 and the square of the speed of light (186,000 miles per second). The bomb bursting in air, as it were, put them in position to defeat the Japanese thereby, but, as the nuclear historian Professor Alperovitz puts it:

> There is also widespread evidence that the bomb was totally involved in American strategy towards Europe ... impressing the Russians became an implicit or explicit reason as well.

That chimed with what had gone before. General Ulysses Grant had ensured that the Northern flag was still there, as it were, in 1865 by assembling a force large enough not so much to defeat as to obliterate his Southern opponents Lee and Jackson and their force. One of his warlord successors, General Curtis Le May, regarded his creation, Strategic Air Command, as in accordance with that strategy by dominating and dispensing with the need for other forms of warfare, a fancy that lasted until SAC gave place to a submarine weapons system in 1962. When the US Navy acquired Trident and shipboard nuclear missiles, their planners evolved New Maritime Strategy, exercised by ten huge aircraft carrier groups, each a slice of US power with multiple capabilities that placed, as a blurb described it:

> about 76% of the earth's land mass and most of the important targets within a missile's range.

All along there was no pretence, as there was and is in Britain, that nuclear weapons are only for deterrence. President-to-be George Bush, father of Dubya, exulted when he was vice president:

> You have a survivability of command and control, a survivability of industrial potential, protection of a percentage of your citizens and you have a capability that inflicts more damage than it can inflict on you. That way you have a winner.

Put in more practical terms by General Nathan Twining, chairman of the Joint Chiefs of Staff:

296

We don't build nuclear weapons for deterrence ... Their deterrence is only a by-product of their war-waging capacity.

Of course there were voices of dissent. Admiral Leahy, President Truman's chief of staff, protested that:

> The use of this barbarous weapon at Hiroshima and Nagasaki was of no material assistance in our war against Japan. The Japanese were already defeated and ready to surrender ... In being the first to use it we had adopted an ethical standard common to the barbarians of the Dark Ages.

General Eisenhower, before becoming president, had warned against the power of the 'military/industrial/economic' complex and declared nuclear war 'insane', adding:

> Japan was at that very moment seeking some way to surrender with minimum loss of face. It was not necessary to hit them with that awful thing.

The most telling protester of all was the last commander of Strategic Air Command, General Lee Butler. He signed up no fewer than 60 retired officers from 17 countries in favour of the abolition of nuclear weapons, including the supreme commander of NATO, General Goodpaster and President Yeltsin's security adviser General Aleksandr Lebed. Like me, but much more erudite, Lee had taught at the US Air Force Academy, coming out, as the phrase was, at the Moscow Forum in 1996. In a brilliant theoretical essay he points out, *inter alia*, that:

> ... deterrence, when raised to its highest level, requires that you make yourself effectively invulnerable to an enemy's attack ... Yet your perfect invulnerability would spell perfect vulnerability for your opponent, which of course he cannot accept. Consequently any balance struck is extremely unstable ... Neither the offense nor the defense has ever remained dominant for any significant period.

Such authorities had their effects. One was a wriggle by NATO, striving to bolster the Bomb and its own credibility with what was dubbed Flexible Response (a metaphor contrived, perhaps, from inconclusive sexual foreplay). That, in oversimplified terms, meant reacting to a Soviet advance with graduated nuclear counter-action, hoping that the use of smaller nuclear weapons would persuade the advancing hordes to halt or even retreat (the near-certainty of immediate nuclear escalation being shelved). If that did not work, ran the argument, there would be an upward progression in the scale of nuclear reaction. Morton Halperin, then a junior assistant secretary in the Pentagon, explained it with such clarity that he had to be sacked:

> We fight with conventional weapons until we're losing. Then we fight with tacticals [nuclear weapons] until we're losing. Then we blow up the World.

A British pundit offered so bizarre an explanation in a broadcast as almost to stop the show:

> The idea of a flexible response is you don't actually blow the World up. You may blow it up – and that's what you rather hope the opposition thinks you will do. But you do it in a graduated, controlled way.

Being a retired chief of the general staff, Field Marshal Sir Nigel Bagnall, it was too late to sack him. A duty neglected.

Such were the Anglo-American elements of my argument. To my mind the apical point was the sheer futility of the Bomb. Not needed for the defeat of Japan, it was no less devoid of purpose in a Cold War in which the threat was trumpeted in the West as *from* the Soviet Union but, after the Fulton declaration of war, was seen in the East as *to* the Soviet Union. As the American elder statesman and former ambassador to the Soviet Union, George Kennan, saw it:

> ... I, as one who has been involved in the observation of Soviet/American relations longer, I believe, than anyone in public life on either side, have never seen any evidence of any desire, intention or incentive on the Soviet side to do any of those things, (attacks on Western Europe, first nuclear strikes or what you will).

And as a Briton, Michael Howard, formerly Regius Professor of Modern History at Oxford wrote in the seventies:

> Few historians now believe that Stalin ever intended to advance his frontiers beyond the territories occupied by his forces in 1945.

I read everything I had time for, notably Howard, as above; Mike Carver's series of books on defence policy and wars of the twentieth century; Gwyn Prins my former mentor at Emmanuel College; and the Americans John Newhouse and Jonathan Schell. They, I hope, gave substance to my talks and to the useful modality of letters to the papers. I have had over 50 published about nuclear matters, almost always by *The Times*, questioning at every opportunity authorities of varying height and might. One was Mrs Thatcher who, having been told by President Reagan that the

'entire world' saluted her and her 'gallant people'

responded no less sickeningly with:

You have restored faith in the American dream, a dream of endless opportunity.

She had taken the opportunity to get from Reagan, as *The Times* leader put it, as much assurance as she needed about Trident. I asked in a letter:

If the deterrent really is British and independent, why does she need an American assurance [from President Reagan] about it? And if that assurance obliges the Americans to keep nuclear weapons in being that they might otherwise get rid of by negotiation, why is she so satisfied?

Answer came there none. Another correspondent was the very same Orr-Ewing, he of the pep talk to my 101 Squadron crews, now a Lord, who had written advising the Government not to repeat the past mistake of keeping the deterrent too small and praising a 'right decision' to make it bigger. In another letter I dismissed his worry, replacing it with:

The real worry is that Lord Orr-Ewing's counterparts in the service of Gaddafi [then acquiring nuclear weapons] must doubtless be offering similar advice – in essence that ... developing the capacity to blow up the world will somehow make it safer.

Marshal of the RAF Sir William Dickson was free of such anxiety, assuring *Times* readers in a letter that we [the British] could rely on the Americans to honour the gentleman's agreement about the use of British bases for launching a nuclear war. If, I asked,

Anglo-US consultation is thus to be relied upon as an element in our nuclear strategy, why do we bother with an independent deterrent whose sole surviving justification is that the Americans might leave us in the nuclear lurch?

Again, answer came there none. So I put another in a letter about the Foreign Secretary Douglas Hurd who had said that 'we' must act to prevent the proliferation of weapons of mass destruction:

Would Mr Hurd or one of his co-apologists explain how the eightfold increase in British strategic nuclear striking power that Trident will import will further his aspiration [to prevent proliferation] on 'our' behalf?

Silence reigned in the letter columns. The most shameful of pro-nuclear pronouncements at the time (1995) came from Malcolm Rifkind, then Defence Secretary, who sought to present Britain's nuclear weapon policy as in accordance with the nuclear non-proliferation treaty's demand for 'effective measures' to prevent proliferation. Calling the attempt evasive and disingenuous, I continued:

Mr Rifkind's version of effective measures seems to consist in withdrawing half our stock of free-fall bombs, all of which are obsolete anyway; no longer deploying Lance, an old tactical missile whose role ended with the Cold War; and lowering what he calls the 'explosive power' [a meaningless term except when defined in terms related to range and accuracy] of the nuclear inventory. The last assertion conceals what matters about the main item in the inventory. Trident, as the Commons Defence Select Committee put it, has accuracy and sophistication which 'does, and was always intended to, represent a significant enhancement of the UK's nuclear capability'.

Along came the first Gulf War. I was delighted when Christopher Lee, anchor man for the daily BBC commentaries on military aspects of events, asked me to join the other 'armchair generals' who did them. Sending up my fellows, I said in a *Times* letter that their:

brilliance of military analysis was matched only by their adherence to prophetic and patriotic principle ... I was struck, however by the similarities between what they had to say and the war commentaries in the quality press, (including, of course, *The Times*) in editions preceding their respective broadcasts. Whether the similarity is due to the excellence of defence journalism or to the capacity of the good soldier to live off the land, as it were, will never be known; and perhaps that is just as well. For my part I was glad of the salve of dealing less with the elementary war-fighting matters that engaged my fellow generals, and more with the unheeded modalities of peace-building which secured the attention but not the motivation of the politicians.

I was able to make one good military point, mystifyingly unique as far as I know, in a more serious letter:

And why, instead of blasting the Iraqi conscripts struggling to escape from Kuwait did [the Coalition forces] not advance on Basra, the capture of which would have dispatched Saddam and settled the problems of Iraq within days?

A few readers reacted well in each instance. But I have seldom had much response to my many letters other than appeals for money and the letting off of steam by nutters. Possibly more effective were those bearing multiple signatures. One such letter was about British obduracy in refusing to stop testing nuclear weapons as had America, France and Russia. My co-signatories, all from BASIC, included James Callaghan, Dennis Healey and Christopher Mayhew. Another combined effort bitterly criticised the Thatcher Government's hollow protestations about non-proliferation while going ahead nevertheless with enhancing the capability of Trident; the other signatories were Harold Pinter the playwright; Hugh (Lord) Jenkins, famous as an outstanding MP for Putney and a friend; Mark Santer, Bishop of Birmingham; and the eminent Professor Dorothy Hodgkin. Having accepted an invitation to join the Committee for a Just Peace in the Middle East, I signed a letter drawing attention to the hatred the Coalition, then as later, was generating in the Arab world. The other signatories were MPs Jeremy Corbyn, a steadfast supporter and later vice-chair of CND; Ken Livingstone; Alice Mahon, a doughty fighter and chair; and the MP and later Lord Dafydd Ellis Thomas. All three letters, I like to think, had some effect in stirring the oceanic sub-currents that eventually affect public opinion.

Concurrent with all this epistolary and vocal activity went travel. Visits to CND branches took me to such pleasant bits of Britain, hitherto unvisited, as Lowestoft and Lancaster, as well as familiar stamping grounds such as Frome, Oxford, Cambridge and my beloved Malvern. To

301

provide local sugar for the anti-nuclear pill I used parts of Daniel Defoe's fascinating *Tour of the Whole Island of Great Britain*, written in 1725/26. CND branch talks I found dull because my invariably appreciative audiences tended to consist only in the converted. One competitive event, however, was in Banbury, debating with Captain Bernard Jenkin RN (ret), brother of Patrick one of my ushers-out from the health world. One of a NATO panel of speakers, he lacked knowledge and training. Not so another opponent, Sir Geoffrey Johnson Smith, an able and charming Tory MP with whom I jousted at Hailsham, in Sussex. The match was marred by a pro-nuclear cleric who so mischaired the meeting that he needed to be shouted at. I obliged. More stimulating still were public school debates in which I took part at Eton, Harrow, Marlborough and (twice) Bradfield. There was always civilised and well-informed opposition from masters and perky, well-briefed boys.

Their very opposites were the louts from the Federation of Conservative Students, who had to be asked to leave from a meeting near Tamworth where I went as part of a tour in a special CND exhibition bus, paid for from a legacy and covering a big area of the Midlands. Julian Lewis MP himself turned up at a meeting to which Bruce Kent had come along in support. He had behaved so badly in previous encounters with Bruce that he, too, was shown the door. Some time later, bereft of an opponent for a broadcast on London Broadcasting, I got hold (metaphorically) of Lewis with retribution in mind. I have to record in all humility, that he did not win the argument.

By far the most rigorous of all my encounters took place in a debate in the Oxford Union, an ancient and highly respected society for training students in the art of debate and a sought-after place to be invited to as a speaker. My first appearance was in 1988 and the topic was of course the Bomb. While I was inveighing against it I was shocked by my opponent Tim Sainsbury, at the time a junior Tory minister, who broke a union convention which restricts the right of interruption to students by interrupting me. The chair did not intervene; and to my lasting regret I gave Sainsbury a civilised answer instead of telling him to sit down. Mercifully his object, which was to disrupt my carefully memorised flow, did not work. Conjecturing that one must expect that sort of thing from a grocer, I sat down to a good reception. As I did so, a female student came over to congratulate me and burst into tears.

It was an honour to be asked back four years later, this time with a much better team. My opponent, I was thrilled but apprehensive to find, was my former boss in the intelligence community Nikko, now Sir

Nicholas, Henderson, full of years and honours but as friendly and funny as ever. He was to argue that:

The Anglo-American relationship is still necessary in the new world order,

assisted, if that is the right word, by his seconder Tom King MP, a former Defence Secretary and later a lord. My seconder was Tam Dalyell MP with whom, after exchanging scripts beforehand, I felt I could work well. I did, familiar with what was to follow and confident enough to enjoy myself. I complimented Sir Nikko on his ability to stroke clichés until they purred like epigrams. I went on to decry American grandiosity, instancing the American cartoon character General Bullmoose who, on seeing the Antarctic, ordered it to be chopped up into ice cubes for marketing. Omnipotence, I continued later:

is of course of no use to the potentate unless he can assert it; and that's what underlies the genius of American generalship for making, and, where expedient, constructing enemies ... it was the Soviet Union, seen as such a threat to America in 1945 that Japan had to be nuked to teach the Soviets a lesson ... the Soviet hordes that never swarmed westwards – not at all because of NATO but because they never intended to. And with that giga-blunder went the one about the Soviet nuclear threat, in reality a fraction of the size it suited American intelligence to say it was, which blasted off the nuclear arms race. There is now a new race course, with neo-Bullmooses leading the charge along it called extended deterrence ... brandishing nukes at ... whatever obstructs the marketing of the ice cubes ... Globo cop, coming soon to a country near you.

Turning to the Anglo partner, I spoke of:

The Gilbertian comic opera we call Defence ... fancy dress rituals to draw the crowds to the Horse Guards and the Mound ... There's hunting – for something for NATO to do: new fiction for old, a replacement for the one about the Soviet hordes. There's the real Defence job of protecting good and necessary things from onslaughts by the 23 Defence Secretaries in 46 years, almost none of whom, the Rt. Hon. the member for Bridg-water [Tom King] included, have stayed long enough to get any idea of what to keep and what to discard.

Bringing the two together:

303

The [Anglo-American] relationship is doing us no good and never did. Lend lease ... meant just what it said: the law was entitled 'An act to promote the *self-defense* of the United States', and the number of the Act, deliberately allotted as some say, was 1776 ... The Marshall Plan was a primer of the European pump so that we could all buy American ...

Large as the famous $937 million loan [to Britain in 1947] was, nearly all of it went in propping up the pound; much as the family silver – not to mention the whole bloody sideboard – was blued for the same purpose.

Further down the decades ... America, still trying to bully [other Countries] with extended deterrence ... vendor in chief of dodgy ice cubes ...

And ending, for the benefit of those whom I had failed to persuade:

a Parthian whiff of the delights they're voting for by hoping they'll have a nice day; and, as we say goodbye, telling them we're missing them already.

In that knockabout setting it went down, as one might say, like a Bomb. But that did not stop Nikko from eviscerating what I had said with humour and skill. Tom King, who had turned from pink to puce on being impugned as incompetent, stalked up and tried to denounce me, asking why I was there. He was not well received. I got no tears this time, but later there was a flattering letter from the president. I found a corresponding debate in the Cambridge Union a tame affair, not least because the two MP opponents of an anti-nuclear motion, one of whom was Churchill junior, cancelled almost at the last minute. After a frantic trawl of my right-wing friends at the president's urgent request, we found two agreeable Cambridge dons, including Professor Alan Lee Williams, one of learned pro-NATO twin academics.

Meanwhile, the annual meetings of Generals for Peace in Vienna were an eye-opener. I knew about Chalfont's accusation in the House of Lords, the Minister's strictures and related yapping in the *Daily Mirror*, and I was wary. I became suspicious when the organiser, host and hander-out of modest expenses payments in cash turned out to be Professor Gerhard Kade, formerly of the notorious Communist puppet the World Peace Council; but he would have been unable to intervene or interfere in our proceedings even if he had wanted to, because for most of the time he was drunk. Worse still, we were given an unconvincing story that the money, which also covered a modest hotel in the suburbs and travel, came from the Dutch Reformed Church in Berlin. There, however, my worries ended. There was never the slightest attempt to influence our choice of topics or what we said of them. The media, of whatever persuasion, would have been welcome; but the only coverage I can remember was from a *Mail on Sunday* feature writer who wrote a mildly critical article in the colour supplement. The clinching point, as I saw it, was that NATO would have been only too welcome to organise and fund a reciprocal series of meetings. That never happened, perhaps for lack of wit and because the case for NATO's existence was so weak. The main achievement of that ill-starred alliance, indeed, was to generate the threat that led to the Warsaw Pact.

All became clearer when we were bidden to the first of two meetings in Moscow. On the second evening of two days of setting the world, or at least Europe, to rights we gave up an opportunity to go to the the Bolshoi Ballet so that we could be entertained in his office by Anatoly Dobrynin, then head of the Communist Party's Foreign Affairs Section. He was urbane, expensively dressed, well rounded and tanned, and looked exactly like a retired right-wing US Senator from Orange County, California. His English was almost faultless because he had been Soviet ambassador both to the USA and the United Nations. He was known for his astuteness and pro-Western sympathies. As we kept going on boiled sweets and bottled water (later missing dinner at our hotel), he told us of the origin of the Generals. He had admired the constructive good sense of the polyglot clutch of senior military and naval officers in the UN Military Staff Committee of which he had had oversight as a secondary function of his UN ambassadorship. As he had despaired of politicians', Western and Eastern, continuing failure to move towards a settlement over Europe he had thought of seeing whether senior officers from both alliances could do better. That was how the teams from both alliances came into being. His account put a new light on the sinister accusations against the Generals in the House of Lords.

The visit ended with a trip to Kiev, where we were to talk to Ukrainian Generals. On the outward journey I found myself sharing a sleeping carriage with the senior Warsaw Pact General, Simonyan (whose son, incidentally was to become one of the self-made tycoons who appeared soon after the Berlin Wall came down). My escorting officer told me that the General was prone to heart attacks. I spent the night on the trundling monster of a train wondering what an attack would sound like and what I should do. Happily we both survived.

Dobrynin disappeared, presumably on retirement, when the Gorbachev era began. The Generals were again summoned to Moscow, this time as part of a huge multinational gathering, known as the Moscow Forum, of people deemed to be influential in their respective countries. The British, apart from Michael and his wife Eirwen, a notable peacebuilder in her own right, and me, mysteriously included the novelist Fay Weldon amongst the assorted trade union and academic lefties. The American contingent, I gathered, was similar but embellished with Gregory Peck and my hero John K. Galbraith, actually a Canadian. We were well housed and fed and offered staggering, as it were, quantities of drink. In return for sitting through a two-hour speech from Gorbachev in a huge auditorium in the Kremlin, and said to have been translated simultaneously into more than 100 languages, we were shown round the wondrous halls, chambers and rooms of the Kremlin fortress and palace, all in scarlet and gold, like Byron's Assyrian cohorts. The message to us all was simple: from now on, Russian foreign policy would be governed by domestic policy. Which, decoded, meant that they were broke and wanted out of the Cold War. Thus the USSR was not going to be just another notch which the US cowboys could put in their stetsons after all.

There was a final Russian hurdle at which I could have fallen. My personal escort was a young woman anxious to improve her English, already remarkably good, and looking like a *Woman's Own* reader from Isleworth. While we were both stuck in the hotel lounge by one of Aeroflot's endemic delays in their service to London, I edified her by reeling off all the English verse I could call to mind, which was quite a lot. At last, we got into the snobs'-panelled back of a Russian limousine with a driver and his attendant, both huge and bull-necked. She soon snuggled up to me and remarked:

I hev very varm feelinks for you.

I could think only of what the two thugs in front could see in the mirror; and I recalled the fate of one Vassal, an English homosexual intelligence officer who had been set up on a Soviet sofa, photographed in action, and blackmailed. The best idea seemed to be to ask to stop and buy some Georgian red wine (very good as plonks go) to take home for Rachel. That we did, after she had swept us to the front of a supermarket queue of uncomplaining proleskis. To my relief the break cooled her ardour.

I was later to be deprived of another dinner, this time in Greece. I was invited to speak at a peace rally in Olympia, no less, which I reached via Athens. I was driven there in his banger by an Orthodox priest and his acolyte, in company with a *Hibakusha* – a survivor, that is – of the atomic attack on Japan. On the way, to my great edification, we stopped at my former bombing target the Corinth Canal. Looking along its length from an entrance lock, I saw how narrow it was and how high and steep were the mountains on the north bank. We were lucky all those years ago, I realised, to have hit it so accurately and to have suffered such small losses from our raids. Olympia itself was a huge grassy amphitheatre with a natural stage in proportion. I was honoured to speak in such historic surroundings at a time well chosen to suit the dinner hour. But only the hour. Speaker followed speaker in ascending order of frightfulness. After the last one had droned to a stop a pop concert began, group after group rendering the night hideous, and the whole event became a penance. At about 2 a.m we were taken back to the town and served goat casserole, on its own except for retsina wine, sweet and tasting of the smell of pine trees. I do not remember a more horrible combination and I was thankful to leave Greece.

Very different was a Generals' jaunt to Dresden via Berlin, well before the Wall came down. There was trouble at the East German frontier post because nobody knew what an air commodore was until enlightenment came from on high. I then had an eerie trip through a series of dark, deserted underground stations, emerging into the utter drear of East Berlin. A steam train took me to a station labelled Dresden. There was also a sign indicating that the next stop was Smolensk, in the USSR, and so I thought it best to alight into the Stygian gloom. There was no sign of the hotel I had been told was next to the station: just dark suburbia with only a bendy bus in sight. I realised that I had got off at the secondary Dresden station and the bus was the only way of getting to the main one. It was full of jolly passengers united in boozy singing. I had no East German money and so, joining in the chorus and trying to look festive, I moved from one bit of bend to the other as the conductor moved from the other to the one. The hotel soon put me in useable funds and I joined my comrades with relief. For the next two days we met uninspiring East German Generals and went to unmemorable receptions. On tour, however, I saw the astonishing contrast between the outer ring of hideous shoebox rebuilding and the carefully preserved, oddly beautiful inner city ruins: all black, many shaped like sculptures with green vegetation in the gaps and crannies.

The ruins made me think of Sir Arthur Harris, Commander-in-Chief of Bomber Command at the time of the attack on Dresden. 'Bomber' Harris had learnt his trade in Iraq in the 1920s, where bombing took place partly to demonstrate that the RAF could, on its own, control territory; rather as

Curtis Le May tried to show that strategic bombing by SAC could replace other ways of waging war. Bombing attacks on unruly tribes did not work without ground support from armoured cars, just as bombing alone could not win wars. But it helped. Harris took over Bomber Command with a directive, no doubt partly written by himself, to

> attack the morale of enemy civil population.

He later wrote to a fellow air marshal that he wanted

> the masonry crashing down on the Boche, to kill Boche, to terrify Boche.

That form of overkill later became known as 'bouncing the rubble,' and was the very antithesis of the professional military use of bombing. No doubt it did to Dresden what Harris wanted; but as the Luftwaffe bombing of Britain showed, the heavier the bombing the greater the determination of the bombed to resist. I remembered the excuse taught at the RAF Staff College – that Dresden had been a nexus of communication vital to the supplying of the German front. I knew on the other hand the testimony of a teenager, Juergen Simonson, who had lived through the raids and, after an odyssey of escape and evasion, had survived to become an Anglican priest and rector of our own parish. As he says in his book:

> The Dresden raids ... were of no direct military value (there were no military targets in Dresden), but hit mainly the civilian population and reduced many precious sites to rubble. The corpses were piled high because there was nowhere to put them.

Another priest with a similarly terrible, brave story is Canon Paul Oestreicher, a fellow vice-president of CND and former dean of Coventry, where the cathedral was part of the setting for a memorable CND conference. I had the pleasure of leading, with him, a procession of protest to the RAF Church at St Clement Danes in the Strand shortly before a statue to Harris was to be unveiled.

In cheerful and often hilarious contrast were my three visits, each two years apart, to the French – somewhere-near-equivalent of Ex-Services CND – as the latter's president and representative. The first was at Narbonne, a pleasant but unremarkable Mediterranean city which I had bicycled through on one of my holidays in the region. The occasion was the biennial congress of ANCAC, the Association Nationale des Cheminots, Anciens Combattants,

Marching with Canon Paul Oestreicher to protest at the Bomber Harris Statue. *Joanne O'Brien*

Victimes de la Resistance et Prisonniers de Guerre. My job was to sit on the platform looking as if I was interested in arguments about veterans' pensions and how the next forming-up to the veterans' minister was to be conducted; and to give an address. My French, garnered from holidays, work for IUHE, as well as books, tapes and listening to the radio, was adequate for most purposes. And I have the big advantage of a nephew from my mother's first marriage, who is a professional translator, to vet and reword my speeches.

Nothing pleases the French more than a visitor who speaks their language tolerably well; and so the address, about my love affair with France since boyhood, was a success. I was taken on the customary ANCAC wine tasting (gulping would have been a better word), coach tours, and round their exhibition, a tribute to the wonderful works of sabotage done by the *cheminots* (railwaymen) of the Resistance: there were pictures of wrecked trains in dozens, all in every posture except upright. There was more of the same at the next gathering which was in Perigeux, regional city of Perigord of foie gras fame. Here the pattern was identical; as, I gathered, it had been for decades. But, having made friends and knowing the ropes I enjoyed the occasion more; and again the borrowed French finery of my speech was well received.

The last congress before I became unfit to go was at Dijon, with an imposing city centre and sad remnants of the brutal German occupation including the shooting butts adapted for mass executions. The sessions took place in a purpose-built centre blending with the Burgundian architecture. It began as usual with an exhortation to work hard, followed in the late morning by a three-hour sit-down lunch that ensured that the afternoon proceedings were conducted with somnolent goodwill. I was moved by the warmth of my reception, particularly after the speech in which I told an anecdote from Churchill's memoirs:

> At perhaps the lowest point in Anglo-French relations in the Second World War the British Navy had to fire on the French fleet in order to deny the use of the warships to the Germans. A British shell hit a French battleship, killing two young sailors, twin brothers from a Provençal village. The parents and other villagers chose to have the funeral at their home. A naval officer escorted the coffins to the village and undertook to bring two Tricouleur flags to cover them at the funeral service. 'No,' said the villagers, 'bring one Tricouleur and one Union flag.' Thus, commented Churchill, did the perception of simple folk touch the sublime.

There was scarcely a dry eye in the Hall. The speech and the little I did for ANCAC during that happy relationship led to my receiving a commemorative medal during a vociferous tribute-paying at the closing session. The next day, after a vinous coach tour sampling the great burgundies and following a marathon lunch, I said a maudlin farewell. Being now an honorary *cheminot* might, I thought, come in useful. It did, especially for putting my bicycle on trains not supposed to carry them during my years of touring holidays in southern France.

All this jaunting, as well as CND Council meetings and producing the written and spoken ephemera required, took a lot of time. So did the giving of evidence at trials stemming from acts of protest at nuclear bases in various parts of the country. One was Norwich, where I spoke up for Bruce Kent at the Crown Court. The humane and courteous judge listened to why I thought Bruce's action at a nuclear base had not amounted to criminal damage; and to my contention that somebody needed to draw attention to what was going on in the name of deterrence. The judge still found him guilty, but I like to think that what amounted to a plea in mitigation had had some effect on the lightness of the sentence to two years' suspended imprisonment, given, in his Lordship's words, to 'a plainly good man'.

In another trial, this time of Barbara Eggleston of Christian CND, Dr John Finnis, a reader in law at Oxford University, wound the magistrates' clerk deftly round his little finger. Effortlessly as it seemed, he got her acquitted, on similar evidence from me, of criminal damage and trespass charges arising from her having written 'Father forgive' on a road inside a nuclear base near Banbury. These and a number of others I found demanding but heartening. They must also have played a part in motivating me to take part in a bit of villainy of which Bruce was the inspired instigator. He wrote a leaflet for distribution to members of the Services employed servicing, guarding or otherwise facilitating the operation of nuclear weapons. It pointed out that, since the weapons were an internationally illegal instrument of war, what those servicing them were doing was itself illegal; and offered the reader help with doing something about it. He formed a squad to execute Operation 'Nuremberg', which was to hand the leaflets to the guards at a nuclear base. We were advised about how to deal with an arrest by John Platts Mills QC, of whom I had known in the Temple where his conduct as a criminal lawyer had not been universally applauded. He was most amusing and genial; but neither he nor our elder son David could give any assurance that, if I was nabbed for Incitement to Disaffection, my pension would not be at risk: 'You might get it back,' said David, 'a judicial review, three years and £30,000 later.'

I decided nevertheless to give it a go. We all drove to Molesworth, a nuclear base in the Midlands. As we approached the fence with bundles of leaflets most of the airmen of the RAF Regiment guarding the perimeter faded away, replaced by the civil police. A few remained, however, to whom we gave leaflets without attracting counter action: to, I must admit, my great relief. I was moved to get a letter from an unknown namesake of my father, George Mackie DFC:

I ... recognise that you and your colleagues were risking, inviting even, prosecution for your actions at Molesworth ... My admiration increases for your moral courage.

I made time for some extended essays, usually strung together from speeches. One, in 1990, was a script for a television documentary that never saw the light of screen, but was useful as a chapter for a paperback published by ex-Services CND. Called 'Unflagging Effort', it harped on the familiar theme of Britain's alien nuclear outfit. It ends:

What keeps me at [my task] is the burgeoning prospect for peace elsewhere. The Soviets have long since lost the terror of invasion that underlay their aggressions and subversions; all they want is a chance to solve their fearsome domestic problems. A majority of European countries realise this and are in a rich productive turmoil of response. Even our American masters are edging towards what they horridly call building down. But as change accelerates everywhere else, Britain alone retains and expands her ludicrous nuclear anachronism. Bevin wanted to fly a Union Jack over it. I would stuff the flagpole somewhere else.

Another piece consisted in a recycled chapter for a Festschrift (celebratory publication to honour eminent people) for Hannah Segal, a doyenne of psychoanalysts with whom I had shared platforms and whom I greatly admired. To my shame I was too busy to accede to the editor's plea for something shorter. Under the title 'Pox Britannica' the modified version included:

Curing the Pox and bringing a befuddled electorate to its senses commits the Peace Movement to administering some bitter pills. Admitting to being, if not a pigmy, then no more than a small nation will not be easy. Nor will learning that alliances are all very well until, like NATO, they lose their reason for existing. Nor will acceptance that Britain is no longer powerful enough to fight other than in combination with other powers. Nor again will understanding that the nuclear threat to Britain resides, paradoxically, in the very nuclear capability that is supposed to protect us. Undignified as it may be, if we had not gone nuclear we would neither rate as a worthwhile target nor qualify as a candidate for nuclear blackmail.

A leg-up to my activities came from my appointment as a vice-president of CND, which is useful as a handle for media work. So did my presidency of Ex-Services CND. With other aged ex-Service men and women I took to standing in Whitehall, opposite the Cenotaph; and with the window of my former office in the Ministry of Defence in sight, handing anti-Bomb leaflets to passers-by. As many takers were tourists, the texts were multilingual. Also wearing my ex-Service (bowler) hat I took part, with the politician Alan Clark as a witness, in the Radio Four programme *The Moral Maze*, consisting in answering questions from a trio of sanctimonious wiseacres of which Clark made short work. So, I hope, did I; greatly impressed by Clark's courteousness as we chatted about his forthcoming diaries while we waited. I also enjoyed jousting on the air with General Sir

Anthony Farrar Hockley, well known as a brilliant soldier and a hero during the Korean War. He had been cantankerous when we first disagreed as Gulf War armchair generals on *Channel Four News*, but later became more genial. Our encounters ended on Sky Television where, I suspect, our esoteric disputations bored the viewers beyond endurance. Another opponent was General Sir John Hackett, an outstanding military historian and classicist, who refused to meet me for a joint performance in a local station broadcast in Birmingham, insisting on separate interviews. I contrived to get him to go first and did not miss the open goal he left. A little better at keeping goal was Lady Olga Maitland, a former MP and a devotee of the Conservative pro-Bomb party line. She also headed a body articulating that persuasion coyly entitled Families for Defence. A sentence from one of its leaflets, which reads as if it came from her own hand, speaks volumes about the rickety structure of illogic that underpins deterrence:

> There are absolutely no grounds for concluding in advance that the evil effect of the use of nuclear deterrence would be inescapably excessive in relation to its objectives.

So there.

Alas, by 1993 I had overdone it and had to stop. I had given everybody who would read, look or listen a peace, as it were, of my mind; and thereby become so pressurised by excess of work that I fell into acute clinical depression and anxiety. I put up metaphorical shutters. Happily, however, the end was not yet.

Chapter 15

Back to Back

Putting the back at the front would, I hoped, make you read on. Now you're back to where you came in, you will have seen that I needed no telling not to go gentle. True, I saw a great deal that was good and beautiful along the way. But for the most part, my theme has been protest and my effort has been to do something about it. Not, alas, to a coherent pattern, but with some fitting together of the pieces. The objective of the armed forces in which I was honoured to serve is peace. So, of course, is that of the peace movement. Health, whether bodily or planetary, cannot flourish without peace; and thus all three are interlinked. My effort to put that unity on film for the Health Education Council failed, but I'm not sure it was all that wrong. Normal service restored, I have relished expressing it in other ways. While I can still do so I look back through the departure lounge window, hoping to escape the fate of poor Mrs Lot (Genesis 19:26).

The best bit was the flying. The RAF prolonged a happy childhood. From the moment I took the King's Shilling I was, after the fashion of Mr and Mrs Sippi in the song, made to feel at home – clothed, housed, warmed, fed and sheltered within a tough but quasi-parental regime. And flying followed a sort of continuum. The riding I learnt from my father's drunken patient had, I later found, an exhilaration comparable to that of being airborne. Squash demanded the instant reactions of the aviator; keeping me, incidentally, on the hop until my forties. So did quasi-flying on a succession of bikes that still continues: the latest being the gleaming Dawes that my son David gave me for my eightieth birthday. Flying was as much in my blood as it was in John Magee's and as much of an addiction as it was for Leonardo.

The ardours of my military service were leavened with laughs. The Officers' Training Corps/Home Guard nightly patrols of the Carthusian playing fields was one instance, involving as it did looking out for German parachutists dressed as nuns equipped with folding motor bicycles. Another came at the end of nights of flying training at Barkston Heath, consisting in frantic efforts in the freezing dawn to hand-crank the

Airspeed Oxford engines into the life on which depended a return to food and sleep at Cranwell. Yet another was being chased home by Italian fighters across the Mediterranean as dawn broke because of idiotically bad staff work. All were made bearable by comrades ready with a reminder:

> If you can't take a joke you shouldn't have joined.

A very present help in trouble (Psalm 46:1). So was the advice in, of all places, the RAF Manual of Air/Sea Rescue, to air crews forced to resort to the inflatable dinghies which all aircraft carried:

> Remain cheerful.

Such comradeship fades with height and might. Flag/field/air rank officerdom leads to jostling and rivalry that sharpen towards the summit. The catapult that projected me into the Temple saved me from that. What a bit of luck.

At a price. Since the catapult's elastic twanged, those I left behind have either ignored me or treated me as a renegade. One nasty slight was being left out of a reunion of previous commanders of 101 Squadron on a grand ceremonial occasion; much mitigated, however, by my dislike of such events. Far worse was the ignoring of my request, as Vice-President of the 3rd Parachute Brigade Memorial Association, for a 101 Squadron fly-past at the 60th anniversary commemoration of the airborne assault on Europe in Normandy which I was helping to arrange (101's part in 1944 was the preparatory flattening of a row of houses obstructing the dropping zones, whose French dwellers had fortunately been displaced by German soldier occupants). I was glad when the great occasion was saluted with a much more impressive fly-past of a Lancaster, a Spitfire and other bits of airborne history by the RAF Battle of Britain Memorial Flight.

My sorrow, not anger, is that the passers of judgement and petty riposters have got it, and me, wrong. My admiration and love for the RAF and its sister Services are unbounded. I share what must be their gall at being misused. One vivid memory is of the first Gulf War. I was appalled by an instruction from the Ministry of Defence to editors not to mention:

> any loss, damage to, air attack upon any naval vessel or military aircraft.

Blatant censorship imposed not by military necessity but to hide politicians' wrong-headedness and bungling.

I ended an article in the CND magazine with a reference to the badly bruised face of Flight Lieutenant John Nichols, pilloried on Al-Jazeera telly:

That leaves us only symbols. One is that poor Goya-like face, battered by Iraqi thugs but set up by war-besotted politicians. Another is the great black [oil] slick epitomising the Gulf's obscene, gargantuan waste and greasing its slide into the abyss.

Little less shaming is the treatment of the Services by politicians in peacetime. The Service ministers, continuing the succession of cynics with little grasp of what they minister to, condone the plundering of resources from soft-touch defence funds to finance hard ones. There can be no other explanation for the bizarre policy announced in 2005 of running down the readiness of the Royal Navy with which, incidentally, it was my privilege to fly, to keep the other two Services going. As the National Audit Office put it:

... the material state of the fleet will degrade, along with its ability to undertake high-readiness tasks over a longer period.

The Admirals put a brave face on their plight by calling the Royal Navy a Versatile Maritime Force for supporting its sister Services, but the gloomy future remains. I hope the spirit of Jolly Jack Tar won't suffer too much. I recall the young rating, keen to impress, who asked his chief petty officer whether he could borrow tools from the chippy shop and use some timber to make a Glub Glub machine. Admiring the lad's enterprise and anxious not seem ignorant, the CPO said he would have to ask the First Lieutenant. Jimmy the One, of the same mind, reported the request to the Captain. Pausing only to praise such initiative and glad to encourage it, the Captain gave permission. Put together on deck, the machine proved to be a large wooden box with a big hole in one of the sides. Anxious to encourage emulation, the Captain assembled the crew to watch a demonstration. The young sailor thereupon pushed the box over the side into the ocean. As it sank, the box went,

Glub glub, glub glub, glub glub ...

The airmen can take no comfort from the sailors' distress. The RAF, many years late, has as a front-line weapon the Euro-fighter, named the Typhoon, which reached the drawing board while Britain still needed protecting from Soviet propeller-driven bombers patrolling the east coast. Now

317

adapted to the needs of several other air forces, we can only hope that it's fit for the wide span of operations demanded of it: interception, strike and ground attack. Other roles were still being filled in the twenty-first century by such candidates for the museum as the VC10, adapted as a tanker from the jet transport of the 1960s and scheduled to last until 2013; and the Nimrod, in service since 1969 and having as its ancestor the Comet, the ill-fated prototype jet airliner of the fifties. No wonder the lower orders put the blame, mistakenly, on their Airships (a derogatory term for air marshals derived, no doubt, from its forbear the Blimp). Airmen too must keep their peckers up; as did the Liberator crew, not mine, on night patrol 2,000 miles out over the Atlantic on an anti-submarine patrol. The captain, after hours of steering the same course, was surprised when the navigator asked for a 60-degree change of heading to the right. Twenty minutes later came another change, this time 120 degrees to the left. When, after another twenty minutes, there came a change back to the original heading his curiosity overcame him. Back at the navigator's chart table, he saw the reason. On the chart was a baked bean, a remnant from the upper gunner's supper, which had fallen from his turret. Desperate to relieve his boredom and fastidious about what he touched, the navigator had steered the aircraft on a triangular course – round the bean.

Always keen to know how affairs turned out, I was fascinated by the result of the great carrier–land base dispute that was part of the discontent that ended my RAF service. The Navy, somewhat pyrrhically, won and, well into the twenty-first century, will eventually get two immensely expensive new carriers. History has shown that the RAF claim to be able to do the job better from land bases is false because most of the bases have gone. But there are riders. One is that nothing can give full protection to carriers from nuclear missile attack. The other is that there are ample American land bases in all parts of the world where operations are conceivable; as a recent chief of Defence staff has said:

> The most demanding expeditionary operations, including intervention against state adversaries, can only plausibly be conducted if US forces are engaged ...

The corollary is not that the use of RAF air strikes is a better proposition. It is that yet another bit of defence capability depends on American consent.

The Army has suffered no less than its sisters. Its worst affliction, however, is the decline of the 100 private armies – the regiments – in which it has long consisted. The county regiments in particular have been

A serving brigadier and a retired air commodore doing a joint unveiling. Hims ancient and modern, as it were. *Le Grain de Selle hors serie. Ville de Sannerville*

the cores of a system which began with the recruitment of illiterate young peasant boys from the fields with signs and devices that called them literally to the colours. My late half-brother William Collingwood brought that home to me through his pride in having joined the Fifth Royal North-umberland Fusiliers, rooted in the north-east where his family originated. Known also as the Old and Bold, they were renowned for their bravery and had a long list of battle honours. With a shorter list but also renowned was his later choice, the Parachute Regiment. Having been intimately linked with the regiment in Normandy and at Arnhem, I have been privileged to help to organise, and to represent 233 Squadron at their reunions, culminating in the enormous 60th anniversary celebrations in 2004. On that occasion I, with our younger son, two grandsons and William's elder daughter in company, backed up the heroic former commander of the Third Parachute Brigade, Brigadier James Hill DSO**

319

Togetherness remembered in the quiet Wiltshire countryside ... *Author*

MC, well into his nineties and at the centre of the regimental commemoration. He already has a square in Sannerville named after him; and, as part of the 2004 ceremonies, James's statue nearby was unveiled by the regiment's colonel-in-chief, Prince Charles.

320

... and on a bicycle pilgrimage to the Parachute Regiment and RAF graves at Ranville in Normandy. *Author*

To the usual gathering of veteran parachutists were added soldiers serving in the regiment and the RAF aircrew who drop and maintain them. These young men and women displayed their prowess in dropping and landing as well as their bearing and sociability at a huge party afterwards. I was moved to write to James:

> I was entranced, humbled but not at all surprised by the superb way in which you carried everything off last week end ... as I'm sure you realised, the faultless way in which you and all your soldier comrades comported yourselves gave everyone a marvellous impression of the British Army. A mere airman, I was nevertheless bursting with pride.

At another ceremony my younger son Gregor and William's daughter Anna jointly laid a wreath on a memorial to a Dakota crew in my stream who were killed, along with all the Paras they were to have dropped except one, on 6 June 1944. The wreath had the Parachute Regiment and the 233 Squadron crests on it, as well as a sentence from the second book of Samuel (1:23):

Saul and Jonathan were lovely and pleasant in their lives and in death they were not divided: they were swifter than eagles, they were stronger than lions.

Esprit de corps and comradeship can be hilarious as well as solemn. At one of the many *vins d'honneur* (boozy municipal parties) our host, the mayor of one of the Norman villages, made over-much in his speech of the gallant Paras who had driven the German soldiers out. One veteran of the occasion cheered some of us up with, in a whisper:

> Oh no we didn't. The Germans had already gone. As we marched through the village there was a hand at every door with a mug of Calvados [apple brandy]. By the time we got to the top of the village we couldn't bloody march, let alone fight.

Of such is the spirit of the county regiments threatened by disbandments and mergers. The problem was well put in 1993 by the chief of Defence staff, lecturing at the Services' sounding board, the Royal United Services Institution. Explaining that the Army would be restructured to offer smaller, more rapidly deployable units able to fight small wars, he foresaw:

> Multiple concurrent small- to medium-sized operations [which] will be the most significant factor in our force planning. Counter terrorism and counter proliferation operations will require rapidly deployable forces able to respond swiftly to intelligence and to achieve precise effects around the world.

Incompatible, unfortunately, with a regimental structure. He was silent, perhaps significantly, about Trident, the gargantuan nuclear consumer of resources that were needed to provide a land force of a decent size. He made routine obeisance to the paramountcy of NATO. He failed, as I saw it, in acknowledging how and where the future of international peace-keeping lies. I begged to differ. When Yugoslavia was bombed in 1999 the NATO generals, I suggested in a long letter for which *The Times* kindly gave me space, were delighted to be given the job, having

> thrived on a strategy of threat and counter threat which, despite the evaporation of [NATO's] Warsaw Pact partner, has ... continued over the years ...

An alternative, I suggested, was:

> ... an untainted, non-threatening body whose 54 members, including Russia, offer an East/West catholicity that could ease the risk of a neo-Cold War, the OSCE [Organisation for Security Co-operation in Europe] could be used to clear up the appalling mess which NATO's action will cause.

adding, three months later, that:

> The sooner NATO exits (without, it is to be hoped, needing pursuit by a [Soviet] Bear) and gives place to the UN, the EU and the OSCE ... the sooner peace will come about.

That was not what happened. As the Defence chief had in effect said, we cannot fight a major war without American help. I spelt that out later in a letter in the *Observer* backing up the renegade minister Clare Short who, I suggested, was:

> ... groping towards a perception of ... British ... subservience to the US [which] has brought us not peace but a thawing permatruce which our so-proclaimed independent nuclear capability has, these 60 years, been supposed to maintain. Being entirely dependent on US goodwill, our nuclear capability has caused all significant defence decisions to be warped by our politicians' never having to forget on which side our nuclear bread is buttered.

Such sound, or perhaps print, and fury and everything relating to my RAF service have not, I have to admit, shown the slightest sign, iota, jot or tittle of result. I find it hard, however, to believe that Trident's glaring pointlessness as literally an old man of the sea burdening our otherwise superb services has not suggested itself to our cash-strapped military. After a poll in 2004 showed much discontent in the Services I suggested in another letter in *The Times*:

> Service people, dispirited for want of proper equipment and unable to agree with the 15 percent of their comrades who believe that defence funds are spent wisely, doubtless have concerns about how the money is spent unwisely. Could those concerns include the use of expensively trained sailors and very costly Trident submarines for cruising the oceans with the missiles pointing at nothing?

However that may be, change will eventually come from outside the Services, whose leaders, whatever they think, have since the beginning of time clung ferociously to everything the politicians vouchsafe them. Trident, moreover, sustains several Flag rank posts as well as the captains, commanders and all below them who man the craft. I took the chance to put what I see as the best way forward when an American ambassador let slip her country's real opinion of a nuclear-armed Britain – utter contempt. I hazarded in a 1993 letter in the *Observer*:

> Perhaps only politeness restrains Her Excellency from remarking in the same strain on other fatuous bits of our Defence furniture. A blue water navy protecting Hong Kong from a Chinese takeaway soon to happen anyway. An army with main battle tanks unusable except on Salisbury Plain. An Air Force whose costly new fighter defends us from what? ... [all] so costly that the useful part of our outfit has to be kept derisorily small. Two thousand or so soldiers in Bosnia with their light armour, sapper and communication units and relatively simple maritime support now provide Britain's last source of military greatness ... replacing her pathetic nuclear posturing with a genuinely world class contribution as a ... peace-keeping nation ... would mean more than ... a ... defence review. We would need to start all over again.

We still do. At one time a suitable engine of change would have been the Cabinet Office where there were plenty of good brains. Whether the modern office, blown up into a department and embellished with a minister, has not been diluted so badly that it cannot make differences, I cannot know. A bad sign is the Joint Intelligence Committee, spoilt at the turn of the century by two bad chairmen in succession. On the other hand a good sign is the easing of excess secrecy of the kind applied to Anthony Armstrong's ('Easy Warriors') white orderly room cat, smug in demeanour because it had been stamped 'Confidential'. One absurd leftover was the marking as 'Restricted' of an exercise folder devoid of content issued to me for a big joint staff exercise in 1967. Another was the refusal of the Cabinet Office when I rang to ask whether I could mention the JIC on telly, even to admit to its existence. Thank goodness for Freedom of Information, one really useful transatlantic import.

In the rear view mirror, my pierhead jump into the law looks a little less lacking in achievement than my time as an airman. In the light of all that has happened since, leaving the RAF eventually turned out not to have been the mistake I had apprehended. Of course I had a much lower base and a much smaller field of play. Lord Donovan, bless him, had been generous in his praise when I left the Inn; and I have no reason to doubt that my Naval successor, though a placeman, consolidated the changes I made. Some at least of the beneficiaries went on to do well. One school friend of our younger son Gregor joined the Inn at my suggestion, worked hard enough to jump the hurdle of being called with height to spare and entered good criminal chambers. He has since specialised in drink-driving offences, so prospering and growing in eminence as to have become a Queen's Counsel. Meanwhile the colourful Rodney Flynn retired from the Inner temple. The new incumbent lost his title of sub-treasurer but is amply compensated for becoming a humdrum chief executive with a salary equivalent to many multiples of our pittances.

The indigent students to whom I reached out have almost certainly become extinct as a species, education for the Bar having been formalised by compulsory training at the Inns of Court Law School; on the lines, it is fair to record, of what I tried to institute for the Middle Temple exclusively. In an echo of the quasi-legal part of my past, I shared the stupefaction of many proper lawyers at the violence done to the ancient liberties of citizens by politicians writhing under the problems of dealing with post-9/11 terrorism. I harked back to a constitutional law case presided over by the eminent Middle Templar, Lord Coke and three other chief justices about the imprisonment of an allegedly unqualified physician. With its aid I denounced in *The Times* two egregious fatuities:

> Charles Clark [Home Secretary] contends that the proposed ID card legislation 'promotes the most fundamental civil liberties in our society'. With that bizarre assertion must be considered the no less flawed proposition, held to be legal until the law lords decided otherwise, that indefinite detention without trial is lawful.
>
> It seems to follow that ad hoc judicial decisions and parliamentary process no longer suffice to safeguard civil liberties from anti-terrorism measures that mutate into legalised terrorism. The time has come to revive the protective power of the judiciary enunciated in 1609 by Lord Coke to nullify a law if it were 'against common right and reason' (Bonham's case).

Coke actually said (Dr Bonham's case (1608) 8 Co. Rep. 113b, 118a) that: 'When an Act of Parliament is against right and reason, or repugnant, or impossible to be performed, the common law will control it and judge that Act to be void.' What a pity that, as Lord Denning said in a lecture in

1980, the sapling planted by Lord Coke failed to take root. In America a large tree of the same genus flourishes as the Supreme Court, whose powers over the legislature have been an often valuable constitutional safeguard. A recent example, recorded by Niall Ferguson in *Colossus*, his monumental study of America, was the ticking-off of President George W. Bush in June 2004: resisting 'an assault on the force of tyranny' could not, said the Court, justify the use by an American President of 'the tools of tyranny'. The rebuke is all the more remarkable in the light of endemic presidential packing of the court with judges picked more on grounds of political propensity than of judicial probity; and as an act of self denial of the Court's infamous cop-out – the right 'not to hear'.

I had a great affection for the Middle Temple and the many good people there, comfortably outweighing the shockers. I wish I had had the confidence to push harder and faster for better training for, as I came to see them, my students. In my next incarnation the absence of windmills amongst the architects, without exception agreeable to work with, meant that my zeal lacked targets for my tilting lance. My refutation of what the Monopolies Commission were threatening to do was superseded by a change in the law which freed the professions from any obligation to become unions. My only achievement, and I look back on it with pleasure, was my merger of Noel Dawson's post and mine. She, I feel sure, took part in converting the large, expensive and unwieldy council into a small board: would that I had thought of the change myself.

Looking back on the Health Education Council, the running of which was the longest and most exacting job in my civil career, I am glad of the troubles which, in all modesty, I had the fulfilment of overcoming:

> ... with a hit-hit here and a hit-hit there
> and a comfortable feeling at night
> that you've let in a little air.

> A little fresh air in the money sty
> knocked a little hole in the holy prison
> done your own little bit, made your own little try ...

as another bit of D.H. Lawrence's poem put it. But not, as it turned out, for long. The job's other great advantage was that I had no abrupt catapulsion into something else. I continued to work in health: first in the International Union and then as a privateer blending work for peace and for health in their broader senses in symbiotic harmony. Just as health means

326

far more than the mere absence of disease, so peace, in its preferable synonym *shalom*, means far more than the mere absence of war. In the European context, I suggested in a letter in *The Times*:

> ... the massed ... alliances, much less their nuclear armamentaria, will have no relevance whatever ... Europe's way forward is to allow them to moulder, acquiring meanwhile comprehensive peace-keeping forces in a system like the one spawned but never hatched by the UN Military Staffs Committee ... preparing itself not as a metamorphosis of the alliances but rather as an apotheosis for the sane use of arms.

Within which lies, I suggest, a useful parallel: with clinical medicine as a militant force for combating disease; and education as a peace-building force for promoting health. Not that the two are distinct: part of health promotion in need of more emphasis is learning not to regard doctors as omniscient high priests and hospitals as surrogate cathedrals. Both should be seen as what they are: useful aids to each of us in the management of our health.

As this dual peace–health activity grew towards the limit of what, in a post-depressive mode, I could tackle, I was saddened by the slow demise of the Health Education Council. Brian Lloyd recruited as my successor Professor Keith Taylor, an agreeable medical don from California. Within three months he left, returning to America because of catastrophic damage to his home there, fortunately able to resume his tenured professorship. He was succeeded by Dr David Player, a good friend and former head of the Scottish Health Education Group. Able as he is, he seemed to have found the job of maintaining the council's organisation too burdensome. He cannot have been helped by the forming of a cluster of advisory groups of council members. That unwise networking must have warped their capacity to accept advice – meaning to do as I and my staff colleagues told them – and to have transmuted that quality into a toxic propensity to interfere. Brian Lloyd had meanwhile been succeeded as Chairman by Sir Brian Bayley, Chairman also of Television South West Holding plc. I was aghast to read soon afterwards of the council's closer working relationships with contraceptive manufacturers and the health food business; both, I had found, knew a soft touch for self-promotion when they saw one. Worse still, the British Nutrition Foundation appeared on the list of national bodies with which the council was cooperating. 'Certain industrial bodies whose objectives are compatible with our own' were identified. And into the annual reports crept oleaginous tributes to 'Secretaries of State, Ministers and officials'. The pass was sold. There followed departure from the New Oxford Street building and obliteration. Happily my other enthusiasm, the International Union for Health Education, having added 'and Promotion' to its title, has gone from strength to strength.

The National Health Service has health educators and the training facilities we instituted still exist. Other sources, notably the retail chemists whom we cultivated as health educators, are increasingly effective. The Department of Health lurches from crisis to crisis, sadly failing to profit from our mistakes in our early days. The worst, under the politician Norman Fowler (doubtless the recipient of one of Sir Brian's tributes) was when AIDS hit this country. The worst of the worst was a poster with the slogan:

> AIDS is not prejudiced.

What, it seems fair to ask, would a semi-literate teenager, terrified in the wake of some sexual peccadillo and desperate for advice, have made of that? True, he or she would have got some help from the telly, slavering at the jaws for anything to do with sex, which made AIDS an excuse for valuable educative programmes of startling frankness about what was and was not risky behaviour. Such education, however, has long been dropped in favour of salaciousness.

For less attention-getting topics, the health rot continues. No young woman, it often seems, considers herself accoutred for walking abroad without a lit cigarette. Abroad may well be plagued with areas made no-go by binge boozers and druggies. There continues an archetypal trio of an overweight infant grazing sweets in a buggy pushed by an obese mother with, as a co-waddler, her own mother, older and even fatter. The child's sugar culture may have started life with a slug of aseptic dextrose to replace the natural K-ration of her mum's colostrum. Life will have continued with sweets as a reward for merit and a forfeit for naughtiness; and later, naughtiness now licenced, as intertwined with sex. One must, of course, be grateful for more and better contents labels, some constituents actually described in understandable terms. I do not claim to have brought that about; but when more and better information for the public about what they were eating became a current topic, I wrote in *The Times* as head of the International Union:

> It is all very well that low fat spreads should be exposed as an expensive way of buying water droplets just as slimming breads provide

comparably expensive air. There may also be advantage in doing away with the Wheatmeal label [which subsequently happened] ... But what the food industry's customers really need is a simple guide not only to the fat content of what it dishes up but also that of other substances, of which the most notable is sugar, concealed in packaged foods and consumed by most of us, almost willy nilly, to excess ...

Which also subsequently happened. Nonetheless fantasy food-selling still abounds. One, as much abused as ever is, bread. A random 2005 example is the Waitrose white Farmhouse loaf; dough lovingly kneaded, no doubt, by the farmer's wife after dosing the flour with:

buttermilk powder, spirit vinegar, vegetable oil and hydrogenated vegetable oil [saturated fat], processing aid calcium sulphate, flavouring, soya flour, emulsifier mono- and diacetyl tartaric esters of mono- and dyglycerides of fatty acids, dextrose (sugar), flour treatment agent ascorbic acid.

The fibre content, reduced to 2.6 per cent, will do the bowel no favours. But that can always be put right with bran cereal, biscuits and other lucrative 'health foods' made with the fibre filched from the flour. As an extra service the red handkerchief used to wrap the mens' lunch for taking to the fields is thoughtfully replaced with film bag PP5 and closure PVC3. A real bucolic idyll.

I continued to link health with my nuclear weapon campaigning. One modality was the short-lived *Times* supplement for the health services (the offer of a job with which I had turned down because it would have meant moving to Oxford). The doctors, it seemed, had lumbered to the collective conclusion that the only realistic medical response to nuclear war was to concentrate on prevention. All very well, I wrote; but you should take it further by focusing on the:

paranoid follies of the so-called strategy of nuclear deterrence. ... The British mixture of post-Empire jingoism and fear that ... the United States would ditch us has generated a strategy which until recently was merely absurd. But now that the latest weapons have put a nuclear capability within reach of thirty or so other little countries our so-called deterrent is a potentially catastrophic example to them all ... Of the lay influences working in ... [the direction of nuclear sanity] ... the most significant for doctors is that of the Anglican working party whose report, 'The Church and the Bomb', indicts nuclear militarism on moral grounds. If doctors intend to take prevention seriously, they should impugn the nuclear strategists no less seriously on grounds of insanity.

But the food and booze industries continued to offer tempting targets. One I shot at with a letter in *The Times*. One food pundit:

> ... having said that food alone doesn't cause obesity, defends 'energy dense' (food industry speak for fattening) items as part of a 'healthy' diet. Condemning them, he warns us, risks 'message dilution' and the alternative is child's play and walking, jogging and riding. That seems to me disingenuous nonsense. Fattening foods cause obesity. Exercise will not make up for excess. While recently reduced to an elaborate cycling machine for exercise, I found that 16 30-minute uphill sessions each consumed about 125 calories – equivalent to less than a single greasy burger bap. The more we all undertake uphill struggles the better. But with them must go resistance to the blandishments of the food industry.

Another was a joust with an advocate for more medical resources for the NHS ('Sickly Britain lags behind in health league'), who ignorantly classify their cost as 'health' spending. Ever helpful, *The Times* allowed me to swat that one:

> Health spending is not throwing money at the NHS. It is, rather, using resources to ease the pressures and change the habits that cause us to overload it. Heart disease, cancer and sexually transmitted diseases have allies such as a food industry which has made some 40% of us obese; cigarette makers whose scarcely restrained sponsorships keep smoking fashionable; and brewers who, amongst others, have so intertwined their product with sex that many, it seems, think that one cannot be enjoyed without the other and none of us gets enough of either ...

There was that hoary quip again. I continue to watch for and seize such opportunities along with any others, for anti-nuclear weapon protest. But I am faced with the reality that, as a movement, peaceniks face a mutating adversary. To the absurdity of nuclear strategy which I tried to retail to the doctors, and its concomitant of creating the threat that it seeks to forfend, is added the evidence that it does not work. In invading Kuwait, Saddam Hussein successfully defied four nuclear powers to nuke Iraq: America, Britain, Israel and France. Nor did the threat of nuclear retaliation deter Russia from invading Afghanistan, Israel from invading the Lebanon, or

Milosevic from invading Kosovo. The new evidence, moreover, has not escaped the perceptions of the influential. One potentate, later to fall from grace and regain it as a presidential place man, let slip that it did not: John Bolton, then US Secretary of State, said in August 2002 that America regarded Saddam as:

> not susceptible to fine theories of deterrence.

Or, it seemed, to coarse ones; as has been tacitly acknowledged by Bolton's Government and its successor. It took Kofi Annan, Secretary-General of the United Nations, to articulate the shift in American policy from deterrence to pre-emption, later there for all to see in the second Iraq war. Ominous Washington rumblings against Iran, Syria, North Korea and Cuba suggest that they may well have joined the coterie of nations classified by America as hostile *before* a threat is manifest. That has led US to extend and redefine defence policy as 'Global Reach', upon which I expatiated in a letter in the *Observer* in 2000:

> ... the Space-Based Infra Red System (SBIRS), to give it its more revealing [than Star Wars] title ... is only incidentally a defence against rogue states ... its purpose is to give the US a secure base for Global Reach, a strategy which, to quote its commander General Ashy in 1996, will use Space Command 'to fight from space and ... into space' ... Global Reach will ... antagonise China and terrify the other Pacific states ... It will nullify UN efforts to ensure, as Kofi Annan puts it, that outer space remains weapons free. And its predication of US impregnability is as flawed as was that of the embryonic predecessor with which Andre Maginot furnished France in the 1930s.

(When the German Army invading France in 1939 came up against the Maginot Line, an enormous defensive system of outworks, they simply steered round it.)

A year later Ashy's braggadocio was endorsed by Defense Secretary Rumsfeld's Space Commission:

> Just as Europe expanded war and its power to the global oceans, the US is expanding war and its power into space and into the planets.

Bad enough in 2001, when megalomanic ravaging of the firmament to the greater glory of the USA had as its object deterrence. Now, with the Arab

One of the million anti Iraq war protesters belting it out. The bouquet was for someone else.
Anon

world in turmoil, oil supply at risk and terrorism defying deterrence, the Pentagon seems certain to be goaded into using space-based weaponry for pre-emptive strikes.

I so relished my dual role as to exceed the limits that the psychiatrist who treated me in my depressive phase had stipulated. I took part in and came to no harm from the gigantic protest march against the second Iraq war in the spring of 2003; and along with other peacenik officials harangued the crowd gathered in Hyde Park:

> ... The onslaught in Iraq is a gigantic weapon of mass destruction in itself, complete with fall-out, all over the Middle East and a half-life of many decades at least. Peace? Couldn't be further off. [because of] hatred from the Arab and Muslim world with what's been done to the Iraqi people, chaos within Iraq and imbroglio, real or threatened ...

332

claiming, in an article in 2005, 'to [have] share[d] in one of the greatest I told-you-so's in history.'

A bigger I-told-you-so lurks, but requital is in doubt because there may be nobody left to tell it. It is that if the nuclear weapon powers go on as they are, they will destroy the world. One such power – Britain – seems bent on doing just that. In 1997 there was a brief halcyon period of mutual nuclear arms reductions by America and Russia, opening a vista of what *The Times* described as a security zone from Vancouver to Vladivostok. Responding to the article, I wrote that Britain:

bucks the trend ... [and], for the narrowest nationalistic reasons, is increasing its so-called independent deterrent fourfold ... Britain continues to propagate the worst long-term incendiary agent of all – nuclear proliferation. Our ... defence ... isn't even European: it's Little England.

Since then Britain and four other declared nuclear powers have committed themselves time and again to the protocol of the 2000 Non-Proliferation Treaty which specifies:

[an] ... unequivocal undertaking to accomplish the total elimination of their nuclear arsenals.

Three have done nothing except filibuster at the review conferences. Britain has done even worse, continuing her role as founder, exemplar and champion of the proliferators' club. Behind that ignoble achievement lies her conflation of national self-esteem and nuclear capability (which, with rich irony, survives only by American grace and favour). Having rooted it in the electoral folk-mind in the 1940s, our politicians dare not question it. A pigmy beside the historians, philosophers, scientists and military men who have fought for sanity, I have done all I can in the contexts of defence, health and journalism to ram home the tantalisingly simple truth on which our fate hangs: that if we don't get rid of nuclear weapons, they will get rid of us.

Comparatively trivial because its lethality, economic and political, is only metaphorical, is our antipathy to Europe. The fictitious headline:

Fog in Channel: Europe isolated

epitomises our insularity and blindness to our destiny. We were not helped by General de Gaulle in 1962 who, out of pique at the way we treated him during World War Two, tripped us at the first fence in 1962. Edward Heath's far-sighted ally Geoffrey Rippon (unique in my experience in fortifying himself with a decanter of claret for the rigours of chairing a meeting), nearly got us over the second. Heath half-finished the job at the third. All was done in the face of the obscurantism that still impedes us. We (you, more probably) may yet get a chance to rescue us from American vassalage by voting us into Europe in heart, soul, constitution and cheque book. But even the politicians who could help the process along dwell on what we would get *out* of full membership to the virtual exclusion of what we could put *in*. As to their opponents, I was glad of a chance to spell out the misconception that afflicts them in, yet again, *The Times*, to reprove Jacques Santer, then at the helm of the EU, for mincing words in describing the damage some of our politicians were doing:

> [They] vie with each other in assuring us of the doughty fight [for British sovereignty] they would put up. Thereby they conveniently ignore the fact that there is little left to fight for: most genuine British economic, military and diplomatic sovereignty has long gone. So – as each party has made a point of not telling us – has much of our power to influence decision-making. Our negativity and intransigence ... in European conclaves, have seen to that. So much Santer could have told us. He could also have fitted out our negotiators with the decent clothing for the conference table of one unassailable truth – that Britain goes fully into Europe or to the wall.

The wall looms.

Admitting to *nul points* for my endeavours over the bomb and Europe, I can only plead that I'm in great and good company. And it was fun to try. As the moment when my ship comes in gets closer, I claim the right to some scattergunnery of other protest. At the periphery of what else matters is the profaning of protest itself. I pick one tiny instance from dozens, because the perpetrator matters and should know better. The telly audience in a programme about pet hates called *Grumpy Old Men* could have done without the gibbering triviality of Michael, as he then was, Grade's complaint about the poor instructions that went with an electrical gizmo:

> it's fuck me I don't know what's going on here.

Good for the ratings, I suppose and a sign of the prolefeed which the BBC under the chairmanship of Lord Grade (whose name, oddly, no longer appears in the list of participants) will doubtless dish up. But, like so much other rubbish, hard to reconcile with the aspiration ensconced in the former Portland Place entrance hall:

> ... *ut messem bonam bona proferat sementis ut immunda omnia et inimica paci expellantur ut quaecunque pulchra sunt et sincera quaecunque bonae famae ad haec avrem inclinans populus virtutis et sapientiae semitam insistat.*

which translates roughly as:

> ... that good seed sown may bring forth good harvest and that all things foul or hostile to peace may be banished hence and that the people, inclining their ear to whatsoever things are lovely and honest, whatsoever things are of good report may tread the paths of virtue and of wisdom.

The slick response is that we have moved on. Moved off, more like; and a long way at that. The hope for love, honesty and good report lies in the nascent BBC Trust. Lord Grade, its Chairman-designate, will need to be in redemptive mode.

Things foul are a speciality of the *Sun*. When, perhaps more significantly than any other event in the twentieth century, the Cold War ended, readers had it explained to them in the headline:

> Demob threat to our lads.

As Chris Horries' excellent history *Stick it up your Punter* relates, *The Sun* later befouled journalism in reporting the Falklands War in 1982. As the prospects for a peaceful settlement faded, it greeted the American offer of peace-brokering talks with:

> Stick it up your junta.

And the drowning of 368 Argentinian conscripts in the shameful sinking of the retreating cruiser *Belgrano* provoked the infamous:

> Gotcha.

At a personal level, an event in an over-exploited model's mending of her life was mercilessly intruded upon with:

Totty Mossy having it off with a toffy.

And so it goes on. Oh for a solar eclipse. And for a *Mirror* cracked from side to side many, no doubt, would say thankshallott.

The Sun, the *Mirror* and its Augean stable companions do nothing to help their blinkered, ignorant readers to cope with the legacy of empire petrified on Boadicea's statue. Legitimate patriotism thus mutates into the rampant nationalism that creates football hooligans and makes some of us ostracise Blacks, Jews, muslims, asylum seekers and other tribes not to our liking; and thence to the mordant insularity of Little England that would have made Nicolas Chauvin (cf. Andre Maginot) blush. With that, and at the same level of protest-worthiness, goes our obsession with all things American, predating and merging with our having to grovel to America to keep our so-called independent deterrent so-called independent. Nor does the subordinacy end there. Ever since silent films gave place to talkies in the 1920s, there have been few mass market commodities than can be sold other than with American advertising copy and voices. Women of all ages, it seems, have guilt feelings about using shampoo that can only be assuaged with an assurance in transatlantic twang that they're wurth it. There are few popular lyrics not couched in mid-Atlantic argot.

Such horrors would be bearable if they did not complement the indigenous wrecking of English which, instead of developing as languages do, suffers from malignant growths. Very few records get by without a track. No story lacks its line. We visit with, meet up, free up. Few get shot but many are gunned down. Headcounts get downsized and the result showcased. Dolls have been subsumed within guys. Chill was what one felt, contracted or did to champagne; now, outed, it has to do with relaxation. One could be forgiven for thinking from the number of 'no problems' that we live in a worry-free Nirvana. So much is described as fabulous or fantastic that the world of make-believe seems full to capacity.

Fortunately there are a few redeeming Anglo-American hilarities. One is the different US–UK organs comprised in the word 'fanny'; another, thanks to Dorothy Parker's aphorism about an American ladies' seminary, is self-explanatory:

If all last fall's Vassar graduates were laid end to end, no one would be in the least surprised.

Of course our language must evolve: 'Time Warner' had to stop meaning an alarm clock and Broadband a lady's corset; and 'extraordinary rendi-

tion' a victim of CIA-speak, could no longer signify the mid-Atlantic cater-
wauling of Elton John. Would that the trend could be towards the short
and simple, despite the occasional penalty for brevity of unclarity. One
such penalty appeared in the helpful instructions on a stick deodorant:

Unscrew top. Push up bottom.

All of which is as nothing compared to some of the cardinal problems
screaming for something better than Lilliputian measures to deal with
Brobdingnagian threats and even the total perversity of making matters
worse. Aircraft, we know, make excellent global heaters; so we build more
airports and make air travel cheaper. We worship the car, strewing in its
tarmac path more of the earth than Columbus discovered; placating it with
human sacrifice; praising it in a calendar of such saints as Ferrari, Porsche
and Mercedes in a psalmody of allure – Laguna, Toledo, Golf, Punto and
Astra to name but a few; all assessed against criteria of time, insanely
seconds from 0 to 60 instead of the other way round. There are few bits of
our planet, like our bodies a property that we only occupy as tenants,
which have not been exploited for financial gain as General Bullmoose
desired. Outside it, not content with exploration, we've turned to
vandalism, for a new-found companion in the firmament (Planet Temple
One) on 4 July (when else?) 2005 by blowing a hole in it with an 18,000
mph rocket. Worst of all, perhaps, are the results of the one characteristic
that distinguishes us from all other animals: our capacity, as Arnold
Toynbee's gigantic study of history points out, to do evil to each other:
800 million people, to quote a Christian Aid example from thousands,
forced to survive on less than a dollar a day as the rest of us wallow in
shaming supermarket superfluity. A telling comparator is the $485 billion
(£270 billion) that America plans to spend in 2006 on so-called Defence,
more than the rest of the rich world combined and about 20 times as
much as the entire 2006 rich world's budget for so-called aid. Aid itself is
rotten at the core in that the part of it consisting in debt relief comes at
the price of free trade: free, that is, for competitors from the rich countries
to swamp producers in the poor countries. That freedom, to quote Christian Aid again, has so far cost Africa an amount equivalent to all the aid
and debt relief it has received over the last twenty years.

First must come stopping the rot, a lot of which is talked by politicians
of the worst offender, America. With religiosity rather than religion
prayed in aid, the seemingly irremovable American Religious Right uses
what a priest friend in Philadelphia calls their selectively edited Bibles to

licence aggression and serve ends antipathetic to fair shares and the peace to which they are prerequisite. The hope must be that the true spirit of America will re-emerge. President James Madison spelt it out at the very beginning:

> Of all the enemies to public liberty war is, perhaps, the most to be dreaded because it comprises and develops the germ of every other. As the parent of armies, war encourages debts and taxes, the known instruments for bringing the many under the domination of the few. In war, too, the discretionary power of the executive is extended ... and all the means of seducing the minds are added to those of subduing the force, of the people ...

Martin Luther King complemented that extraordinarily prescient passage nearly 200 years later:

> If we do not act, we shall surely be dragged down the long, dark and shameful corridors of time reserved for those who possess power without compassion, might without morality and strength without sight.

That there was no such action moved Frank Griswold, the senior Anglican bishop in America, to say of what has happened in the Middle East:

> We are loathed, and I think the world has every right to loathe us, because they see us as greedy, self-interested and almost totally unconcerned about poverty, disease and suffering.

Not so much unconcerned, I suggest, as blind to reality. One source of illumination was North America's greatest thinker, John K. Galbraith, who was Canadian. I met him, incidentally, at the Moscow Forum and again at a congressman's breakfast briefing when I was working for BASIC in Washington. Tall, magisterial and good-looking even in old age, he exuded a combination of the friendly, the perspicuous and the authoritative before leaving, as he explained with unaffected modesty, to brief the president. He talked in 1989 about truth to an assembly of young ladies graduating not at Vassar, but at Smith College, Massachusetts:

> Institutional truth bears no necessary relation to simple truth. It is, instead, what serves the needs and purposes of the large and socially pervasive institutions ... [for example] ... our great foreign policy appa-

ratus – the State Department, the National Security Council and the CIA ... Be especially in conflict with the turgid tendencies of institutional truth on military and foreign policy ... To the adherents of the institutional truth there is nothing more inconvenient, nothing that so contributes to discomfort than open, persistent, articulate assertion of what is real.

US military and foreign policy thrives on the institutional truth that Global Reach and its seaborne counterpart New Maritime Strategy (dominating the oceans) will maintain a Pax Americana. The reality is that the dominees will perceive it as a Pox Americana of threat and react with unending turmoil. The institutional truth about resources is that the rich world can continue to dictate how much of them they will vouchsafe to the poor world. The reality is that if the poor of the world aren't given their perceived share (*share*, not aid, relief or other conscience-salve) they will seize it. Meanwhile the yardstick of our duty towards them should be the reply of the small girl in Malawi to an aid worker who asked her whether the large baby under whose weight she was staggering along was not too heavy for her:

> How can he be too heavy? He's my brother.

Nuclear weapons, says institutional truth, deter the letting off of other nuclear weapons. The more we rely on them to do that, says reality, the more certain we are to blow up the world. It is institutional to question global warming and the shrinking quantum of resources left to deal with the problems to which it is central. It is real to accept what stares us in the face and get on with putting it right. Institutional use of the Bible is as a handbook of excuses for whatever the exigencies of racism and belligerence may demand; and bolstering what John Maynard Keynes called capitalism:

> The extraordinary belief that the nastiest of men, for the nastiest of motives, will somehow work for the benefit of all.

One devotee of that nostrum and a mistress of Institutional Bible-bending is Margaret Thatcher, who in 1988 doubtless staggered her audience of Scottish clerics with her apologia for savaging the social services and handing the proceeds to the well off:

We are told we must work and use our talents to create wealth. 'If a man will not work he shall not eat' wrote St Paul to the Thessalonians. [2 Thessalonians 2:10] Indeed, abundance rather than poverty has a legitimacy which derives from the very nature of Creation.

Abundance, yes: wealth, no. And anyway the troublesome Christians of first-century Thessaly were as different from the disadvantaged of twentieth-century Britain as could be.

The Bible depends as a source of Simple Truth on recognising it as what it is: a library of books by all sorts and conditions of authors on what, over 1,400 years, they thought about God: full of the contradictions and inconsistencies of poetic licence and using metaphor and allegory in ways for which latter-day readers find it difficult to allow; but an underpinning, nevertheless, for a long and happy life.

I could go on. Perhaps Dylan Thomas, having started me off, should shut me up:

Dylan [wrote Rayner Heppenstall] talked copiously, then stopped. 'Someone's boring me,' he said, 'I think it's me.'

I echo Dylan. Besides, that's all the time I have: a great deal of it, let me add, for the some of the people who've stuck with me all this way.

Backispiece

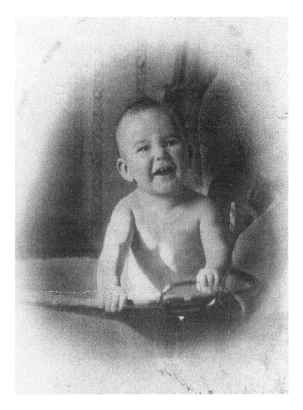

That's all folks. Enjoying second childhood, I hope it was all as much fun to read as it was to write.

Index

345

346

351